ettie knight.

GUINNESS WORLD RECORDS 2024

Hold tight – we're off on a thrill-a-minute ride into *Guinness World Records 2024*! When selecting superlatives for this year's book, the editors took inspiration from our beautiful blue planet, so expect bucket-loads of wet-and-wonderful world records. We're starting right here at Atlantis Aquaventure in Dubai, UAE, which boasts a record 50 waterslides among its 105 attractions – the **most waterslides in a waterpark**. And if you don't like getting your hair wet, don't worry: there's plenty more record-breaking action to enjoy on dry land (and beyond!) To find out what's in store for '24, just turn the page…

CONTENTS

Take a deep breath and dive into the fully revised and updated *Guinness World Records 2024*! This year's theme is the Blue Planet, and we have a sea of aquatic superlatives for you, alongside our pick of the thousands of new records that have *flooded* in over the past 12 months…

YOUNG ACHIEVERS
BELLA J DARK

REYANSH SURANI

Young Achievers
As part of GWR's ongoing mission to inspire record breakers of all ages, we introduce six more under-16s who've shown courage, determination and passion beyond their years. Look out for a Ukrainian contortionist, an Australian drummer and an Indian yoga teacher, among others.

Q&As with record holders

BASKETBALL WIZARDS
HARLEM GLOBETROTTERS

Hall of Fame

GWR Hall of Fame
Meet the latest inductees of the GWR Hall of Fame: those record breakers who truly embody what it means to be Officially Amazing! This year, we welcome into the family the likes of music legend Elton John, wheelchair-tennis stars Shingo Kunieda and Diede de Groot, basketball dynamos the Harlem Globetrotters and a posthumous spot for history's **longest-serving female monarch**.

YOUR RECORD-BREAKING BUCKET LIST AWAITS!
Many people tell us that setting a record is high on their bucket list… To celebrate this, we're revealing the 100 most popular "things to do before you die", as ranked by our friends at Bucketlist.net. You'll find everything from skydiving to whale-watching, each with a related record. Where will *your* life goals rank?

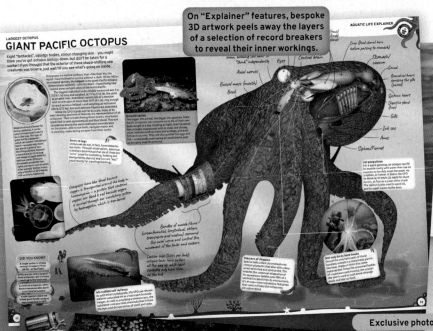

On "Explainer" features, bespoke 3D artwork peels away the layers of a selection of record breakers to reveal their inner workings.

AQUATIC LIFE EXPLAINER

LARGEST OCTOPUS
GIANT PACIFIC OCTOPUS

TALLEST & SHORTEST

SHORTEST MAN

Exclusive photography

Continue the story online at guinnessworldrecords.com
Whenever you see this symbol, visit guinnessworldrecords.com/2024 for bonus video content. Our video team has curated a selection of clips from the world's most awe-inspiring record holders. Don't miss the opportunity to see the records explode into life!

Myths & Magic

HISTORY

History chapter
Step back in time in a special segment for *GWR 2024*, as we take a quirky look at the record breakers of yesteryear. Egyptians, pirates, catapulting knights and even real-life witches and vampires all vie for your attention in this chronicle of the superlative past.

EDITOR'S LETTER

It's been another bumper year of record breaking at GWR, with more than 36,000 applications received. Starting here with some highlights from the UK, you'll discover our pick from the 7,416 claims that were finally approved. Let's find out who's Officially Amazing...

Breaking a world record and proudly showing off that official Guinness World Records certificate is high on many people's bucket lists. Attesting to this is the fact that we hear from thousands of individuals, groups and communities from all corners of the globe who strive to push boundaries and be recognized for their efforts. It's a privilege for us to play a small part in celebrating and promoting these remarkable feats, and the result is the book you now hold in your hands.

Inspired by the idea of "things to do before you die", for this edition we've partnered with BucketList.net – a website that collates the public's dreams and ambitions and ranks them in order of popularity. So, starting at the bottom of p.18, you'll find a list of the world's top 100 life goals,

each with a related GWR title. What's on *your* bucket list? Seeing the Taj Mahal (the **most searched-for UNESCO World Heritage Site**)? Gazing out from the top of the Eiffel Tower (the **tallest iron structure**)? Or perhaps encountering blue whales in the wild (the **largest animal**)? Can you guess what tops most people's to-do lists? If you can't wait to read through the whole countdown, skip to No.1 on p.242.

BLUE PLANET

The theme for this year's edition is our watery world, so when selecting records we've taken our inspiration from all things aquatic. We dive in straight away with the fourth and final cover in the "Discover Your World" series by the award-winning Rod Hunt. This time, Rod leads us down beneath the waves to the deepest parts of the ocean to encounter all manner of submarine superlatives!

Fastest time to top 10 pancakes
Heart Breakfast's Amanda Holden celebrated Shrove Tuesday in traditional style on 21 Feb 2023 by topping off 10 pancakes with lemon juice and sugar in 29.39 sec. It was third time lucky for the radio star, as her two previous record challenges had flopped live on air. Amanda served up her delicious dishes in London's Leicester Square.

Most scones assembled in one minute
Radio presenter Melvin Odoom prepared four scones – topped with clotted cream and jam, naturally – at Horse Guards Parade in London on 5 Jun 2022. The one-minute challenge took place in celebration of Queen Elizabeth II's Platinum Jubilee. Melvin took on his good friend and showbiz sidekick Rickie Haywood-Williams in this high-tea head-to-head.

Inside, we open with the BLUE PLANET chapter (*pp.14–27*), which explores Earth's rivers, lakes, oceans and seas. This is followed by AQUATIC LIFE (*pp.30–49*), which – as the name suggests – brings you up close to fish, molluscs and others creatures of the deep (though look out for a bonus feature about some record-breaking pets on dry land).

Other chapters also dip their toe into the watery theme: look out for features on ships (*pp.162–65*) and shipwrecks (*pp.146–47*), submarines (*pp.116–17*) and sailors (*pp.120–21*). We also reveal the superlatives behind lighthouses (*pp.158–59*), ice swimming (*p.123*) and even merfolk (*pp.80–81*).

Most donuts around a motorcycle performing a wheelie
From scones and pancakes to donuts... On 20 Aug 2022, Paul Swift drove 10 circles around motorcyclist Jonny Davies in 60 sec at The British Motor Show in Farnborough. Jonny had to maintain a wheelie throughout the attempt.

A day later, Paul executed the **tightest parallel park by electric car**, slotting one MINI E between two parked cars with just 30 cm (11.8 in) to spare. And all in a time of just 3 sec!

To control the sliding car in such tight parallel parking, the driver typically uses the clutch to rapidly engage and disengage the engine. In electric cars, this is not possible, adding extra complexity to the challenge.

Tom Enoch

This aspiring fitness coach is on a mission to inspire people with Down syndrome by achieving 21 GWR titles – a nod to "trisomy 21", the other name for his genetic disorder. Tom's already broken 17 records in the intellectual impairment (II) category, including the **most weight deadlifted in three minutes** (1,475 kg; 3,251 lb) and **one minute** (1,110 kg; 2,447 lb), the **longest handstand wall hold** (33.65 sec) and the **most squats in three minutes** (93).

Officially Amazing visitors to GWR HQ

Editor-in-Chief Craig Glenday regularly welcomes extraordinary record breakers to our London headquarters for a Q&A. This year…
1. Jade Kingdom talked about being the **first woman with Down syndrome to complete a sprint triathlon**, at the London Triathlon on 7 Aug 2021.
2. The **first female quadriplegic competitive racing driver** – Nathalie McGloin – popped in to share her experiences of life in the fast lane.
3. Mountaineering consultant Thaneswar Guragai invited three Nepalese climbers – Nirmal "Nims" Purja, Mingma "David" Gyabu Sherpa and Mingma Tenzi Sherpa – to pick up certificates for recent Himalayan ascents.
4. Paraplegic Simon Kindleysides also collected his certificate for the **most stairs climbed in a robotic walking device in eight hours** – he'd ascended 1,444 steps at the capital's Leadenhall Building on 12 Mar 2022.

For a change of pace, turn to the HISTORY chapter (*pp.136–51*), where we take a potted tour through the ages to chronicle records relating to pyramids and mummies, castles and knights, pirates and buccaneers, and witches and werewolves. Our artistic partners at 55Design have pushed the boat out to make this a fun and engaging visual treat, rather than an exhaustive history textbook.

EXPLAINERS

For a different perspective, we've taken a three-dimensional approach in the EXPLAINER features that introduce each chapter. Our digital artists guide you around the **most expensive car** (*pp.156–57*), expose the inner workings of the **largest animatronic dinosaur** (*pp.180–81*), and reveal what's going on inside the body of the world's **largest octopus** (*pp.32–33*), among other things. And you can continue your journey online to find out even more about these remarkable record holders – just follow the QR codes you'll find dotted throughout the book.

We continue to pay tribute to our most celebrated record holders in the GWR Hall of Fame. Those selected for inclusion are considered to fully

Most promotions to the English football top flight by a manager
Neil Warnock (*pictured*) steered four different clubs to the summit of the English league pyramid between 1990/91 and 2017/18: Notts County, Sheffield United, QPR and Cardiff City. He matched the feat of Steve Bruce, who got Birmingham City and Hull City promoted twice apiece from 2001/02 to 2015/16.

Back, left to right: Nirmal "Nims" Purja, Thaneswar Guragai and Mingma "David" Gyabu Sherpa. Front: Mingma Tenzi Sherpa. Find out about their record-breaking climbs on pp.118–19, 124 and 132.

EDITOR'S LETTER

Most shaving-cream pies thrown in different faces in one minute
Mwaka Mudenda splatted cream pies into the faces of 24 volunteer victims on *Blue Peter* on 17 Mar 2023. Mwaka is a co-host on the show, which first aired on the BBC in 1958 – making it the **longest-running children's TV programme**.

Fastest time to put on five jumpers
Richie Driss took just 27.6 sec to pull on a quintet of sweaters on the set of *Blue Peter* on 16 Dec 2022. He went one-on-one with fellow presenter Joel Mawhinney during the show's Christmas special, using festive jumpers in a range of sizes.

embody the spirit of Guinness World Records, and most closely reflect our mission and values. This year's inductees include an oceanographer, a freestyle footballer, a pioneering adventurer and a mould-breaking sports team – every one of them an inspiration to anyone looking to make a positive difference in the world.

YOUNG ACHIEVERS

On pp.104–09, we profile six more under-16s who've made an early start on earning their place in the record books. This new GWR generation includes an Australian drummer, a British novelist and an Indian yoga teacher – plus a remarkable young acrobat from Ukraine who continues to break records despite facing the challenge of living in a war zone. These inspiring youngsters go to prove that age is never a barrier to achieving great things.

Talking of which, in *GWR 2023* we introduced a new project to encourage those under the age of 16 to have a go at setting a record. You'll find out how some of these junior stars progressed on pp.10–11. There, you'll also discover other ways in which kids can access content specially curated for them – and how they can go about getting their names listed in the next edition!

GWR GURUS

Helping the editors compile the book is a huge team of experts and advisors from across a vast spectrum of topics, so I'd like to take this opportunity to welcome all of our newest recruits. Among those joining us for the first time are individuals such as anime and manga expert Andrea Horbinksi; comedy chronicler Bruce Dessau;

Most Charleston swivel steps in 30 seconds
On 20 Oct 2022, Helen Skelton performed 24 of these classic dance moves on the set of *Blue Peter* – a show she had once co-presented. This equalled Giovanni Pernice's (ITA) record, set five years earlier, also on *Blue Peter*.

Most back Charleston kick steps in 30 seconds
Professional dancer Amy Dowden shot to fame after joining BBC's *Strictly Come Dancing* in 2017. On 4 Nov 2022, she executed 19 quickfire kick steps – under the watchful eye of adjudicator Joanne Brent – on companion show *It Takes Two*.

Stock up on GWR gear!
Did you know that there's now an online store where you can buy a range of Guinness World Records goodies? There's everything from mugs, backpacks and water bottles to T-shirts and hoodies (adults' and kids' sizes), as well as the main event, of course: the *GWR* annual! Pictured here modelling the merchandise are the Chennai Hoopers – record-breaking hula-hoopers from India. You too could look as cool as them! Visit **gwrstore.com** to browse and buy, and be sure to tag us on social media with your goodies!

BONUS CONTENT

Find out more...
We simply can't fit all our record-breaking action into *GWR 2024*... so we're offering you a virtual ocean of bonus content online! Keep your eyes peeled for divers, merfolk and rays bearing QR codes; scan these with your phone's camera and you'll be directed straight to GWR TikTok videos, Facebook posts, Instagram stories and web articles. You'll even be able to find official guidelines on how to earn yourself a GWR certificate!

Watch out too for the ▶ play button – it means that a record is accompanied by a video from our YouTube channel. Scan the QR code above and you'll be taken straight there. Finally: if you're a Snapchatter, unlock even more video content by scanning the Snapcodes dotted throughout the book. Open the app, point the camera at the GWR-themed Ghostface Chillah and away you go! Enjoy!

Largest collection of No.1 singles

Dave Watson owns 1,258 UK chart-toppers, including shellac, vinyl and CD singles, as verified in Dunstable, Bedfordshire, UK, on 5 Dec 2022. His first purchase was 1988's "Don't Turn Around" by Aswad, which cost just 99p. The hardest record to get was Lita Roza's "(How Much Is) That Doggie in the Window?" (1953), which eluded him until internet search engines arrived.

mythologist and folklorist Ceri Houlbrook; merfolk maven Sarah Peverley; and maritime historian Sam Willis. A big thank you to all those who've helped us curate the book – you can find a more comprehensive list on pp.252–53.

ACCESSIBLE EBOOK

Making record breaking accessible to as many people as possible is an important goal for everyone at GWR – in terms of both attempting records and also reading about them. So I'd like to offer special thanks to the non-profit technology company Benetech for enabling us to create an accessible ebook version of this year's edition. Benetech have now delivered more than 20 million books for people with print disabilities, and

we're proud to make our annual available in the UK through the Royal National Institute of Blind People and their RNIB Bookshare platform.

My final thanks are reserved for those thousands of wannabe record holders who continue to include "break a record" on their bucket lists. Keep those claims coming in – Guinness World Records would be nothing without your boundless enthusiasm!

Craig Glenday
Editor-in-Chief

Most neck ties worn at once

In Feb 2023, Imruh Asha, the Fashion Director for British style magazine *Dazed*, organized a series of shoots in Paris, France, with the photographer Andrea Artemisio. Among those who modelled for the project was David Aparecido Dos Santos Araújo (BRA), who wore 330 ties. *See below for more.*

Most people crocheting simultaneously

BBC Radio Derby and its listeners joined forces to get 960 individuals stitching at Derby Arena on 24 Feb 2023. The crafty collective came together for the station's "Make a Difference: Make a Blanket" appeal, to crochet and distribute blankets to those in need over the winter. The 2,000 blankets made on the day were donated to food banks and local charities.

Largest trousers

For *Dazed* magazine's feature on record-breaking fashion (*see above right*), couture stylist Anh Quynh Duong (USA) recreated a pair of ASOS tapered sweatpants with a total length of 13.07 m (42 ft 11 in) and a waist of 9.22 m (30 ft 3 in). The titanic trews were unveiled in Paris, France, on 8 Feb 2023.

GWR DAY

Each year, thousands of people around the globe take on a mind-boggling array of challenges in celebration of Guinness World Records Day. The event was first held in 2004 to celebrate the anniversary of *Guinness World Records* becoming the world's **best-selling copyright book**. The 19th annual day of record breaking took place on 10 Nov 2022 and was built around the theme of "super skills" – the special (and often unorthodox!) talents that people devote their lives to honing in the hope of becoming Officially Amazing.

To kick off the day's festivities, GWR invited four record contenders to put their abilities to the test in front of the UK's Houses of Parliament in London: speedcuber George Scholey, loose-limbed YouTube sensation Liberty Barros, hula hooper Amazí and freestyle footballer Ben Nuttall (*see opposite*). The talented quartet were more than up to the task – and they were only part of the astonishing array of super skills on show across the world that day...

▶ **Most basketball arm rolls in one minute (three basketballs):** 56, by Junji Nakasone (JPN) in Kōtō, Tokyo, Japan.

Fastest 30-m car pull with the teeth: 18.13 sec, by Saleh Yazan (SYR) in Lattakia, Syrian Arab Republic.

All flags indicate the attempt location

Dinesh is a parkour athlete who holds multiple GWR titles for gymnastic feats.

Fastest time to set up and topple 10 books: 13.07 sec, by Rocco Mercurio (ITA) in Reggio Calabria, Italy.

▶ **Most blindfolded standing backwards somersaults in one minute:** 21, by Dinesh Sunar (NPL) in Orlando, Florida, USA.

▶ **Most consecutive football touches while hanging with one hand in 30 seconds:** 87, by Ammar Ahmed Alkhudhiri (UAE) in Dubai, UAE.

▶ **Most lanyards worn at once:** 509, by Salacnib "Sonny" Molina (USA) in Woodstock, Illinois, USA (*see also pp.100–01*).

Most hula-hoop rotations on the arm in the bridge position in 30 seconds: 98, by N Sidhiksha Lakshanyaa (IND) in Chennai, Tamil Nadu, India.

▶ **Fastest time to tie three pairs of shoelaces in a bow:** 9.99 sec, by Álvaro Martín Mendieta (ESP) in Rivas-Vaciamadrid, Spain.

▶ **Most consecutive football touches on a quad bike performing a wheelie:** 70, by freestyler Ammar Ahmed Alkhudhiri (*above right*) and driver Abdulla Saeed Alhattawi (both UAE) in Dubai, UAE.

▶ Most Smarties eaten with chopsticks while blindfolded in one minute: 25, by Avery Chin (MYS) in Kuala Lumpur, Malaysia.

▶ Most forks in a beard: 126, by Joel Strasser (USA) in Kuna, Idaho, USA.

Bar at least 90 cm off the ground

▶ Most bunny hops on to a bar (rear wheel) in one minute: 14, by Zhang Jingkun (CHN) in Qingdao, Shandong, China.

Most single-leg backward skips over a rope blindfolded in 30 seconds: 117, by Cristian Sabba (ITA) in Milan, Italy.

▶ Most arrows caught by hand in one minute: 17, by Anthony Kelly (AUS) in Armidale, New South Wales, Australia.

▶ Most alternating single-arm handstands in one minute: 32, by Nicolas Montes de Oca (MEX) in Barcelona, Spain.

▶ Fastest 400 m joggling backwards with three objects: 1 min 35.36 sec, by Christian Rodríguez (ESP) in Toledo, Spain.

▶ GWR Day record breaking in London (*from left to right*)...
• **Most rotating puzzle cubes solved in 24 hours**: 6,931, by George Scholey
• **Fastest 20 m backbend knee-lock walk**: 22.53 sec, by Liberty Barros
• **Most hula hoops spun simultaneously on stilts**: 25, by Amazí, aka Mariam Olayiwola
• **Most football crossovers in one minute**: 53, by Ben Nuttall (all UK).

9

NO GROWN-UPS ALLOWED!

KIDS RECORDS

Here at GWR, we don't think it's fair if adults get to have all the fun. That's why we've introduced an Under-16s category! Whether it's putting on socks or identifying Pokémon characters, there are loads of GWR challenges that are perfect for young people. You'll find some on these pages, but there are a whole lot more on the GWR Kids website (see right). So, get practising! Who knows – next year, it might be YOU appearing in the GWR book...

India's eco-conscious siblings Sathvika Sree and Lakshine Vel Vivek achieved the **fastest time to sort two bags of recyclable materials (team of two)** in 39.5 sec.

For the full list of records in our new under-16s category, scan the QR code below to go straight to the GWR KIDS WEBSITE. You'll find profiles of our current record holders too... so you can check out the competition! Have you got what it takes to be OFFICIALLY AMAZING?!

Ashwin Sudhan Palani Kumar (IND) loves nothing more than attempting world records in his spare time! The Chennai schoolboy has held five different titles, including the **most cans stacked into a pyramid in 30 seconds** – 28 – and the **most times to hit a target with a paper aircraft in three minutes** – 33. Do you dare take him on?

Our brand-new GWR title for **most tosses of a pancake in one minute** is waiting for its first record holder. Pick up a pan and step up to the challenge – can you make the minimum of 15 tosses in 60 sec?

Josiah Tom Joss (right) of Niles, Illinois, USA, has set the **fastest time to win a 1 v 3 match on Nickelodeon All-Star Brawl** – 44.72 sec. His brother Jayden (above) is also a former record holder for the **fastest hat-trick with the goalie on FIFA 22**.

US readers can check out the GWR Zone on Sensical, the safe and free online streaming platform for younger viewers. You'll find made-for-kids videos about some of our funniest, craziest and most inspiring records. Whether it's dogs dancing a conga or death-defying pogo-stick jumps, you'll find something to make your jaw drop!

THINK YOU CAN MAKE ME AT HIGH SPEED? THEN MAYBE YOU COULD BECOME A WORLD RECORD HOLDER TOO. GET TIPS ON SENSICAL.

WOW!

YOUNG ACHIEVERS

Turn to p.104 to find a special section devoted to junior record holders. There, you'll meet amazing talents such as gymnast Sofia Tepla and juggler Simeon Graham.

Hi! My name is Fenrir Antares Powers, and I'm a su-purr-lative puss because I'm the **tallest domestic cat**. Find out how I meow-sure up on Sensical!

I'm Zaila Avant-garde, and I have the record for the **most bounce juggles in one minute (four basketballs)** – 255! I'm also a US spelling bee champion!

KIDS

GWR's own Kids website is jam-packed with cool stunts, cute animals and crazy collections. Get to know our youngest record holders in our exclusive behind-the-scenes videos. You can also play games and test your knowledge with our fiendish quizzes – all made just for you! And make sure you check out our GWR Kids channel on YouTube. Our new series, "Game the Record", focuses on GWR's Under-16s records.

They call me Bini the Basketballing Bunny. Why? Because I can slam this ball seven times in a minute: the **most basketball dunks by a rabbit**!

Hi, I'm Wylie J Brys, and I was just 4 years 337 days old when I became the **youngest person to discover a new dinosaur fossil**. I found the 100-million-year-old remains near a shopping mall in Texas! Does this mean I'm 0-fossil-y Amazing?!

Hi, I'm McCauley Hoover. Last summer, I searched GWR for "skateboard records for girls", and now I've broken two: the **most frontside (33) and backside grinds in one minute (34)**.

Yoo hoo! Meet Aneeshwar Kunchala from the UK – he's the **youngest documentary presenter**. He was just 7 years 288 days old when "COP27 – Six Ways to Save Our Planet" aired on 5 Nov 2022.

THE ONE THING

Watch on... **Da Vinci**

What's "The One Thing" that you can do better than everyone else? In this fun, inspirational TV series, 26 record breakers share the secrets of their success – and try to teach our presenters just one skill (yeah, good luck with that!). Among the talent on offer are some youngsters who've shown that youth is no barrier to being the best...

I'm ballerina Bianca Ciocirlan and I've given my dancing a 21st-century twist by performing the **most seated pirouettes on a hoverboard in 30 seconds**. Can you beat my record of 10 spins?

You aiming to be a big shot? I'm Kaden Galatiuk, and I can tell you how to achieve the **most hockey pucks hit into a target on inline skates in one minute**. My record to beat is 38. Good puck luck!

I'm Creole. Can you pluck up the courage to take on my chicken trainer Zoe Tomas? She helped me achieve the **fastest completion of an agility course by a chicken** – thanks to her, I finished in just 1 min 0.02 sec!

Hey, I'm Dashaun Jiwe Morris II – aka "Dflash". I completed the **most one-handed mini-American football catches in one minute** – 23. Let me show you how I did it...

11

CHARITABLE EFFORTS

As well as being a pinnacle of personal achievement, record breaking offers limitless opportunities for anyone seeking to help a worthy cause. Millions of people have used a record-based challenge to turn the spotlight on their charity of choice, raising both funds and awareness along the way. GWR is proud to have been able to provide a platform to many philanthropic individuals over the decades.

Here, we're showcasing just a handful of charity-driven records, including the latest cohort of record-breaking runners from the London Marathon. This event never fails to rally thousands of fundraisers; indeed, the pre-COVID-19 edition in 2019 amassed an unprecedented haul of £66.4 m ($85.7 m) – the **most money raised at a marathon**.

Most awareness ribbons...
- **Made in one hour (team):** To see in World Cancer Day on 4 Feb 2022, Emirates Oncology Society (UAE) created 2,828 ribbons in eight colours – representing various forms of the disease.
- **On a car:** In a bid to educate the public about different types of cancer and also to encourage early screenings, siblings Amaar, Baraa, Rawan and Muaaz Amir (all SAU) decorated a vehicle with 5,637 ribbons of 16 different colours in Dhahran, Saudi Arabia, on 26 Jun 2022.

Most heads shaved in one hour
On 20 Nov 2015, 462 brave souls raised over $60,000 (£39,300) by relinquishing their locks for the Bald Angels Charitable Trust in Kerikeri, New Zealand. The record was attempted to raise money for struggling families in Northland, which has one of the highest rates of poverty in the country.

Largest awareness ribbon
To mark Breast Cancer Awareness Month in Oct 2022, Trillo City Council (ESP) rallied more than 500 volunteers to adorn the top of Tetas de Viana in Guadalajara, Spain, with a pink ribbon measuring 5,620.5 m² (60,498 sq ft) – an area greater than 21 tennis courts. Most of those involved had been affected by breast cancer in some way.

Most sweaters donated in one hour
For his birthday on 28 Jan 2022, Lakshyaraj Singh Mewar (IND), prince of the former state of Mewar in Udaipur, India, donated 2,800 sweaters to charity. It was the fifth year running that he had marked his birthday with a good deed. On the same day, he also provided 2,800 food parcels, forming the **longest line of hunger-relief packages**.

Longest time in direct contact with snow
On 13 May 2022, engineer Valerjan Romanovski (LTU, b. POL) buried his entire body (excluding his head) in snow for 105 min 2 sec in Kraków, Poland. Bettering the previous record by nearly 45 min, Romanovski took on this challenge not only to prove his cold endurance (*for more of that, see pp.70–71*), but also as part of his ambassador duties for the DKMS Foundation, a charity that helps individuals with blood cancer.

Most consecutive Christmas No.1s on the UK's Official Singles Chart
LadBaby, aka Mark and Roxanne Hoyle (both UK), scored their fifth Christmas No.1 with "Food Aid" on 29 Dec 2022. The cover of Band Aid's 1984 classic "Do They Know It's Christmas?" follows four other festive hits since 2018, including "Sausage Rolls for Everyone" in 2021. Profits from the sales of "Food Aid" were divided between The Trussell Trust, a charity seeking to end the need for food banks in the UK, and The Band Aid Charitable Trust.

Most hair donated by an individual
Pro squash player Zahab Kamal Khan (USA) chopped off 155 cm (5 ft 1 in) of her 190-cm-long (6-ft 3-in) tresses to donate to Children with Hair Loss in McLean, Virginia, USA, on 26 Aug 2021. Up until Dec 2021, Zahab also held the record for **most hairclips on the head** (1,100).

On 2 Oct 2022, the London Marathon saw thousands of athletes taking to the streets in their fancy-dress costumes to raise money for a charity close to their heart. In total, 25 new records were set, here listed in order from the fastest...

Fairy (male): Andy Kirkup (UK) 2:38:26

Pyjamas (male): David Jones (UK) 2:47:15

Handcuffs (male): David Henson (UK) 2:54:57

Non-racing wheelchair (male): Stephen Salmon (UK) 2:56:07

Witch (female): Sarah Dudgeon (UK) 3:11:52

Scientist (male): Gower Tan (UK) 3:14:16

Hospital patient (male): Donato Esposito (UK) 3:19:23

Badminton player (male): Andrew Roberts (UK) 3:23:33

Vampire (female): Victoria Carter (UK) 3:23:48

Mythical creature (male): Jérémie Maillard (FRA) 3:26:38

Toga (female): Emanuela Pizzoni (ITA) 3:27:18

Stationery item (female): Belinda Neild (UK) 3:38:22

Mythical creature (female): Kristina Beadle (UK) 3:43:41

Largest gummy candy
A dolphin-shaped gummy weighing 1,212.5 kg (2,673 lb) was made by the Iranian confectionery brand Shiba in Tehran, Iran, on 27 Jan 2022. The 64-cm-tall, 207-cm-wide (2-ft 1-in x 6-ft 9-in) sweet was partly created to promote the conservation of these much-loved marine mammals.

Largest donation of turkey in 24 hours
TikTok chefs Nick DiGiovanni (USA) and Lynn Davis (JPN) supplied 64,463.44 kg (142,117 lb 8.8 oz) of the Thanksgiving staple to food banks in Boston, Massachusetts, USA, on 14 Nov 2022. *See some of the cooks' supersized snacks on p.95.*

Farthest vehicle pull in 24 hours
John Darwen (*above*) and his brother-in-law James Baker (*right*; both UK) each hauled a 1.5-tonne (1.6-ton) van for 51.499 km (32 mi) on 25–26 Aug 2022. They raised more than £2,500 ($3,100) for Cancer Research UK and Redeeming our Communities Garden Services, a charity based in Blackpool, Lancashire, that empowers local unemployed people. They smashed their previous record of 35.701 km (22.2 mi), set in Oct 2021.

Most money raised by camping
Max Woosey (UK) slept in a tent pitched in his garden for three years (2020–23), raising £700,000 ($840,800). All the proceeds went to the North Devon Hospice, a charity that cared for his 74-year-old neighbour during his final days. For his epic camp-out, Max was awarded the British Empire Medal in 2022.

Largest gathering of Santas
A ho-ho-horde of 18,112 Father Christmases amassed in Thrissur, Kerala, India, on 27 Dec 2014 to raise money for the needy. The event was organized by Thrissur Citizenry and Thrissur Archdiocese (both IND) for the charitable Buon Natale Programme.

Greatest distance on a treadmill in one week
Jamie McDonald (UK) covered 843.94 km (524.40 mi) in Gloucester, UK, on 29 Apr–6 May 2019 for the Superhero Foundation, a charity he founded for sick children. Following the attempt, Jamie was awarded the Pride of Britain "Fundraiser of the Year" award.

Star (male): Matt Brooks (UK) 3:44:00

Harlequin (male): Martin Porter (UK) 3:51:35

Glass (male): Joan Pons Laplana (UK) 3:58:52

Traditional Welsh dress (female): Kranti Salvi (IND) 4:03:51

Aircraft (male): Thomas Langdown (UK) 4:23:03

Confectionery item (female): Kellie Clark (UK) 4:24:06

Six-person costume: Tristan Clark, Freddie Wright, Freddie Flanagan, John Lavelle, George Peirson and Hugh Williams (all UK) 4:25:12

Body part (female): Sadie Smith (UK) 4:26:43

Carrying golf clubs (male): Will Ridgway (UK); 4:30:22

Non-racing wheelchair (female): Lexi Alyx Chambers (UK); 4:32:11

Police uniform (female): Beth Goucher (UK) 4:45:03

Book (male): Philip Beer (UK) 5:34:31

BLUE PLANET

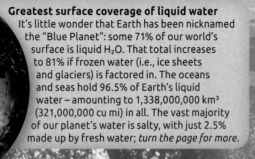

Greatest surface coverage of liquid water
It's little wonder that Earth has been nicknamed the "Blue Planet": some 71% of our world's surface is liquid H₂O. That total increases to 81% if frozen water (i.e., ice sheets and glaciers) is factored in. The oceans and seas hold 96.5% of Earth's liquid water – amounting to 1,338,000,000 km³ (321,000,000 cu mi) in all. The vast majority of our planet's water is salty, with just 2.5% made up by fresh water; *turn the page for more.*

		Liquid water volume	% of world
Ganymede		35.4 ZL	69%
Titan		18.6 ZL	44%
Callisto		5.3 ZL	33%
Europa		2.6 ZL	18%
Earth		1.335 ZL	0.12%

As far as we know for certain, Earth has the **most liquid water in the Solar System** – some 1,361,620,510 km³ (1.3 ZL [zettalitres]; 326,670,100 cu mi) either on its surface or within its atmosphere. That said, some scientists speculate that there are a few worlds on which an ocean of liquid water may exist beneath an icy crust many kilometres thick.

Ganymede is the biggest of Jupiter's satellites and the Solar System's **largest moon**, with a diameter of 5,262.4 km (3,269.9 mi). NASA planetary scientist Steve Vance – who posited the figures in the graphic here – estimates that it may hold as much as 35.4 ZL of liquid water, which would equate to more than two-thirds of its total volume! Water on Earth, by comparison, only makes up a tiny 0.12% of the planet's volume.

This photo was snapped by astronaut Thomas Pesquet from the *International Space Station* in 2021.

A millilitre of surface seawater near the coast can harbour 1 million bacteria and 10 million virus particles.

WATER ON EARTH

It covers 71% of the globe as a liquid, but also takes the form of ice and vapour. Without it, there would be no human race – or any life as we know it – and our planet would be radically different. Arguably, no other substance has contributed more to shaping our world.

Our planet exists in a cosmic sweet spot: its distance from the Sun and the composition of the atmosphere combine to keep our "Blue Planet" blue. If it were farther from the Sun, all its water would freeze into ice; any closer, and rising temperatures would melt frozen regions, sea levels would rise and submerge most of the dry land, making it an even "Bluer Planet".

The vast majority of water on Earth lies within the oceans. The tiny remainder is fresh water, which contains less than 1% salt. Most of that is frozen, largely within ice sheets in Antarctica and Greenland. Lakes and rivers make up only a minuscule proportion of the fresh water distributed across the world, yet provide most of the water we use daily. All life on Earth, including the human race, may rely on water, but how did it get here in the first place?

When our Sun was still young, it was orbited by a protoplanetary disk – a rotating mass of gas and dust. Over time, dust grains clumped together, along with ice and water, forming asteroids. Many scientists believe that such bodies, formed in cold, distant regions of the Solar System, brought water to Earth when they crashed into it. One theory is that hydrogen ions within solar winds penetrate the surface of asteroids that pass through them and alter their chemical composition, creating H_2O within their minerals. In 2022, it was confirmed that a meteorite that landed in Winchcombe, UK, carried water whose chemical composition was an almost perfect match for that on Earth.

Life support

Many people credit land-based plants such as trees for providing the air we breathe, but at least half of the atmosphere's oxygen is generated by tiny marine organisms such as algae and bacteria. Not only that, but the ocean is critical to mitigating against climate change, soaking up around 25% of all CO_2 emissions.

The Pacific Ocean takes up 30% of Earth's surface

Oceans contain 99% of the habitable space on Earth and are home to 50–80% of all life

SALT WATER: 97.5%

FRESH WATER: 2.5%

GLOBAL WATER

Of all the water found on our Blue Planet, 97.5% is saline (i.e., salty). Of this, 96.5% is held within Earth's vast oceans, seas and bays. (*See the volumes of each of the five major oceans listed left, from smallest to largest.*) The other c. 1% of saline water is found in landlocked lakes, such as the Dead Sea (*see p.18*), and in underground reservoirs. That means that approximately just 2.5% of Earth's total H_2O is fresh – i.e., not salty (*see below*).

As much as 60% of the human body – and 90% of our blood – is water, hence why it's so vital to stay hydrated.

Deep blue sea

What gives the world's oceans their distinctive colour? Orange and red wavelengths in sunlight are absorbed by water molecules at the surface. But blue and violet light penetrate farther, and so are the dominant hue that we see, at least in the open ocean. Eventually, as you descend, all light peters out, shrouding the deepest parts of the sea in permanent night. Nearer land, the presence of other particles such as silt and sand, or tiny plants known as microalgae, can make the water appear brown or green.

WATER VOLUME OF THE FIVE OCEANS

Arctic 18,750,000 km³

Southern 71,800,000 km³

Indian 264,000,000 km³

Atlantic 310,410,900 km³

Pacific 660,000,000 km³

Source: NOAA

GLOBAL FRESH WATER

Just 2.5% of Earth's water is fresh – and yet even much of that isn't readily available to us. A staggering 98.8% of all fresh water is either locked up or hidden out of sight: 68.7% is frozen solid, bound in ice caps and glaciers, while 30.1% is trapped deep beneath the planet's crust as groundwater in vast subterranean aquifers. A tiny 1.2% of fresh water exists as a liquid (or vapour) on the surface, as illustrated in the final graphic below.

Wells can be drilled into some aquifers and the water pumped out. About 40% of crops worldwide are irrigated with groundwater

ATMOSPHERIC WATER VAPOUR: 3%

Clouds

LIVING ORGANISMS: 0.26%

Plants and animals

RIVERS: 0.49%

GROUND ICE AND PERMAFROST: 69%

SOIL MOISTURE: 3.8%

GROUNDWATER: 30.1%

SURFACE FRESH WATER: 1.2%

ICE CAPS AND GLACIERS: 68.7%

The white colour of ice and snow helps to deflect the Sun's energy, which is why its melting could cause an alarming cascade effect of further global warming

The white planet
More than two-thirds of Earth's fresh water exists in glaciers and snow. The Antarctic Ice Sheet (the **largest glacier**, *see p.23*) alone is around double the size of the USA and Mexico combined, and a mind-boggling 3,050 m (10,000 ft) at its deepest. NASA estimates that if this all melted, global sea levels would rise by about 60 m (200 ft).

WETLANDS: 2.6%

Swamps, bogs and marshes

GLOBAL FRESH WATER ON THE SURFACE

Only 1.2% of Earth's non-frozen fresh water exists on the planet's uppermost layer. Most of the water we use comes from natural lakes and rivers (*see the largest lake and the longest river on p.18*), bolstered by artificial reservoirs built to capture meltwater or rain. The impact of climate change and industry is being felt most keenly by aquatic ecosystems on the surface, which may reconfigure our world's watery make-up as time goes on – e.g., regions of permafrost are thawing, lakes are shrinking, and water retention is affected by deforestation and the repurposing of wild land for urban development and agriculture.

LAKES: 20.9%

Source: US Geological Survey, Water Science School; percentages are rounded

INLAND WATERS

LONGEST RIVERS

The Nile flows north from Burundi (its most southerly source) in Central Africa to the Mediterranean Sea, passing through 10 other countries along the way. It is not just its continent's longest river but the world's. Laid out in a straight line, it could link the cities of Paris and Delhi. The Amazon is a close second place; while just missing out on the "longest" title, it does claim a plethora of other riverine records (see right).

Antarctica: Onyx – 32 km

Oceania: Murray – 2,508 km

Europe: Volga – 3,692 km

North America: Missouri – 3,767 km

Asia: Chang (Yangtze) – 6,300 km

South America: Amazon – 6,400 km

Africa: Nile – 6,695 km

Highest river
The Yarlung Tsangpo's source lies 6,020 m (19,750 ft) above sea level at the foot of the Angsi Glacier in Tibet, China.
The **lowest** is the Jordan River. Where it empties into the Dead Sea (see below), it is 436 m (1,430 ft) below sea level.

Greatest river by discharge
South America's Amazon outputs 200,000 m³ (7.1 million cu ft) of fresh water into the ocean every second. That's 17% of the global total and enough to fill the Dead Sea in under a week! This can rise to 340,000 m³ (12 million cu ft) in the wet season.
The Amazon is fed by the **largest river basin**, covering 7.04 million km² (2.72 million sq mi) across eight nations – 14 times the size of Spain. At its broadest (not in flood), the Amazon spans 11 km (6.8 mi), also making it the **widest river**.

Largest freshwater lake
• **By surface area**: One of the five Great Lakes, Superior covers 82,414 km² (31,820 sq mi) of Canada and the USA.
• **By volume**: Lake Baikal in Siberia, Russia, has a capacity of c. 23,615 km³ (5,666 cu mi). Dipping to 1,642 m (5,387 ft) in its central basin, it's the planet's **deepest lake** too.
• **In the tropics**: The 59,947-km² (23,146-sq-mi) Lake Victoria (aka Nyanza, Nam Lolwe or Nalubaale) is Africa's biggest lake by area. It's the primary reservoir of the River Nile (see left).

Largest tropical wetland
Approximately 0.03% of Earth's fresh water is found in swamps, bogs and marshes, of which the Pantanal in South America is among the most significant. Located principally in Brazil, but also Bolivia and Paraguay, this 160,000-km² (61,780-sq-mi) wetland is a haven for flora and fauna, including jaguars. In the rainy season (Dec–May), some 70–80% of the Pantanal is flooded.

Largest ephemeral lake
As the name suggests, ephemeral lakes come and go. Kati Thanda (aka Lake Eyre) in South Australia, located in a basin that forms the country's lowest natural point, is the largest such non-permanent body of water. When the dry salt pan floods every eight years or so, Kati Thanda can grow to 9,690 km² (3,740 sq mi) – similar in size to the city of Melbourne. Proliferations of algae and bacteria can transform the water shades of pink and orange.

Largest lake
The Caspian Sea is Earth's biggest inland body of water, with a surface area of 371,000 km² (143,244 sq mi). Bordered by Kazakhstan, Russia, Azerbaijan, Iran and Turkmenistan, the shoreline of this saltwater lake is c. 7,000 km (4,350 mi).

Tallest waterfall
Kerepakupai Merú (aka Salto Ángel, or Angel Falls) in eastern Venezuela descends 979 m (3,212 ft) in total, with the **longest single drop** being an uninterrupted 807-m (2,648-ft) cascade.

Deepest hypersaline lake
The Dead Sea on the Israel-Jordan border averages 120 m (393 ft) deep, but bottoms out at c. 306 m (1,004 ft). Also the **lowest exposed body of water**, it lies 436 m (1,430 ft) beneath mean sea level. With a salinity almost 10 times greater than that of seawater, salt-encrusted rocks are a common sight along its shores.

Widest waterfall
Raging around islets and over rocky crags, the Khône Falls on the Mekong River in southern Laos have a total crest width of 10,783 m (35,377 ft) between the western and eastern banks. This is four times the span of South America's Iguazú Falls. Although exceptional horizontally, this series of cascades and rapids has a maximum vertical drop of just 21 m (69 ft).

100

SHOWER IN A WATERFALL
Follow in the soggy footsteps of millions who have been hopping on to boats to get soaked beneath the roiling waters of Niagara Falls on the US-Canada border since 1846. You'll be in good company: with up to 22.5 million pilgrims heading here each year, it's the **most visited waterfall**.

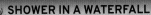

Air pocket

Semi-open cenote (young)

Open cenote (mature)

Cave

Sea

Porous limestone (karst)

Halocline (where fresh water meets salt water)

Coastal aquifer

Cenotes are the visible part of an "anchialine" system: one that seems landlocked but is linked to the ocean.

LONGEST FLOODED CAVE SYSTEM

From the surface, Mexico's Yucatán Peninsula appears fairly bereft of water, but looks can be deceiving… Beneath the surface lies a labyrinth of water-filled caverns and tunnels – effectively an underground river network.

The most extensive contiguous section – the Sac Actun System – measures at least 371.9 km (231.1 mi) long, as of the most recent survey conducted in 2019. It claimed the record in 2018, when it was confirmed that the Sac Actun ("White Cave") and Dos Ojos ("Two Eyes") cave networks were linked. This aquatic maze has been carved out from the limestone landscape over millennia via erosion from both below (by the sea) and above (by rain); *see Yucatán's karst topography in top corner.*

Offering a glimpse into Sac Actun's hidden world are some 220 *cenotes* – natural pools left exposed by collapsed sinkholes. They come in many shapes and sizes, from the 40-m-deep (131-ft) El Pit (*main image*) to the shallower, jungle-edged Nicte-Ha (*inset*).

Although the main rocky base of El Pit visited by recreational divers lies 40 m down, adjoining caverns actually descend much farther, up to 121 m (397 ft) underground.

From the Mayan, Nicte-Ha translates as "Flower of the Water" – referring to the many waterlilies that grow in this cenote.

OCEANS & SEAS

OCEANIC LAYERS

The open ocean boasts the greatest vertical extent of any biome – up to 11 km (6.8 mi). Ocean ecologists divide it into layers or "zones". Sealife has adapted to thrive in the varying levels of sunlight and pressure, from the light-saturated surface to the deepest, darkest trenches...

Epipelagic (Sunlight Zone)
Altiphotic: 0–40 m
Mesophotic: 40–130 m

Rariphotic: 130–310 m; the **newest ocean zone**, formally defined in 2018

500 m

Mesopelagic (Twilight Zone)
310–1,000 m

1,000 m

2,000 m

Bathypelagic (Midnight Zone)
1,000–4,000 m

3,000 m

4,000 m

Abyssopelagic (Abyssal Zone)
4,000–6,000 m

5,000 m

See pp.116–17

6,000 m

Hadopelagic (Hadal Zone/ Trenches)
6,000+ m

Largest tidal bore
Tidal bores occur when an incoming tide enters a narrow bay or estuary and generates waves that travel up-river, against the usual flow. The phenomenon occurs in several places, but most dramatically in China's Qiantang River. At extreme spring tides, the bore waves have been known to reach 9 m (30 ft) high and move at 40 km/h (25 mph).

Largest ocean
The Pacific covers 161,760,000 km² (62,456,000 sq mi) – more than 16 times the size of the USA – and represents 44.7% of Earth's oceans, or 31.7% of its entire surface.

At 15,558,000 km² (6,007,000 sq mi) – smaller than Russia – the Arctic is the **smallest ocean**. Its average depth of 1,205 m (3,953 ft) also makes it the **shallowest ocean**.

Largest sea
Seas are smaller bodies of water than oceans, partly enclosed by a land mass but still connected to an ocean. At *c.* 3,500,000 km² (1,350,000 sq mi), the South China Sea occupies the greatest area. It borders China, the Philippines, Malaysia, Brunei, Indonesia, Singapore and Vietnam.

The 11,350-km² (4,380-sq-mi) Sea of Marmara in Türkiye is the **smallest sea**. It connects the Black Sea to the Aegean in the Mediterranean, which itself feeds into the Atlantic.

First proven rogue wave
Rogue or freak waves are those an order of magnitude larger than the waves that precede or follow them. Notoriously difficult to record or measure, they were long considered to be the tall tales of old sailors. But on 1 Jan 1995, the reality of rogue waves was confirmed by an up to 25.6-m (84-ft) monster that struck the Draupner platform in the North Sea.

The **tallest wave measured by buoy** – and ratified by the World Meteorological Organization – was 19 m (62 ft) high, logged in the North Atlantic between Iceland and the UK on 4 Feb 2013.

First protected waves
On 18 Feb 2016, Peru enacted Ley de Rompientes ("Law of the Breakers"), forbidding any offshore construction up to 1 km (0.6 mi) from Punta Malabrigo. The legislation seeks to safeguard the region's waves, known as Chicama or Mamape, which are world-famous among surfers for their consistency. They are among the longest waves in the world, rolling up to 4 km (2.5 mi) before breaking.

Warmest ocean
Covering *c.* 20% of Earth's surface, the Indian Ocean has the warmest waters of all the oceans, as most of it lies in the tropics. Its average minimum surface temperature is around 22°C (72°F), but it can reach 35°C (95°F) in the Persian Gulf. Its coolest stretches are found in the south, towards Antarctica, where it meets the Southern Ocean.

Greatest tidal range
The world's highest tides occur in the funnel-shaped Bay of Fundy, which divides the peninsular province of Nova Scotia in Canada from New Brunswick (Canada) and Maine (USA). Burntcoat Head (*below*), in Nova Scotia's Minas Basin, experiences the most extreme average spring range: 14.5 m (47 ft 6 in). Tides here flood and ebb over 3.2 km (2 mi) of muddy shore, from the lower water mark to the head of the bay.

Low tide allows visitors to walk out on the mud flats

At high tide, the sea fully surrounds Flowerpot Island

RIDE IN A LIMOUSINE
There are stretch limos and then there are *strrreeetttch* limos! On 1 Mar 2022, the 30.51-m (100-ft 1-in) *American Dream* regained its title as the **longest car** after being restored to its former glory by Michael Manning and Michael Dezer (both USA). You can take 74 friends along for the ride!

The Oceanic Pole of Inaccessibility was first identified in 1992 by Croatian-Canadian survey engineer Hrvoje Lukatela.

LARGEST BIOME

The open ocean – excluding waters close to the shore – is known as the "pelagic zone". Globally, it contains around 1.33 billion km³ (319.1 million cu mi) of water, with a maximum depth of almost 11 km (6.8 mi). This vast watery realm contains many of the largest animals on Earth (*see pp.44–45*) but also huge conglomerations of smaller sealife such as plankton and fish shoals that form the basis of the entire marine ecosystem.

The **remotest place in the ocean** is Point Nemo in the South Pacific (*left, yellow dot*), located at 48.87°S, 123.39°W. The nearest dry land is *c.* 1,451 nautical miles (2,688 km; 1,670 mi) away on three virtually equidistant islands: Pitcairn to the north (*pink dot*); Rapa Nui, aka Easter Island, to the north-east (*green*); and the Antarctic Maher Island to the south (*orange*).

Largest oceanic "garbage patch"

Earth's oceans are under threat from humanity's trash, including 8 million tonnes (8.8 million tons) of plastic pollution per year. Owing to currents, much of it ends up in swirling vortices known as gyres. Debris polluting the North Pacific Central Gyre is some of the most prolific, covering an area at least the size of Texas, USA. According to a 2001 study, it contains 5.114 kg of plastic for every 1 km² (29 lb 3 oz per sq mi) of seawater.

TAKE DANCE LESSONS

Whether you're keen to glide around a ballroom or cut some shapes at the disco, there are many ways you *can-can* boogie your way into the record books. Bandana Nepal (NPL), for example, jived for 126 hr straight on 23–28 Nov 2018, waltzing away with a certificate for the **longest dance marathon**.

ICESCAPES

Most intact woolly mammoth
In Aug 2010, a 39,000-year-old female juvenile woolly mammoth (*Mammuthus primigenius*) was found in Siberian permafrost. Dubbed "Yuka", it is 3 m (9 ft 10 in) tall and weighs 5 tonnes (11,020 lb). The icy surroundings had kept the carcass (including fur, the brain and liquid blood) in near-pristine condition.

PERMAFROST: NATURE'S FREEZER
Permanently frozen land covers around 15% of Earth. The **deepest permafrost** is in Siberia, Russia, where historically the ground has remained icy to a depth of *c.* 1,000 m (3,280 ft). With a warming climate, however, this is undoubtedly reducing. And as it does, ancient flora and fauna that have been in the deep freeze for millennia are now starting to thaw…

In 2012, new plants were grown from the frozen fruit of 32,000-year-old *Silene stenophylla* found near the Kolyma River. This is the **oldest resurrected plant tissue**.

In May 2018, two nematode worm species were reanimated, having lain in Arctic permafrost for up to 42,400 years. They had undergone the **longest animal cryobiosis**.

The **oldest liquid blood** was drawn from a young male Lenskaya horse found in Yakutia in Jun 2018. It has been radiocarbon-dated to at least 41,000–42,000 years old.

In 2021, an exceptionally well-preserved lion cub was unearthed near the Senyalyakh River, above the Arctic Circle. Dating back 28,000 years, it had even retained its whiskers.

A cave bear that had died during the last ice age was uncovered on the island of Bolshoy Lyakhovsky in 2020. Its fur, internal organs and soft tissues were all intact.

First photo of a snow crystal
On 15 Jan 1885, Wilson Bentley (USA) snapped a single snow crystal on his family's farm near Jericho in Vermont, USA. The crystals here were also photographed by Bentley *c.* 1902. On the night of 27 Jan 1887, a winter storm dropped snowflakes (snow-crystal clusters) that were "larger than milk pans" over the Clark Fork River valley near Missoula, Montana, USA. Reports suggest they were up to 1 ft 3 in (38 cm) wide and 8 in (20 cm) thick – the **largest snowflakes**. *Check out the **largest snow crystal** on p.27.*

Longest subglacial river
Using computer modelling and radar images, scientists have inferred that a 460-km-long (286-mi) river flows from below the interior of the East Antarctic Ice Sheet, to the underside of the Filchner-Ronne Ice Shelf and then into the Weddell Sea. The discovery was published in Oct 2022.

As global temperatures rise, rivers are starting to flow over the surface of ice sheets too. The **longest supraglacial river** – observed by satellite on the Amery Ice Shelf in East Antarctica on 22 Jan 2015 – stretched for 120 km (75 mi).

Highest glacier
The Khumbu Glacier in north-east Nepal ranges in altitude from 4,900 m to more than 8,000 m (16,080–26,250 ft). It drains from the West Cwm between Everest and the Lhotse–Nuptse Ridge, and is a key route for scaling the world's **highest mountain** (*see pp.118–19*) from the south.

Largest tropical glacier
Earth's two largest ice caps in the tropics are both in the Peruvian Andes. The Coropuna Ice Cap had a surface area of 42.3 km² (16.3 sq mi) – about the same as 26,800 NHL ice rinks – as of 2021. It most likely overtook the Quelccaya Ice Cap, once the larger of the two, some 40 years ago.

Largest iceberg ever
On 12 Nov 1956, the USS *Glacier* sighted an iceberg estimated by eyewitnesses to be more than 31,000 km² (12,000 sq mi); this would have made it larger than Belgium. Located west of Scott Island in the Southern Ocean, it was said to be *c.* 335 km (208 mi) long and 97 km (60 mi) wide.

Measured by satellite imagery, the **largest iceberg** now is A23A, as of 6 Jan 2023. It had maximum dimensions of 40 x 34 nautical miles (74 x 63 km; 46 x 39 mi) – more than 4,000 km² (1,540 sq mi). Unusually long lived, A23A was "born" from Antarctica's Filchner-Ronne Ice Shelf in 1986.

Greatest concentration of pingoes
Found in permafrost regions, pingoes (or hydrolaccoliths) are mounds of earth with an ice core, formed as frozen groundwater is forced upwards. The Tuktoyaktuk Peninsula in western Arctic Canada is home to some 1,350, the biggest of which is the 49-m (161-ft) Ibyuk Pingo (*above*). The **tallest** overall is Kadleroshilik Pingo near Prudhoe Bay in Alaska, USA, at 54 m (177 ft) high.

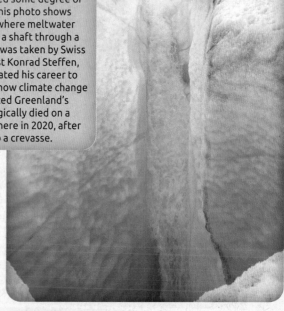

Greatest ice-sheet melt in one day
On 31 Jul 2019, the Greenland Ice Sheet – the second-largest glacier – shed more than 24 billion tonnes (26.5 billion tons) of meltwater. That's enough to fill 10 million Olympic swimming pools! About 60% of the total sheet experienced some degree of melting. This photo shows a moulin (where meltwater carves out a shaft through a glacier). It was taken by Swiss glaciologist Konrad Steffen, who dedicated his career to assessing how climate change has impacted Greenland's ice. He tragically died on a field trip there in 2020, after falling into a crevasse.

2002 **2003** **2019**

Fastest glacier retreat on land
Between the summers of 2003 and 2005, global warming brought about a retreat of 350 m (1,148 ft) at Triftgletscher (Trift Glacier) in the Swiss Alps. Glacier melt has created a large lake (the Triftsee) in front of its terminus. This lake only served to accelerate the shrinkage by warming the glacial ice and causing further chunks to break off. Between 2000 and 2021, the glacier reduced in length by nearly 1.9 km (1.2 mi).

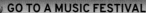

GO TO A MUSIC FESTIVAL
Sure, there's Coachella and Glastonbury, but if you prefer your live music served in the great outdoors, then where better to "chill" out than at the **longest-running ice music festival**? The Ice Music Festival, replete with icy instruments, has been held annually in Norway since 2006.

LARGEST GLACIER

The Antarctic Ice Sheet covers a contiguous 13,924,000 km² (5,376,100 sq mi) of Antarctica – most of the continent, including its floating sections, or "ice shelves". It has an overall volume of 26,920,000 km³ (6,458,450 cu mi).

At a point where the sheet sits over the Astrolabe Subglacial Basin, to the south of the Adélie Coast, it is 4,897 m (16,066 ft) deep – Earth's **thickest ice**.

The interior of the continent may receive as little as 50 mm (2 in) of precipitation per year. As a "desert" is defined as an area with no to very little rainfall, this also makes the Antarctic Ice Sheet the **largest desert**.

There's no fear of overheating in this desert, though. A low of -89.2°C (-128.6°F) logged at the Vostok research station on 21 Jul 1983 is the all-time **coldest temperature recorded on Earth**.

Largest ice shelf

An ice shelf forms when a glacier meets the ocean and starts to float, creating a large platform connected to the ice inland. As of 2021, the Ross Ice Shelf was some 800 km (500 mi) wide and covered 511,371 km² (197,441 sq mi). Its leading edge can tower 50 m (160 ft) above the sea.

In 2010, a camera on a submersible robot spotted the **first ice-dwelling sea anemone** on the underside of the Ross Ice Shelf. Named *Edwardsiella andrillae*, very little is known about how these cold-tolerant cnidarians survive.

Emperor penguins (*Aptenodytes forsteri*) were listed as critically endangered in 2022 owing to climate change.

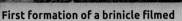

First formation of a brinicle filmed

Brinicles are pipes of frozen water that develop beneath sea-ice as a result of sinking columns of supercold, supersaline water. If a brinicle reaches the seabed, in shallow conditions, icy tendrils can spread across the ocean floor, freezing and killing any organisms in its path. The process was first filmed by the BBC for the series *Frozen Planet* in 2011, in the Antarctic's McMurdo Sound.

HOT WATER

Hottest ocean water measured

In Aug 2008, an international team of scientists announced they had logged water at a temperature of 464°C (867°F) issuing from a hydrothermal vent on the seabed 3,000 m (9,842 ft) down in the Atlantic Ocean. The vents are conduits for discharges of sea water, superheated by molten magma below Earth's crust. At this depth, water above 407°C (764°F) becomes "supercritical" and lighter than usual.

Deepest hydrothermal vents

In 2013, UK scientists reported the discovery of hot-water vents at a depth of 4,968 m (16,299 ft). They are located in the Cayman Trough in the Caribbean Sea.

The **tallest hydrothermal vents** measure *c.* 55 m (180 ft) – higher than Nelson's Column in London, UK. They were found by the *Atlantis* research ship of the Woods Hole Oceanographic Institution (USA) in Dec 2000. Dubbed "The Lost City", they are part of a system of vents on the Mid-Atlantic Ridge.

Steamboat (up to 137 m)

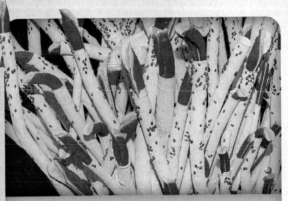

Fastest-growing marine invertebrate

Giant tube worms (*Riftia pachyptila*) have been recorded colonizing a new site and reaching 1.5 m (4 ft 11 in) long in less than two years. They live around seabed hydrothermal vents and form a mutually beneficial relationship with bacteria. Where deposits of iron sulphide are present, the vents' discharge is tinted – hence their nickname of "black smokers" (*inset*).

Tube worms aren't the only extremophile organisms to survive within this ecosystem fuelled by heat and volcanic minerals (rather than sunlight). Perhaps the toughest of them all is the so-called Strain 121, a microbe belonging to the ancient group of bacteria-like lifeforms known as archaea. The **most heat-tolerant organism**, it can endure temperatures of 121°C (249°F).

Old Faithful (up to 55 m)

Tallest active geyser

Steamboat Geyser can produce jets more than 90 m (295 ft) tall, and reached a record height of 137 m (449 ft) – taller than Giza's Great Pyramid – in Jul 2020. It's located in the USA's Yellowstone National Park, home to the **greatest concentration of geysers** – in excess of 500. Of these, some 250 are active, including Old Faithful (*left*).

In total, the park, which sits atop a supervolcano, has more than 10,000 geothermal features – at least half of the world's known examples. This includes thousands of hot springs, among them the stunning Grand Prismatic Spring (*right*), as well as many mudpots and fumaroles. .

The **tallest geyser ever** was Waimangu Geyser, located near Rotorua on the North Island of New Zealand. First documented erupting in 1900, its jets could surge in excess of 460 m (1,510 ft) – higher than Malaysia's Petronas Towers. It has been dormant since 1 Nov 1904.

Largest island created by volcanic eruptions

Covering 102,775 km² (39,681 sq mi), Iceland was formed from lava that spewed from the Mid-Atlantic Ridge and cooled into basalt. Ongoing volcanic activity is responsible for the country's popular geysers and hot springs (*example above*); it enables Iceland to generate 66% of its primary energy from geothermal sources.

The **most northerly active geyser field** is also found in Iceland: Hveravellir in Reykjahverfi, 18 km (11 mi) south of the town of Húsavík, lies at 65.9°N.

Highest geyser field

The Dagejia geothermal field – which features some 100 hot springs, about 20 of which are geysers – is *c.* 5,100 m (16,730 ft) above sea level. It is located near the head of the Yarlung Tsangpo River (*see p.18*) in southern Tibet, China.

Largest hot spring

Waimangu Cauldron (aka Frying Pan Lake) is a natural hot spring with a surface area of *c.* 3.8 ha (9.3 acres) – larger than five soccer fields. It sits in the Echo Crater on New Zealand's North Island. The lake's average temperature of 50–60°C (122–140°F) is ideal for thermophilic micro-organisms. Less than 50 km (31 mi) away lies the world's **most southerly active geyser field** – Ōrākei Kōrako, at a latitude of 38.4°S, some 35 km (22 mi) from the city of Rotorua.

Most frequent geyser

Between 20 and 27 Oct 2012, scientists recorded the activity of the "El Jefe" geyser at the El Tatio geothermal field in northern Chile – the largest in the southern hemisphere. The mean interval between its eruptions over the six days was a mere 132.2 sec, about half the time that it takes to boil a full electric kettle.

Deepest underwater volcanic eruption

In Dec 2015, an autonomous underwater vehicle found a stretch of dark, glassy lava at a depth of some 4,450 m (14,600 ft), west of the Mariana Trench in the Pacific Ocean.

VISIT ROME
No trip to Italy's capital city would be complete without stepping inside its iconic Colosseum – the **largest amphitheatre**. Completed in 80 CE, it covers 2 ha (5 acres) and had a capacity of 87,000 spectators, who would have seen combat between gladiators, slaves and wild beasts.

Tourists flock to the Kawah Ijen volcano not only for its strikingly colourful acid lake. The site boasts other unusual phenomena such as billowing fumaroles and "blue fire". The latter occurs when sulphurous gas escaping from cracks in the volcano are ignited by lava and encounter the oxygen-rich air.

Kawah Ijen's crater hosts one of the few remaining active artisanal sulphur mines. It contributes greatly to the local economy, despite the inhospitable conditions and impact on the health of those who work here. After it has been processed, the sulphur is used for a range of purposes, from the manufacture of fertilizer to bleaching sugar.

LARGEST HYPERACID LAKE

The oval-shaped crater lake in the Kawah Ijen volcano, on the Indonesian island of Java, has an area of around 0.6 km^2 (0.2 sq mi), a maximum depth of 200 m (660 ft) and a volume of 27.5 million m^3 (971 million cu ft). The lake owes its vibrant turquoise hue to high levels of chemicals such as sulphuric and hydrochloric acid. The water has a pH value of less than 0 – the most acidic level on the pH scale – making it corrosive enough to eat through metal; for context, car battery acid has a pH of 1. The average water temperature is 37°C (99°F) – the same as that of the human body.

Hydrothermal water, infused with gases from subterranean magma, lend the lake its high acidity levels.

ROUND-UP

Largest lake ever

Formed some 12 million years ago (MYA), Megalake Paratethys extended from the European Alps to what is now Kazakhstan in Central Asia (*see map below*). At its peak, *c.* 10 MYA, it covered 2.8 million km² (1.08 million sq mi) and was home to endemic species such as seals and even miniature whales. Today, the Black, Caspian and Aral seas are its main surviving fragments. Paratethys' full scale was set out by paleo-oceanographer Dan Palcu, in *Scientific Reports* in Jun 2021.

Lowest Antarctic sea-ice extent

On 21 Feb 2023, Antarctica's sea ice spanned a record low of 1.79 million km² (691,122 sq mi), as measured by satellite. Unlike in the Arctic, which has seen a dramatic decline in summer sea ice since the 1970s, coverage in the Antarctic gradually expanded from the late 1970s. However, research shows that the overall increase in its area reversed around 2014 and is now showing a downward trend.

The **lowest Arctic sea-ice extent** was logged on 17 Sep 2012, with only 3.39 million km² (1.3 million sq mi) of ice at the end of the Arctic summer. Each winter, the Arctic Ocean freezes over and forms sea ice that is just a few tens of centimetres thick and which shrinks the following summer. At the current rate of decline, the annual average is diminishing by about 80,000 km² (30,900 sq mi) – an area similar in size to Austria – each year.

Greatest concentration of deep-sea brine pools

Deep-sea brine pools are hypersaline, anoxic (oxygenless) lakes that form on the seafloor; their high salt content makes them denser than the surrounding ocean. There are at least 25 complexes of brine pools at the bottom of the Red Sea, more than anywhere else on Earth. The only other locations known to host these pools are the Mediterranean Sea and the Gulf of Mexico.

The **deepest brine pool** lies within the latter, in the Orca Basin, some 2,200 m (7,220 ft) below sea level. Its water has a salt content of around 300 g/litre (40 oz/gal), which is approximately eight times greater than that of the Gulf of Mexico itself.

Highest dewpoint temperature

The "dewpoint" is one method of assessing humidity, which – when taken with air temperature as measured by a thermometer – can give a more accurate sense of the experienced heat. At 3 p.m. on 8 Jul 2003, the city of Dhahran in Saudi Arabia recorded a dewpoint temperature of 35°C (95°F), accompanied by a dry-bulb air temperature of 42°C (107.6°F). This equated to a total heat index (i.e., the temperature that "it feels like" to the human body) of 81.1°C (178°F).

Highest terrestrial weather station

On 9 May 2022, a team of scientists and Sherpas installed a weather-monitoring system 8,810 m (28,904 ft) above sea level atop Bishop Rock on the Nepalese side of Everest, the **highest mountain**. The National Geographic/Rolex expedition was a collaboration between Appalachian State University (USA), King's College London (UK), Tribhuvan University (NPL) and the Nepalese government's departments of Hydrology and Meteorology, and National Parks and Wildlife Conservation.

Largest water-vapour injection into Earth's atmosphere

The eruption of the submarine Hunga Tonga-Hunga Ha'apai volcano in the South Pacific on 15 Jan 2022 released 146 million tonnes (160.9 million tons) of steam into the stratosphere, up to 53 km (33 mi) high. The plume contained the equivalent of 58,000 Olympic swimming pools of water.

The explosive event triggered the **most volcanic lightning** (*inset*), caused by ash-generated static electricity. On 13–15 Jan, 589,754 discharges were detected at the site. It also caused the **fastest atmospheric waves**, peaking at 968 km/h (601 mph) – close to the speed of sound – in the stratosphere. They lasted for 12 hr and travelled around the planet six times!

Most Blue Flag beaches (country)

The Foundation for Environmental Education is an international voluntary programme that recognizes coastal regions that uphold a strict series of high standards. Criteria include water quality, environmental management and accessibility. As of 2022, Spain boasts more Blue Flag beaches – 621 – than any other nation, followed by Greece with 581 and Türkiye with 529. Pictured is the beach of Peñarronda in Asturias, in north-west Spain.

GO TO CANADA

Stunning nature, epic winter sports and a chance to tick off the No.1 bucket-list goal (*see p.242*) – what's *not* to like about the second-largest country? Make time for a funicular ride up Montreal's Olympic Stadium Tower – the **tallest leaning tower**, at 165 m (541 ft 4 in), with a tilt of 45°.

Greatest rainfall in one month
In monsoon season, clouds form over the Bay of Bengal and drift inland until they reach the Khasi Hills of eastern India. Here, the change in altitude causes the water vapour to condense, unleashing huge downpours. In Jul 1861, a total of 9,300 mm (366 in) of rain fell over the town of Cherrapunji (aka Sohra) in Meghalaya. At this rate, the rain would have filled an Olympic diving pool in just 16 days. This contributed to the **one year** record too: Cherrapunji received 26,470 mm (1,042 in) of rainfall between 1 Aug 1860 and 31 Jul 1861.

Largest snow crystal
On 30 Dec 2003, ice-crystal expert Kenneth Libbrecht (USA) used a portable microscope to measure a snow crystal that was 10 mm (0.39 in) from tip to tip in Cochrane, Ontario, Canada. It's known as a "fernlike stellar dendrite", in a nod to its frond-like structure.
*For the **largest snowflake** (a clump of snow crystals), see p.22.*

100%

Deepest freshwater cave
Surveys of the Hranice Abyss in eastern Czechia have been taking place since 1960 – carried out by human divers and more recently robots – and yet the sinkhole's full depth is still unknown. In Aug 2022, the Czech Speleological Society updated the *measured* extent of this karst chasm to 519.5 m (1,704 ft), of which 450 m (1,476 ft) is flooded. Above-ground tests conducted in 2020 indicate that trenches at the base of the cavern system might descend as far as 1 km (0.6 mi).

Deepest blue hole
Sometimes called "pupils of the sea", blue holes are sheer-sided underwater sinkholes, often found in reef areas, that appear as dark circles from the surface. The most profound example, at 300.89 m (987 ft 2 in), is the Dragon Hole, which lies off the Paracel Islands in the South China Sea.

Most powerful upward lightning event
On 14 May 2018, a massive discharge of lightning known as a "gigantic jet" was recorded over south-west Oklahoma, USA. It shot upwards from a cloud top some 80 km (50 mi) into the ionosphere – the boundary between Earth's atmosphere and space. The discharge transferred 300 coulombs of electrical charge, which is between 60 and 300 times more than a typical lightning bolt.

The **longest-lasting lightning** lit up the sky over Uruguay and northern Argentina on 18 Jun 2020, with a flash that persisted for 17.102 sec. Most lightning discharges last a mere 0.2 sec. The event was verified by the World Meteorological Organization (WMO) on 1 Feb 2022.

Greatest rainfall in...*
• **One minute**: 31.2 mm (1.23 in) in Unionville, Maryland, USA, on 4 Jul 1956.
• **One hour**: 304.8 mm (12 in) in Holt, Missouri, USA, on 22 Jun 1947.
• **24 hours**: 1,825 mm (71.8 in) at Foc-Foc, on the Indian Ocean island of Réunion, on 7–8 Jan 1966.
• **48 hours**: 2,493 mm (98.1 in) in Cherrapunji (*see above*), Meghalaya, India, on 15–16 Jun 1995.
All rainfall records ratified by the WMO

In 2022, 91% of coral surveyed in the Great Barrier Reef suffered some degree of bleaching, owing to warming waters.

Warmest average global ocean surface temperature
In 2022, the heat content for the upper 2,000 m (6,560 ft) of Earth's oceans was 245.4 zettajoules (245.4 billion trillion Joules) above the 1981–2010 average. This amount of energy is enough to boil 700 million kettles every second for a year. The trend of warming oceans (a record that has been broken four years in a row) is a major contributor to the global decline in marine habitats such as coral reefs.

OWN A BUSINESS
Hit a *sweet* spot in the market and your fledgling enterprise could really go the distance... Take Ichimonjiya Wasuke, a traditional confectionery seller and café in Kita-ku, Kyōto, Japan, which is the world's **oldest candy store**. Inaugurated *c.* 1000 CE, it is currently operated by the 25th generation of the founding family.

SYLVIA EARLE

A quanaut Sylvia Earle has devoted her life to the exploration and protection of Earth's oceans. Her iconic underwater expeditions and contributions to the development of SCUBA and submersible technology have earned her the title "Her Deepness".

Sylvia fell in love with the ocean at an early age. "I was three years old and a big wave knocked me over," she recalled. "I wasn't frightened, I was excited." She learned to SCUBA dive at Florida State University, where she majored in botany and collected more than 20,000 samples of algae for her PhD. In 1970, Sylvia was selected to head the *Tektite II* mission, spending a fortnight with four other scientists in a submerged habitat 15 m (50 ft) below the surface of the Atlantic Ocean, off the US Virgin Islands. It was there, while studying local coral reefs, that she first witnessed directly the impact of pollution on marine ecosystems.

In the 1970s/80s, Sylvia ventured on several record-breaking descents (*see 1 and 5*) that not only pushed the boundaries of aquatic exploration, but also made her a figurehead for the advancement of women in science. She founded Deep Ocean Engineering and was closely involved with designing its *Deep Rover* submersible. In 1990, Sylvia became the National Oceanic and Atmospheric Administration's **first female chief scientist,** where she made use of her knowledge of oil spills to advise on the environmental costs of the Gulf War.

Now in her 80s, Sylvia remains a passionate crusader for the oceans. In a fitting tribute to a scientist and campaigner who has spent more than six decades exploring the seas, in Nov 2022 a state-of-the-art polar expedition ship bearing her name was launched, hoping to discover more of our world's watery wonders.

VITAL STATISTICS

Name	Sylvia Earle (née Reade)
Birthplace	Gibbstown, New Jersey, USA
Birth date	30 Aug 1935
Current GWR titles	5, including first *TIME* Hero of the Planet and **deepest solo sub descent (female)**
Hours logged underwater	7,500+ (312 days) on 100+ expeditions
Honours	Explorers Club Medal, SeaKeepers Award, NOGI Award, Rachel Carson Prize

HALL OF FAME

1: Sylvia prepares for a dive in the *DeepSee* submersible near Panama. After almost 40 years, she still holds the women's record for the **deepest solo descent by submersible** – 1,000 m (3,280 ft) – on board *Deep Rover* off San Clemente Island, USA, in 1985.

2: In 1970, Sylvia led the **first all-female aquanaut research team** – the *Tektite II* mission, with Alina Szmant, Ann Hartline, "Peggy" Lucas Bond (all USA) and Renate True (BRA). The aquanauts were viewed as trailblazers in the scientific community.

3: Sylvia met then-US president Barack Obama on Hawaii's Midway Atoll in 2016. Obama's administration had just expanded the Papahānaumokuākea Marine National Monument to make it the world's **largest marine protected area (IUCN)**. Today, it covers 1,508,870 km² (582,578 sq mi) – which is three times the size of Spain.

4: The Emmy-Award-winning Netflix documentary *Mission Blue* (2014) brought Sylvia's attempts to protect the oceans to a wider audience. Founded by her in 2009, the NGO seeks to preserve "Hope Spots" – global marine habitats identified as being critical to the ocean's wellbeing.

5: On 19 Sep 1979, Sylvia donned a *JIM* diving suit and descended 381 m (1,250 ft) to the seafloor off Hawaii, where she performed the **deepest untethered sea walk by a woman**. She spent two hours exploring the seabed, walking among green-eyed sharks and bioluminescent fish. The suit – named after diver Jim Jarrett – had a metal body, a Perspex viewing dome and articulated limbs.

Sylvia shows Barack Obama images of a newly discovered fish to be named after him: *Tosanoides obama*.

3

5

The Mission Blue project has set up 140-plus "Hope Spots", covering 57 million km² (22 million sq mi) of ocean.

4

NETFLIX
A NETFLIX DOCUMENTARY
MISSION BLUE
A WORLD WITHOUT THE OCEAN, IS A WORLD WITHOUT US.
AUGUST 15

Find out more about Sylvia in the Hall of Fame section at www. guinnessworldrecords.com/2024

AQUATIC LIFE

Largest seadragon

Seadragons are marine vertebrates related to seahorses. Of the family's three known species, the weedy seadragon (*Phyllopteryx taeniolatus*) reaches the greatest size, growing up to 45 cm (1 ft 5 in) from snout to tail tip. As the name implies, weedy seadragons live among seaweed and coral in coastal waters off southern Australia and Tasmania, where its patterned body and leaf-like appendages provide excellent camouflage. Although also called common seadragons, this species' numbers have sadly been in decline in recent years, most likely as a result of habitat destruction.

Very few baby seadragons have been born in captivity. One place that successfully bred them was the...

100%

...Birch Aquarium at the Scripps Institution of Oceanography in California, USA, with two hatchlings in 2020.

A single brood takes around eight weeks to incubate and can contain 250 baby seadragons!

After fertilization, seadragon eggs are carried around by the male on their tails until they hatch.

GIANT PACIFIC OCTOPUS

Eight "tentacles", squidgy bodies, colour-changing skin – you might think you've got octopus biology down, but don't be taken for a sucker! If you thought that the exterior of these shape-shifting sea creatures was bizarre, just wait till you see what's going on inside…

Octopuses are marine molluscs that – like their kin, the squid – have evolved to survive without a shell. Of the 300 or so octopod species, the **largest** is the giant Pacific octopus (*Enteroctopus dofleini*) – GPO for short – found living near coastal areas on both sides of the North Pacific.

The biggest individual to be reliably measured was 4 m (13 ft 1 in) long and weighed, at 71 kg (156 lb), the same as an adult man. Anecdotal reports tell of a monster with an arm span of more than 30 ft (9.1 m) – big enough to reach across a helipad – and weighing an estimated 600 lb (272 kg), but such extreme figures are contested.

While the GPO stands out for its scale, many of its most amazing anatomical features are representative of all octopuses. That includes having three hearts, nine brains (each limb is semi-autonomous) and blue blood. They are considered among the most intelligent invertebrates on the planet, able to use tools, navigate mazes and, in captivity, make daring escapes from their tanks!

When an animal is known for being a colossus, it can be easy to forget that it wasn't born that way. The eggs of giant Pacific octopuses – which can number 100,000 per batch – are each only about the size of a grain of rice. Hatchlings (*below*) measure a mere 6 mm (0.23 in) long and weigh 22 mg (0.0008 oz). While as adults GPOs are formidable predators (*see right*), youngsters are on many other animals' menus. In fact, only a handful of GPO babies will survive to adulthood.

Eclectic tastes
The bigger the animal, the bigger the appetite. Giant Pacific octopuses can consume up to 4% of their own body weight in a day. Hunting at night, their favoured fare includes crustaceans such as crabs and shrimp, other molluscs such as clams and scallops, and even fellow octopuses. They will also gobble fish eggs and fish – occasionally even taking on small sharks such as the spiny dogfish pictured.

Arms vs legs
Octopuses do not, in fact, have tentacles but limbs. Through observation, aquarium scientists determined that six of these are "arms" (used for swimming, hunting and manipulating objects) and two are "legs" (used mainly for crawling/climbing).

Octopuses have blue blood because oxygen is transported around the body in haemocyanin – a protein that contains copper; our blood is red because oxygen is carried through our circulatory system by haemoglobin, which is iron-based

Bundles of muscle fibres (circumferential, longitudinal, oblique, transverse and median) surround the axial nerve and control the movement of the limbs and suckers

Suction cups (200+ per limb); octopus limbs have suckers all the way up, while squid tentacles only have them at the end

DID YOU KNOW?
A single sucker is strong enough to support 16 kg (35 lb) – or four cats!

GPOs are one of the longest-lived octopuses, but still only reach up to five years old.

As with all octopuses, GPOs have a venomous bite, but it is not fatal to humans.

A new species called the frilled giant Pacific octopus was recognized in 2017.

Ink-redible self defence
As with most cephalopods, the GPO can release melanin-saturated ink as a last resort to evade danger. As well as providing a smokescreen, the substance contains toxic chemicals that irritate the eyes and disrupt senses of smell and taste.

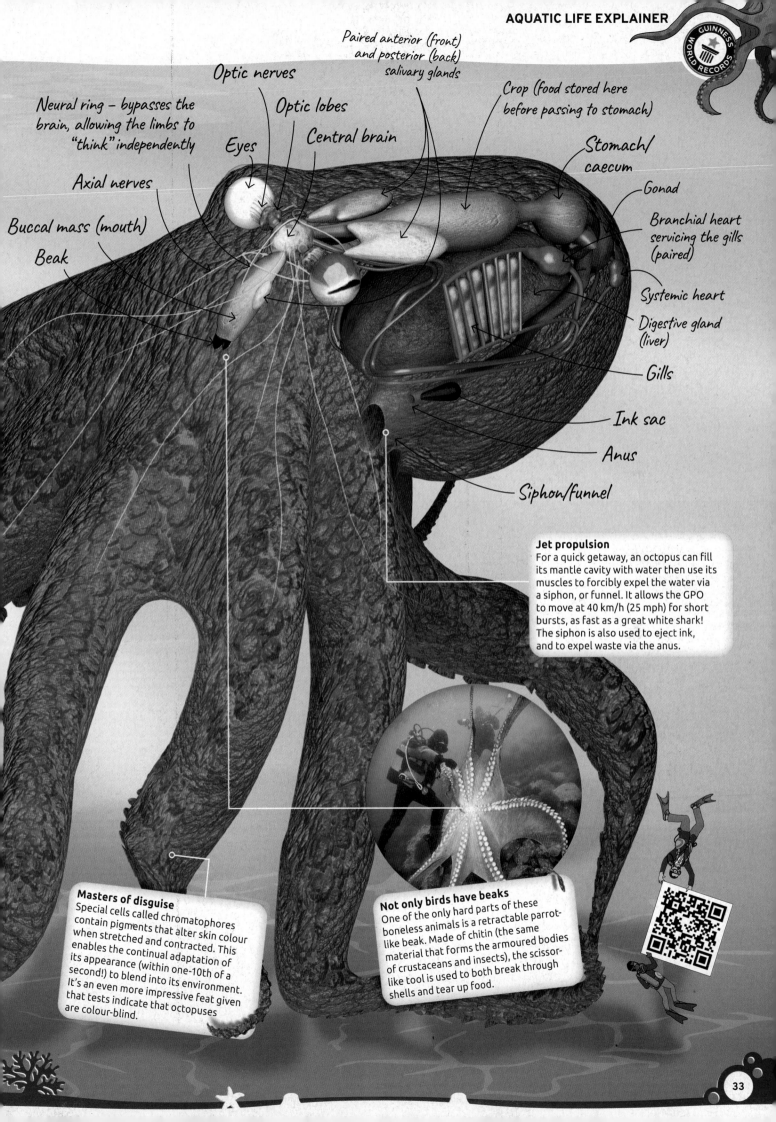

Neural ring – bypasses the brain, allowing the limbs to "think" independently

Optic nerves

Paired anterior (front) and posterior (back) salivary glands

Optic lobes

Crop (food stored here before passing to stomach)

Eyes

Central brain

Stomach/ caecum

Axial nerves

Gonad

Buccal mass (mouth)

Branchial heart servicing the gills (paired)

Beak

Systemic heart

Digestive gland (liver)

Gills

Ink sac

Anus

Siphon/funnel

Jet propulsion
For a quick getaway, an octopus can fill its mantle cavity with water then use its muscles to forcibly expel the water via a siphon, or funnel. It allows the GPO to move at 40 km/h (25 mph) for short bursts, as fast as a great white shark! The siphon is also used to eject ink, and to expel waste via the anus.

Masters of disguise
Special cells called chromatophores contain pigments that alter skin colour when stretched and contracted. This enables the continual adaptation of its appearance (within one-10th of a second!) to blend into its environment. It's an even more impressive feat given that tests indicate that octopuses are colour-blind.

Not only birds have beaks
One of the only hard parts of these boneless animals is a retractable parrot-like beak. Made of chitin (the same material that forms the armoured bodies of crustaceans and insects), the scissor-like tool is used to both break through shells and tear up food.

110

Most teeth for a crocodilian
Gharials (*Gavialis gangeticus*), aka gavials, native to the Indian subcontinent, have up to 110 razor-sharp teeth in their slender snouts. These deadly dentures are specialized for snapping up fish in rivers with fast-moving currents.

DID YOU KNOW?

Just 2.5% of water on Earth is fresh; the rest is saline and lies mainly in the oceans.

Most is locked up in ice or underground; only c. 1.2% is surface water (*see pp.16–17*).

Even so, 10% of animal species and 50% of fish species reside in freshwater habitats.

LARGEST
FLAMINGO COLONY

The soda lakes of East Africa host a permanent population of 1.5–2.5 million lesser flamingos (*Phoeniconaias minor*), with most of these in northern Tanzania. This represents 75% of all lesser flamingos but also the largest proliferation of any flamingo species on Earth.

The collective noun informally used to describe a flock of flamingos is a flamboyance.

Lightest freshwater fish
A fully mature male dwarf pygmy goby (*Pandaka pygmaea*) is c. 10 mm (0.3 in) long and weighs just 4–5 mg – about one-sixth that of a typical staple, or over 7,000 to the ounce. Females are slightly larger. They are found in shady waterways in the Philippines, as well as in the brackish mangroves of Singapore and Indonesia. As small as this goby is, a rival fish claims the tiny crown based on length (*see right*).

Oldest freshwater fish
A female bigmouth buffalo (*Ictiobus cyprinellus*) collected near Pelican Rapids in Minnesota, USA, was age-authenticated to 112 years old. This species is part of the sucker family native to North America's Mississippi Basin and Hudson Bay. A 2019 study of the fish's otoliths (earstones) revealed that up to 90% of some bigmouth populations were octogenarians – far exceeding the previously assumed top age of just 26 years. Among those analysed, five were centenarians. *See also the oldest fish in captivity ever on p.46.*

Most aquatic spider
The only species of spider to spend its life almost entirely submerged is the diving bell spider (*Argyroneta aquatica*). It dwells within a bubble of air, brought from the surface in a "net" of air-trapping hairs. Although occasionally venturing to the surface to replenish its air supply, this arachnid hunts, reproduces and lays its eggs all underwater.

Most biodiverse lake (fish)
While it may be the world's ninth-largest lake by surface area, the 29,544-km² (11,407-sq-mi) Lake Malawi (aka Nyasa) in eastern Africa teems with more types of fish than any other. It hosts at least 700 species of cichlid (some ichthyologists posit 1,000); all but four are endemic. Unique species of catfish, tetra and eel also dwell here.

Longest mustelid
No member of the weasel family (Mustelidae) grows longer than the giant otter (*Pteronura brasiliensis*), a native of rivers and wetlands in South America. From nose to tail tip, it can span 1.8 m (6 ft) – the same as an adult man is tall – and weigh up to 32 kg (70 lb). By weight, they can be surpassed by the shorter but stockier sea otter (*Enhydra lutris*; *see p.36*).

Largest waterfowl
Two extant species of swan share this title: the mute swan (*Cygnus olor*), which is heavier, and the trumpeter swan (*C. buccinator*), which has a greater wingspan. Native to Europe, the mute swan has a typical weight in adult males (cobs) of 15 kg (33 lb), though one exceptional specimen – documented by German naturalist Walter von Sanden in 1935 – was 22.5 kg (49 lb 9 oz). North America's trumpeter swan sports a wingspan of up to 2.5 m (8 ft 2 in).

Loudest penis
The 2-mm-long (0.08-in) water boatman *Micronecta scholtzi* is a surface-skimming insect with an unusual "chat-up" song. When a male rubs its penis against a ridge on its abdomen (a process called stridulation), it produces a chirping noise up to 99.2 dB – akin to listening to an orchestra while sitting in the front row.

Strongest bite force (relative to body size)
During tests, a black piranha (*Serrasalmus rhombeus*) with a mass of 1.12 kg (2 lb 7.5 oz) and a length of 36.8 cm (1 ft 2 in) logged a bite of 320.27-N (32.6-kgf; 71.9-lbf) – 29 times its own weight. Proportionately, this makes its chomp even more powerful than that of the *T. rex*, which likely had the **strongest bite ever** at 53,735 N (5,479 kgf; 12,080 lbf).

LARGEST FRESHWATER...
Mammal
The hippo (*Hippopotamus amphibius*, or "river horse") of sub-Saharan Africa averages 1,400 kg (3,090 lb) but can reach up to 3,630 kg (8,000 lb). It is more than 1,000 times heavier than the **smallest aquatic mammal**: the American water shrew (*Sorex palustris*), which is 8–18 g (0.28–0.63 oz).

Turtle
Yangtze giant softshell turtles (*Rafetus swinhoei*) measure over 1 m (3 ft 3 in) long and up to 250 kg (550 lb). Once distributed across China and Vietnam, only three known living specimens remain today, also making it the **rarest turtle**.

Crustacean
Endemic to Tasmania, Australia, the Gould's giant crayfish (*Astacopsis gouldi*) can reach 80 cm (2 ft 7 in) long, about the same as a collie dog. It's also the **largest freshwater invertebrate** overall.

Poorest vision in a dolphin
Inhabiting murky rivers such as the Ganges in southern Asia, *Platanista* river dolphins are effectively blind. They are the only dolphins without a functioning lens in their eyes. What's more, the optic opening of each eye is so tiny – no more than a pinprick in diameter – that virtually no light can enter. They have come to rely entirely on echolocation to navigate and track down prey.

WRITE A SONG
Budding songwriters should take inspiration from YouTuber Jonathan Mann (USA). As of 14 Mar 2023, he'd penned 5,186 tunes in as many days: the **most consecutive days writing a song**. His quirky numbers include "Duet with Siri", "Non-Existent Cat" and "Baby Yoda Baby Baby Yoda".

The previous **largest freshwater fish specimen** – and still a lead contender among the **largest freshwater fish species** – also hailed from the Mekong River. This massive Mekong giant catfish (*Pangasianodon gigas*), caught in Thailand in 2005, tipped the scales at 293 kg (646 lb) and was 2.7 m (8 ft 10 in) from head to tail.

600%

Shortest freshwater fish
At the other end of the fishy scale is a tiny carp called *Paedocypris progenetica*. Found in 2006 in acidic peat swamps on the South-east Asian islands of Borneo and Sumatra, one full-grown female was a mere 7.9 mm (0.31 in) long. *See also the lightest freshwater fish, opposite.*

► LARGEST FRESHWATER FISH (SPECIMEN)

A 300-kg (660-lb) female giant freshwater stingray (*Urogymnus polylepis*) was collected from the Mekong River in Cambodia on 13 Jun 2022. Assessed by scientists from the US-Cambodian "Wonders of the Mekong" (WOTM) project, she had a disc width of 2.2 m (7 ft 2 in); including the tail, her total length was 3.98 m (13 ft). Locals gave her the name Boramy ("Full Moon"). Dr Zeb Hogan, who presents TV series *Monster Fish* and directs WOTM, said: "This is an absolutely astonishing discovery and justifies efforts to better understand the mysteries surrounding this species and the incredible stretch of river where it lives."

The record ray was returned to the Mekong with a tracker to help us learn more about these enigmatic river titans.

ON THE COAST

Longest whiskers
Pinnipeds (e.g., seals) boast the largest whiskers, or vibrissae, in the animal kingdom. An Antarctic fur seal (*Arctocephalus gazella*) found in 1968 had a 48-cm (1-ft 6-in) whisker; his total 'tache spanned 106.5 cm (3 ft 6 in).

TOP 5 COUNTRIES: LONGEST COASTS*

Philippines: 36,289 km
Russia: 37,653 km
Indonesia: 54,716 km
Norway: 83,281 km
Canada: 202,080 km

Canada has more than double the length of coastline of any other sovereign nation on Earth. Its total comprises the mainland and its many islands, which number into the tens of thousands. The **largest island**, Greenland (with 44,087 km of coast), would be fourth but has been omitted here, as it's a territory of the Kingdom of Denmark.

*CIA World Factbook

Densest fur
The sea otter (*Enhydra lutris*) has up to 160,000 hairs per cm² (more than 1 million per sq in) on parts of its body. Lacking internal blubber, the otter's thick coat traps a layer of insulative air close to the skin, helping it withstand the cold coastal waters of the North Pacific. *Discover one of its freshwater relatives on p.34.*

Heaviest starfish
A specimen of the aptly named heavy starfish (*Thromidia catalai*) weighing *c.* 6 kg (13 lb 3 oz) – about the same as a bowling ball – was caught off Îlot Amédée, New Caledonia, on 14 Sep 1969. This up-to-70-cm-wide (2-ft 3-in) invertebrate feeds by blanketing prey with its stomach and digesting them.

Fastest-growing seaweed
Giant kelp (*Macrocystis pyrifera*) can grow 0.5 m (1 ft 7.6 in) in a day – 1,250 times faster than human hair! Found off rocky

Largest horseshoe crab
Common horseshoe crabs (*Limulus polyphemus*) measure up to 60 cm (1 ft 11 in) long and are native to the Atlantic coast of North America and the Gulf of Mexico. These aquatic relatives of arachnids are living fossils that have barely altered since they emerged some 445 million years ago, 200 million years before the dinosaurs.

Highest-living shark
Epaulette sharks (*Hemiscyllium*) have been observed hunting in intertidal pools several metres above sea level. Originally described in 1788, these carpet sharks grow up to 1 m (3 ft 3 in) long. In May 2022, one was filmed by Forrest Galante "walking" on land for the first time as it dragged itself between rock pools in Papua New Guinea.

shores in the Pacific, this alga secures itself to the seabed with a root-like "holdfast" and grows towards the sunlit surface with the aid of gas-filled floats (pneumatocysts). Its fronds can reach 60 m (196 ft), also making it the **longest seaweed**.

Longest bill
The beak of the Australian pelican (*Pelecanus conspicillatus*) grows up to 47 cm (1 ft 6 in) long – about the same size as this *GWR* book when open. It can hold 13 litres (2.8 gal) of water.

Largest sea slug
Sometimes found in tidepools, the California black sea hare (*Aplysia vaccaria*) grows up to 99 cm (3 ft 2 in) long – twice that of a newborn baby! It can weigh nearly 14 kg (30 lb 13 oz).

Largest bacterium
Discovered in mangroves on the Caribbean island of Guadeloupe in 2009, *Thiomargarita magnifica* measures 1 cm (0.39 in) long. It is the first-ever single bacterium to be visible to the naked eye. The new species was described in the journal *Science* in Jun 2022.

Length of the largest bacterium

Largest green-turtle rookery
During the breeding season, up to 60,000 female green turtles (*Chelonia mydas*) amass on Raine Island off Queensland, Australia, to lay their eggs. As many as 15,000 individuals have been recorded nesting at the same time along a 1.8-km (1.1-mi) beach. This mass gathering is believed to have occurred for 1,000 years.

Largest bear
Adult male polar bears (*Ursus maritimus*) typically weigh 400–600 kg (880–1,320 lb), with a nose-to-tail length of up to 2.6 m (8 ft 6 in). They are the **largest land carnivores**, hunting seals, young walruses and even beluga whales. Males are up to twice the size of females – most likely as an evolutionary advantage when battling to win a mate in the breeding season. Polar bears are found throughout the Arctic, along shorelines in the summer and on ever-diminishing sea-ice during the winter.

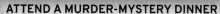

ATTEND A MURDER-MYSTERY DINNER
When death is served up with the soup course, will you be able to unmask the killer? Prepare for a night of knives-out drama by watching Agatha Christie's *The Mousetrap*: the **longest-running play**. The whodunnit has been engrossing audiences in London's West End since 25 Nov 1952.

SPOTTER'S GUIDE TO PUFFINS

Atlantic puffin (*Fratercula arctica*)

The **smallest puffin**, at 28–30 cm (11–12 in) from beak to tail tip, the Atlantic puffin is native to the UK, Iceland, Norway and north-east Canada, as well as a visitor to a few more southerly locations. In Jan 2020, it was revealed that this species uses sticks clutched in its beak as backscratchers – making it the **first tool-using seabird** to be documented.

Tufted puffin (*F. cirrhata*)

Also known as the crested puffin, this species sprouts a bright yellow tuft of feathers during the breeding season. It is the **largest puffin**, with adults reaching a length of 40 cm (1 ft 3 in) and weighing around 1 kg (2 lb 3 oz). Tufted puffins can be found along the North American coastline and in Russia and Japan by the Western Pacific. They can dive to depths of 350 ft (106 m).

Horned puffin (*F. corniculata*)

The horned puffin earns its name from the black spike that extends above the eye in breeding adults. It can often be found nesting in cliff-face crevices in the Gulf of Alaska, the Aleutian Islands and along the Russian coastline. It can carry as many as 65 small fish in its beak at once.

Spiny tongues help to keep wriggly fish securely in their beaks to take back to pufflings (baby puffins).

Puffins' black-and-white plumage inspired their genus name *Fratercula* – "little brother", or a monk.

LARGEST PUFFIN SUPER-COLONY

The Vestmannaeyjar archipelago (Westman Islands) off south-west Iceland hosts some 830,000 breeding pairs of Atlantic puffins (*F. arctica*) during the Apr–Aug nesting season, approximately 20% of this species' worldwide population. These calculations are based on "apparently occupied burrows"(AOBs) – nesting holes that can stretch 1 m (3 ft 3 in) underground.

These charismatic birds with their colourful bills spend almost two-thirds of their lives at sea, resting while bobbing on the water. Atlantic puffin numbers have been dwindling for many years, owing to oil spills, reduced levels of their preferred food and a rise in extreme weather events.

GO TO AMSTERDAM

The capital of the Netherlands is a UNESCO World Heritage Site and a haven for tourists, boasting a rich cultural heritage, vibrant nightlife and more canals than Venice. Don't leave without paying a visit to Anne Frank House and learning about the life of the ill-fated author of the **best-selling diary**.

SUNLIGHT ZONE

Longest zooids
A type of siphonophore, the Portuguese man o' war (*Physalia physalis*) is a colonial animal made up of thousands of separate organisms, known as zooids. The longest of these are its stinging tentacles that can grow up to 50 m (164 ft).

Nelson's Column in London, UK: 51.59 m (169 ft 3 in)

Also known as the epipelagic, the "sunlight zone" is the top 200-m (660-ft) layer of ocean where photosynthesis is still viable. Although making up only about 3% of Earth's oceans, it's home to around 90% of all marine life.

Longest reef
Situated off Queensland, Australia, the Great Barrier Reef (GBR) – actually a chain of nearly 3,000 individual reefs – extends for *c.* 2,300 km (1,430 mi). The GBR represents 10% of all the planet's coral-reef ecosystems.

Longest sea snake
The yellow sea snake (*Hydrophis spiralis*) of the family Elapidae can grow to 2.75 m (9 ft). Native to the Indian Ocean, this venomous marine reptile preys on eels and is cathemeral, i.e., active by day and night.
   The **fastest-swimming snake** is the yellow-bellied sea snake (*H. platurus*), capable of bursts of 1 m (3 ft 3 in) per sec.

Fastest shark
The shortfin mako (*Isurus oxyrinchus*) is capable of cutting through the water at 56 km/h (34.8 mph). Built for speed, its skin is covered in crystalline mineral scales called dermal denticles, which minimize drag. The mako is also the **highest-leaping shark**, propelling some 6 m (20 ft) out of the water.

Largest sea urchin
Found in kelp-rich coastal areas of the north-east Pacific, giant red sea urchins (*Mesocentrotus franciscanus*) have spines up to 8 cm (3.1 in) long and an outer skeleton ("test") that can exceed 18 cm (7 in) in diameter.
   It is *c.* 30 times bigger than the **smallest sea urchin**: the 5.5-mm-wide (0.22-in) *Echinocyamus scaber*, which is native to waters off New South Wales, Australia.

Most poisonous fish
The pufferfish (family Tetraodontidae) of the Red Sea and Indo-Pacific region contain a powerful neurotoxin called tetrodotoxin (TTX), derived from bacteria that live in the invertebrates that they eat. A lethal dose for a human adult could be as little as 16 mg (0.0005 oz) – a single pufferfish can contain enough TTX to kill 30 people.

Largest ciliated animals
Ctenophores ("comb bearers"), aka comb jellies, are primitive marine invertebrates that derive their name from the unique plates of fused hair-like cilia used to propel them through the water. A ribbon-like, surface-dwelling species known as Venus's girdle (*Cestum veneris*) can reach 1.5 m (4 ft 11 in) long.

Longest whale tooth
The spiralled ivory tusk of the male narwhal (*Monodon monoceros*) can exceed 3 m (9 ft 10 in). Although its uses are still debated by scientists, it's thought the horn-like teeth of these "Arctic unicorns" may sense subtle changes in the water.

Oldest non-colonial animal
A quahog clam (*Arctica islandica*) dredged off the seabed near Iceland in 2006 was later found to have lived for 507 years. The mollusc, dubbed Ming, was examined by sclerochronologists from Bangor University's School of Ocean Sciences (UK).

Most widely distributed reptile
Leatherback turtles (*Dermochelys coriacea*) can be found as far north as the Arctic Circle and as far south as the southernmost tip of New Zealand – a latitude range of 115°.

Fastest marine mammal
On 12 Oct 1958, a bull killer whale (*Orcinus orca*) in the north-east Pacific was timed swimming at 55.5 km/h (34.5 mph) – faster than a galloping horse. Reaching up to 10 m (32 ft) long and weighing 10 tonnes (22,050 lb), these cetaceans are, despite their common name, the **largest dolphins**. Inhabiting all oceans, they are highly intelligent predators that work in packs (pods) – hence why some call them the "wolves of the sea".

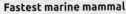

SLEEP IN A CASTLE
Wannabe Sleeping Beauties looking for 40 winks in surroundings straight out of a fairy tale should add the world's **tallest castle** to their itineraries. Indeed, the 65-m (213-ft) Neuschwanstein Castle in Bavaria, Germany, inspired the iconic Cinderella Castle at Walt Disney World.

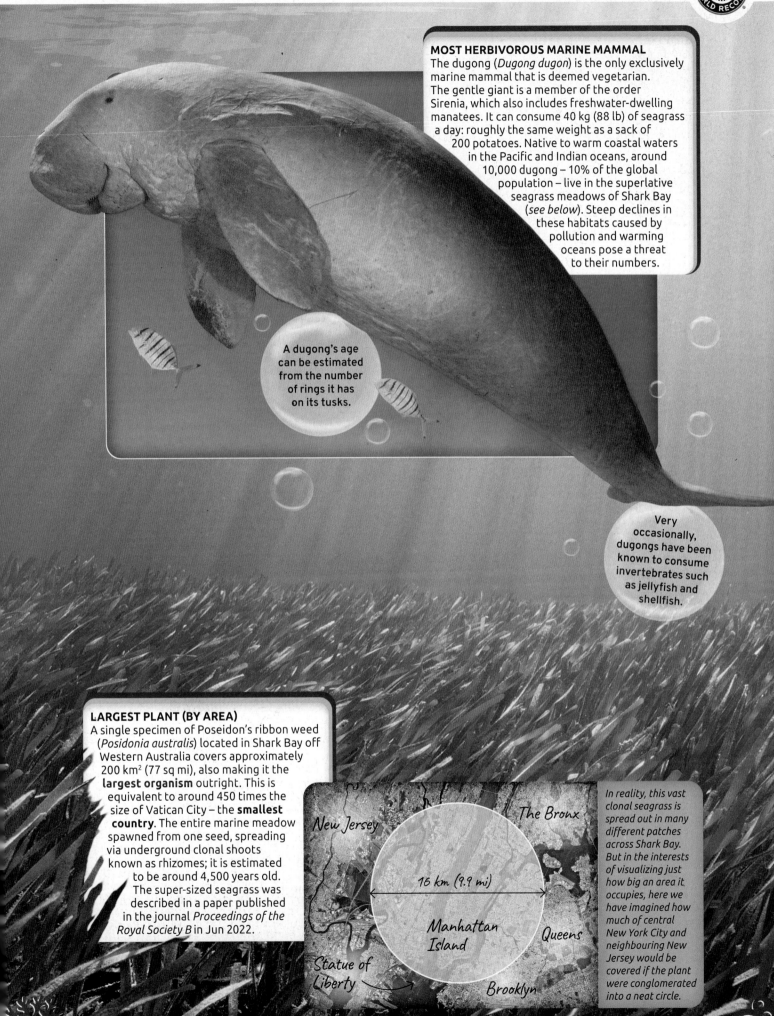

MOST HERBIVOROUS MARINE MAMMAL

The dugong (*Dugong dugon*) is the only exclusively marine mammal that is deemed vegetarian. The gentle giant is a member of the order Sirenia, which also includes freshwater-dwelling manatees. It can consume 40 kg (88 lb) of seagrass a day: roughly the same weight as a sack of 200 potatoes. Native to warm coastal waters in the Pacific and Indian oceans, around 10,000 dugong – 10% of the global population – live in the superlative seagrass meadows of Shark Bay (*see below*). Steep declines in these habitats caused by pollution and warming oceans pose a threat to their numbers.

A dugong's age can be estimated from the number of rings it has on its tusks.

Very occasionally, dugongs have been known to consume invertebrates such as jellyfish and shellfish.

LARGEST PLANT (BY AREA)

A single specimen of Poseidon's ribbon weed (*Posidonia australis*) located in Shark Bay off Western Australia covers approximately 200 km² (77 sq mi), also making it the **largest organism** outright. This is equivalent to around 450 times the size of Vatican City – the **smallest country**. The entire marine meadow spawned from one seed, spreading via underground clonal shoots known as rhizomes; it is estimated to be around 4,500 years old. The super-sized seagrass was described in a paper published in the journal *Proceedings of the Royal Society B* in Jun 2022.

New Jersey

The Bronx

16 km (9.9 mi)

Manhattan Island

Queens

Statue of Liberty

Brooklyn

In reality, this vast clonal seagrass is spread out in many different patches across Shark Bay. But in the interests of visualizing just how big an area it occupies, here we have imagined how much of central New York City and neighbouring New Jersey would be covered if the plant were conglomerated into a neat circle.

TWILIGHT ZONE

As you descend through the ocean, sunlight decreases and pressure increases – two challenges its inhabitants have to overcome. The mesopelagic ("twilight zone") represents the layer between 200 m and 1,000 m (660–3,280 ft); beyond it lies the bathypelagic ("midnight zone"), spanning from 1,000 to 4,000 m (3,280–13,120 ft).

MOST ASYMMETRICAL VERTEBRATES

As larvae, flatfishes (Pleuronectiformes) start out looking much the same as other fish, with symmetrical body features. But as they develop, they become uniquely lopsided. One eye migrates across the head until it sits alongside the other eye, becoming inclined towards the twisted mouth; the fins, however, stay laterally flattened. The side of the body bearing both eyes now becomes the fish's dorsal (upper) flank and remains pigmented, whereas the ventral (under) side loses its pigmentation.

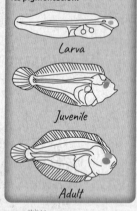

Larva

Juvenile

Adult

100%

Smallest migrant
Copepods (small crustaceans) are planktonic life forms that average 1–2 mm (0.04–0.08 in) long. They live mainly at the bottom of the ocean to avoid predators. But at night they ascend in their billions to feed at the surface, in the **largest animal migration**. With some 14,000 known species, copepods are among the most diverse groups of animals.

Darkest animals
The black skin of *Oneirodes* deep-sea anglerfish absorbs up to 99.95% of all light. Although sunlight does not reach their habitat, light from bioluminescent prey could reveal their whereabouts. Multiple layers of black pigment (melanin) in their skin, however, render them virtually invisible.

Another anglerfish, *Photocorynus spiniceps*, is the **smallest vertebrate**. One mature adult male, collected at a depth of 1,425 m (4,675 ft) in the Philippine Sea, measured just 6.2 mm (0.24 in) – akin to a medium grain of rice. The findings were published by Theodore W Pietsch (USA).

Fastest starfish
Starfishes are not generally known for their speed, but the sunflower sea star (*Pycnopodia helianthoides*) has been timed at a rate of 1 m (3 ft 3 in) per minute. It moves by means of its 15,000 tube feet, attached to 16–24 limbs. This large predatory species lives in the Pacific Ocean between Alaska and southern California.

Largest marine crustacean (leg span)
The taka-ashi-gani or giant spider crab (*Macrocheira kaempferi*) lives off southern Japan. It has an average body size of 25 x 31 cm (10 x 12 in) and a leg span of 2.4–2.7 m (8–9 ft). The largest known specimen had a 3.69-m (12-ft 1.2-in) leg span – similar in length to a Mini Cooper car. These colossal crabs live as deep as 600 m (1,970 ft) and feed on worms, molluscs and other crustaceans.

Hottest fish eyes
The swordfish (*Xiphias gladius*) utilizes special organs to heat its eyeballs to 28°C (82°F), even in cold water at depths of 2,870 m (9,416 ft). This enables it to track fast-moving prey, such as squid, far more clearly.

Greatest morphological variation in a fish
A 2009 study led by ichthyologist G David Johnson of the Smithsonian Institution shed light on a twilight-zone mystery. DNA analysis revealed that what had been three distinct fish families – distinguished by their drastically differing appearance – were, in fact, the adult males, adult females and larvae of a single family. Previously, the juveniles were designated as tapetails (Mirapinnidae), males as bignoses (Megalomycteridae) and females as whalefish (Cetomimidae); this research confirmed that all three belong to the latter.

Deepest shark
The Portuguese dogfish (*Centroscymnus coelolepis*) has been found foraging on the seabed 3,700 m (12,140 ft) beneath the surface. Few sharks venture below 3,000 m (9,840 ft).

Deepest dive by a...
• **Sea snake**: an unidentified species of *Hydrophis*, 245 m (803 ft) logged on 16 Nov 2014.
• **Bird**: emperor penguin (*Aptenodytes forsteri*), 564 m (1,850 ft) – as reported on 19 Jul 2006.
• **Reptile**: leatherback turtle (*Dermochelys coriacea*), 1,280 m (4,200 ft) on 16 Dec 2006.
• **Pinniped**: northern elephant seal (*Mirounga angustirostris*), 1,529 m (5,016 ft) in May 1989.
• **Mammal**: Cuvier's beaked whale (*Ziphius cavirostris*), 2,992 m (9,816 ft) – from data collected in 2010–12.

Largest eye-to-body ratio
The eyes of the *Vampyroteuthis infernalis* (literally "vampire squid from hell") may attain a diameter of 2.5 cm (0.9 in), while its adult body length is typically 28 cm (11 in) – a ratio of 1:11. First discovered in 1903 by Carl Chun, it has been found to favour tropical waters at depths in excess of 600 m (1,970 ft).

The squid's name derives from its cloak-like array of legs and dark red colour. In fact, it's completely harmless.

89

GO SAILING
Bid farewell to dry land and embrace the life aquatic! The **longest non-stop solo yachting race** is the Vendée Globe, starting and finishing at Les Sables d'Olonne in France. It covers approximately 22,500 nautical mi (41,670 km; 25,890 mi), so you might want to start with some shorter jaunts!

The sharks' eyes often host worm-like parasites (*pictured*) that can cause blindness; luckily, they don't rely on sight alone.

LONGEST-LIVED VERTEBRATE

According to a 2016 study, the rarely seen Greenland shark (*Somniosus microcephalus*) can live up to 392 years old – and perhaps even longer. This deep-dwelling fish grows just 1 cm (0.4 in) per year and only becomes sexually mature at 150 years old! It is widely distributed across the cold waters of the North Atlantic at depths of around 2,000 m (6,560 ft), where the temperature is a frigid -1°C (30°F). Scientists believe that this habitat has contributed to its longevity and lengthy maturation, as the shark has evolved a slow metabolism in order to adapt to its cold surroundings.

Largest bioluminescent vertebrate

The kitefin shark (*Dalatias licha*) can grow to 1.8 m (5 ft 11 in) from nose to tail. It lives at depths of 200–600 m (660–1,970 ft), usually close to the seafloor, and is found worldwide. Both its ventral surface and its two dorsal fins glow by means of a combination of hormones, with light emitted via "photophores" scattered across its skin. The purpose of its bioluminescence remains uncertain, but may aid with hunting in the gloomy twilight zone.

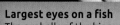

Largest eyes on a fish

The eyeballs of the bigeye thresher shark (*Alopias superciliosus*) can span up to 12.5 cm (4.9 in), exceeding even those of the **largest fish**, the whale shark (*see pp.44–45*). Unusually, their sight organs are taller than they are wide, shaped more like an upside-down pear, rather than being spherical.

INTO THE ABYSS...

Below 4,000 m (13,120 ft) in the ocean lies the abyssal zone, an inhospitable netherworld cast in permanent darkness. Deeper still, within vast trenches in the seabed, the temperature hovers just above freezing and the crushing pressure is 1,000 times that at sea level. Welcome to the hadal zone – named after Hades, king of the underworld in Greek myth – which begins at 6,000 m (19,685 ft) below the surface.

The first observation of the hadal world was made on 23 Mar 1875 by scientists on board the research ship HMS *Challenger*. While stationed south of the Mariana Islands in the Pacific Ocean, a sounding of 4,475 fathoms (8,184 m; 26,850 ft) was logged. The expedition's name lives on in the oceans' **deepest point** (*see pp.116–17*).

Despite these extreme conditions, life has found a way to survive even here. In 1901, the **first hadal organisms collected** – spoonworms, starfish, brittlestars and demersal (bottom-dwelling) fish – were trawled by the *Princess Alice II* from 6,035 m (19,800 ft), within the Zeleniy Mys Trough in the North Atlantic.

Since then, many more abyssal and hadal extremophiles have been discovered, some by marine biologist and GWR consultant Dr Alan Jamieson (*left*). He is pictured with the **largest amphipod crustacean**, *Alicella gigantea*, which can reach 34 cm (1 ft 1 in) long. So, join us now as we embark on a deep-sea superlative safari – don't forget your flashlight!

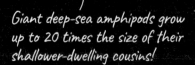

Giant deep-sea amphipods grow up to 20 times the size of their shallower-dwelling cousins!

Largest grenadier fish
Grenadiers are also known as rattails, owing to their elongated, tapering rears. Some species have been found as deep as 6,500 m (21,325 ft), having adapted to their dark environment by evolving bulbous eyes and light-producing organs to lure prey. The largest of their kind is the giant grenadier (*Albatrossia pectoralis*), growing to 2.1 m (6 ft 10 in) long. Native to the northern Pacific, the greatest known depth for *A. pectoralis* is 3,500 m (11,483 ft).

Deepest crinoid
The Crinoidea class of marine invertebrates includes a group of animals known as sea lilies. They fasten themselves to hard surfaces – such as coral or rocks – using a stalk, and feed on floating food detritus and plankton with their feathery arms. One sea lily, *Bathycrinus kirilli*, has been trawled from 9,735 m (31,939 ft) in the Izu-Ogasawara Trench in the western Pacific Ocean.

Deepest octopus
In 2019, a dumbo octopus (*Grimpoteuthis*) was spotted foraging near the seafloor at 6,957 m (22,825 ft) in the Indian Ocean's Java Trench. This extended the previous maximum depth for this genus by 1,812 m (5,945 ft), and is the first irrefutable evidence of a cephalopod (i.e., the group including octopuses, squid and cuttlefish) living in the hadal zone. The octopus's body is soft, semi-gelatinous and capable of resisting the immense pressure found at these depths. It derives its common name from two specialized flippers on its head that resemble elephant ears – hence the link to the Disney character.

Longest fins on a fish (relative to body size)
The tripodfish (*Bathypterois grallator*) is c. 30 cm (1 ft) in length, but each of its two pelvic fins and its lower caudal fin boast an extremely long ray that may measure more than three times the fish's body length! When held downwards, these three rays stiffen, enabling the aptly named tripodfish to lodge itself in the sandy sea floor to catch passing food. *B. grallator* is distributed widely throughout the Atlantic, Pacific and Indian oceans.

Deepest echinoderm
Echinoderms are a group of marine invertebrates that includes starfish, sea urchins and sea cucumbers. The latter are small deep-sea animals typified by squidgy bodies, mouths surrounded by finger-like tentacles, and caterpillar-like feet. Sea pigs (*below*), which inhabit the abyssal zone, are atypical of sea cucumbers in that they "walk" on long, leg-like tube feet. The deepest-living echinoderm of them all is the sea cucumber *Prototrochus bruuni*, one specimen of which was retrieved from 10,730 m (35,203 ft) in the Tonga Trench in the south-west Pacific in 1977.

*Animals not to scale

ATTEND THE OLYMPICS
If there were a gold medal for Olympic fandom, it would have to go to Harry Nelson of California, USA. He attended 19 iterations of the elite sporting contest between Los Angeles 1932 and Rio 2016 – the **most Olympic Summer Games attended**. Track and field events were his favourite to watch.

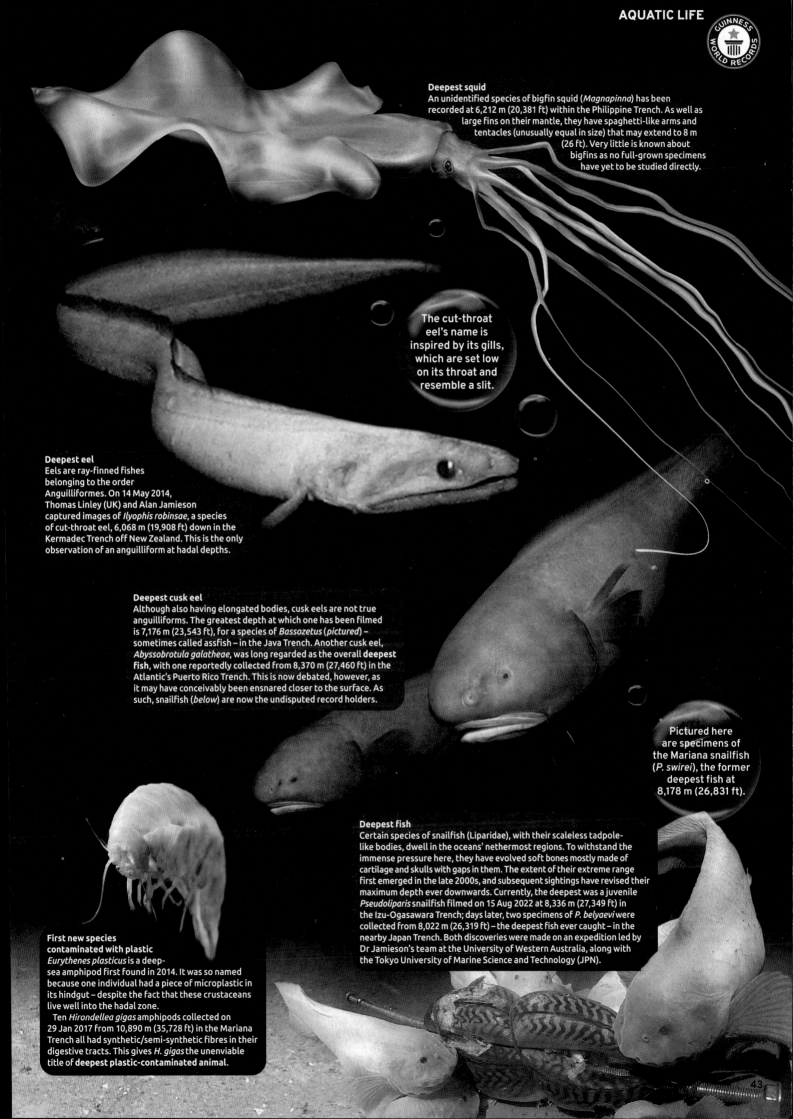

Deepest squid
An unidentified species of bigfin squid (*Magnapinna*) has been recorded at 6,212 m (20,381 ft) within the Philippine Trench. As well as large fins on their mantle, they have spaghetti-like arms and tentacles (unusually equal in size) that may extend to 8 m (26 ft). Very little is known about bigfins as no full-grown specimens have yet to be studied directly.

The cut-throat eel's name is inspired by its gills, which are set low on its throat and resemble a slit.

Deepest eel
Eels are ray-finned fishes belonging to the order Anguilliformes. On 14 May 2014, Thomas Linley (UK) and Alan Jamieson captured images of *Ilyophis robinsae*, a species of cut-throat eel, 6,068 m (19,908 ft) down in the Kermadec Trench off New Zealand. This is the only observation of an anguilliform at hadal depths.

Deepest cusk eel
Although also having elongated bodies, cusk eels are not true anguilliforms. The greatest depth at which one has been filmed is 7,176 m (23,543 ft), for a species of *Bassozetus* (*pictured*) – sometimes called assfish – in the Java Trench. Another cusk eel, *Abyssobrotula galatheae*, was long regarded as the overall **deepest fish**, with one reportedly collected from 8,370 m (27,460 ft) in the Atlantic's Puerto Rico Trench. This is now debated, however, as it may have conceivably been ensnared closer to the surface. As such, snailfish (*below*) are now the undisputed record holders.

Pictured here are specimens of the Mariana snailfish (*P. swirei*), the former deepest fish at 8,178 m (26,831 ft).

First new species contaminated with plastic
Eurythenes plasticus is a deep-sea amphipod first found in 2014. It was so named because one individual had a piece of microplastic in its hindgut – despite the fact that these crustaceans live well into the hadal zone.
Ten *Hirondellea gigas* amphipods collected on 29 Jan 2017 from 10,890 m (35,728 ft) in the Mariana Trench all had synthetic/semi-synthetic fibres in their digestive tracts. This gives *H. gigas* the unenviable title of **deepest plastic-contaminated animal**.

Deepest fish
Certain species of snailfish (Liparidae), with their scaleless tadpole-like bodies, dwell in the oceans' nethermost regions. To withstand the immense pressure here, they have evolved soft bones mostly made of cartilage and skulls with gaps in them. The extent of their extreme range first emerged in the late 2000s, and subsequent sightings have revised their maximum depth ever downwards. Currently, the deepest was a juvenile *Pseudoliparis* snailfish filmed on 15 Aug 2022 at 8,336 m (27,349 ft) in the Izu-Ogasawara Trench; days later, two specimens of *P. belyaevi* were collected from 8,022 m (26,319 ft) – the deepest fish ever caught – in the nearby Japan Trench. Both discoveries were made on an expedition led by Dr Jamieson's team at the University of Western Australia, along with the Tokyo University of Marine Science and Technology (JPN).

43

MARINE MEGAFAUNA

The blue whale has the **heaviest tongue**, weighing about 4 tonnes (8,820 lb)

Since classical times, tales have abounded of giant sea monsters such as the Kraken lurking beneath the waves... Yet the marine organisms that actually reside in our oceans are every bit as incredible as those of fable and fantasy (head to pp.32–33 to see inside one such ocean giant). Here, we have arranged eight behemoths of the blue in order of their largest recorded specimens, also shown to scale alongside a human diver.

1. Lion's mane jellyfish
Average length: 9 m (30 ft), including tentacles
Found in the cold waters of the Arctic and North Pacific Ocean, *Cyanea capillata* is the **largest jellyfish**. It can weigh as much as 1 tonne (2,200 lb), despite being composed largely of water and soft parts. In 1870, a lion's mane found washed up in Massachusetts Bay, USA, had a bell diameter of 2.3 m (7 ft 6 in) and tentacles that stretched 36.5 m (120 ft) – akin to three-and-a-half school buses!

2. Blue whale
Average length: 25 m (82 ft)
The ocean colossus *Balaenoptera musculus* is the **largest animal ever**. A female measured at a whaling station in the South Atlantic in 1909 had a length of 33.57 m (110 ft 1 in) – the same as three London double-decker buses. The blue whale also has the **largest heart** – 199 kg (440 lb) – and the **largest lungs** – a capacity of 5,000 litres (1,320 gal). Even their babies are behemoths: newborn calves can be 8 m (26 ft) long and weigh 2–3 tonnes (4,400–6,600 lb), the **largest offspring**.

3. Whale shark
Average length: 10–12 m (32–39 ft)
Favouring equatorial waters, the whale shark (*Rhincodon typus*) is today's **largest fish**. A female caught in the Arabian Sea, off India, in May 2001 measured 18.8 m (61 ft 8 in) long. Research published in Jul 2022 revealed that the whale shark feeds on not only krill – as long assumed – but also seaweed, making it the **largest omnivore**.

4. Giant oarfish
Average length: 6 m (19 ft)
The ribbon-shaped giant oarfish (*Regalecus glesne*) has a skeleton composed of bone tissue rather than cartilage, distinguishing it from sharks and rays. The oarfish is the **longest bony fish**. One super-sized specimen observed on 18 Jul 1963 by a team of marine scientists off New Jersey, USA, had an approximate length of 50 ft (15.2 m).

5. Giant squid
Average length: 3–9 m (9–29 ft)
Little is known about the elusive giant squid (*Architeuthis dux*), with only a few intact specimens available for study. Growing to almost 13 m (42 ft 8 in), they are the **largest cephalopod** (the class of molluscs that includes squid, octopuses and cuttlefish). The closely related colossal squid (*Mesonychoteuthis hamiltoni*) is typically shorter but heavier, with one logged at 495 kg (1,091 lb). Both squid are the biggest animals without inner skeletons – i.e., the **largest invertebrates**.

6. Southern elephant seal
Average length: 5 m (16 ft)
The southern elephant seal (*Mirounga leonina*) of the subantarctic islands is both the **largest seal** and the **largest pinniped** overall. A 6.85-m-long (22-ft 6-in) bull was killed in the South Atlantic on 28 Feb 1913. It weighed at least 4 tonnes (8,820 lb) – about the same as *nine* grand pianos.

7. Great white shark
Average length: 4.3–4.6 m (14–15 ft)
The **largest predatory fish** is the great white shark (*Carcharodon carcharias*). There are many accounts of great whites growing beyond 6 m (19 ft); as of 2022, the largest-known living individual was "Deep Blue", a 50-year-old female estimated to be 6.1 m (20 ft) long and more than 2 tonnes (4,400 lb).

8. Sunfish
Average length: 1.8 m (6 ft)
These disc-shaped dwellers of tropical waters can often be found sunbathing near the surface. A bump-head sunfish (*Mola alexandrini*) is the **heaviest bony fish** on record, with one deceased individual found in the waters off the Azores, Portugal, on 9 Dec 2021 weighing 2.74 tonnes (6,049 lb). Its total length was 3.25 m (10 ft 8 in). *For more, see p.46.*

Longest colonial animal
Apolemia uvaria is a type of free-floating "super-animal" composed of numerous minute stinging organisms known as zooids. A kind of predatory drift net, it has the catchy nickname "long stringy stingy thingy". An enormous specimen sighted forming a spiral off Western Australia on 16 Mar 2020 had an estimated total length of 119 m (390 ft) – three times that of the biggest lion's mane jellyfish (*see 1*).

VISIT THE GREAT BARRIER REEF
Lying off Queensland, Australia, the **longest reef** measures 2,300 km (1,429 mi) and is one of the world's most celebrated sites of natural beauty. More than a million people visit every year, to swim among the clownfish, manta rays and sharks. (*See p.38 for more.*)

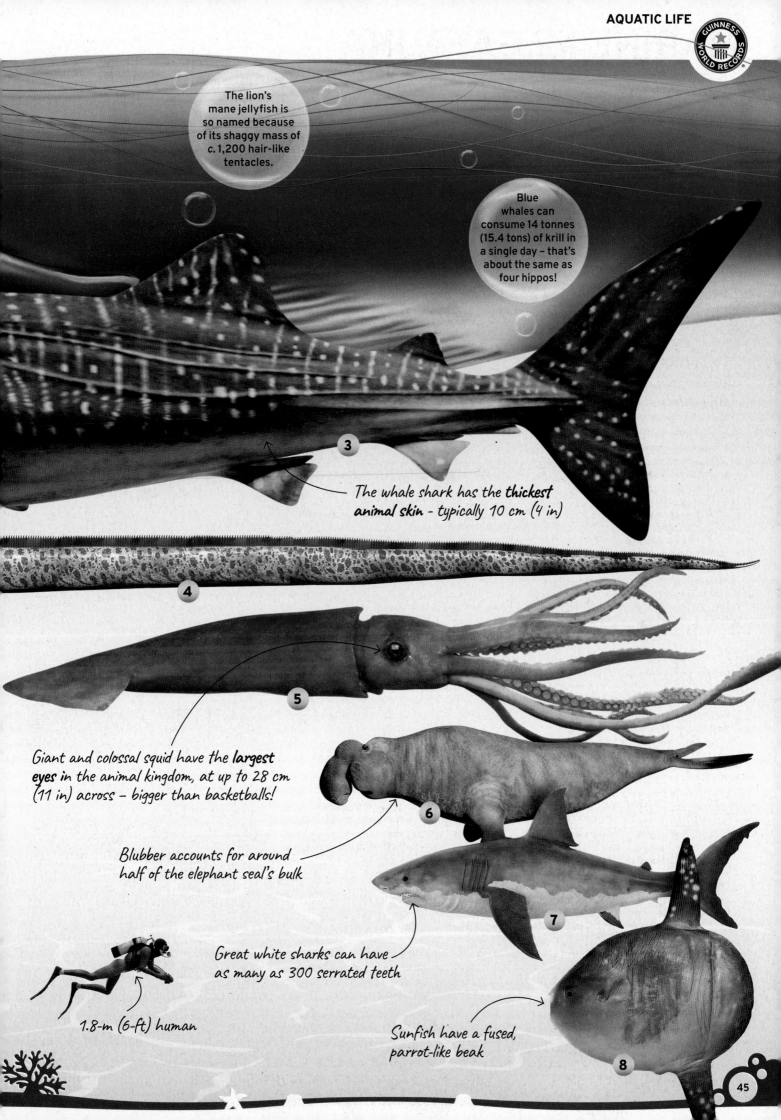

The lion's mane jellyfish is so named because of its shaggy mass of c. 1,200 hair-like tentacles.

Blue whales can consume 14 tonnes (15.4 tons) of krill in a single day – that's about the same as four hippos!

3

The whale shark has the **thickest animal skin** - typically 10 cm (4 in)

4

5

Giant and colossal squid have the **largest eyes** in the animal kingdom, at up to 28 cm (11 in) across – bigger than basketballs!

6

Blubber accounts for around half of the elephant seal's bulk

7

Great white sharks can have as many as 300 serrated teeth

1.8-m (6-ft) human

Sunfish have a fused, parrot-like beak

8

ROUND-UP

Oldest heart

The extraordinary discovery of a preserved heart dating back to the Late Devonian Period, some 380 million years ago (MYA), was announced in Sep 2022. Comprising two discrete chambers, it was found inside a fossilized specimen of the fish *Mcnamaraspis kaprios*, disinterred from the Gogo rock formation in Western Australia. A very rare type of mineralization had kept not just the heart but many of the other soft internal organs intact, including its liver, stomach and intestine.

Oldest ichthyosaur

On 13 Mar 2023, a study in *Current Biology* revealed that fossils of an as-yet-unnamed marine reptile found in Svalbard, Norway, in 2014 – but only recently examined – dated from 250 MYA. The dolphin-like sea creature was about 3 m (9 ft 10 in) long. Scientists posit that such an advanced species must have predated (and therefore survived) the "Great Dying" – a mass-extinction event that wiped out up to 90% of all life on Earth *c.* 251.9 MYA.

First seaweed pollinated by animals

The marine red alga *Gracilaria gracilis* is pollinated by the Baltic isopod (*Idotea balthica*). This woodlouse relative carries tiny spermatia (male gametes) from male algae to females. Without it, the process would rely solely on random water flow. The **first marine flower animal pollinators** were identified in 2016 as the larvae of crustaceans and bristleworms, which transfer seagrass pollen.

Oldest fish in captivity ever

A male Australian lungfish (*Neoceratodus forsteri*) aptly named Granddad was estimated after scale analysis to have been around 109 years old when he died in 2017. Purchased in 1933 from Taronga Zoo and Aquarium in Sydney, Australia, he was brought to the John G Shedd Aquarium in Chicago, Illinois, USA. Over the course of 84 years there, he was seen by more than 100 million visitors.

Oldest predator

Auroralumina attenboroughii is a 560-million-year-old extinct cnidarian (a group that includes jellyfish and sea anemones). Dating to the Ediacaran Period, it lived *c.* 20 million years earlier than the next oldest-known predatory animals – ancient jellyfishes. *A. attenboroughii* is represented by a 20-cm-tall (8-in) specimen found in Charnwood Forest, Leicestershire, UK. It has two branching polyps in a rigid organic skeleton, with evidence of simple tentacles for catching prey. The sea creature was named after naturalist David Attenborough (UK) – the **most enduring TV presenter**, with a career spanning 69 years 219 days as of 9 Apr 2023.

Longest non-stop migration by a bird

In 2022, a satellite-tagged, juvenile bar-tailed godwit (*Limosa lapponica baueri*) flew some 13,560 km (8,425 mi) across the Pacific Ocean, without stopping once for food or rest. It left Alaska, USA, on 13 Oct, reaching Tasmania, Australia, 11 days 1 hr later. The five-month-old bird was dubbed "234684" – the number of its tag. Airborne day and night while migrating, such birds may burn up more than half their body weight.

Birds sustain themselves on epic flights by shrinking their internal organs to make way for energy-rich fat.

Heaviest bony fish

Adult sunfish (*Mola*) reach an average length of 1.8 m (6 ft) and weigh about 1 tonne (2,200 lb). But the heaviest recorded specimen – a deceased bump-head sunfish (*M. alexandrini*, pictured) – was nearly three times that weight, at 2,744 kg (6,049 lb). It was found near Faial Island in the Azores, off the Portuguese coast, on 9 Dec 2021. (*See also pp.44–45.*)

Longest fish migration (return journey)

A male common shortfin mako shark (*Isurus oxyrinchus*), dubbed Hell's Bay, swam more than 21,000 km (13,050 mi) in the Atlantic Ocean over a period of 600 days. Tagged and tracked by researchers at Florida's Nova Southeastern University (USA), his epic journey was the equivalent of swimming halfway round the globe. He advanced from Ocean City in Maryland, USA, northwards along the US eastern seaboard to Nova Scotia, Canada, then down just south of Bermuda before heading back to Ocean City.

Largest water walker

A number of animals have evolved ways to walk over water for seconds at a time – one of the most iconic being the Jesus Christ lizards, or basilisks, of Latin America. However, the largest-known creatures capable of this improbable feat are the sailfin dragons (*Hydrosaurus*) of south-east Asia. Like basilisks, they run bipedally, with their flattened toes creating a cushion of air on the water's surface. Their long, sturdy tails also help them to balance. The largest specimen on record, an *H. microlophus*, was 1.07 m (3 ft 6 in) long – and was likely even longer once as it was missing its tail tip.

LEARN TO RIDE A MOTORCYCLE
If the open road is calling, why not follow in the tyre tracks of Benka Pulko (SVN)? She embarked on a five-year two-wheeled tour between 1997 and 2002, riding 180,016 km (111,856 mi) through 69 countries and seven continents. This stands as the **longest solo motorcycle journey**.

Shortest-lived turtle species

Turtles and tortoises are among the longest-lived animals. The greatest known lifespan for the chicken turtle (*Deirochelys reticularia*), however, is just 21 years. To help offset this, juveniles mature quickly and females may produce two clutches of eggs in a year.

By contrast, a Seychelles giant tortoise (*Aldabrachelys gigantea hololissa*) called Jonathan, who lives on the island of St Helena, is the **oldest land animal**, aged *c.* 190 in 2022.

Deepest hydrozoan

Hydrozoans are soft-bodied sea creatures related to jellyfish. One species, provisionally identified as *Pectis profundicola*, was filmed at 10,063 m (33,015 ft) in the Philippine Trench in the

north-west Pacific, during a 2021–22 expedition by the DSV *Limiting Factor* (*see pp.116–17*). This is 997 m (3,271 ft) deeper than previously known.

Observations on this field trip also revised the extent of the **deepest tunicate** (aka sea squirt) down to 8,077 m (26,499 ft), for an Octacnemidae specimen in the Izu-Ogasawara Trench. Both new findings were published on 9 Feb 2023.

Largest macroalgal bloom

Abundant accumulations of *Sargassum* brown seaweed are steadily rising. In Jun 2022, the Great Atlantic Sargassum Belt reached a new peak, with a monthly mean coverage of 6,989 km² (2,698 sq mi). The bloom stretched from the Gulf of Mexico all the way to the west coast of Africa. Possible catalysts for this growth explosion include warming ocean waters and rising levels of sewage and fertilizer.

Largest penguin species ever

On 8 Feb 2023, a paper in the *Journal of Paleontology* revealed that the newly described prehistoric penguin *Kumimanu fordycei* had weighed around 154 kg (340 lb) – three times heavier than today's **largest penguin species**, the emperor (*Aptenodytes forsteri*). *K. fordycei* fossils were found in boulders dating back 55.5 million–59.5 million years in North Otago on New Zealand's South Island.

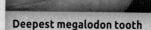

Deepest megalodon tooth

In Jun 2022, the tooth of an extinct megalodon shark (*Otodus megalodon*; example above) was retrieved from a depth of 3,089 m (10,134 ft). It was found some 240 km (150 mi) south of Johnston Atoll in the Pacific Ocean. Megalodons were the **largest fish ever**, possibly reaching as much as 20 m (65 ft) in length. *For today's **largest fish**, see pp.44–45.*

Largest waterlily species

Native to El Beni in north-east Bolivia, *Victoria boliviana*'s floating pads can exceed 2.8 m (9 ft 2 in) across. Carlos Magdalena of the UK's Royal Botanic Gardens, Kew (*shown left with his six-year-old son, Mateo, and botanical artist Lucy Smith*) played a key role in identifying the new species, as revealed in Jul 2022. It had been mistaken for another giant waterlily (*V. amazonica*) for nearly 200 years.

A *V. boliviana* pad grown at La Rinconada ecopark (*below*) in Santa Cruz, Bolivia, spanned 3.2 m (10 ft 6 in) on 3 Feb 2012, making it the **largest waterlily leaf**. The border of the pad stood 17 cm (6.7 in) tall. Its surface area of 7.55 m² (81.3 sq ft) – akin to about two king-size beds – also makes it the **largest undivided leaf** of any plant on record.

La Rinconada ecopark is owned by Gaston Ribero, aka Tonchi – pictured right.

V. boliviana's short-lived flowers are as big as car steering wheels and turn from white to pink overnight.

VISIT LONDON

There are so many sights in the UK's bustling capital, it can be hard to know where to start... One way is to make a game of it, like Alex Radford (UK) did on 5 Aug 2018. The **fastest time to visit every location on the London Monopoly® board on foot** is 1 hr 45 min 35 sec. FYI, you only have to take a photo *outside* a jail!

DOMESTIC ANIMALS

OLDEST...

▶ **Cat:** On 10 Nov 2022, Flossie (UK, b. 29 Dec 1995) had her age verified at 26 years 316 days. The venerable feline had been signed into the care of the Cats Protection charity for rehoming. She has since been matched with a new owner.

Dog: Bobi (PRT, b. 1992), 30 years 243 days as of 9 Jan 2023.

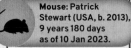
Mouse: Patrick Stewart (USA, b. 2013), 9 years 180 days as of 10 Jan 2023.

Chicken: Peanut (USA, b. 2002), 20 years 272 days as of 28 Jan 2023.

Alpaca: Hawthornden Wainui (NZ, b. 1998), 25 years 47 days as of 18 Feb 2023.

Fastest time to jump 10 hurdles by a rabbit
On 30 Jan 2023, Penelope ran a 10-fence steeplechase in just 7.16 sec while filming for *Lo Show dei Record* in Milan, Italy. Each fence was 25 cm (10 in) high. Penelope's owner, Ole Roski (DEU), was on hand to provide encouragement.

Another TV star – Creole – took on a series of jumps, ramps and a seesaw to set the **fastest time to complete an agility course by a chicken**: 1 min 0.02 sec, on 14 Feb 2023. Creole was guided by 13-year-old Zoe Amaya Tomas (USA).

Highest bar jump by a guinea pig
On 15 Aug 2022, Abby the American crested guinea pig, owned by Grace Hoiness (USA), cleared a 22-cm-high (8.6-in) bar in Bend, Oregon, USA. This beat a 19-year-old record.

▶ Most dogs in a conga line
Wolfgang Lauenburger (DEU) led a column of 14 upright *wunder-hunds* – Emma, Filou, Fin, Simon, Susy, Maya, Ulf, Speck, Bibi, Katie, Jennifer, Elvis, Charly and Cathy – in Stukenbrock, Germany, on 25 Aug 2022. That year, his dog Maya also set the **most rollovers in one minute** (62) and **most spins in 30 seconds** (49).

▶ Fastest time to weave five poles by a blind horse
On 29 Oct 2022, Endo navigated five poles in 6.93 sec in Corvallis, Oregon, USA. The Appaloosa gelding was ridden by owner Morgan Wagner (USA). Endo – whose eyes had to be removed owing to a medical condition – also set unsighted records for the **highest free jump** (106 cm; 3 ft 5 in) and **most flying changes in one minute** – 39.

Shortest dog
Pearl, a two-year-old Chihuahua, was just 9.14 cm (3.59 in) tall from paw to shoulder when measured by a vet on 23 Aug 2022 in Orlando, Florida, USA. She beats the record once held by her own relative, Miracle Milly, who stood 9.65 cm (3.79 in) in 2013. Pearl is the pride and joy of Vanesa Semler (PRI), who also owned Milly.

▶ Most consecutive medical samples identified by dogs
The charity Medical Detection Dogs (UK) has trained canines to use their powerful olfactory ability to discern a record 28 different types of disease/condition. On 24 Nov 2022, a squad of five Labradors and retrievers correctly sniffed out 24 successive samples – including COVID-19, Parkinson's and prostate cancer – in Great Horwood, Buckinghamshire, UK.

Farthest jump by a dog
Laurel Behnke's (USA) seven-year-old whippet Sounders leapt 36 ft 6 in (11.12 m) into a dock-diving pool in Gig Harbor, Washington, USA, on 30 Jul 2022. The jump was authenticated by judges from North America Diving Dogs.

Longest tongue on a dog
Black Lab-German shepherd cross Zoey has a 12.7-cm (5-in) licker, as ratified on 27 Oct 2022 in Metairie, Louisiana, USA. The Williams family are the recipients of her generous kisses!

The **longest eyelash on a dog** is 17.8 cm (7 in), belonging to a Newfypoo named Coco, as measured on 18 Nov 2022. Her owner is Rachelle Parks (USA).

Most tricks performed by a guinea pig in one minute
Coco the Abyssinian guinea pig executed 16 tricks – including spins, jumps and interacting with objects – in High Point, North Carolina, USA, on 6 Mar 2022. He added the **30 second record** (10) on 16 Nov 2022. The cunning cavy was adopted in 2018 by Gwen Ford (USA), who was inspired by Coco's energy and curiosity to begin training; he is now a certified champion, with 70-plus skills in his repertoire.

High five

Ring a bell

Pick a card

Push a ball

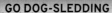

GO DOG-SLEDDING
Glide across a wintery landscape, pulled by a team of huskies. The **longest annual dog-sled race** is the 1,688-km (1,049-mi) Iditarod Trail across Alaska, USA. Racers endure extreme weather conditions, with temperatures as low as -73°C (-100°F). Inaugurated in 1967, it's also the **oldest dog-sled race**.

Largest horn spread on a cow

On 8 Oct 2022, the distance between Sweet Maxi's horn tips was 284.16 cm (9 ft 3.9 in) – about the same as two ice-hockey sticks – as verified at a Texas Longhorn Breeders Association of America competition in Corsicana, Texas, USA. Sweet Maxi is owned by Kali and Mike Smith (both USA), who describe her as "a big puppy dog".

The record **steer horn spread** is 323.74 cm (10 ft 7.4 in) on 8 May 2019, for a Texas longhorn named Poncho Via from Goodwater, Alabama, USA. He resides with the Pope family.

The withers is the ridge between the shoulder blades

Tallest cow ever

A Holstein named Blosom (d. 2015) measured 190 cm (6 ft 2.8 in) from the hoof to the withers on 24 May 2014 in Orangeville, Illinois, USA. She was cared for by Patty Meads-Hanson (USA), who first met Blosom when she was an eight-week-old calf. According to Patty, the bovine behemoth loved having her chin rubbed and ears scratched.

TALLEST STEER

A 13-year-old Brown Swiss steer named Tommy stood 187 cm (6 ft 1 in) from hoof to withers on 11 Dec 2022 in Cheshire, Massachusetts, USA. He was rescued at just two days old by Fred Balawender (USA, *right*), who has cared for him ever since. The 3,000-lb (1,360-kg) ox eats a 5-gal (22-litre) bucket of grain a day, along with a bale-and-a-half of hay and as many apples as he can gobble! Tommy has become an unlikely *moo*-vie star on social media, with one video of the gentle giant receiving more than 14 million views on TikTok.

FREESTYLE TRAILBLAZER
LAURA BIONDO

Soccer has long been a part of Laura Biondo's life, but there have been a few twists along the way... Now in her mid-30s and a seasoned freestyler, she's on a mission to engage the stars of the future – particularly young girls. For her, it's time that **gender stereotypes were shown the red card once and for all.**

Laura was born in Venezuela to an Italian family, and spent time growing up in the USA and Italy. After being introduced to football by her brother at the age of 10, she began her formal training with the Schulz Academy in Florida. Laura would go on to play for several teams in Italy's major soccer league. In her late teens, a knee injury stopped her soccer career in its tracks, but an unfazed Laura decided to treat this as a new opportunity. While on the sidelines, she taught herself to juggle and manipulate the ball – and it was at that moment that she realized another path lay open to her: freestyle football.

Since that epiphany, she has become one of the field's leading lights – and the only Latin American to be crowned world champion. In 2011, she also became the first female freestyler to be recognized by GWR, setting the women's record for the **most "around the world" tricks in one minute** – 43, later updated to 63. A run with Cirque du Soleil on its critically acclaimed show *Luzia* highlighted how freestyle offers a bridge between athletics and theatre. The ever-growing list of mega-brands on her resumé – everyone from UEFA, Sony, Google and Lamborghini – is proof of the insatiable demand for this new sport-art paradigm.

All along, Laura has refused to let tradition or societal expectations stand between her and her goals. Now serving as the Head of Women's Development for the World Freestyle Football Association, she is seeking to pass that gender blindness on to the next generation.

Laura is quadrilingual: she fluently speaks Spanish, English, Italian and French.

VITAL STATISTICS

Name	Laura Biondo
Birthplace	Caracas, Venezuela
Birth date	27 Jan 1989
Current GWR titles	8, inc. **most football touches with the head in one minute** (206) and **most clipper tricks in one minute** (33)
Medals won	Superball World Open Championships (2 gold, 2 silver, 4 bronze); Latin American Championships (1 gold, 1 silver); European Championships (2 gold, 1 silver)
Cirque du Soleil shows	1,000+ performances in *Luzia*

1: Laura's soccer training began in Boca Raton, Florida, where she played as part of the travel team at the Schulz Academy. Later, she went on to play for Weston Fury (*pictured*).

2: In 2016, Laura became the first Venezuelan to work with Cirque du Soleil, as she joined the cast of *Luzia* – a vibrant tale that celebrates Mexican culture. In the show, Laura teamed up with fellow freestyler Abou Traore to wow audiences with their ball control. *Luzia* has now been seen by some 2 million people.

3: Laura has amassed a sizeable collection of awards, medals and trophies – including 15 GWR certificates – since kick-starting her football-freestyle career in the late 2000s.

4: Soccer stars such as Ronaldinho (*pictured*) and the USA's Mia Hamm have been two of Laura's greatest influences. In the early days, her attempts to mimic her heroes' tricks didn't always go to plan… But she started to see her efforts improve after many hours of training and was soon competing at the highest level.

5: Laura isn't afraid to think outside the box when it comes to taking on new challenges. On 19 Jun 2020, she combined her passions for fitness and ball skills by completing the ⬤ **most football touches on a treadmill in one minute**, executing 170 keepy-uppies in Miami, Florida, where she now lives.

Find out more about Laura in the Hall of Fame section at www. guinnessworldrecords.com/2024

"Freestyle is an art… because we can express ourselves through a ball and transmit an emotion."

HUMANS

Oldest wing walker
For Ivor Button (UK, b. 10 Dec 1926), the sky truly is the limit. On 9 Apr 2022, aged 95 years 120 days, he soared over Rendcomb Aerodrome in Gloucestershire, UK, strapped to the wings of a biplane. Ivor's passion for planes started at the age of six, when his parents took him to see a flying circus.

The **women's** record is held by Elizabeth "Betty" Bromage (UK, b. 12 Mar 1929). She was 93 years 145 days old when she completed a loop-the-loop and barrel roll over the same airfield on 4 Aug 2022. Unlike Ivor, Betty caught the wing-walking bug late in life. She began aged 87, after seeing a chocolate-bar advert that featured the daredevil skill and deciding, "I could do that!"

For more Super Seniors who consider age to be just a number, fly over to pp.56–57.

GUINNESS WORLD RECORDS

CERTIFICATE

The oldest wing walker (male) is Ivor Button (UK, b. 10 December 1926) who is 95 years and 122 days old, as verified in Cirencester, Gloucestershire, UK, on 9 April 2022

OFFICIALLY AMAZING

RECORD HOLDER

GUINNESS WORLD RECORDS

CERTIFICATE

The oldest wing walker (female) is Elizabeth "Betty" Bromage (UK, b. 12 March 1929) who is 93 years and 145 days old, as verified in Cirencester, Gloucestershire, UK, on 4 August 2022

OFFICIALLY AMAZING

RECORD HOLDER

The soaring seniors flew atop a Boeing Stearman; Betty's flight (*right*) included inverted aerobatics.

G-IIIY

AeroSuperBatics
EXCELLENCE IN WINGWALKING

HEAVIEST PERSON EVER

JON BROWER MINNOCH

In 1978, an American taxi driver was estimated by his doctors to weigh nearly eight times more than the average man, making him the world's **heaviest person ever**. It might be an iconic record, but it's an unenviable title that comes with a host of medical complications...

Jon Brower Minnoch was born in Washington, USA, in 1941. His health problems began in childhood – by the age of 12, he already weighed 178 kg (392 lb; 28 st), and was almost double this by the time he was 25.

He continued to grow, and by Mar 1978, his resulting heart, respiratory and circulation problems required urgent medical treatment. "I was being crushed by my own weight," he later explained. It took a dozen firemen to lift him on to a makeshift stretcher, after which he was taken by ferry to University Hospital, Seattle. He was too heavy to be weighed, but the hospital's endocrinologist, Dr Robert Schwartz, diagnosed generalized oedema (fluid accumulation) and estimated his mass at more than 635 kg (1,400 lb; 100 st).

The 6-ft 1-in (185.4-cm) Minnoch was promptly put on a 1,200-calorie daily diet, which saw him drop to 216 kg (476 lb; 34 st). Ultimately, though, no treatment would be effective. His weight fluctuated for the rest of his life, and in 1983, aged just 41, he died of complications from his oedema.

The cause of Minnoch's weight gain was never identified, beyond excessive calorie intake, but his case helped doctors to study the effects of morbid obesity on a person. Here, we look inside the body of one such patient to see how extreme weight gain takes its toll on almost every aspect of our anatomy and physiology.

Excessive body fat has been linked to higher incidence of dementia; stroke risk is also increased

Airway restriction leading to sleep apnoea (arrested breathing)

Swollen tissue around the eyes can restrict vision

Oesophageal cancer
Being overweight can increase the risk of tumours in a range of body parts and organs; indeed, obesity causes more than one-quarter of all cases of oesophageal cancer in the UK. This is one of the most difficult cancers to treat, along with that of the pancreas and gallbladder.

Cirrhosis of the liver

Pancreas unable to produce enough insulin, resulting in risk of type-2 diabetes

Gastrointestinal issues
Constipation, haemorrhoids and diarrhoea can all be brought about by an excess of body weight. Other related health problems include colon polyps, gallstones and acute pancreatitis.

Skinfold rashes

Hardened arteries, leading to heart disease and risk of cardiac arrest

Visceral Fat
Fat that builds up inside the abdominal cavity, around internal organs, is known as visceral or hidden fat; it should account for about 10% of your overall fat content. Inactivity, and a diet high in saturated fats and carbohydrates (sugars), will cause an increase in fats. With morbid obesity, an increase in visceral fat can seriously affect the functioning of vital organs such as the liver and intestines, and lead to a higher risk of diabetes.

Body Fat
Adipose tissue – aka body fat – stores calories in the form of lipids, from which your body creates energy. Fat also aids in the secretion of hormones, and provides the body with a degree of cushioning and insulation, among other things. Body fat is considered healthy when it accounts for roughly 20–30% of body weight in women and 10–20% in men (depending on age).

There are two main types of body fat – visceral (*see right*) and subcutaneous – and excessive amounts of either is bad for your health. The latter is found just beneath the skin, and accounts for c. 90% of your body fat. Subcutaneous fat – which, unlike visceral fat, is visible – is typically the first sign of obesity, and can be measured by doctors using skinfold callipers.

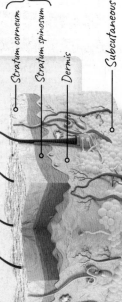

Stratum corneum
Stratum spinosum } *Epidermis*
Dermis
Subcutaneous fat

Poor circulation

Obesity can lead to the formation of blood clots, which impact on the smooth flow of blood through the veins. Should a clot pass to a vital organ such as the heart or lungs, it could prove fatal.

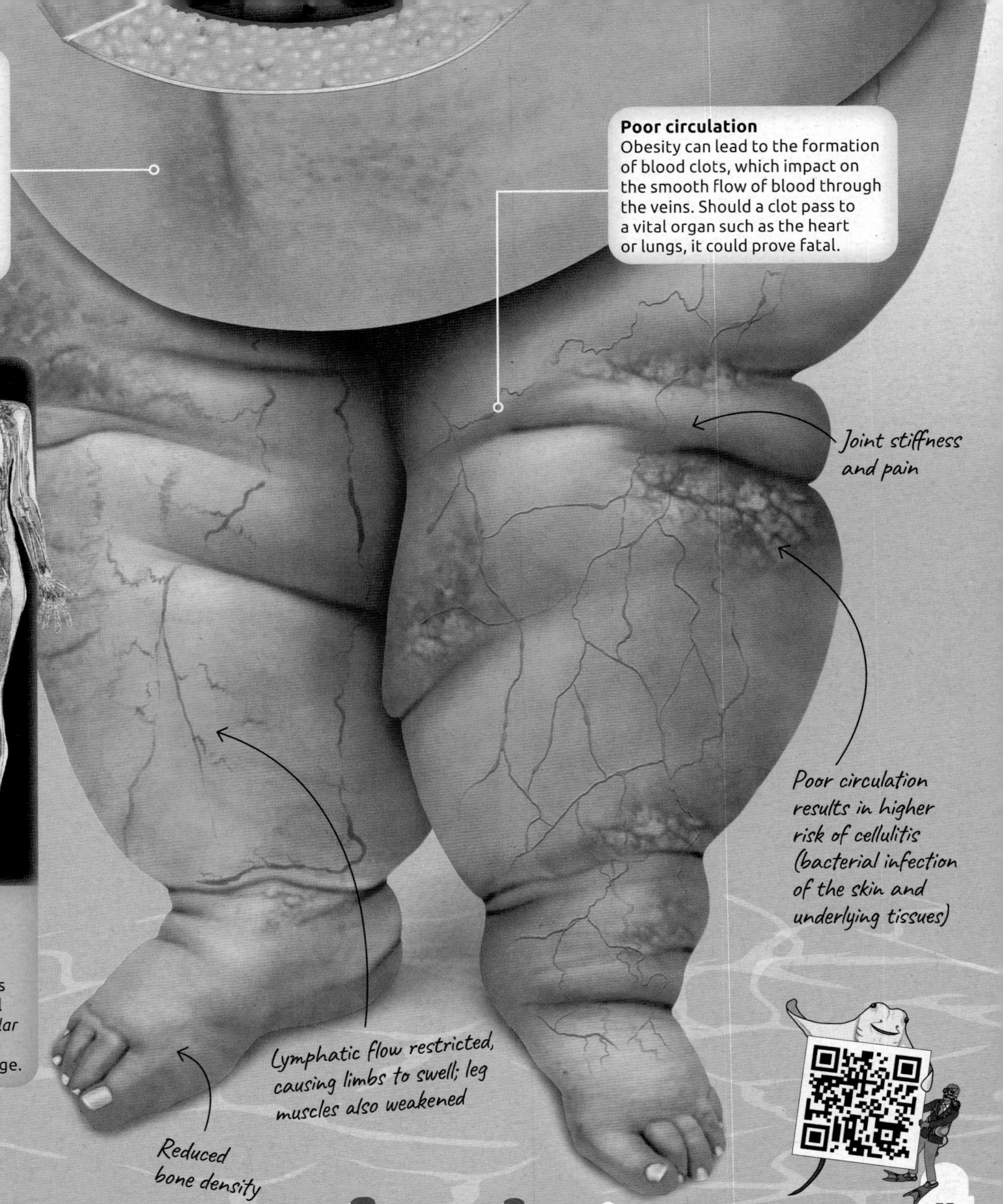

Joint stiffness and pain

Poor circulation results in higher risk of cellulitis (bacterial infection of the skin and underlying tissues)

Lymphatic flow restricted, causing limbs to swell; leg muscles also weakened

Reduced bone density

Anasarca

Also known as generalized oedema (or edema), this condition – not a disease but a symptom of underlying conditions – results in water retention and swelling throughout the body. It can cause severe discomfort, immobility, impaired vision and, in extreme cases, organ failure and death. Minnoch presented with generalized (body-wide) oedema that ultimately resulted in his untimely death.

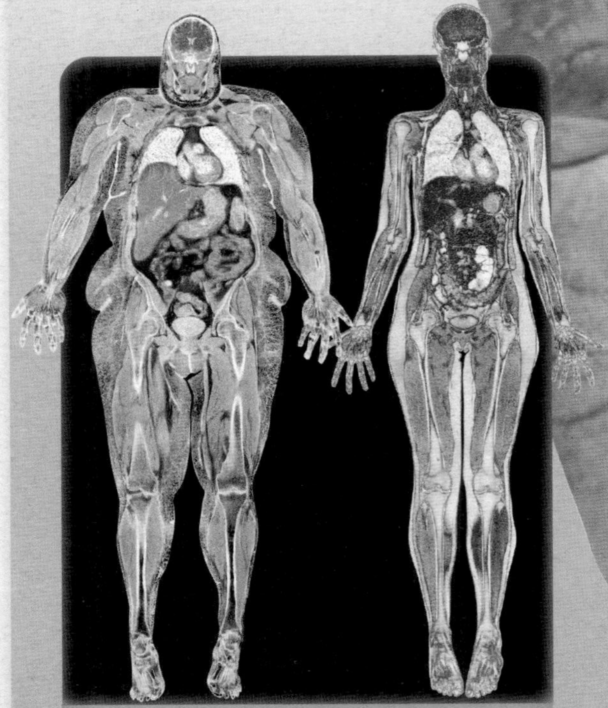

Obesity: the inside story

The magnetic resonance imaging (MRI) scans pictured above contrast the body of an obese woman with that of a lean one. Compare the two, and you'll see that the one on the left has more compressed lungs and enlarged internal organs, including the liver (*the orange triangular shape below the lungs*). Layers of fat have also built up over the muscles in the left-hand image.

HEAVIEST HUMANS

Below, we list the only individuals known to have exceeded 500 kg (1,102 lb), along with their peak weights, as recorded or estimated by medical professionals.

Jon Brower Minnoch
(USA, 1941–83). (See above.)
*1,400 lb
(100 st;
635 kg)*

Khalid bin Mohsen Shaari
(SAU, 1991–). First reported in Aug 2013 with body mass index of 204; slimmed to 710 lb (50 st 10 lb; 322 kg) in just six months.
*1,345 lb
(96 st 1 lb;
610 kg)*

Juan Pedro Franco Salas
(MEX, 1985–). By Sep 2020, had reduced to around 458 lb (32 st 10 lb; 207.7 kg) as a result of exercise, dieting and stomach-reduction surgery.
*1,311 lb
(93 st 9 lb;
594.6 kg)*

Manuel Uribe (MEX, 1965–2014). First reported in Jan 2006; weighed 869 lb (62 st; 394 kg) at the time of his death.
*1,232 lb
(88 st;
558.8 kg)*

Walter Hudson (USA, 1944–91). At peak weight, recorded the **widest waist**, measuring 9 ft 11 in (3.02 m) in circumference; weighed c. 900 lb (64 st 4 lb; 408.2 kg) at time of death.
*1,201 lb
(85 st 11 lb;
544.7 kg)*

Robert Butler (USA, 1972–2015). In 2006, weighed 900 lb (64 st 4 lb; 408.2 kg); reached peak size in the year of his death, from sepsis.
*1,200 lb
(85 st 10 lb;
544.3 kg)*

Francis J Lang, aka Michael Walker (USA, 1934–82). Attributed his excessive weight gain to prescription drug abuse.
*1,187 lb
(84 st 11 lb;
538.4 kg)*

Johnny Alee (USA, 1853–87). Underwent exponential weight gain in childhood. Reportedly too heavy to support his own body weight by the age of 15.
*1,132 lb
(80 st 12 lb;
513.4 kg)*

Carol Yager (USA, 1960–94). Shed c. 121 lb (8 st 8 lb; 54.8 kg) over three months – without the aid of surgery – prior to her death from multiple organ failure.
*1,128 lb
(80 st 8 lb;
511.6 kg)*

Eman Ahmed Abd El Aty (EGY, 1980–2017). Second-heaviest woman; died from a range of obesity-related complications, despite losing c. 716 lb (51 st 2 lb; 325 kg) in the preceding months.
*1,102 lb
(78 st 10 lb;
500 kg)*

SUPER SENIORS

TOP 10 OLDEST...

1 — Oldest person
María Branyas Morera
(USA/ESP, b. 4 Mar 1907)
116 years 14 days

2 — Fusa Tatsumi
(JPN, b. 25 Apr 1907)
115 years 327 days

3 — Edith "Edie" Ceccarelli
(USA, b. 5 Feb 1908)
115 years 41 days

4 — Tomiko Itooka
(JPN, b. 23 May 1908)
114 years 299 days

5 — Inah Canabarro Lucas
(BRA, b. 8 Jun 1908)
114 years 283 days

6 — Hazel Plummer
(USA, b. 19 Jun 1908)
114 years 272 days

7 — Nina Willis
(USA, b. 14 Jan 1909)
114 years 63 days

8 — Ushi Makishi
(JPN, b. 15 Feb 1909)
114 years 31 days

9 — Oldest man
Juan Vicente Pérez Mora
(VEN, b. 27 May 1909)
113 years, 295 days

10 — Elizabeth Francis
(USA, b. 25 Jul 1909)
113 years 236 days

Source: Gerontology Research Group; correct as of 18 Mar 2023

OLDEST...

Person

María Branyas Morera (*see left*) succeeded to the title of **oldest woman** and **person** after the passing of France's Sister André, aka Lucile Randon, on 17 Jan 2023. At 118 years 340 days, Randon was the fourth-oldest person ever, as well as the **oldest nun** and **oldest COVID-19 survivor**.

Morera was born in San Francisco, California, to a Catalan family who returned to Spain in 1915. She currently resides at a nursing home in Olot, Catalonia. She attributes her longevity to "order, tranquillity, no regrets, no worries and staying away from toxic people", as well as a lifelong abstinence from cigarettes, alcohol and fad diets.

Competitive soccer player

Australia's David Mudge (b. 26 Jan 1943) was 79 years 89 days old when he played for Kissing Point FC against North Turramurra in a Northern Suburbs Football Association match on 25 Apr 2022. Sadly for him, Kissing Point lost 6–0.

Oldest equestrian vaulter

As of 17 Oct 2021, Maureen Marsha Fitzgerald (ZAF, b. 25 Apr 1944) continued to perform horseback gymnastics, aged 77 years 175 days old, as verified in Johannesburg, South Africa. Fitzgerald competed in the 2021 Gauteng Vaulting Championships to achieve this title. She was once South African champion in gymnastics and participated at the World Games in 1966.

Oldest tandem parachute jumper

Rut Linnéa Ingegärd Larsson (SWE, b. 12 Sep 1918) dropped from the skies at the age of 103 years 259 days, with parachutist Joackim Johansson, on 29 May 2022. The leap took place at Linköpings Fallskärmsklubb in Motala, Östergötland, Sweden. A latecomer to aerial adventure, Larsson first paraglided aged 90, and made her debut parachute jump in 2020.

Person to perform a headstand

Ishwar Nath Gupta (IND, b. 14 May 1936) turned his world view upside down aged 86 years 232 days, in Rourkela, Odisha, India, on 1 Jan 2023.

Surfer

Having only taken up surfing after turning 80, Seiichi Sano (JPN, b. 23 Sep 1933) was still hitting the waves in Yokohama, Japan, by 8 Jul 2022, aged 88 years 288 days. His advice to other would-be record setters? "Whether it be surfing or world records, it's a can-do attitude that will get you there, not logic."

HALO skydiver

Larry Connor (USA, b. 7 Jan 1950) performed a high-altitude, low-opening (HALO) skydive aged 72 years 291 days. He jumped from 25,693 ft (7,831 m), free-falling at up to 160 mph (257 km/h), as verified on 25 Oct 2022 in Davis, California, USA.

Cyclist from Land's End to John o' Groats

On 17 Sep 2022, Martin Harvey (UK, b. 27 Sep 1935) completed a ride between Great Britain's most extreme points at the age of 86 years 355 days. He cycled with his daughters to raise funds for St Giles Hospice, in memory of his late wife, Jackie.

Gina Harris (UK, b. 23 Apr 1940) claimed the **women's** title on 27 May 2022, finishing her charity ride aged 82 years 34 days.

Dance instructor

Ulla Kasics (CHE, b. 19 Jan 1926) was still putting her students through their paces at the age of 96 years 170 days, as verified in Zurich, Switzerland, on 8 Jul 2022. She founded her own dance school in 1954 and still teaches there four days a week.

Oldest person to bag the Munros

On 13 Aug 2022, Nick Gardner (UK, b. 3 Apr 1940) scaled the last of the 282 Munros – Scotland's mountains above 3,000 ft (914 m) – aged 82 years 132 days. He'd climbed his first Munro in Jul 2020, and it took him just over two years to complete the full complement. The admirable feat of endurance also "bagged" more than £80,000 ($97,220) for Alzheimer Scotland and the Royal Osteoporosis Society.

BUY A CAR

Just remember where you've parked it... especially if you're visiting the West Edmonton Mall in Alberta, Canada. This enormous shopping complex boasts the world's **largest parking lot**, which is big enough to accommodate 20,000 cars, with overflow facilities nearby for 10,000 more!

83

Ginny works out for an hour three times a week, and does yoga twice a week. She's also a regular swimmer.

OLDEST COMPETITIVE FEMALE NINJA ATHLETE

Virginia "Ginny" MacColl (USA, b. 31 Oct 1951) competed in the US National Ninja League (NNL) on 29 Jan 2022 aged 70 years 90 days. Competitors tackle a series of obstacle-course challenges, in a contest that takes place under the auspices of the World Ninja League. The super-fit septuagenarian – who entered the Season VII Qualifier in the Traditional (Masters) category – appeared on *American Ninja Warrior* (*ANW*) in 2017–18, yet didn't start gym work until the age of 63.

Ginny's pictured right with her daughter, Jessie Graff (USA), a martial-arts expert, stunt woman and fellow *ANW* star. On 26 Nov 2022, they joined forces in Santa Monica, California, USA, to break the women's record for the **most consecutive tandem pull-ups** (14).

Kozak's refusal to be limited by longevity has earned him the affectionate nickname "Ageless Ninja".

The **oldest competitive ninja athlete** overall is Dave Kozak (USA, b. 29 Mar 1947), who was aged 74 years 230 days when he took part in an NNL qualifier on 14 Nov 2021. A former fighter pilot, Kozak has 188 combat missions under his belt.

HAIR

WONDROUS WORLD OF WHISKERS

Whether you sport a Garibaldi or an Alaskan whaler, the World Beard and Moustache Championships provide the ultimate opportunity for pogonophiles (beard-lovers). Held every two years, the competition is categorized by style, with a "whiskerina" section for women. The 2017 event, hosted by the Austin Facial Hair Club (USA), attracted 738 participants – the **largest beard and moustache championships.**

At the 2022 US National Beard and Moustache Championships – held at The Gaslight Social in Casper, Wyoming, USA – Paul Slosar (USA) displayed the **longest moustache.** Tip to tip, his "English" 'tache measured 63.5 cm (2 ft 1 in) on 12 Nov.

At the same event on 11 Nov, a line of 69 hirsute competitors joined forces to create the **longest beard chain**, stretching 45.99 m (150 ft 10 in). They linked their whiskers – each measuring at least 20 cm (7.8 in) – using hairclips.

Longest head hair
No human – or indeed animal – has grown their hair longer than Xie Qiuping (CHN). On 8 May 2004, after 30 years of avoiding scissors, Xie combed out her locks to an incredible 562 cm (18 ft 5.5 in).

Other (singular) superlative sproutings include:
- **Abdomen**: Elaine Martin (USA) – 16.77 cm (6.60 in).
- **Arm (female)**: Sarah Hetrich (USA) – 13.57 cm (5.34 in).
- **Arm (male)**: David Reed (USA) – 21.7 cm (8.54 in).
- **Back**: Michael Johnson (UK) – 16.60 cm (6.53 in).
- **Chest**: Vittorio Lullo (ITA) – 28.20 cm (11.10 in).
- **Ear**: Anthony Victor (IND) – 18.1 cm (7.12 in).

▶ Longest beard
On 15 Oct 2022, Sarwan Singh's (CAN) beard was measured at 254 cm (8 ft 4 in) in Surrey, British Columbia, Canada. As a devout Sikh, Sarwan adheres to the articles of faith known as the "Five Ks", one of which ("Kesh") forbids the cutting of hair. He has held this record since 2008.

Tallest hairstyle
Syrian stylist Dani Hiswani created a 290-cm-tall (9-ft 6-in) coiffure for model Akhdiya Mirzokarimova in Dubai, UAE, on 16 Sep 2022. Dani sculpted wigs and hair extensions into the shape of a Christmas tree, replete with baubles.

The ▶ **tallest Mohawk** is 129.4 cm (4 ft 2 in) and belongs to Joseph Grisamore (USA), as verified on 16 Apr 2021.

Fastest time to complete five skin-fade haircuts
On 23 Aug 2022, Enrico Springfield (ZAF) gave five customers a skin fade in 18 min 57 sec at his Southside Barbershop in Johannesburg, South Africa. The attempt was filmed for TV show *Stumbo Record Breakers*.

Heaviest weight held while suspended by the hair
Circus artist The Flying Brain (aka Stephanie Morphet-Tepp, USA) hangs in mid-air from her super-strong locks while she performs. While suspended in Denver, Colorado, USA, on 10 Nov 2022, she bore a weight of 125.7 kg (277 lb) for 10 sec.

Longest hair on a teenager
Sidakdeep Singh Chahal (IND) has grown his hair to a length of 146 cm (4 ft 9.5 in), as verified in Mar 2023 in Greater Noida, Uttar Pradesh, India. The impressively tressed teen – now 15 years old – washes his hair twice a week, dedicating at least an hour each time to showering, drying and brushing it before tying it into a bun.

The ▶ **longest hair on a teenager ever** is 200 cm (6 ft 6 in), grown by fellow Indian Nilanshi Patel. She finally cut her hair in 2021, donating it to a museum.

▶ Largest afro (female)
Aevin Dugas's (USA) hair is her crowning glory, extending 25 cm (9.8 in) high and with a total circumference of 165 cm (5 ft 4.9 in). The awesome afro was measured on 11 Sep 2022 in Gonzales, Louisiana, USA. "When I first went natural, it was literally as if a weight lifted off my head," she told GWR.

Largest afro (male)
On 10 Aug 2022, the afro belonging to Amir Manuel Menendez (USA) was measured at a height of 19.67 cm (7.7 in) in Anaheim, California, USA. Its circumference was 226 cm (7 ft 4.9 in). Amir was aged just 13 years old at the time, meaning that he also qualified for the **teenage** version of this record. He described his eye-catching hairstyle as "unique and cool".

SEE A SHOW ON BROADWAY
New York City's Theater District plays host to some of the finest musical productions in the world. If you're going to take in a musical, why not make it the **highest-grossing Broadway show**? Disney's *The Lion King* had earned $1.8 bn (£1.5 bn) as of the week ending 5 Mar 2023.

LONGEST COMPETITIVE MULLET

Tami Manis of Knoxville, Tennessee, USA, sports a "business-in-the-front, party-in-the-back" hairstyle that extends to a length of 172.72 cm (5 ft 8 in). At the 2022 USA Mullet Championships – where judges assess "length, style, uniqueness and showmanship" – Tami competed in the "Femullet" division and finished in second place. She attributes her ability to grow her extraordinary tresses to "good genes".

The mullet haircut has ebbed in and out of popularity over the years. In 2010, the Cultural Ministry of Iran banned the style for being "too decadent". The USA Mullet Championships is the **largest mullet competition**, receiving upwards of 1,000 applicants every year.

Tami last had the back of her hair cut on 9 Feb 1990 – which she now calls her mullet's birthday.

Longest competitive mullet (male)
"Big Rich" Price of Strongsville, Ohio, USA, is the proud owner of a 99.06-cm-long (3-ft 3-in) mullet. At the 2021 USA Mullet Championships, he made it through to the final 25 in the "mane" event and finished in 13th place. Big Rich is the founder of a not-for-profit organization dedicated to saving unwanted pet fish.

STAND ON THE EQUATOR

Bestride the world by standing in both the Northern and Southern hemispheres. Explorer Mike Horn (ZAF) decided to up the ante by completing the **first non-motorized circumnavigation along the Equator**. Between 2 Jun 1999 and 27 Oct 2000, he circled the planet on foot and by bicycle, canoe and trimaran.

HANDS

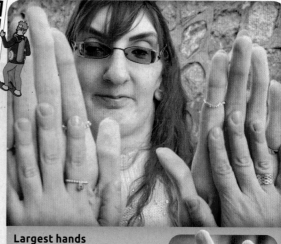

Largest hands ever
Male: Robert "Bob" Pershing Wadlow (USA, 1918–40), the ▶ **tallest person ever** (see p.62), had hands that measured 32.3 cm (1 ft 0.7 in) from the wrist to the tip of the middle finger. Bob's hand span was not recorded, but estimates suggest a reach of 40 cm (1 ft 3.7 in) – a piano interval of 18 white keys! *For the living record, see right.*
Female: Zeng Jinlian (CHN, 1964–82), the **tallest woman ever**, had a wrist-to-fingertip length of 25.5 cm (10 in).

Widest hand span
Mohamed Shehata (EGY) can open his left hand to a width of 31.3 cm (1 ft 0.3 in). During a medical examination in Cairo, Egypt, on 27 Apr 2021, Mohamed was also recorded as having the **widest arm span**, at 250.3 cm (8 ft 2.5 in).
    The **women's** record is held by Rumeysa Gelgi (see right), who can separate the tips of her right thumb and pinkie by 22.6 cm (8.9 in).

Polydactyly derives from the Greek for "many digits". The opposite is oligodactyly: "few digits".

Largest hands

▶ **Female**: Rumeysa Gelgi's (TUR) right hand measures 24.93 cm (9.8 in) from the wrist to the tip of the middle finger. It's no surprise: Rumeysa was confirmed as the world's **tallest woman** in Safranbolu, Türkiye, on 23 May 2021.
Male: Similarly, the world's **tallest man** – fellow Turk Sultan Kösen – holds the men's record, with a wrist-to-fingertip length of 28.5 cm (11.2 in; *right*).

▶ Longest fingernails on a pair of hands
Diana Armstrong (USA) has nails totalling 1,306.58 cm (42 ft 10.4 in), as verified in Minneapolis, Minnesota, USA, on 13 Mar 2022. Each nail is twice the height of Jyoti Amge, the world's **shortest woman** (see pp.62–63).
    The ▶ **longest single fingernail** ever belonged to India's Shridhar Chillal, who stopped trimming the nails of his left hand in 1952. His coiled thumbnail measured 197.8 cm (6 ft 6 in) on 17 Nov 2014. In 2018, he lost his record for **longest nails on one hand**; after 66 years of growth, he had his 909.6-cm (29-ft 10-in) nails cut with a Dremel rotary saw.

Loudest finger-knuckle crack
Metacarpophalangeal-joint distraction produces an audible (and harmless) "snap" as pockets of fluid in the knuckles are popped. On 25 May 2012, Miguel Ángel Molano (ESP) registered a sound-meter reading of 83.2 dB when popping his joints In Bilbao, Spain.

Most family members to walk on all fours
Five (out of 19) adult siblings of the Ulaş family of Türkiye are compelled to walk on their feet and the palms of their hands. The Ulaşes struggle to maintain balance when on two feet, resulting in a quadrupedal gait known as a "bear walk". The cause appears to be a rare genetic mutation.

▶ MOST FINGERS AND TOES
The current owner of the most digits is Devendra Suthar (IND), who has 28 independent fingers and toes distributed equally between his hands and feet, as verified in Himatnagar, Gujarat, India, on 11 Nov 2014. Devendra plies his trade as a carpenter with extra diligence: "I work mostly with saws and hammers... [and] have to always be careful to avoid the fingers."
    The **all-time** record for polydactylism is held by Akshat Saxena (IND, inset above), who was born with 14 fingers and 20 toes, as confirmed on 20 Mar 2010. A successful surgical operation has since reduced his haul of fingers and toes to 10 apiece.

First USB prosthetic
In May 2008, Finnish computer programmer Jerry Jalava lost part of a finger when his motorcycle struck a deer. While waiting for a regular fingertip prosthetic, Jerry had a 2-GB "finger drive" made to fit, allowing him to carry his data around with him constantly. He peels back the nail to access the memory stick.

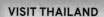

VISIT THAILAND
The "Land of Smiles" is famous for its beaches but before you head to the coast or islands, pay a visit to the Wat Traimit temple in the capital, Bangkok. There, you'll find the **largest golden statue**. The 3-m-tall (10-ft) Buddha is made from 5.5 tonnes (12,125 lb) of solid gold and is worth an estimated $270 m (£244 m)!

FEET

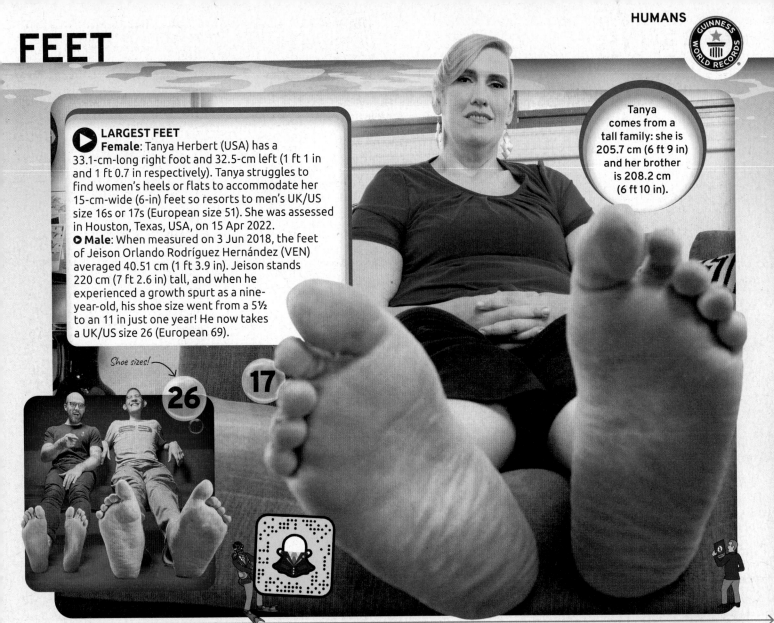

LARGEST FEET
Female: Tanya Herbert (USA) has a 33.1-cm-long right foot and 32.5-cm left (1 ft 1 in and 1 ft 0.7 in respectively). Tanya struggles to find women's heels or flats to accommodate her 15-cm-wide (6-in) feet so resorts to men's UK/US size 16s or 17s (European size 51). She was assessed in Houston, Texas, USA, on 15 Apr 2022.
Male: When measured on 3 Jun 2018, the feet of Jeison Orlando Rodríguez Hernández (VEN) averaged 40.51 cm (1 ft 3.9 in). Jeison stands 220 cm (7 ft 2.6 in) tall, and when he experienced a growth spurt as a nine-year-old, his shoe size went from a 5½ to an 11 in just one year! He now takes a UK/US size 26 (European 69).

Shoe sizes!

Tanya comes from a tall family: she is 205.7 cm (6 ft 9 in) and her brother is 208.2 cm (6 ft 10 in).

Longest toenails
Louise Hollis (USA) gave up trimming her toenails back in 1982. When measured at their longest in 1991, the combined length of all 10 nails came to 220.98 cm (7 ft 3 in) – meaning that each toenail was, on average, as long as the width of this page!

Average length of Louise Hollis's toenails!

Most Toe Wrestling World Championships won
Male: Barefoot battles have been contested annually in Wetton, North Staffordshire, UK, since 1976. Contestants must push an opponent's foot to the other side of a ring ("toerack") using only their toes. In 2022, Alan "Nasty" Nash (UK) was finally beaten after a record-breaking run of 17 wins, starting in 1994. He lost his crown to Ben "Toetal Destruction" Woodroffe in a gripping final, after which this sporting leg-end announced his retirement.

Oldest prosthesis
A false toe crafted from wood and leather was found attached to an ancient Egyptian mummy dating to between 950 and 710 BCE. Artificial body parts were common in Egyptian burial rites, but most were added after death for cosmetic or religious reasons. This particular prosthesis, found in a tomb near Thebes (Luxor) in 2000, had been made for a noblewoman. Dubbed the Cairo Toe, the nearly 3,000-year-old prosthetic is unique because it is jointed and flexible, with signs of wear that indicate it served a practical purpose.

Female: Mixed toe-wrestling is not allowed because of the danger of "myxomatoesis". In the women's category, the most vic-toe-rious is Lisa "Twinkletoes" Shenton (UK), with five wins in 2009–11 and 2018–19.

Heaviest weight lifted by the toes
For a third time, Marcello Ferri (ITA) demonstrated that he has the strongest toes in the world, using just his halluces (big toes) to lift metal plates weighing 41.3 kg (91 lb) in Pesaro, Italy, on 6 Feb 2022. He first broke the record in Jan 2021, and continues to better his personal bests as a way of honouring a promise he made to his late father.

Farthest walk on the toe knuckles
On 21 Dec 2021, Spencer Thurgood (UK) tested his metatarsophalangeal joints to their limit by walking 49.62 m (162 ft 9 in) on folded toes. He did this barefooted on a running track in Cambridge, UK, bettering the record by 18.12 m (59 ft 5 in); he might have walked farther but could only find a 50-m tape measure!

Greatest foot rotation
Aaron Ford (USA) can turn each of his feet until they face backwards. At an orthopaedic assessment in Lehi, Utah, on 17 Jan 2020, he was able to rotate his left foot 173.03° – as averaged over three measurements using an electronic goniometer – and hold it there for 10 sec. His right foot averaged 167.93°.

LARGEST FEET EVER

Male: Excluding cases of the disfiguring disease elephantiasis, the largest feet ever measured belonged to Robert Wadlow, who wore US size 37AA shoes (UK size 36 and roughly European size 75) – the equivalent foot length of 47 cm (1 ft 6.5 in). To acquire bespoke shoes (costing $2,100 or £1,995 in today's money), Bob modelled for a footwear company at the age of 11.
Female: China's Zeng Jinlian had 35.5-cm-long (1-ft 2-in) feet, needing a UK/US-size 20 or 21 shoe (European 56).

TALLEST & SHORTEST

1. ○ Shortest woman

Jyoti Amge (IND) was 62.8 cm (2 ft 0.7 in) tall when first measured on 16 Dec 2011. Formerly the **shortest female teenager**, Jyoti is also the **shortest actress**, having played the character Ma Petite in FX TV's *American Horror Story*.

2. ○ Shortest man

Afshin Ghaderzadeh (IRN) measured 65.24 cm (2 ft 1.68 in) in Dubai, UAE, on 13 Dec 2022. He is the fourth-shortest man ever verified by Guinness World Records. *(See below for more.)*

3. ○ Shortest identical male twins

Canada's Zachary and Tristan Lelièvre (b. 19 Sep 2003) had an average height of 114.88 cm (3 ft 9 in) as of 7 Jan 2021. Born with achondroplasia, the twins play elite badminton with the Montreal International Club and harbour hopes to compete in the 2024 Paralympic Games.

4. ○ Shortest female twins

At the age of 27, Elisabeth and Katharina Lindinger (both DEU) averaged 128 cm (4 ft 2 in) in height, as verified on 25 Jan 2021.

5. ○ Greatest height differential in a married couple (same sex)

There is a gap of 84.94 cm (2 ft 9.45 in) between Christie Chandler and Seneca Corsetti (both USA), who met while teaching at the same school and tied the knot in Jun 2021. Christie is 182.22 cm (5 ft 11.74 in), while Seneca is 97.28 cm (3 ft 2.29 in).

Shortest non-twin siblings
Bridgette and Brad Jordan of Sandoval in Illinois, USA, measured 69 cm (2 ft 3 in) and 98 cm (3 ft 2.5 in) tall respectively – a combined height of 167 cm (5 ft 5.5 in). Their restricted growth was the result of a form of primordial dwarfism. They both had starring roles in the TLC reality show *Big Tiny*, which brought their lives to the attention of millions of viewers. Sadly, Brad passed in Feb 2017 at the age of 25; Bridgette – who, prior to Jyoti Amge *(see below)*, was the shortest living woman – died in Jun 2019, aged 30.

(both CHN) have a combined height of 423.47 cm (13 ft 10.72 in). He stands 236.17 cm (7 ft 8.98 in) tall, while she measures a still-statuesque 187.3 cm (6 ft 1.74 in). They were married in Beijing on 4 Aug 2013.

6. ○ Tallest woman

Rumeysa Gelgi (TUR) stands 215.16 cm (7 ft 0.7 in) tall, as verified on 23 May 2021 in Safranbolu, Türkiye. Previously the **tallest female teenager**, she says achieving a GWR title has "motivated me to pursue my goals and have a more confident outlook in life" and hopes that this record will help to raise awareness of overgrowth syndromes such as hers.

7. ○ Tallest teenager

On 19 Dec 2020, Olivier Rioux (CAN, b. 2 Feb 2006) measured 226.9 cm (7 ft 5.33 in), as verified in Beloeil, Quebec, Canada. Olivier tells us that he had his eye on this record title since he was 10 years old! The NBA wannabe is currently honing his basketball skills at Florida's famed IMG Academy.

8. Tallest married couple

Former sports stars Sun Mingming and his wife Xu Yan

9. ○ Tallest man

Türkiye's Sultan Kösen has been the **tallest person** on Earth since 11 Feb 2009. His extreme height – 251 cm (8 ft 2.8 in) – is the result of a now-excised pituitary tumour. He also has the **largest hands** *(see p.60)*. Despite his stature, Sultan is still 21 cm (8.3 in) shorter than Robert Wadlow (USA), the **tallest person ever** at 272 cm (8 ft 11.1 in).

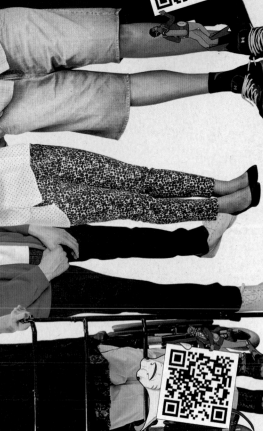

▲ SHORTEST MAN

Standing just 65.24 cm (2 ft 1.68 in) tall, Afshin Esmaeil Ghaderzadeh (IRN) was confirmed as the shortest living man during a visit to the GWR office in Dubai, UAE, on 13 Dec 2022. Mohamed, as he's known to his friends and family, is from the Kurdish region of Bukan County in northern Iran, and turned 20 years old on 13 Jul 2022. He weighed in at 6.5 kg (14 lb 5 oz) – about the same as a large domestic cat.

Included on this page are snapshots from Afshin's whistlestop trip to Dubai to be measured for his world record.

... then makes a quick visit to Maher Watter of Handy Tailor to be measured up for a new suit.

The world's media meet Afshin for the first time in a press conference held at his hotel.

To get ready for his meeting with the media, Afshin is treated to a trim and a shave at the barber's shop...

Posing with GWR Editor-in-Chief Craig Glenday for a portrait by photographer Mustapha Azab.

Smallest hands (male)

It's not just his diminutive stature that makes Afshin special: his hands are also record breakers in their own right. His right hand (print shown) measures 6.4 cm (2.51 in) from the base of the palm to the tip of the middle finger, while his left hand measures 6.7 cm (2.63 in), as verified in Milan, Italy, on 3 Mar 2023.

Being measured – three times in a single day – by Dr Bindu Devarajan, a GP from the Ahalia Group.

Mother Khatoun and father Esmaeil meet with adjudicator Kanzy El Defrawy at the GWR office.

No trip to Dubai is complete without a visit to the top of the Burj Khalifa, the tallest building.

VISIT THE LOUVRE

The Parisian art gallery has a total surface area of c. 73,000 m² (785,765 sq ft), making it the **largest palace used as a museum**. In 2021, nearly 3 million visitors jostled to see the Louvre's most popular exhibit: Leonardo da Vinci's *Mona Lisa*, which in 1911 became the **most valuable object stolen**. (It was found in 1913.)

FAMILY ALBUM

Sullivan   Lorne (now Alex)   Isaac

Longest interval between birth of triplets

Lorne McBurney (b. 20 Sep 2004) was born 17 days 18 hr 55 min ahead of his brothers Isaac and Sullivan (b. 8 Oct 2004) in Lee's Summit, Missouri, USA. All three siblings were born prematurely and weighed less than 2 lb (900 g) each. Their parents are Kara and Scott McBurney (all USA).

Most family members born on the same day
For the nine members of the Mangi family of Larkana, Pakistan, 1 Aug is one big birthday. Ameer (father), Khudija (mother) and their seven children – Sindhoo, Sasui, Sapna, Aamir, Ambar, Ammar and Ahmar – were all born that day. Eleven years (1992–2003) separates the first- and last-born. (See also nonuplet record, right.)

Rarest form of discordant twinning

Sienna "Sinny" Bernal was born with a form of primordial dwarfism so uncommon that it isn't formally classified. But even rarer is the fact that she is the monozygotic twin of Sierra (both USA). Born on 22 Dec 1998, the "discordant" sisters display the **greatest height differential in identical twins**: when last measured, Sinny stood 132 cm (4 ft 4 in) tall, while Sierra was 170 cm (5 ft 7 in).

Most premature twins
Adiah Laelynn and Adrial Luka Nadarajah (both CAN) were born 126 days early at Mount Sinai Hospital in Toronto, Canada, on 4 Mar 2022. They were born at a gestational age of 22 weeks, some 18 weeks earlier than a full-term pregnancy. Adiah and Adrial weighed 330 g (11.6 oz) and 420 g (14.8 oz) respectively at birth – lighter than a pint of milk.

Most premature triplets

Rubi-Rose, Payton-Jane and Porscha-Mae Hopkins (all UK) were born to Michaela White and Jason Hopkins at a gestational age of 22 weeks 5 days (159 days) – or 121 days prematurely. They arrived at Southmead Hospital in Bristol, UK, on 14 Feb 2021; their weight totalled just 1,284 g (2 lb 13.3 oz), making them also the **lightest triplets**.

SEE AN ACTIVE VOLCANO
Calling all hot heads! For a front-row seat at an explosive event, head to Mount Stromboli, which sits on a small island in the Tyrrhenian Sea, off the coast of Italy. It has been releasing ash and lava a few times an hour since at least 700 BCE, making it the **longest continuously erupting volcano**.

The nonuplets are pictured here in a family gathering at the Ain Borja Clinic in Dec 2022, aged 19 months.

Boys: Mohammed VI, Oumar, Elhadji and Bah. Girls: Kadidia, Fatouma, Hawa, Adama and Oumou.

Friday,

Most children delivered at a single birth

On 6 May 2021, Associated Press announced the birth of nine children to Mali's Halima Cissé and father Abdelkader Arby at the Ain Borja Clinic in Casablanca, Morocco. Cissé gave birth prematurely on 4 May 2021 – at 30 weeks – via Caesarean section; each of the five girls and four boys weighed within the range of 500 g– 1 kg (1 lb 1 oz–2 lb 3 oz). Nonuplets are extremely rare – indeed, this is the first known incidence of nine babies surviving birth.

In terms of birthdays, this also ties with Pakistan's Mangi household (*see left*) for the **most family members born on the same day**, although the latter was achieved over 11 years.

MEDICINE

PANDEMICS

We're now in year four of the **first coronavirus pandemic**, and while the severity of COVID-19 has declined in many places, the World Health Organization is anxious to stress that it is still not over. As of 27 Mar 2023, there had been 761 million reported cases, making it the **most widespread coronavirus outbreak**. With 6.8 million deaths, it is also the **deadliest**, dwarfing the impact of its cousins MERS and SARS.

DID YOU KNOW?

The **earliest recorded pandemic** was the Plague of Athens in 430 BCE.

The **longest lasting** is the Seventh Cholera Pandemic – ongoing from 1961 to this day.

In 2005, a glitch created the **first videogame pandemic**, Corrupted Blood, which spread through the *World of Warcraft* community, triggering virtual lockdowns.

The **deadliest pandemic** was the Black Death, which killed 50–100 million people between 1346 and 1353.

The global response to the pandemic involved an unprecedented research effort. The first result of this, BioNTech's (DEU) and Pfizer's (USA) Tozinameran vaccine, was approved for use just 337 days after COVID-19 was identified – the **fastest vaccine development**.

337

Most whole blood donated by a woman

Between 25 Mar 1987 and 30 Sep 2022, Josephine Michaluk of Alberta, Canada, gave blood 203 times. Her donations add up to 99.1 litres (209 US pints) – that's 20 times the amount of blood in an adult. And those are just the donations that can be verified: she started in 1965, before donations were recorded.

First...

• **Separation of conjoined twins**: Swiss surgeon Johannes Fatio successfully separated two infant girls who were joined at the sternum in Basel, Switzerland, between 24 Nov and 3 Dec 1689.

• **Use of mouth-to-mouth resuscitation**: On 3 Dec 1732, William Trossach used chest compressions and artificial ventilation to revive a man who was carried, seemingly dead, out of a fire in a coal mine in Alloa, Clackmannanshire, UK.

• **Heart transplant**: A team of 30 doctors led by Christiaan Barnard (ZAF) replaced the heart of Louis Washkansky at the Groote Schuur Hospital in Cape Town, South Africa, on 3 Dec 1967. Washkansky survived for 18 days with the new heart.

Largest collection of...

• **Human brains**: The Brain Collection at the University of Southern Denmark, located in Odense, has 9,479 preserved specimens, some dating back as far as the late 1940s. Samples from this collection are made available to researchers studying neurological disorders.

• **Ingested objects**: The Mütter Museum at The College of Physicians of Philadelphia, Pennsylvania, USA, houses 2,374 objects that were swallowed or inhaled by the patients of the physician Chevalier Quixote Jackson. The collection includes a miniature trumpet, opera glasses and several sets of dentures.

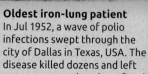

Oldest iron-lung patient

In Jul 1952, a wave of polio infections swept through the city of Dallas in Texas, USA. The disease killed dozens and left many more paralysed, confined to negative-pressure respirators known as "iron lungs" (*left*). One of those infected was six-year-old Paul Alexander. Despite being confined to the iron lung for many hours every day, Alexander graduated from high school and went on to earn a degree in law. Using a technique known as "frog breathing" to sustain himself outside the machine, he went on to run his own legal practice and represent clients in court. Alexander, who is now retired, has been making daily use of his iron lung for 70 years.

Longest...

• **Submergence survived**: In 1986, two-year-old Michelle Funk of Salt Lake City, Utah, USA, spent 66 min underwater having fallen into an icy creek. She was revived at Salt Lake City's Primary Children's Hospital and went home eight weeks later.

• **Dream**: On 29 Apr 1994, David Powell (USA) settled down for a night's rest at the North Puget Sound Center for Sleep Disorders near Seattle, Washington, and drifted off into a 3-hr 8-min period of REM (rapid eye movement) sleep. A typical REM cycle lasts between one and two hours.

• **Bout of yawning**: In 1888, the case of a 15-year-old girl who yawned continuously for five weeks was reported in the *Memphis Journal of the Medical Sciences*. According to the author, Dr Edward W Lee, the period of oscitation began following a tooth extraction and continued until it was treated with "ammonium salts and bed rest".

• **Survival without food**: As part of a weight-loss study, Angus Barbieri (UK) subsisted on a diet of tea, coffee, water and vitamins for 382 days between Jun 1965 and Jul 1966. His weight dropped from 214 kg (471 lb) to 80.7 kg (178 lb).

• **Sneezing fit**: British teenager Donna Griffiths experienced a bout of sternutation on 13 Jan 1981 and couldn't make herself stop. For the next 976 days, she reportedly sneezed around 100 times an hour, eventually stopping on 16 Sep 1983.

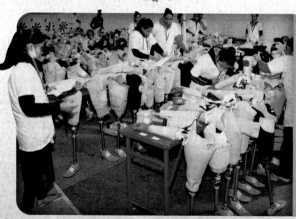

Most people fitted with prosthetic limbs in eight hours

On 3 Dec 2021, the Shree Swaminarayan Multispecialty Hospital in Vadtal, Gujarat, India, hosted an event that saw 710 people receive new prostheses. The event was organized by the hospital and volunteers from local Swaminarayan temples, who assisted with the fittings.

ATTEND CARNIVAL IN RIO DE JANEIRO

Samba your way through the bustling streets of Rio de Janeiro, Brazil, during the **largest carnival**. The costumed performers from the city's samba schools dance their way past a crowd of more than 7 million people on their way to the Sambadrome stadium.

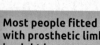

Skully's skeleton was discovered at a site called Liang Tebo, a cavern that can be reached only by a week's hike through the rainforest. The archaeologists camped out at the site during the 11-day excavation, living in the same cave that Skully had called home 31,100 years ago.

Skully belonged to a people who left cave paintings across the island of Borneo.

OLDEST AMPUTATION

In 2022, a group of Indonesian and Australian archaeologists uncovered something remarkable in Kalimantan, Indonesia. They found a 31,100-year-old skeleton, dubbed TB1 (or more informally "Skully"), that was missing its left foot and lower leg, but that did not show any signs of blunt-force injury or infection.

Instead, it appeared that this was the consequence of a surgical amputation that had taken place when Skully was a child, most likely because they had a foot injury that was either not healing or that had become infected. Skully's survival suggests that their stone-age surgeon had a good working understanding of human anatomy; crucially, their community could also manage the careful post-operative care required to avoid a fatal infection.

The tibia and fibula of Skully's left leg had been cleanly cut. A crushing injury, such as from a rockfall, would have caused extensive fracturing above the severed section, while an animal bite (from a crocodile, for example) would have caused an infection whose effects would have been visible on the bone. The cut ends of the bones had healed over with newer growth.

Skully lived for around 10 years after their risky operation, and eventually died of unrelated causes.

ROUND-UP

Widest mouth
GWR was sad to hear of the passing of Francisco Domingo Joaquim "Chiquinho" (AGO) in Jan 2023. His world-beating mouth was 17 cm (6.69 in) across when measured in Rome, Italy, on 18 Mar 2010.

The **largest mouth gape** – i.e., the distance between the upper and lower incisors – is 10.196 cm (4.014 in), by Isaac Johnson (USA). He can fit a soda can or even a baseball into it!

The equivalent **women**'s record is a gape of 6.52 cm (2.56 in), by Samantha Ramsdell (USA). She also has the women's title for **widest mouth** – 10.33 cm (4.07 in) – as confirmed in Norwalk, Connecticut, USA, on 29 Nov 2022. Her massive maw can accommodate everything from an entire apple to a large portion of McDonald's French fries.

Shortest club DJ
Dance-music devotee "YEYE" (aka Yeison Enrique Delgado Castro, COL) stood just 102.46 cm (3 ft 4 in) tall, as verified in Caracas, Venezuela, on 12 Nov 2022. A fruit seller by day, the dedicated DJ has performed for more than 10 years across Latin America.

Heaviest weight lifted by tongue
On 22 Feb 2022, Thomas Blackthorne (UK) raised a slab weighing 13 kg (28 lb 10 oz) – about the same as two bowling balls – with just his tongue. His other titles include the **heaviest object sword-swallowed** – a 38-kg (83-lb 12-oz) demolition hammer!

Largest gathering of people with the same first and last name
On 4 Feb 2023, a group of 256 female citizens named Milica Jovanović convened in Belgrade, Serbia, from all over the country. Both those women born with the name and those who had adopted it – through marriage, for example – were eligible to attend.

Largest gathering of people born prematurely
Dr A K Jayachandran and Neo Bless Moulana Hospital (both IND) brought together 612 individuals born before their time in Perinthalmanna, Kerala, India, on 13 Nov 2022.

Greatest height differential in twins (female)
A disparity of 75 cm (2 ft 5.5 in) separates sisters Yoshie and Michie Kikuchi (both JPN), as verified on 23 Feb 2023 in Okayama, Japan. Michie has a form of dwarfism, which accounts for the difference. The non-identical siblings were chosen as torchbearers for the 2020 Tokyo Olympics. *For the identical-twins record, see p.64.*

Fastest time to name all human bones
It took Banan Sultan Nassereddine (LBN) a mere 5 min 37 sec to identify images of all 206 bones in the human body at Safir High School in Ghazieh, Lebanon, on 2 Aug 2022. The knowledge will stand her in good stead: she wants to become a doctor.

Oldest human embryos used in a successful pregnancy
The birth of twins Lydia and Timothy Ridgeway (both USA) on 31 Oct 2022 via *in vitro* fertilization involved the use of embryos that were 30 years 192 days old. Stored in liquid nitrogen at roughly -196°C (-320°F) since 22 Apr 1992, they were donated to the US National Embryo Donation Center in Knoxville, Tennessee, in 2017, before being passed on to parents Rachel and Philip Ridgeway from Vancouver, Washington, USA.

Shortest comedian
Tanyalee Davis (CAN/USA) stood 100.65 cm (3 ft 3.6 in) tall when measured in Bradenton, Florida, USA, on 6 Feb 2023. Davis has a form of dwarfism known as diastrophic dysplasia, a disorder of the bones and cartilage that typically results in short stature. She describes herself as the "Ferrari of comedy – low to the ground and kind of racy"! (*See also p.197.*)

Since joining TikTok in Sep 2020, Davis's quips and dance routines have won her 3.2 million followers and 37 million likes!

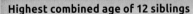

Highest combined age of 12 siblings
The brothers and sisters of the Hernández Pérez family (ESP) had an aggregate age of 1,058 years 249 days as of 4 Aug 2022. The oldest is José (b. 30 Dec 1924), then aged 97 years 217 days, while the youngest is Luis (b. 4 Apr 1946), at 76 years 122 days. The count was confirmed in Moya, Las Palmas, Spain, where the siblings have lived all their lives.

FLY A PLANE
Kiss *terra firma* goodbye for a while and experience the freedom of the open skies. The USA's Colonel Clarence Cornish was a lifelong enthusiast: he flew planes from 6 May 1918 until 4 Dec 1995 – the **longest career as a pilot**, at 77 years 212 days. He died just 18 days after his final flight.

First green-screen tattoo

In Aug 2018, a *Rick and Morty* tattoo featuring a chroma-key element (*right*) – by artist Roy Lee Rowlett – went viral. However, the first use of green-screen tattooing came a few weeks earlier on 21 Jul, when Josh Herman (USA) inked a TV on to Tyler Smith in Denver, Colorado, USA. When viewed with a smartphone app, the green area becomes a media player for photos or video.

"It's called a green screen Morty"

Youngest Mensa member

Isla McNabb (USA, b. 19 Nov 2019) was a certified member of the famous IQ society at the age of 2 years 195 days, as verified in Louisville, Kentucky, USA, on 2 Jun 2022. She attempted an intelligence test after proving she could read at just 2 years old, and her score was in the 99th percentile.

Most body modifications for a married couple

Between them, Gabriela Peralta (URY) and Victor Hugo Peralta (ARG) have 91 body mods, as verified in Milan, Italy, on 13 Feb 2023. They include piercings, implants, ear expanders and ear bolts, while both of them can boast a broad and intricate range of tattoos. Victor sums up their collective outlook as: "Enjoy life, enjoy the art."

Most joints cracked consecutively

The clicking sound generated when we crack our bones – known as "crepitus" – is caused by hydrogen bubbles popping in the synovial fluid, a lubricant between the bones. On 25 Jan 2023, Olle Lundin (SWE) cracked 46 of his joints one after the other in Uppsala, Uppland, Sweden.

Youngest person to have a wisdom tooth extracted

Ryan Scarpelli (USA, b. 3 Sep 2011) was only 9 years 327 days old when he had a wisdom tooth removed, as affirmed in Leesburg, Virginia, USA, on 27 Jul 2021. The tooth was on top of his second molar and would have prevented it from dropping. Ordinarily, wisdom teeth don't emerge until our late teens.

Most Marvel comic-book characters tattooed on the body

Rick Scolamiero (CAN, *right*) has 34 images of Marvel superheroes inked on to his skin. He was also lucky enough to have his wrist signed by the great Stan Lee himself, which he had permanently inked. The count took place in Alberta, Canada, on 9 Mar 2023, and made Scolamiero a joint holder with Ryan Logsdon (USA), whose 34 tats were ratified in Louisville, Kentucky, USA, on 3 Dec 2022.

> While at GWR HQ, Stoeberl used his tongue (wrapped in clingfilm) to paint a portrait of Editor-in-Chief Craig Glenday!

Most technological implants

Biohacking magician Anastasia Synn (USA) has augmented her body with an array of functional implants such as magnets, RFID tags and microchips. At an official count in Milan, Italy, on 2 Feb 2023, Synn revealed 52 augmentations. She uses them in her stage act, and – among other things – to unlock her front door!

Fastest time to remove five Jenga blocks with the tongue

Nick Stoeberl (USA) took just 55.52 sec to dislodge a quintet of wooden blocks with his lengthy licker at the GWR offices in London, UK, on 20 Feb 2023. Stoeberl has the distinct advantage of possessing the world's **longest tongue**, at 10.1 cm (3.97 in) from lip to tip.

Most tattoos of the same comic-book character

Costas Moutsios (GRC) has nine tattoos of Batman, as authenticated in Athens, Greece, on 10 Mar 2022. Altogether, his Dark Knight designs have cost Moutsios €3,440 (£2,875; $3,780).

RIDE A SEGWAY
These electric-powered two-wheelers are an eco-friendly means of getting around – and fun to spin on too! The **most people performing 360s on Segways simultaneously** is 108, by Sony (USA) prior to the premiere of *Paul Blart: Mall Cop 2* in New York City, USA, on 11 Apr 2015.

69

WIM HOF

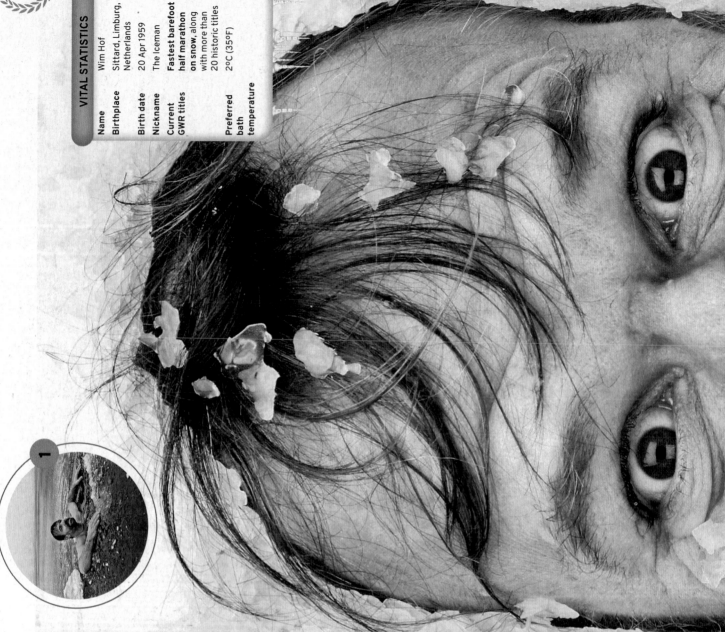

Chill-seeker Wim Hof (NLD) has become famous for his feats of sub-zero stamina, climbing mountains and plunging into icy lakes. "The Iceman" believes that the cold can hold the key to health and happiness.

Wim's love affair with the cold began when he was 17 years old. Walking through a local park in Amsterdam, he saw a half-frozen canal and decided to take a dip – "I just undressed and got in," he recalled. He returned to the canal the next day and continued to swim in it throughout the winter. He went on to develop a special breathing technique – what he calls the Wim Hof Method – which he claims helps his body deal with icy conditions, and which he has practised every day since. When he was filmed by a TV crew rescuing a man who'd fallen through lake ice, word of his unusual abilities began to spread.

Wim decided to turn his talents to record breaking, claiming multiple GWR titles swimming under ice and submerging himself in freezing baths. In 2007, he attempted to climb Everest, the **highest mountain**, wearing only shoes and shorts. He reached an altitude of 7,400 m (24,300 ft) before a foot injury forced him to abandon the expedition. In 2016, Wim attempted a similar feat on Mount Kilimanjaro, leading a sparsely dressed team to the summit, where temperatures can plummet as low as -20°C (-4°F).

Wim continues to enthuse about the invigorating effects of the cold on people's wellbeing. He has been the subject of countless TV shows and documentaries; he says famous names such as Oprah Winfrey and Justin Bieber have tried his breathing method. The Iceman shows no sign of thawing any time soon...

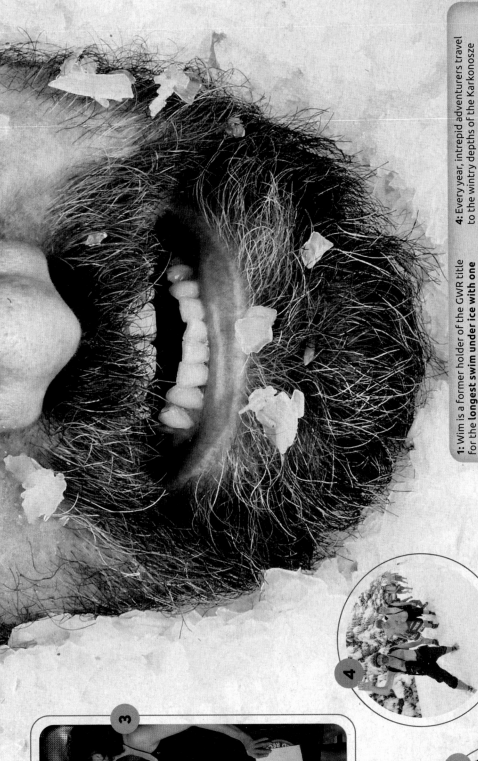

1: Wim is a former holder of the GWR title for the **longest swim under ice with one breath (no fins, no diving suit)**. On 16 Mar 2000, he swam 57.5 m (188 ft 7 in) under the frozen surface of a lake near Kolari in Finnish Lapland, wearing only trunks and a pair of goggles. The current record is 80.99 m (265 ft 8 in), set by David Vencl (CZE) on 23 Feb 2021.

2: For his 2022 BBC series *Freeze the Fear with Wim Hof*, the Iceman took a group of celebrities, including *Strictly Come Dancing* pro Dianne Buswell, to the Italian mountains, where he guided them through a series of sub-zero challenges.

3: Wim has broken the record for the **longest duration full-body contact with ice** on multiple occasions, recording a best time of 1 hr 53 min 2 sec on 18 Oct 2013. The men's record now stands at 3 hr 28 sec, by Valerjan Romanovski (POL) on 23 Oct 2021.

4: Every year, intrepid adventurers travel to the wintry depths of the Karkonosze biosphere reserve on the Poland-Czechia border for the Wim Hof Expedition. There, the Iceman leads recruits on a five-day training programme. The Expedition culminates in a mountain climb in the Sudeten range.

5: On 26 Jan 2007, Wim travelled to the Finnish Arctic Circle to run the **fastest barefoot half marathon on snow** – 2 hr 16 min 34 sec. His feat was recorded on Discovery Channel's *The Real Superhumans and the Quest for the Future Fantastic*.

6: Wim believes that his self-devised system – based on breathing, cold therapy and commitment – can help people connect not only with nature, but also one another. He has participated in a number of scientific studies in the hope of proving the benefits of the Wim Hof Method.

Find out more about Wim in the Hall of Fame section at www.guinnessworldrecords.com/2024

RECORDOLOGY

Largest collection of Care Bears memorabilia
As of 23 Jan 2023, American make-up artist Nicholas Cherrywood had 1,234 items related to the Care Bears franchise. His collection includes books, movies, stationery, clothing and – of course – dozens of versions of the classic teddy bears. Nicholas's relationship with the Kingdom of Caring began with a pair of plush toys – Grumpy Bear and Cheer Bear – that he was given during an extended stay in hospital as a child. Nicholas even changed his name to reference a character from *The Care Bears Movie* (CAN/USA, 1985).

As a child, Nicholas used his bears to express himself, carrying Cheer Bear on good days or Bedtime Bear when he was tired.

LARGEST VEGETARIAN BURGER

MrBEAST'S VEGGIE BURGER

From speed-eating to marathon serving sessions, the humble burger has played a part in some of GWR's most popular culinary records. In 2022, a virtual restaurant set out to make a super-sized version, with one important twist – no meat allowed!

As the **most subscribed YouTuber** – with a mind-boggling 112,193,139 fans, as of Nov 2022 – "MrBeast" (aka Jimmy Donaldson, USA) knows all about large numbers. So when his "MrBeast Burger" virtual restaurant set about creating the **largest vegetarian burger**, they didn't hold back.

A team of 43 people got to work in Greenville, North Carolina, USA, preparing for the burger's unveiling on 29 Sep 2022. Inside a refrigerated trailer, a pair of stainless-steel cooking moulds were each packed with 1,900 lb (861 kg) of the restaurant's "Impossible" burgers – made from soy protein concentrate, water, salt, and sunflower and coconut oils. The patties were transferred via forklift to a propane oven and cooked for 10 hr at around 400°F (204°C). Under the watchful eye of a food-safety officer, the vast veggie treats were slathered in BBQ sauce and then rested in the oven in order for the juices to settle.

At assembly time, the patties were laid between two giant brioche buns and garnished with 200 lb (90.7 kg) each of onions, lettuce and cheese. The finished burger tipped the scales at a record-breaking 2,092.4 kg (4,612 lb 15 oz). Finally, as per GWR food-wastage guidelines, the behemoth burger was divided up and distributed to local charities.

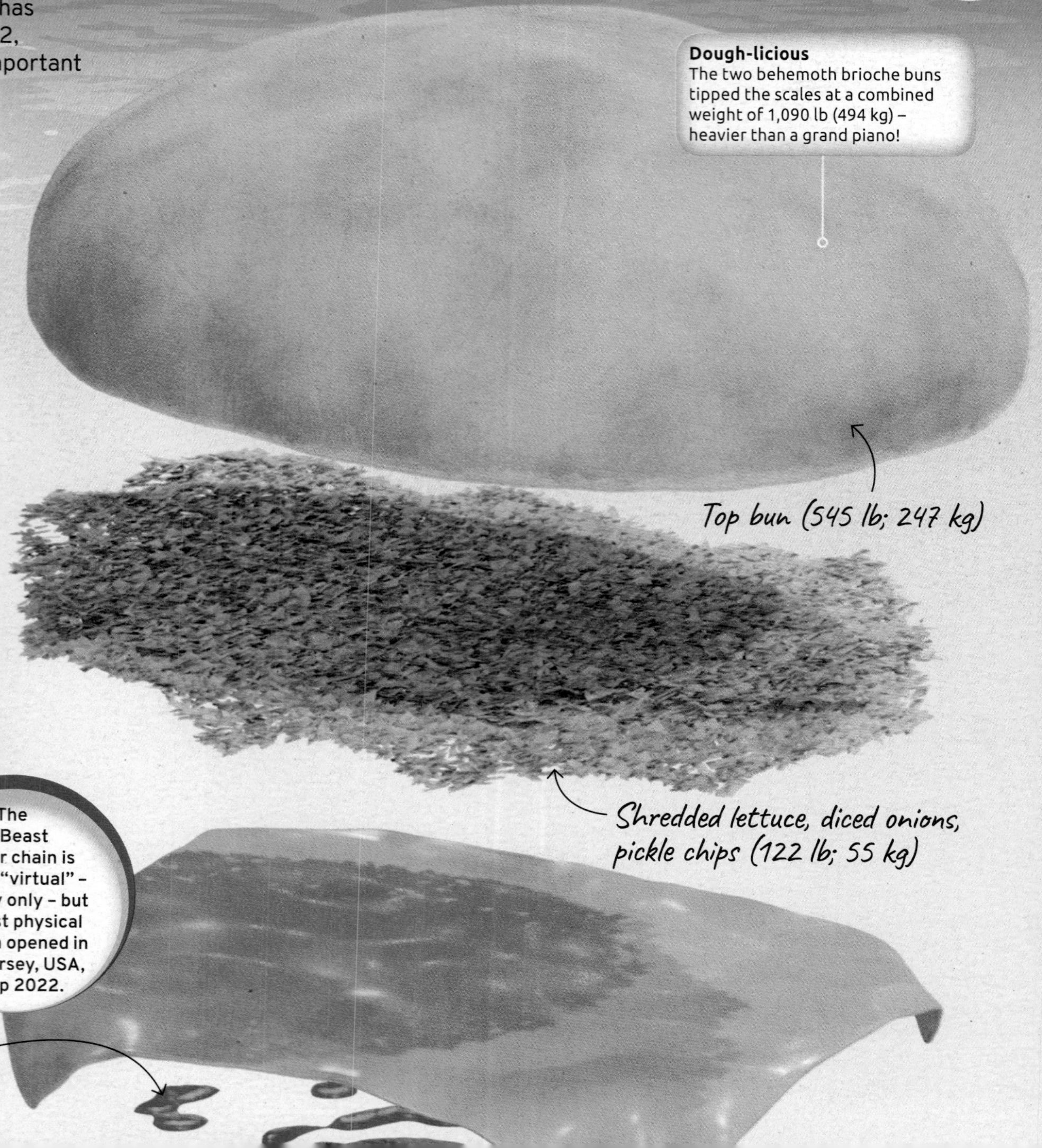

Dough-licious
The two behemoth brioche buns tipped the scales at a combined weight of 1,090 lb (494 kg) – heavier than a grand piano!

Top bun (545 lb; 247 kg)

Shredded lettuce, diced onions, pickle chips (122 lb; 55 kg)

BBQ sauce (50 lb; 22 kg)

The MrBeast Burger chain is usually "virtual" – delivery only – but the first physical location opened in New Jersey, USA, in Sep 2022.

GRILLED GIANTS

Largest hamburger
A triple burger and bun weighing a total of 1,164.2 kg (2,566 lb 9 oz) was served up by six Bavarian cooks led by Josef Zellner (all DEU) on 9 Jul 2017 in Pilsting, Germany (*right*). It was later chopped up into 3,000 portions.

Largest hamburger patty
Loran Green and Friends of Hi Line Promotions (all USA) grilled a slab of Montana ground beef weighing 6,040 lb (2.7 tonnes) in Saco, Montana, USA, on 5 Sep 1999. More than 3,500 people looked on (and drooled!) at the Sleeping Buffalo Resort.

Largest vegan burger
On 18 Nov 2021, Finnebrogue Artisan (UK) prepared a 162.5-kg (358-lb 4-oz) meat- and dairy-free burger in Downpatrick, County Down, UK. The patty was a scaled-up version of their "Naked Evolution Burger" and took 9 hr to cook. It was topped with vegan bacon, crispy onions, vegan cheese, burger sauce, lettuce, tomatoes and pickles.

Cheese (200 lb; 90 kg)

Bottom bun
(545 lb; 247 kg)

2 x patties (total
1,800 lb; 816 kg)

BBQ sauce
No burger is complete without condiments, and the MrBeast vegetarian burger was no exception. The restaurant's standard "Build Your Own Double Impossible Burger" uses one teaspoon of barbecue sauce; its record-breaking big brother, however, required 50 lb (22 kg) of the same dressing. It was made to exactly the same recipe, using tomato, vinegar, sweetener and spices. Once the two patties had been splashed with sauce, they were returned to the oven and rested for 4 hr at 175°F (79°C).

Brioche buns
MrBeast's standard 3.5-in-wide (8.8-cm) burger buns were going to need some serious upscaling if they were going to break the record. The giant brioche rolls were made to the same recipe, using wheat, milk powder, yeast, salt, canola oil, sugar and sesame seeds. The dough was kneaded by a pro baking team using industrial mixers. They were then baked at 350°F (176°C) in a propane oven: 6 hr for the top bun and 5 hr for the bottom.

Super stack
Once assembled, the finished MrBeast veggie burger stood 0.87 m (6 ft 10 in) tall, with a diameter of 2.1 m (7 ft).

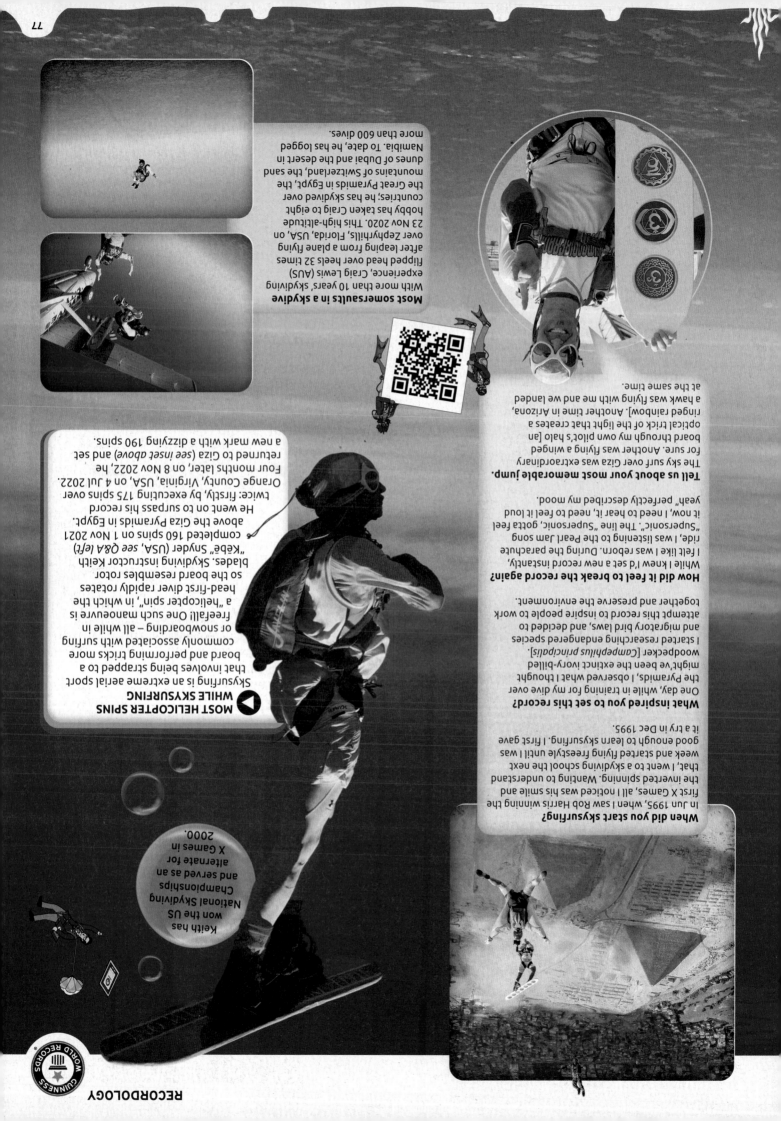

MOST HELICOPTER SPINS WHILE SKYSURFING

Skysurfing is an extreme aerial sport that involves being strapped to a board and performing tricks more commonly associated with surfing or snowboarding – all while in freefall! One such manoeuvre is a "helicopter spin", in which the head-first diver rapidly rotates so the board resembles rotor blades. Skydiving instructor Keith "Kebe" Snyder (USA, *see Q&A left*) completed 160 spins on 1 Nov 2021 above the Giza Pyramids in Egypt. He went on to surpass his record twice: firstly, by executing 175 spins over Orange County, Virginia, USA, on 4 Jul 2022. Four months later, on 8 Nov 2022, he returned to Giza (*see inset above*) and set a new mark with a dizzying 190 spins.

Keith has won the US National Skydiving Championships and served as an alternate for X Games in 2000.

Most somersaults in a skydive

With more than 10 years' skydiving experience, Craig Lewis (AUS) flipped head over heels 32 times after leaping from a plane flying over Zephyrhills, Florida, USA, on 23 Nov 2020. This high-altitude hobby has taken Craig to eight countries; he has skydived over the Great Pyramids in Egypt, the mountains of Switzerland, the sand dunes of Dubai and the desert in Namibia. To date, he has logged more than 600 dives.

When did you start skysurfing?
In Jun 1995, when I saw Rob Harris winning the first X Games, all I noticed was his smile and the inverted spinning. Wanting to understand that, I went to a skydiving school the next week and started flying freestyle until I was good enough to learn skysurfing. I first gave it a try in Dec 1995.

What inspired you to set this record?
One day, while in training for my dive over the Pyramids, I observed what I thought might've been the extinct ivory-billed woodpecker [*Campephilus principalis*]. I started researching endangered species and migratory bird laws, and decided to attempt this record to inspire people to work together and preserve the environment.

How did it feel to break the record again?
While I knew I'd set a new record instantly, I felt like I was reborn. During the parachute ride, I was listening to the Pearl Jam song "Supersonic". The line "Supersonic, gotta feel it now, I need to hear it, need to feel it loud yeah" perfectly described my mood.

Tell us about your most memorable jump.
The sky surf over Giza was extraordinary for sure. Another time I was flying a winged board through my own pilot's halo [an optical trick of the light that creates a ringed rainbow]. Another time in Arizona, a hawk was flying with me and we landed at the same time.

UPSIDE DOWN

Most swords swallowed simultaneously
Professional sword-swallower Franz Huber (DEU) slid nine blades down (well, up!) his gullet while suspended in Milan, Italy, on 10 Feb 2022. It is the third time that Franz has broken this record, having first swallowed five swords inverted in 2016 and then seven swords in 2017. As per the rules, each blade must be at least 38 cm (15 in) long.

Most balls juggled
On 3 Feb 2018, aerial circus performer Zane Jarvie (NZ) juggled five balls while hanging on a trapeze in Perth, Western Australia. The feat was equalled by serial record breaker David Rush (USA) in Boise, Idaho, USA, on 1 Dec 2021.

The **most juggling catches while upside down** is 1,769, set by Araki Terumi (JPN) in Shizuoka-ken, Japan, on 16 Feb 2012. Araki was wearing "gravity boots" and suspended from a bar.

Longest time holding breath underwater (male)

Fastest 100 m on forearm crutches
On 6 Mar 2014, Tameru Zegeye (ETH) covered 100 m (328 ft) in 57 sec while balancing on crutches in Fürth, Bavaria, Germany. Born with irregular feet, circus star Tameru was determined to show that nothing was out of reach. He began walking with his hands at a young age to increase upper-body strength.

On a single breath, Sobhan Bahri (IRN) remained submerged while inverted for 4 min 40 sec on 30 Jun 2017 in Bushehr, Iran.

Fastest 5-m inverted rope climb
On 21 Oct 2001, Tuomo Kostian (FIN) completed a 5-m (16-ft 4-in) rope climb in 13.7 sec, despite going up feet first. For the attempt to count, his whole body had to cross the 5-m line. Also putting her best foot forward was Nele Bruckmann (DEU), who set the **farthest inverted pole climb in one minute**. On 1 Sep 2007, she reverse-clambered 9.73 m (31 ft 11 in) on a TV show in Cologne, Germany.

Most aircraft in an inverted acrobatic flight
During a hometown display on 29 Oct 2006 in Pirassununga, São Paulo, the Brazilian Air Force's Esquadrilha da Fumaça ("Smoke Squadron") beat their own flight-flipping record from 2002. A total of 12 T-27 Tucanos performed a half-loop in close formation, then held position upside down for more than 30 seconds.

Most people doing a handstand simultaneously
A group of 399 people experienced a rush of blood to the head for at least 10 sec in Wevelgem, Belgium, on 17 Sep 2006. The equivalent **headstand** record is 2,945 people, achieved at a Shirshasana yoga event organized by Gyanjyot Vidyalaya, Maulik Ashwin Sudani, Hari Krishna Exports and Euro India Fresh Foods (all IND) in Gujarat, India, on 3 Dec 2017.

Most handstand push-ups in one minute (female)
CrossFit athlete Rachel Martínez (USA) executed an abs-busting 12 vertical push-ups on behalf of the sports clothing brand Reebok in New York, USA, on 1 Feb 2017.

Most spins of a hula hoop on one foot while doing a headstand in one minute
Multi-tasker J Jessica (IND) claimed her debut GWR title by rotating a hoop 213 times on her left foot while perched on her head in Chennai, Tamil Nadu, India, on 11 Jul 2020. The **most hula hoops spun while hanging upside down** is 23, set by Jenny Doan (AUS) in Denver, Colorado, USA, on 29 May 2022.

Fastest time to solve a rotating tetrahedron
An inverted Lim Kai Yi (MYS) unscrambled a 3D pyramidal puzzle in 7.74 sec in Georgetown, Malaysia, on 20 Jul 2022.

◀ **Most stairs climbed on the head**
While in a headstand position (and wearing padding for some protection), acrobatic athlete Li Longlong (CHN) bounced up 36 steps consecutively on the set of *CCTV Guinness World Records Special* in Jiangyin, Jiangsu, China, on 5 Jan 2015. The rules stipulate that there can only be a five-second break between each step and no other body part than the head may touch the steps.

Li previously shared the record with compatriot Zhao Xiaolong: both climbed 34 steps in Dec 2012.

DEXTEROUS DANGLING

Daryl's inverted puzzle feats

4x4x4 cube	Solve time: 37.25 sec
3x3x3 cube (one-handed)	Solve time: 17.12 sec
Two 3x3x3 cubes simultaneously	Solve time: 56.61 sec

All set on 18 Apr 2021

Daryl Tan Hong An (SGP) holds nine records for unscrambling rotating puzzles, including several underwater (see *p.78*) and others while upside down (see *below*). Along with a passion for speedcubing, he's also an avid runner, which is why he took on the **fastest 100 m solving a cube** (13.63 sec) on 19 Jun 2021. Daryl aims to inspire children to put down their electronic gadgets and to try out a physical puzzle (see p.86).

RIDE IN A HELICOPTER

You might have rotor-powered ambitions to pilot a beast like a Chinook or an Apache, but why not think outside the box? Japan's Gen Corporation have created the 70-kg (154-lb) H-4: a single-seat flying machine that's the **world's smallest helicopter**. As a bonus, it can fit in your garage!

79

UNDERWATER FEATS

Most couples married underwater
On Valentine's Day 2001, 34 couples gargled "I do" under the sea off Ko Kradan in Thailand. The wet wedding was organized by Thai Airways International and the Trang Chamber of Commerce.

34

DEEPEST...

Model photoshoot: On 26 Jun 2021, Steve Haining (aided by Mareesha Klups) snapped model Ciara Antoski (all CAN) at a depth of 6.4 m (21 ft) alongside the eerie *W L Wetmore* shipwreck in Lake Huron, Ontario, Canada.

Postbox: A marine mailbox located 10 m (32 ft 9 in) below the surface in Susami Bay, Japan, is serviced by a local land-based post office. Up to 1,500 waterproof postcards are deposited here annually.

Bike ride: Lowered by SCUBA divers to 28 m (92 ft), Vittorio Innocente (ITA) cycled along the seabed to 66.5 m (218 ft) off Santa Margherita Ligure, Italy, on 21 Jul 2008.

Wedding: Hiroyuki Yoshida (JPN) and Sandra Smith (USA) got hitched 130 m (426 ft) underwater in Song Hong Lake, Thailand, on 30 Sep 2013.

Concert: Pop star Katie Melua (UK, b. GEO) and her band played a gig at 303 m (994 ft) beneath the waves on 1 Oct 2006. They performed inside one of the legs of Statoil's Troll A gas rig, off Bergen, Norway.

Longest walk on a single breath
Female: Freediving champion Amber Fillary (ZAF) completed a 109-m (357-ft) subaquatic stroll on one breath in Dahab, Egypt, on 28 Nov 2021. She also made the **longest swim under ice without a diving suit** (90 m; 295 ft) in Norway (*see p.123*).
● **Male:** Vitomir Maričić (HRV), who holds several diving records, walked for 107 m (351 ft) in Opatija, Primorsko-Goranska, Croatia, on 17 Sep 2021. The week after, Vitomir went on to claim a gold and a bronze at the AIDA Freediving World Championship in Limassol, Cyprus.

Most cannonball dives in three minutes
On 24 Jun 2022, Walid Mohamed Bakr (EGY) fulfilled a goal to appear in the *GWR* book by executing 37 "dive bombs" in New Valley, Egypt, bettering the previous mark by one dive.
   The **most people cannonball diving simultaneously** is 298, arranged by LAGO Gent Rozebroeken to mark the leisure centre's 10th anniversary in Ghent, Belgium, on 25 Jun 2022.

Most swords swallowed simultaneously underwater
The Space Cowboy, aka Chayne Hultgren (AUS), slipped four blades down his throat while in a swimming pool in Milan, Italy, on 11 Jul 2014. He currently holds 17 records, including the **most underwater somersaults while sword swallowing** – two – set in Australia on 9 Feb 2017.

Largest underwater painting
On 30 Sep 2020, Saddam Killany (EGY) spent nine hours painting a 7.92-m² (85.25-sq-ft) canvas off Dahab, Egypt. It was to thank essential workers during the COVID-19 pandemic.

Longest underwater human chain
The Indonesian Women's Diving Organisation recruited 578 of its members to take a dip and link arms off Manado, North Sulawesi, Indonesia, on 1 Aug 2019.

Most puzzle cubes solved underwater
After two months of breath training, multi-record holder Daryl Tan Hong An from Singapore made a splash by setting four records on 18 Apr 2021. He unscrambled the **most 2x2x2 cubes** (26), **3x3x3 cubes** (16), **3x3x3 cubes one-handed** (eight) and **tetrahedrons** (15), allowing himself only a single breath for each attempt. Clearly a fan of turning convention on its head, Daryl has also set records for solving puzzles while hanging upside down (*see p.76*).

Largest underwater clean-up in 12 hours
A group of 597 volunteers rallied by the environmental non-profit Oceanum Liberandum (PRT) collected more than 3 tonnes (3.3 tons) of litter from the harbour in Sesimbra, Portugal, on 24 Sep 2022. A day before, the NGO had curated the **largest underwater photography exhibition**, featuring 150 aquatic-themed shots.

Nessie?

First marathon distance on foot underwater
Lloyd Scott (UK) emerged from Loch Ness in Scotland, UK, on 9 Oct 2013 after a 12-day, 42-km (26-mi) marathon walk beneath the frigid waters. He did the whole loch-bed trek in an 80-kg (176-lb) vintage diving suit. The leukaemia survivor spent a month training before setting out to raise money for the charity Children with Leukaemia.

GRADUATE HIGH SCHOOL
Donning that graduation gown will be the proud culmination of many years in education. While you're formally dressed, why not tick off another bucket-list goal? The **fastest marathon wearing a graduation gown** is 3 hr 32 min 8 sec (**female**) and 3 hr 31 min 11 sec (**male**)!

Jason's artworks are created using eco-friendly materials such as stainless steel and pH-neutral concrete.

MOST UNDERWATER ART INSTALLATIONS

Environmental sculptor Jason deCaires Taylor (UK) has completed 13 aquatic art installations around the world (11 marine examples and two in freshwater), which comprise hundreds of sculptures.

His first project (*inset, top left*), completed in 2006 in the wake of 2004's Hurricane Ivan, was a series of 75 sculptures that formed Molinere Bay Underwater Sculpture Park off Grenada in the Caribbean.

His most recent (*main and inset, bottom left*) is his take on an underwater forest, consisting of 93 artworks, created for the Museum of Underwater Sculpture Ayia Napa in Cyprus, which opened on 31 Jul 2021.

All of Jason's aquatic art seeks to draw attention to ocean conservation and coastal communities, and is also designed to become part of the natural habitat over the passage of time.

MERFOLK

Oldest depiction of a merperson
Images of *kulullû* ("fish-men", *left*) and *kuliltu* ("fish-women") appear in ancient Mesopotamian art dating to the end of the 3rd millennium BCE. The oldest surviving examples are found on stone cylinder seals that would imprint personalized designs on to lumps of clay used to secure administrative documents, doors and bags, among other valuable things.

Oldest merperson movie
La Sirène (FRA, 1904) is a silent movie by the French director Georges Méliès of the Star Film Company. In the 3-min 58-sec film, Méliès plays a magician who conjures a mermaid from a fish tank and transforms her into a woman.

Largest collection of mermaid-related items
Self-proclaimed "Mergirl" Laurie Koller (USA) has amassed 726 pieces of sea-siren *mer*-morabilia, as verified on 15 Oct 2015. Her collection includes figurines, vases, pillows, bathing costumes – and a dustpan. Laurie also sports four mermaid tattoos (not counted towards the total).

Jacqueline "Sirenita" Granda of Quito, Ecuador, spent 16 years building the **largest collection of *Little Mermaid* memorabilia**. As of 16 Jan 2016, it contained 874 items – including dolls, clothing, board games and plasters, all relating to Ariel and other characters from the Disney franchise.

DID YOU KNOW?
Early mermaid tales may have been inspired by sightings of the dugong, a large marine mammal (*see p.39*).

HIGHEST-GROSSING MERFOLK MOVIES

Movie	Gross
1. *Mei Ren Yu* (*The Mermaid*, CHN, 2016)	$525,018,479
2. *The Little Mermaid* (USA, 1989)	$222,299,758
3. *Splash* (USA, 1984)	$62,599,495
4. *Aquamarine* (USA, 2006)	$22,978,953
5. *The Mermaid: Lake of the Dead* (RUS, 2018)	$2,990,620

The Numbers, as of 14 Mar 2023; excludes aquatic humanoids such as Aquaman or films where merfolk are minor characters

Most translated mermaid story
Hans Christian Andersen's *Den lille havfrue* (*The Little Mermaid*) has been published in at least 100 languages, from Abkhazian to Zulu. The Danish fairy tale was first published on 7 Apr 1837 as part of a short-story compendium. It is set for a live-action Disney adaptation in 2023, starring Halle Bailey as Ariel (*above*).

First accredited mermaid course
The Professional Association of Diving Instructors launched its Mermaid Programme in Dec 2020 to cater to an increasing interest in "mermaiding" – swimming with a monofin in a fabric or silicone tail. Aspiring Ariels can learn skills such as breath-holding, dives, turns and somersaults, and also receive instruction in water safety and environmental awareness.

Largest merperson sculpture
Located fittingly by the sea at Shankumugham Beach in Thiruvananthapuram, Kerala, India, *Jalakanyaka* is an enormous concrete mermaid reclining in a shell-shaped pool. The figure, with long flowing hair and a finned tail, measures 7.6 m (25 ft) in height and 26.5 m (87 ft) in length – longer than a standard cricket pitch. *Jalakanyaka* is the work of Kerala's royal sculptor Kanayi Kunhiraman (IND).

Highest jump from water wearing a monofin
On 17 Nov 2020, Omar Syed Shaaban (EGY) leapt to a height of 2.3 m (7 ft 6 in) at a pool in Cairo, Egypt. The 21-year-old student and decorated junior swimmer broke a record that had stood for almost a decade. Monofins are typically used in underwater sports such as free diving.

Most expensive merperson painting sold at auction
John William Waterhouse's *The Siren* (1900) fetched £3,835,800 ($5.08 m), including buyer's premium, at Sotheby's in London, UK, on 12 Jul 2018. It was purchased anonymously and remains in a private collection.

Most expensive mermaid
The "Feejee Mermaid" was bought by the US sea captain Samuel Barrett Eades in 1822 for 5,000 Spanish dollars – about £110,000 ($126,600) today. Sold as the mummified corpse of a submarine humanoid, it was, in fact, the merged remains of a monkey and a fish, perhaps made in Japan. The Feejee Mermaid was exhibited in South Africa, the UK and the USA, arousing huge public interest and provoking fierce speculation over its veracity. It was bought by the US showman PT Barnum, who gave the exhibit its name, and is believed to have been destroyed in a fire in the late 19th century. Shown here is another example of an embalmed "mermaid", made from papier-mâché.

Japanese mermaid mummies were originally devotional objects representing *ningyo* ("human-fish" spirits).

TAKE A COOKING CLASS
Treat your tastebuds by honing your culinary skills under the expert eye of a master meal-maker. One person who needed no help in the kitchen was the late Joël Robuchon (FRA), who accrued the **most Michelin stars for a chef**: 32, across restaurants in 13 different countries.

LARGEST UNDERWATER MERMAID SHOW

On 28 Apr 2021, the Atlantis Sanya Resort on Hainan Island, China, staged a submarine spectacle starring 110 mermaids. The venue teamed up with the Professional Association of Diving Instructors (*see also left*) to scour the country for swimmers capable of performing "aquabatics" in a fast-flowing current. Following an intensive training regime, the mermaids showed off their skills inside the Ambassador Lagoon, a giant aquarium at the heart of the resort that contains 13,500 tonnes (14,880 tons) of water and is home to 250 marine species including moon jellies, moray eels and rays.

Largest gathering of merfolk

On 2 Jun 2022, to mark the Queen's Platinum Jubilee (*see pp.214–15*), a total of 378 wannabe merfolk donned coloured wigs and fishtails to chill out around Tinside Lido (*right*) in Plymouth, Devon, UK. Organizers Pauline Barker and Devon and Cornwall Wild Swimming (both UK) described the turnout as "mermazing".

On 4 Nov 2022, this record was topped by cruise line Virgin Voyages (BMU), who assembled 457 merfolk in Bimini, The Bahamas (left).

SUPERLATIVE SKILLS

Sport-stacking stars
The competitive stacking and unstacking of plastic cups in specific sequences – and at high speed – is governed by the World Sport Stacking Association (WSSA). In Mar 2021, the WSSA announced a record reset following a change to their standard timer design. Listed below are the new record holders from the major categories.

Event	Time	Name
3–3–3 (male)	1.419 sec	Chan Keng Ian (MYS, *above*)
3–3–3 (female)	1.632 sec	Sama Basaw (CHN)
3–6–3 (male)	1.788 sec	Chan Keng Ian
3–6–3 (female)	2.041 sec	Kim Si-eun (KOR, *below*)
Cycle (male)	4.881 sec	Chan Keng Ian
Cycle (female)	5.255 sec	Kim Si-eun
Doubles cycle	5.996 sec	Sama Basaw and Yu-Chun Chou (CHN)
Relay timed 3–6–3	12.591 sec	William Orrell, Andrew Dale, William Allen, Dalton Nichols and Tyler Hollis (all USA)

All figures as of 16 Jan 2023

Farthest archery target hit
On 2 Sep 2022, Dude Perfect's Tyler Toney (USA) struck a standard 122-cm (4-ft) World Archery target with an arrow fired from a distance of 330 m (1,083 ft) in Sadler, Texas, USA. That's about the length of three American football fields.

The sports entertainment team were all about archery in 2022. On 31 Aug, Tyler also achieved the **greatest height to shoot and catch an arrow** – 55 m (180 ft 5 in), in Midlothian, Texas. On the same day, James Jean (USA) shattered a clay pigeon fired from a machine at 77.2 km/h (48 mph) – the **fastest-moving target hit with an arrow**.

Fastest mile on a kick scooter
On 16 Aug 2022, Michael O'Connor (CAN) celebrated his 57th birthday in style by completing a mile-long (1.6-km) course on a push scooter in 4 min 45.19 sec in Thunder Bay, Ontario, Canada. "I decided to race against Father Time and see what was possible," Michael said afterwards.

Fastest time to complete five *kendama* spike catches
A *kendama* is a traditional Japanese skill toy consisting of a wooden handle with three cups, a spike and a ball on a string. On 2 Feb 2022, Gideon Huddleston (USA) landed the ball on the spike five times in just 13.38 sec in Ishinomaki, Miyagi, Japan.

Longest throw and catch of a hot-dog sausage into a bun
On 14 Jul 2022, catcher David Rush and thrower Russell Phillips (both USA) completed a 55.8-yard (51.02-m; 167-ft 5-in) reception of a frankfurter into a waiting bun in Boise, Idaho, USA. The guidelines stated that the meaty missile had to measure 14–18 cm (5.5–7 in); vegetarian and vegan alternatives were also acceptable. David reclaimed a record he had previously held in 2019.

Largest human waterskiing pyramid formation
On 10 Sep 2022, a total of 93 members of the Mercury Marine Pyramid team (USA) waterskied in an interlocked formation for 200 m (656 ft) along the Rock River in Janesville, Wisconsin, USA. The daredevil display unit – drawn from a number of local ski teams – beat their own record of 80, set on 18 Aug 2018.

Most standing jumps on horseback in 30 seconds
Amanda Staalsoe (DNK) is a proponent of equestrian vaulting, a federated sport that involves performing gymnastic-like moves while riding a horse. In Roskilde, Denmark, on 22 Jan 2023, while partnered with Charlie, Amanda made 13 standing jumps from the saddle. On the same day, she also achieved the **most scissor transitions in 30 seconds** (five), repeatedly switching her riding position from forwards to backwards, and lifting her legs high in a "scissoring" action between each turn.

Most pull-ups from a helicopter in one minute
This record was broken three times in 2022. On 6 Jul, YouTuber Arjen Albers completed 24 pull-ups from the landing gear of a hovering helicopter at Hoevenen Airfield in Belgium, only to be beaten by co-presenter Stan Browney (aka Stan Bruininck, both NLD), with 25. Then, on 5 Nov in Yerevan, Armenia, Hamazasp Hloyan (ARM) increased the record to 32 lifts.

Farthest throw of a rubber chicken
Oscar Lynagh (AUS) launched the plucked poultry prop 32.49 m (106 ft 7 in) on 24 Jul 2022 in Melbourne, Australia, smashing the record by more than 7 m (22 ft).

Greatest vertical height stair-climbing in one hour
On 6 Nov 2022, Christian Roberto López Rodríguez (ESP) ascended 1,457 m (4,780 ft) by making repeated climbs of a 363-step tower in Albacete, Spain. In Mar 2022 in Toledo, Spain, he also set the **one week** record, ascending 100,475 m (329,645 ft) – the equivalent of climbing from Earth into space.

Fastest time to assemble Mr Potato Head
It took Lim Kai Yi (MYS) a mere 5.43 sec to slot together a standard Mr Potato Head toy in Butterworth, Malaysia, on 9 Aug 2022. Kai Yi is a multiple speed-puzzling record holder, with 39 current GWR titles for, among other things, manipulating Jenga bricks, Rubik's Cubes, marbles and tangrams.

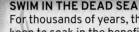
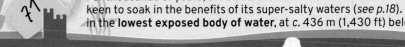

SWIM IN THE DEAD SEA
For thousands of years, the Dead Sea on the Israeli–Jordanian border has attracted visitors keen to soak in the benefits of its super-salty waters (*see p.18*). If you go for a dip, you'll be floating in the **lowest exposed body of water**, at c. 436 m (1,430 ft) below sea level.

Dmytro pulled the metro car along using a 2-mm-thick (0.078-in) cable around his neck.

HEAVIEST TRAIN PULLED BY THE NECK
On 10 May 2022, strongman Dmytro Hrunskyi (UKR) hauled a subway car weighing 32,500 kg (71,650 lb) – about the same as five and a half elephants – using a wire looped around his neck. The carriage, housed in a metro depot in Dnipro, Ukraine, tipped the scales at almost 400 times Dmytro's own body weight. At just 82.4 kg (12 st 13 lb), he is proud to show that smaller strongmen are just as capable of extraordinary feats of strength as their supersized peers. To qualify for the record, he had to tow the car at least 5 m (16 ft).

ADOPT A CHILD
It's never too late to bring a new face into the family. On 9 Jun 2015, Muriel Banks Clayton (USA, b. 22 Jul 1922) became the **oldest adoptive parent** at the age of 92 years 322 days; her daughter, Mary Banks Smith (USA, b. 5 Mar 1939), became the **oldest adoptee** aged 76 years 96 days.

POGO-STICKING

Fred's "new" stick is a cutdown Flybar Master

1. Highest backflip: 2.82 m (9 ft 3 in), by Curt Markwardt (USA) in Costa Mesa, California, USA, on 26 Jul 2012.

2. Most cars jumped over: six, by Tyler Phillips (USA) in Milan, Italy, on 3 Feb 2022.

3. Tallest usable pogo stick: 2.91 m (9 ft 6 in), by Pogo Fred (aka Fred Grzybowski, USA) in Toronto, Canada, on 7 Aug 2011. *See also shortest, right.*

4. Most balloons popped in one minute: 57, by Mark Aldridge (UK) on *Lo Show dei Record* in Rome, Italy, on 1 Apr 2010.

5. Most consecutive backflips: 21, by Henry Cabelus (USA) in New Hope, Pennsylvania, USA, on 5 May 2022. Cabelus also holds records for the **highest jump** (3.41 m; 11 ft 2.2 in), **fewest bounces in one minute** (37) and **fastest 100 m** (20.19 sec).

6. Most consecutive jumps while skipping: 4,030, by Abigail Webster (USA) in Wellesley, Massachusetts, USA, on 23 Oct 2021.

7. Fastest solve of a Rubik's Cube while jumping: 9.613 sec, by Xia Yan (CHN) in Xi'an, Shaanxi, China, on 7 Jan 2021.

8. Highest stickflip: 3.65 m (12 ft), by Dalton Smith (USA) in Pittsburgh, Pennsylvania, USA, on 24 Jun 2022. Also **longest jump** (5.52 m; 18 ft 1 in).

9. Fastest mile: 7 min 40 sec, by Drew McQuiston (USA) in Pittsburgh on 24 Jun 2017.

10. Most consecutive jumps: 88,047, by Jack Sexty (UK) in Philadelphia, Pennsylvania, on 2 Jul 2015. Also: **farthest distance jumped in 24 hours** – a 26.2-mi (42.1-km) marathon – in Manchester, UK, on 6–7 Apr 2014.

11. Shortest usable pogo stick: 36.8 cm (1 ft 2.5 in), by Pogo Fred in Boston, Massachusetts, on 1 Feb 2023.

12. Greatest distance juggling while jumping: 6.44 km (4 mi), by Ashrita Furman (USA) on Rapa Nui (Easter Island), Chile, on 28 Jan 2010. Also **longest time jumping underwater** (3 hr 40 min), **fastest mile dribbling a basketball** (23 min 2.91 sec) and **most skips in one minute** (178).

LEARN TO SWIM

It's fun, it keeps you fit and – who knows – one day it could even save your life. All you need is a bathing costume (although that's optional: *see Bucket List 36 on p.175!*), goggles and a swim cap. The **most swim caps worn at once** is 75, by Hristo Terziyski (BEL) in Kalmthout, Belgium, on 4 Apr 2014.

SKATEBOARDING

Most consecutive ollies
Jean-Marc Johannes (ZAF, *left*) pulled off 323 of these hands-free aerials on *Stumbo Record Breakers* in Cape Town, South Africa, on 12 Aug 2022. This equalled the record achieved by David Tavernor (UK) on 23 Aug 2021.

At the same event, pro skater Jean-Marc also performed the **most 360 frontside spins in 30 seconds** – seven.

Most "Baby Leaf" tricks in 30 seconds
In this manoeuvre, the skater starts with the board upside down on his feet before flipping it up and landing on it. Ramel Bulana (PHL) aced 21 of these turnover tricks in half a minute in Mabalacat, Philippines, on 7 Aug 2022.

Most half-cab blunt fakies in one minute
Skaters start with the dominant foot on the nose, then perform an ollie fakie with a backside 180° spin, landing in a blunt position. Oska Sullivan (UK) executed 29 of these in 60 sec at Hop Kingdom, London, UK, on 5 Jul 2022. (*See below for more record breaking at Hop Kingdom.*)

Longest 50-50 grind (IS2)
On 15 Jan 2022, Dan Mancina (USA) completed a 6.85-m (22-ft 5-in) 50-50 grind in Royal Oak, Michigan, USA. IS2 is a category for visually impaired challengers. Dan orientates himself using sounds – and a guide stick – when he skates.

Most consecutive ollies blindfolded
On 21 May 2022, Jido (aka Ryusei Ouchi, JPN) racked up 142 ollies while unsighted in Tokorozawa, Saitama, Japan. On the same day, he also broke the **one minute** record (33). Although visually impaired, Jido chose to compete in the non-IS categories, which insist on the use of a blindfold.

Longest ramp jump
Some records are broken frequently; others resolutely stand the test of time. On 8 Aug 2004, pro skater Danny Way (USA) achieved a monumental 24-m (79-ft) 360 air on a Mega Ramp at X Games X in Los Angeles, California, USA. That's around three times longer than a London double-decker bus!

Fastest standing speed downhill (team)
The Virgin Media Speed Demons (UK) reached 84.95 km/h (52.78 mph) on skateboards in Dalby Forest, Pickering, UK, on 9 Apr 2022. Peter Dashwood-Connolly, Jonathan Braund, Aaron Skippings (all UK) and Jennifer Alina Schauerte (DEU, b. USA) linked hands in a chain on the 100-m (328-ft) slope.

Most countries visited by electric skateboard (continuous)
Between 10 and 25 Aug 2021, Stefano Rotella (ITA) passed through Italy, Austria, Germany, Czechia, Slovakia and Hungary on his battery-powered Loaded Omakase board.

The **most countries visited by skateboard in 24 hours** is four, by Michael Kolbe (DEU). Starting in Perl, Germany, he skated through France and Luxembourg, ending in Messancy, Belgium, on 27 May 2022.

Fastest electric skateboard
Raine Kent (AUS) hit 132.37 km/h (82.25 mph) – almost twice the top speed of a greyhound – in Bullsbrook, Western Australia, on 17 Sep 2022. He dramatically outpaced the previous record of 95.83 km/h (59.55 mph), which had stood since 2015. A mechanical engineer, Raine designed the board himself.

HOP KINGDOM
On 5 Jul 2022, this London venue hosted a day of one-minute record challenges, in the presence of GWR adjudicators:
1. Jamie Griffin (IRL) achieved the **most varial heelflips** – 23 – and **most heelflips** – 28, breaking the previous record by 13.
2. Alex DeCunha (UK) performed the **most kickflips blindfolded** – 23. He also has two long-standing records, for **most kickflips in 30 seconds** – 18 – and **most no comply flips in one minute** – 56.
3. Miklós Peller (HUN) nailed the **most nollie heelflips** – 19.

Alex honed his love of street skating in Milton Keynes. The city's urban architecture has made it a magnet for skaters.

CUBING

Smallest Rubik's Cube
A 5.6-mm-wide (0.2-in) puzzle cube created by Tony Fisher (UK) was unveiled on 10 Jun 2010. The frosted-plastic conundrum could be manipulated like a normal-sized Rubik's Cube with the aid of tweezers.

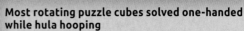

100%

Fewest moves to complete a 3x3x3 rotating puzzle cube
The first World Cube Association record for fewest moves was set in 2003, by Czechia's Mirek Goljan with 29. The current record is held by Sebastiano Tronto (ITA), who took just 16 moves to unscramble a cube at the FMC (Fewest Moves Count) global event on 15 Jun 2019.

The **average** record for fewest moves is 21, by Cale Schoon (USA) on 19 Jan 2020. He solved three 3x3x3 cubes in 23, 18 and 22 moves at the North Star Cubing Challenge in New Brighton, Minnesota, USA.

Fastest time to solve a rotating puzzle cube in freefall
On 19 Mar 2021, Nitin Subramanian (USA) took 30.14 sec to crack a cube while skydiving over Waialua in Hawaii, USA. He also holds the record for **most puzzle cubes solved while running 5 km** – 77, on 21 Jan 2019 in Cupertino, California, USA.

Fastest average time to solve a...
• **Rubik's clock**: 3.56 sec, by Jacob Chambers (UK) in Droitwich Spa, Worcestershire, UK, on 18 Sep 2022.
• **Square-1 cube**: 5.02 sec, by Max Siauw (USA) on 29 May 2022 in Boston, Massachusetts, USA.
• **Megaminx**: 28.56 sec, by Leandro Martín López (ARG) in Buenos Aires, Argentina, on 19 Nov 2022.

Largest collection of rotating puzzles
Florian Kastenmeier (DEU) had amassed 1,519 rotating puzzles in Mindelheim, Bavaria, Germany, as of 28 Feb 2022. His prized possession is a Rubik's Cube from the first production line in Hungary dating to 1977.

Fastest average time to solve a Skewb puzzle cube
Zayn Khanani (USA) cracked three Skewbs in an average time of 1.56 sec on 3 Sep 2022. He was competing in the first round of the Pretzel Mania 2022 event in Pennsylvania, USA. Zayn also holds the **single Skewb** record – 0.81 sec, set on 9 Jul 2022 in Toronto, Ontario, Canada.

DID YOU KNOW?
Hungarian architecture professor Ernő Rubik invented his puzzle cube in 1974.

More than 450 million Rubik's Cubes have been sold since 1980.

A 3x3x3 cube has 43,252,003,274,489,856,000 (43 quintillion) combinations.

Most rotating puzzle cubes solved one-handed while hula hooping
Josiah Plett (CAN) cracked 531 cubes with his left hand while hula hooping in Victoria, British Columbia, Canada, on 20 Feb 2021. He beat the previous record, which he had seen on TV, by more than 500 solves. Josiah was already the proud owner of the **two-handed** version of this record – 1,015 – having broken that a week earlier.

Most rotating puzzle cubes solved on a skateboard
On 13 Oct 2022, George Scholey (UK) rearranged 500 puzzle cubes while navigating a course on his skateboard in London, UK. His record attempt took around 1 hr 40 min.

George followed up with the **most rotating puzzle cubes solved in 24 hours** – 6,931 – in London on 9–10 Nov 2022. He beat the previous record by more than 1,100, averaging an incredible 12 sec per solve. *For more GWR Day action, turn back to pp.8–9.*

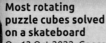
George began solving puzzle cubes at the age of 13. He is now a brand ambassador for Rubik's.

Fastest average time to solve a 3x3x3 rotating puzzle cube
On 30 Oct 2022, GWR visited the Kewbz UK Championship in Coventry to present two record-breaking speedcubers with their certificates. Max Park (USA, *left*) and Tymon Kolasiński (POL) share the record for the fastest average solve of a 3x3x3, clocking 4.86 sec at separate events in 2022. *See below for more lightning-fingered feats, as ratified by the World Cube Association.*

Cube		Time	Holder	Date
3x3x3	single	3.47 sec	Yusheng Du (CHN)	24 Nov 2018
	average*	4.86 sec	Tymon Kolasiński (POL)	30 Jul 2022
			Max Park (USA)	24 Sep 2022
2x2x2	single	0.47 sec	Guanbo Wang (CHN)	26 Nov 2022
	average*	1.01 sec	Zayn Khanani (USA)	22 Jan 2023
4x4x4	single	16.79 sec	Max Park	3 Apr 2022
	average*	19.88 sec	Max Park	3 Apr 2022
5x5x5	single	33.02 sec	Max Park	13 Mar 2022
	average*	37.00 sec	Max Park	11 Mar 2023
6x6x6	single	59.74 sec	Max Park	31 Jul 2022
	average†	1 min 8.56 sec	Max Park	9 Oct 2022
7x7x7	single	1 min 35.68 sec	Max Park	24 Sep 2022
	average†	1 min 42.12 sec	Max Park	24 Sep 2022

*Average time of five solves minus the best and worst attempts
†Mean of three solves

EXPLORE THE AMAZON RAINFOREST
Take a trip to South America to visit one of Earth's most outstanding areas of natural beauty, where howler monkeys, jaguars and tree frogs reside among almost 400 billion trees. The Amazon is the **largest tropical rainforest**, covering up to 6.56 million km² (2.53 million sq mi).

PAPER PLANES

A larger paper aircraft than the Carolo was constructed in 2018 in Fitchburg, Massachusetts, USA. Project Soar measured 19.5 m (64 ft) long and weighed 680 kg (1,500 lb) but was unable to fly and was therefore ineligible for this GWR title.

Largest paper aircraft
The brainchild of students at the Technical University of Braunschweig (DEU), *Carolo Wilhelminchen* had a wingspan of 18.21 m (59 ft 8 in). Its construction required around 70 m² (750 sq ft) of paper and 200 tubes of superglue. To prove its airworthy status, on 28 Sep 2013 the plane was launched from a platform and flew 18 m (59 ft).

The invention of the paper plane as we know it today is often attributed to the American aviation engineer Jack Northrop, co-founder of Lockheed, in the 1930s. However, the Chinese supposedly flew poison-tipped paper darts at their enemies more than 2,000 years ago; people in Japan – home of origami – are also thought to have experimented with folded paper designs around the same time. In more recent history, there are written accounts from the 14th century of Leonardo da Vinci building models of his conceptual aircraft designs from parchment.

Longest time aloft for a paper aircraft
Takuo Toda (JPN) launched a plane that stayed in the air for 29.2 sec at the Fukuyama Big Rose in Hiroshima, Japan, on 19 Dec 2010. Takuo, the chairman of the Japan Origami Airplane Association, folded his design *Sky King* from a single sheet of paper, with no cuts or gluing.

Fastest time to fold and throw a paper aircraft
On 3 Aug 2019, Akimichi Hattori (JPN) created and launched a paper plane in 7.03 sec at the Maker Faire Tokyo event in Japan. To qualify for the record, Akimichi had to make a seven-fold aircraft and then throw it at least 2 m (6 ft 6 in).

Most paper aircraft caught by mouth in one minute
Ashrita Furman caught 17 paper planes in his mouth in 60 sec in New York City, USA, on 15 Mar 2013. The missiles were thrown by Bipin Larkin (both USA).

Most times to hit a target with a paper aircraft in three minutes
On 14 Aug 2022, Subramanian Palani Kumar (IND) fired 62 planes into a bucket in 180 sec in Dharmapuri, Tamil Nadu, India. He also set the **one minute** record with 25. The receptacle had a maximum diameter of 30 cm (11 in) and he had to stand at least 3 m (9 ft 10 in) away.

Most paper aircraft...
· **launched simultaneously**: 12,672, by fans of soccer club FC Porto at the Estádio do Dragão in Portugal on 2 Nov 2007.
· **made in one hour (team)**: 12,026, by 703 people from the AXA China Region Insurance Company in Hong Kong, China, on 21 Aug 2019.
· **thrown into watermelons in one minute**: 13, by Nong Junning (CHN) in Nanning, Guangxi, China, on 11 Jul 2018. The martial-arts master embedded his paper planes into the fruit from a distance of 2 m (6 ft 6 in).

Farthest flight by a paper aircraft
With support from Nathaniel Erickson and Garrett Jensen, Dillon Ruble (all USA) threw a paper plane 88.31 m (289 ft 9 in) in Crown Point, Indiana, USA, on 2 Dec 2022. The trio studied aerospace and mechanical engineering, and their aircraft design was inspired by hypersonic aerospace vehicles. The record-breaking throw took four months to plan.

Largest paper-aircraft competition
The Paper Airplane World Championship – first staged in 2006, and held every three years under the auspices of the Red Bull Paper Wings event – attracted 61,210 competitors in 2022. After more than 500 "qualiflying" rounds, 171 contestants from 57 countries descended on Red Bull's Hangar-7 at Austria's Salzburg Airport for the Super Final. There were three categories: Distance, Airtime and Aerobatics. No cutting, tearing or gluing allowed!

Longest time aloft
Rana Muhammad Usman Saeed (PAK) set an event record in the 2022 Airtime category with a square-shaped plane design that stayed in the air for 16.39 sec.

Farthest throw
Lazar Krstić (SRB) won the 2022 Distance category with an event-record throw of 61.11 m (200 ft 5 in) – farther than three ten-pin bowling alleys combined!

Most wins
Jovica Kozlica (HRV) is the only person to win two Red Bull Paper Wings events: the 2006 and 2009 Distance categories. His farthest winning throw travelled an impressive 54.43 m (178 ft 6 in).

First female winner
Kateryna Agafonova (UKR) soared to victory in the 2019 Aerobatics category. Her 60-sec rhythmic gymnastics routine earned her the only perfect 10 of the competition.

MINIGOLF

Oldest minigolf course
The nine-hole Ladies' Putting Green – aka The Himalayas, on account of its undulating playing surface – was established at St Andrews Links (the **oldest golf course** – see p.230) in Fife, UK, in 1867. It was designed by Open-winning golfer Old Tom Morris to allow women to play the game. The first all-female competition here offered a gold locket as the top prize.

Most holes played in one hour
On 19 Mar 2022, Alex Russell (USA) sank 231 putts in 60 min at the All Star Sports course in Wichita, Kansas, USA. He averaged one hole every 15.5 sec.

The **24-hour** record is 4,729 holes, by David Pfefferle (USA) at Westerville Golf Center in Ohio, USA, on 28–29 May 2008. He walked 55 mi (88.5 km) during his epic round and raised $6,000 (£3,030) for charity.

Most perfect rounds in international competition
Walter Erlbruch (DEU) completed 15 perfect rounds (i.e., 18 holes in 18 shots) between 1990 and 2015. His latest stroke masterclass was at the Minigolf World Championships in Lahti, Finland, on 19–22 Aug 2015.

Walter's compatriot Bianca Zodrow holds the **women's** record: five perfect rounds between 1995 and 2005.

Deepest subterranean course
Zip World's 18-hole Underground Golf is situated 500 ft (152 m) below ground in the disused Llechwedd slate mine near Blaenau Ffestiniog in Gwynedd, UK. Opened on 29 Jul 2022, the course is spread across four levels and takes around 90 min to play. Hard helmets are provided!

In its heyday in the 1930s, the USA had as many as 25,000 minigolf courses across the nation.

Highest concentration of courses
As of Sep 2022, there were 33 minigolf venues (boasting 50-plus 18-hole courses) along the 60-mi (100-km) stretch of coast known as the "Grand Strand" in South Carolina, USA. The greatest hotspot is the seafront at Myrtle Beach City (above) – the so-called "Minigolf Capital of the World" – where the pursuit really took off in the 1970s.

Start · Finish · *Longer than seven bowling lanes!*

Longest hole
The fearsome 18th hole at Shipwreck Amusements in Cortland, New York, USA, measures 140.05 m (459 ft 6 in) from tee to hole. The par-54 monster comprises four sections and encircles almost the entire pirate-themed course. On the final stroke, players have a chance to putt to win a free game. The centre is owned by Patricia and Stephen Jordan (both USA).

Most wins of the World Crazy Golf Championships
Tim "Ace Man" Davies (UK) has five crazy golf world titles to his name, won in 2003–06 and 2008 at the 18-hole Arnold Palmer Putting Course in Hastings, East Sussex, UK.

The **women's** record is two, by Olivia Prokopová (CZE) in 2013 and 2017. This member of the US ProMiniGolf Association Hall of Fame saw off 66 competitors to claim her second title.

Youngest competitor at the WMF World Championships
Keiichi Kondo (JPN, b. 27 Jun 2011) was just 8 years 118 days old when he competed as part of Japan's adult team at the World Minigolf Sport Federation (WMF) World Championships on 23 Oct 2019 in Zhouzhuang, Jiangsu, China.

The **most WMF Youth World Championship wins** is three, by Kenny Marc Schmeckenbecher (DEU) in 2022. Two junior golfers hold the **female** record of two wins: Sarah Schumacher (DEU) and Alena Doleželová (CZE), in 2016–18.

902

Most courses visited
In 2006, Richard Gottfried (UK) embarked on a putting pilgrimage that has seen him visit 902 different crazy golf courses, many (800-plus) with his wife, Emily. He played a round at more than 560 of these during their self-titled "Crazy World of Minigolf Tour".

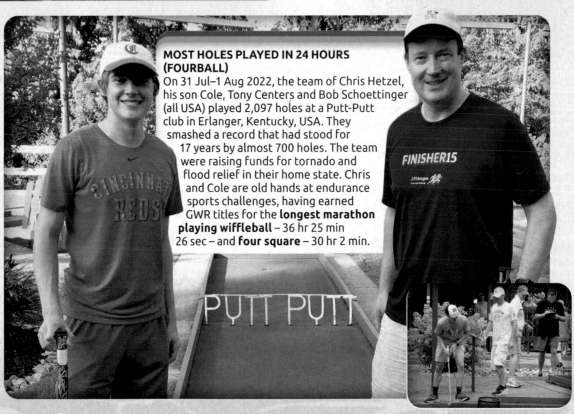

MOST HOLES PLAYED IN 24 HOURS (FOURBALL)
On 31 Jul–1 Aug 2022, the team of Chris Hetzel, his son Cole, Tony Centers and Bob Schoettinger (all USA) played 2,097 holes at a Putt-Putt club in Erlanger, Kentucky, USA. They smashed a record that had stood for 17 years by almost 700 holes. The team were raising funds for tornado and flood relief in their home state. Chris and Cole are old hands at endurance sports challenges, having earned GWR titles for the **longest marathon playing wiffleball** – 36 hr 25 min 26 sec – and **four square** – 30 hr 2 min.

FINISHER15 · PUTT PUTT

67

MAKE A BUCKET LIST
What are your hopes and dreams of a lifetime? If you're stuck for ideas, check out the 2007 movie *The Bucket List* (USA). The comedy-drama starred Morgan Freeman and Jack Nicholson, who has earned the **most Oscar nominations for an actor** – 12; he won three times, in 1974, 1984 and 1998.

FLYING DISC

Longest flying-disc throw on ice skates
A disc released by Rob McLeod (CAN) stayed aloft for 14.14 sec at the Silver Skate Festival in Edmonton, Alberta, Canada, on 17 Feb 2018. On the same day, he also set the **farthest throw and catch on ice skates** – gliding 92.4 m (303 ft 1 in) over the ice to catch his disc before it landed.

Farthest thrown mini flying disc
Professional disc golfer Simon Lizotte (DEU) hurled a mini flying disc 160.9 m (527 ft 10 in) at the Fall Desert Wind Open in Primm, Nevada, USA, on 24 Oct 2014. Mini flying discs can be no larger than 4.5 in (11.43 cm) in diameter.

The **women's** record is held by Jennifer Allen (USA), who covered a distance of 92.4 m (303 ft 1 in) at the High Desert Distance Challenge, also in Primm, on 27 Mar 2016. The previous day, Jennifer had claimed the women's overall **standard disc** distance record (see table, right).

Farthest thrown upside-down flying disc
On 23 Sep 2021, Seth Dey (USA) sent an inverted flying disc 176.66 m (579 ft 7 in) in American Fork, Utah, USA. To qualify, the disc had to remain upturned for the full flight.

Most consecutive passes by a pair
On 23 Jul 2022, serial record breaker David Rush teamed up with Chris Knight (both USA) to exchange 12,345 flying-disc passes without a drop in Boise, Idaho, USA. They played for just under four hours. The pair had already executed the **most passes in one hour** – 5,341, on 27 Jul 2020 – and **one minute** – 110, on 14 Dec 2018.

Longest flying-disc marathon
On 22–25 Mar 2013, Eastern Washington University's Ultimate team (USA) completed an epic game lasting 85 hr 1 min in Cheney, Washington, USA. There were 30 players in all, with two seven-person teams competing on a rotating shift.

Farthest throw and catch on ice skates (female)
Jill Duffy (CAN) caught a flying disc that she had launched from 31.1 m (102 ft) away at the Silver Skate Festival in Edmonton's Hawrelak Park on 11 Feb 2017. At the same event, fellow Canadian Jennie Orsten achieved the **longest flying-disc throw on ice skates (female)** – 6.22 sec.

Farthest disc-golf ace
On 21 Aug 2022, Caleb Hall (USA) threw a 611-ft (186.23-m) "hole in one" on the 14th hole of the Boulders course at North Cove Leisure Club in Marion, North Carolina, USA. This bettered the previous mark by 81 ft (24.7 m).

WORLD FLYING DISC FEDERATION

Record		Name	Date
Farthest thrown	338 m (1,108 ft)	David Wiggins Jr (USA)	28 Mar 2016
	173.3 m (568 ft)	Jennifer Allen (USA)	26 Mar 2016
Maximum time aloft	16.72 sec	Don Cain (USA)	26 May 1984
	11.81 sec	Amy Bekken (USA)	1 Aug 1991
Farthest throw, run and catch	94 m (308 ft)	Christian Sandstrom (SWE)	9 Jul 2003
	60.02 m (196 ft)	Judy Horowitz (USA)	29 Jun 1985
Highest score for self-caught flight	166.19 pts	Niclas Bergehamn (SWE)	16 Jul 1996
	110.35 pts	Anni Kreml (USA)	20 Jan 1994

All standard discs, male/female; figures correct as of 16 Dec 2022

Farthest throw and catch on inline skates (female)
On 24 Sep 2022, Ashley Wager (CAN) rolled 16 m (52 ft 6 in) to catch a disc that she had thrown at Grey Eagle Casino in Calgary, Alberta, Canada. She also added the **longest flying disc time aloft on inline skates (female)**: 5.28 sec.

Farthest mini disc throw caught by a dog
On 13 Nov 2021, a border collie-whippet cross called Sailor snapped up a miniature flying disc thrown from 40 m (131 ft 3 in) away by owner Rob McLeod (see above left) in Calgary, Alberta, Canada.

> The basket was set up in six locations, each with three teeing-off points, for a full round of 18 "holes".

HIGHEST-ALTITUDE ROUND OF DISC GOLF
On 19 Oct 2016, (*from left*) Jason Hornosty, Frederique Boisvert (both CAN), Chip Morgan (USA) and Jaryd Leibbrandt (AUS) played a game of disc golf in the Nepalese village of Gorak Shep – a lofty 5,180 m (16,995 ft) above sea level. The idea began with globetrotter Chip, who carried the disc-golf equipment up to Everest base camp initially intending to play there, but discovered the terrain was a little too treacherous!

MARATHON EFFORTS

Professional yogi Yash Mansukhbhai Moradiya (IND) has five endurance records for maintaining dynamic yoga poses, including the scorpion, aka *Vrschikasana* (*above*), held for 29 min 4 sec in Dubai, UAE, on 22 Feb 2022. The 21-year-old prepared for almost two years to obliterate the previous mark of 4 min 47 sec. Yash credits self-confidence as the foundation for his feats (*see his other records below*).

POSE PERFECT

Longest time to hold the...

Eight angle
26 min 26 sec
21 Jun 2022

Peacock
30 min 53 sec
21 Jun 2022

Scale
29 min 51 sec
22 Feb 2022

Wheel
55 min 16 sec
21 Jun 2022

POLE POSITION

Some of the earliest proponents of endurance feats were the Stylites, dating back to the 5th century ᴄᴇ. These Christian ascetics made a virtue of standing on a pillar, or *stylos*. They spent months – or even years – there while preaching, fasting and praying in the hope that such sacrifice in life would ensure the salvation of their eternal souls.

DID YOU KNOW?

The first Stylite was Simeon Stylites the Elder; it's said he lived on a pillar for 37 years!

On the inside of a Stylite's tower, a channel ran from top to bottom to use as a toilet.

In the 1990s, the monk Maxime Qavtardze lived atop the Katskhi Pillar in Georgia...

...spending more than 20 years there before making his final descent in 2015.

Playing piano
Romanian pianist Thurzó Zoltán gave a 130-hr recital from 19 to 25 Sep 2022 in Oradea, Romania. As with all modern GWR marathon records, he was permitted a 5-min rest break every hour, which could be saved up.
This was Thurzó's second record: on 13 Jun 2022, he gave the **highest-altitude grand-piano performance**: 5,325.7 m (17,473 ft) above sea level near Everest base camp.

Dancing (relay)
A team of 16 led by Joshua Usoro (all NGA) took turns to boogie for 53 hr 28 min 47 sec in Lagos, Nigeria, on 4–6 Apr 2019. Having failed this record in 2017, Joshua practised for two years to ensure the attempt was a success.
Sisters Rubisha and Alisha Shrestha (both NPL) danced their heart out for 41 hr 5 min to claim the **longest dance marathon by a pair** in Kathmandu, Nepal, on 25–27 May 2019.

Playing basketball
Players from New York and Canada hit the court of Nardin Academy with The Revelas Family Foundation (USA) in Buffalo, New York, USA, to bring attention to mental-health issues affecting young adults. The team raised more than $60,000 (£43,330) by playing basketball for 120 hr 2 min from 6 to 11 Aug 2021.

Playing accordion
Music teacher Christelle De Franceschi (FRA), who has played the accordion since the age of seven, performed for 51 hr 43 min 40 sec in Saint-Amand-les-Eaux, France, on 25–27 Jun 2022. "The accordion has been my fellow traveller for more than 45 years," she said. "I wanted to share this extraordinary adventure with many people."

Playing harp
Ukrainian-born harpist Kateryna Oliinyk plucked her way to GWR glory on 25–26 Oct 2022 playing for 31 hr 1 min 54 sec in Dubai, UAE, where she now resides. The diverse set list featured songs by Lady Gaga, Metallica and Andrea Bocelli.

Crocheting
On 29–30 May 2021, Alessandra Hayden (USA) crocheted for 34 hr 7 min in Gig Harbor, Washington, USA, to earn a place in the records book that she has long loved to read. Using the tapestry technique, she produced a 1.52-m² (16.3-sq-ft) blanket and a 1.77-m-long (5-ft 6-in) shawl.

Reading aloud
As part of the IV World Nomad Games, Rysbai Isakov (KGZ) recited the 18th-century poem *Epic of Manas* for 124 hr in Bursa, Türkiye, from 22 to 27 Sep 2022. Rysbai was keen to share this Kyrgyz national epic with a wider audience.

Ninepin bowling
Uroš Stoklas (SLV) bowled for 24 hr exactly in Radlje ob Dravi, Slovenia, on 15–16 Apr 2022. In that time, he threw almost 3,000 balls and racked up a total of 291 strikes.

The Sandbaggers Rugby Club raised more than £70,000 ($87,000) and also won a local hero award.

Playing beach touch rugby
A 22-member squad of GPs, anaesthetists and surgeons from the Sandbaggers Rugby Club (all UK) played for 34 hr 6 sec in Branksome, Dorset, UK, on 20–21 May 2022. The match was organized to raise money for two motor neurone disease charities after their teammate Andrew Vaughton was diagnosed with the condition in 2021.

TAKE A ROAD TRIP WITH FRIENDS
Many of us have dreamed of hitting the road, Kerouac style, but does it ever go beyond planning? It did for Jim Rogers and Paige Parker (both USA), who drove to 111 countries and three territories between 1 Jan 1999 and 5 Jan 2002 – the **most countries visited in a continuous car journey**.

LONGEST RAP MARATHON

English teacher Daniel Alcon, aka DAlcon (UK), skipped sleep for two nights to rap for 39 hr 37 min in Valencia, Spain, from 1 to 3 Apr 2022. Daniel has been vocal about his mental-health issues and took this opportunity to promote the charity Key Changes – a support service and music label dedicated to musicians who have faced similar problems.

The rules stated that the beats had to be continuous; Daniel was permitted only 30 seconds to collect his breath between tracks, and he was given a five-minute break for every hour that he performed.

This was Daniel's second attempt after rapping for 35 hr in 2021, only to find out that Liam Reeves (IRL) had done 36 hr 36 min!

A former holder of this record was Harvey Daniels (USA), who also goes by Frzy. On 11–12 Jan 2020, he rapped for 31 hr 52 sec in Pittsburgh, Pennsylvania, USA, to raise funds for the music-industry charity MusiCares.

More recently, Polish rapper Radosław Blonkowski (aka Rademenez) was GWR's rap-endurance heavyweight. He freestyled for 36 hr exactly in Zielona Góra, Lubuskie, Poland, on 20–21 Nov 2021.

PECULIAR PASSIONS

▶ **Most baubles in a beard**
Joel Strasser (USA) fitted 710 festive balls into his beard on 2 Dec 2022. Joel's been a regular fixture in *GWR* since 2018. Just see what else he's lodged into his facial fuzz...

MOST IN A BEARD

Items	Count
Forks	126
Clothes pegs	359
Pencils	456
Chopsticks	520
Paper straws	534
Golf tees	607
Toothpicks	3,500

...IN ONE MINUTE

Items	Count
Pencils	59
Chopsticks	86

Figures correct as of 13 Feb 2023

Tallest stack of hats worn
On 14 May 2022, Anthony Kelly (AUS) proved he had a head for hats by wearing a 107.5-cm-tall (3-ft 6-in) stack of them in Armidale, New South Wales, Australia.

Longest thread of beads made by an individual in one hour
Syeda Anisa Murshed (BGD) created a 42.3-m-long (138-ft 9-in) string of 1,700-plus wooden beads in Dhaka, Bangladesh, on 12 Aug 2022. She has 20 years' experience of beadwork.

Longest chain of bottle tops
On 3 Jul 2022, a 10.93-km-long (6.79-mi) cord adorned with more than 2 million bottle caps was presented in the Netherlands. It was patiently assembled by the villagers of Zijtaart over two years, in a project arranged by volunteer organization 24 Uur van Zijtaart (NLD). The attempt was staged to help put the village on the map, but also to support people with Duchenne muscular dystrophy.

▶ **Farthest throw of a washing machine**
Johan Espenkrona (SWE) likes to show off his powerlifting prowess by hurling kitchen appliances. On 15 Feb 2022, he threw a washing machine 4.45 m (14 ft 7 in) in Milan, Italy.

Smallest wooden spoon
Navratan Prajapati Murtikar (IND) carved a tiny spoon just 2 mm (0.078 in) long, as confirmed on 22 Jun 2022 in Jaipur, Rajasthan, India. Navratan is a marble sculptor by trade, but having proven his eye for detail, he now has ambitions to develop a miniature craft museum.

Farthest throw of a golf club
Tyson Allen (USA) believes that golf is much more fun *without* the balls! On 14 Oct 2021, he launched a Callaway "Mack Daddy 3" 56° wedge a distance of 71.69 m (235 ft 2 in) at Emporia State University in Kansas, USA.

Fastest time to sort 500 g of Peanut M&M's
It took Samuel Mornement (AUS) just 1 min 33.03 sec to sort a pack of M&M's into separate colours. The speedy sweet sweep took place in Perth, Western Australia, on 9 Jul 2022.

Largest display of miniature chairs
Over 28 years, Eladio Rivero Sánchez (ESP) has honed his passion for whittling scaled-down wooden seats. On 27 May 2022, he presented 4,147 of them – varying in size from 1.5 cm to 40 cm (0.5–15.7 in) – in Torrevieja, Spain.

Tallest house of cards built in eight hours
Tian Rui (CHN) raised a structure that stood 50 levels tall from playing cards in Qingdao, Shandong, China, on 10 Nov 2022. It reached a vertiginous height of 3.37 m (11 ft). This represents the **12-hour** record for the category as well. Earlier that year, on 3 Jul, the stacking ace also set a new **one-hour** record – 27 levels.

Largest display of model ships in bottles
The Arendal Bymuseum in Norway is home to a remarkable exhibit of 655 bottled boats, each hand-made by local craftsman Kjell Birkeland (NOR). Sometimes known as "impossible bottles", the items were counted on 15 Feb 2013.

The **largest impossible bottle** is *Nelson's Ship in a Bottle*, a 1:30-scale replica of Vice Admiral Horatio Nelson's warship HMS *Victory*, with sails of African wax-print fabric. Measuring 4.7 m (15 ft 5 in) long and 2.8 m (9 ft 2 in) wide, the artwork was created by British-Nigerian artist Yinka Shonibare. It was displayed in London's Trafalgar Square in 2010, and later moved to the National Maritime Museum in Greenwich.

In 1956, Arthur V Pedlar (UK) constructed the **smallest ship in a bottle**. The design was based on a galleon with three masts, five sails and three flags, and was delicately placed inside a 1-cc medical phial measuring 2.38 cm (0.93 in) long and 0.9 cm (0.35 in) wide. The neck diameter was a mere 0.2 cm (0.07 in).

Richard "hit the wall" after 18 hr, but the 51-year-old swung back into action after a 12-min power nap!

Longest marathon on a swing
Richard Scott (UK) embraced his inner child by swinging for 36 hr 32 min in Kinross, Tayside, UK, on 14–15 May 2022. When he saw that the previous record was "only" 34 hr, Richard thought, "I could do that." He told GWR, "I was the fittest I had been in my life so why not? Turns out it wasn't as easy as I thought...!"

MEET SOMEONE FAMOUS
...and when you do, why not immortalize the encounter with an autograph? Celebrity signatures can be serious money-spinners down the line. The **most valuable autograph** is that of Apple co-founder Steve Jobs (USA), which was worth £50,000 ($60,290) on average as of 2022.

COMPETITIVE BIG FRUIT & VEG

Outsized produce has cropped up in *Guinness World Records* since our very first edition in 1955. Below, we present a hand-picked selection of recent holders in this enduring category, as ratified by the UK's National Vegetable Society and the Great Pumpkin Commonwealth.

Garden giant	Record	Grower
1 Longest leek	143.2 cm (4 ft 8.3 in)	Derek Hulme (UK)
2 Heaviest tomato	5.284 kg (11 lb 10.4 oz)	Julie and Del Faust (both USA)
3 Heaviest eggplant/ aubergine	3.36 kg (7 lb 6.6 oz)	Peter Glazebrook (UK)
4 Longest broad bean	39.6 cm (1 ft 3.59 in)	Ian Simpson (UK)
5 Heaviest luffa	2.616 kg (5 lb 12.2 oz)	Ian Neale (UK)
6 Tallest potato plant	2.847 m (9 ft 4.1 in)	Kevin Fortey (UK)
7 Longest cucumber	113.4 cm (3 ft 8.6 in)	Sebastian Suski (POL/UK)
8 Largest jack-o'-lantern circumference	614.7 cm (20 ft 2 in)	Travis Gienger (USA)
9 Longest runner bean	76.9 cm (2 ft 6.2 in)	Lee Herrington (UK)
10 Heaviest field pumpkin	121.6 kg (268 lb 1 oz)	Mark Baggs (UK)

Figures correct as of 13 Feb 2023

Heaviest jack-o'-lantern
Stefano Cutrupi (ITA) grew the **heaviest pumpkin**, at 1,226 kg (2,702 lb 14 oz), as confirmed in Italy in Sep 2021. A month later, he transported his giant gourd to the annual pumpkin festival in Ludwigsburg, Germany, where it was given a facelift by German carver Udo Karkos (*above*). Despite having lost 8.5 kg (18 lb 11 oz) to water loss in the interim, it was still a record weight.

Dubbed "Maverick", Travis Gienger's giant gourd was given a glaring eagle's face by carver Mike Rudolph.

ATTEND MARDI GRAS IN NEW ORLEANS
An appetizing gumbo of music, dance and mouth-watering food, this annual carnival attracts more than a million revellers. While you're there, check out the city's spookier side. The **largest voodoo doll** – a 6.6-m-tall (21-ft 8-in) effigy dubbed "Charlie" – was created here in 2010 by priestess Catherina Williams (USA).

FOOD FEATS

Chilli champions

The **hottest chilli pepper** is Smokin Ed's Carolina reaper, grown by Ed Currie of PuckerButt Pepper Company (USA). It measures an average of 1,641,183 Scoville Heat Units (SHU). Regular tabasco sauce measures around 400 SHU.

Also known as the ghost pepper, the bhut jolokia (1,001,304 SHU) is so hot it has been smeared on fences as an elephant repellent! The **fastest time to eat 10 bhut jolokias** is 30.70 sec, by Togo's Amedonou Kankue in Milan, Italy, on 19 Jun 2014.

Spice cadet Greg Foster (USA, *see right*) is always ready to turn up the heat. On 14 Nov 2021, he consumed the **most bhut jolokias in one minute**, munching through 110.50 g (3.98 oz) in San Diego, California, USA.

On 8 May 2021, Lance Rich and Matthew Burnham (both USA) ticked an item off their bucket list when they shared the **longest habanero kiss** in Shreveport, Louisiana, USA. The pair ate one chilli each before locking (numb) lips for 3 min 36.86 sec.

Largest serving of...

Macaroni and cheese: On 29 Jul 2022, to celebrate 50 years of production at their Logan facility in Utah, USA, Schreiber Foods served up a massive mac and cheese weighing 2,151 kg (4,742 lb 2 oz). This is about the same as an adult black rhino. The dish took four hours to make and was offered with a pulled-pork topping prepared by a local BBQ champion.

Nachos: A similarly sized portion of nachos (2,209 kg; 4,870 lb) was presented by the Smorgasburg Los Angeles open-air food market in California, USA, on 25 Sep 2022. The record attempt was staged in honour of the small-screen return of Paramount+ and Mike Judge's *Beavis and Butt-Head*, the cartoon duo with the catchphrase "Nachos rule!"

Largest spritz cocktail

The Fiordaliso shopping centre in Rozzano, Italy, concocted an alcoholic apéritif on 30 Jun 2022 that came to 1,050 litres (277 gal) – akin to nearly seven bathtubs. The colossal cocktail required 700 bottles of Prosecco, 350 bottles of Aperol and 180 bottles of sparkling water.

33 sec

▶ **Fastest time to eat 10 Carolina reaper chillies**
On 17 Sep 2022, Greg Foster (USA) wolfed down 10 of the **hottest chillies** (*see left*) in 33.15 sec in San Diego, California, USA. Greg, who owns a hot sauce company, describes the feat as like eating "liquid lava" and advises having milk and ice cream on standby. He also holds the **three Carolina reapers** record – 8.72 sec.

▶ **Most chicken feet eaten in one minute**
On 5 Aug 2022, Vuyolwethu Simanile (ZAF, *below centre*) gobbled up 121 g (4.26 oz) of grilled poultry paws in 60 sec on *Stumbo Record Breakers* in Durban, South Africa. Vuyolwethu saw off the challenge of four of her colleagues from the Mashamplanes Lounge restaurant, where spicy chicken feet is a signature dish; she consumed nearly twice as much as her nearest rival.

▶ **Fastest time to drink two litres of soda**
Competitive eater Eric "Badlands" Booker (USA) chugged a beaker of Coca-Cola Zero in 18.45 sec on 19 May 2021 in Selden, New York, USA. On 20 Feb 2022, Eric added the **one litre of soda** record – 6.80 sec – and **one litre of tomato sauce through a straw** – 1 min 18.90 sec – in front of a live crowd in Ridgefield, Washington, USA.

Fastest time to drink 500 ml of sparkling water

On 26 Feb 2022, Chris Stewart (UK) downed half a litre of fizzy water in 3.23 sec in Birmingham, UK. He fulfilled a lifelong ambition to claim his very own GWR title.

Fastest time to wrap five portions of chips

In celebration of the UK's National Fish and Chip Day on 27 May 2022, Zohaib Hussain (UK) wrapped five portions of chips in 40.13 sec at the Zero Plus Fish Bar in Cardiff, UK. He beat the previous record by more than 4 sec.

▶ **Most hot dogs eaten in three minutes**
Nicholas Wehry wolfed down 12 hot dogs – each a minimum length of 7 in (17.8 cm) and served in a bun with at least one condiment – in Tampa, Florida, USA, on 22 Oct 2022.
Nicholas is married to fellow competitive eater Miki Sudo (both USA), the reigning female record holder for **most hot dogs eaten at Nathan's Hot Dog Eating Contest** (48.5 in a row in 2020) and for the **most wins** (seven). She broke the **one-minute** record – also on 22 Oct – with six dogs; she then went on to shave 0.88 sec off Leah Shutkever's record for **fastest time to eat a burrito**, downing a 550-g (19.4-oz) wrap in just 31.47 sec. *For more on Shutkever, see p.96.*

Most expensive hamburger (single portion)

A "Golden Boy" burger created by chef Robbert Jan de Veen (NLD) was bought for €5,000 (£4,295; $5,967) on 28 Jun 2021. The dish boasted a wagyu beef patty, champagne-battered onion rings, king crab, caviar and a gold-leaf-covered bun made using Dom Pérignon champagne. Robbert donated the money from his first Golden Boy order to a local food bank.

BE A BRIDESMAID

Bridal showers, bachelorette parties, dress fittings, helping the bride on her big day... There's a lot for bridesmaids to do. Perhaps that's why Tina Ackles (USA) asked 168 maids to share the role for her wedding in Tampa Bay, Florida, USA, on 18 Apr 2015 – the **most bridesmaids to one bride**!

LARGEST DOUGHNUT CAKE

On 3 Apr 2023, TikTok chefs Nick DiGiovanni (USA) and Lynn Davis (JPN) teamed up at the Oakleaf Cakes Bake Shop in Boston, Massachusetts, USA, to create a giant pink-iced doughnut cake weighing 102.5 kg (226 lb). The toroidal, sprinkle-covered confection – constructed from layers of sponge and buttercream, and wrapped in fondant – weighed more than the two chefs combined.

The epicurean influencers had previously joined forces to produce the **largest chicken nugget** (*below*), weighing 20.96 kg (46 lb 3 oz); the **largest cake pop** (*below right*), at 44.24 kg (97 lb 8 oz); and the **widest sushi roll** (*right*): a salmon, cucumber and rice wrap covered in seaweed and spanning 2.16 m (7 ft 1 in) – wider than a king-sized bed!

SWEET STUFF

Largest brownie

A chocolate brownie weighing 152 kg (335 lb) – about the same as a mountain gorilla – was served up by Betty Crocker MENA in Jeddah, Saudi Arabia, on 23 Sep 2022. A total of 210 regular packs of brownie mix were combined with 504 eggs and 23.1 litres (6.1 gal) of oil before being baked for three hours.

Longest candy-wrapper chain

Elizabeth Allen (USA) has tied together 10,000 Starburst wrappers to encourage Furman University in Greenville, South Carolina, USA, to continue its reuse and recycle programme. The chain was assessed there on 30 Jul 2021.

The ongoing record for the **longest gum-wrapper chain** currently stands at 2,583,335 Wrigley's wrappers. Gary Duschl (USA) had it surveyed in 2020, when it was found to be more than 20 miles long: 32,555.68 m (106,810 ft) to be precise.

Largest bag of candy

On 20 Aug 2022, Broadway Sweets of Johannesburg in South Africa filled a 5-m-tall (16-ft 5-in) bag with 1,025 kg (2,259 lb) of Stumbo "Cola Burst" candies. The scaled-up packet was weighed and measured for *Stumbo Record Breakers*, a documentary series in which the South African confectioner celebrates the country's cultural heritage.

▶ Fastest time to eat a Chocolate Orange

Competitive eater and social-media superstar Leah Shutkever (UK) unwrapped and wolfed down a Terry's Chocolate Orange in just 57.14 sec on 21 Oct 2020. The multi-record-breaking mukbanger currently holds 22 GWR titles, with a few of her sweetest accomplishments listed on the left. Other, more savoury superlatives include the **most chicken nuggets eaten in one minute** (19, totalling 352 g; 12.42 oz), **fastest time to eat a hot dog with no hands** (18.15 sec) and **most sausages swallowed in one minute** (12).

6
Hot-cross buns (3 min)

10
Jam doughnuts (3 min)

12
Chocolate truffles (no hands, 1 min)

20
Marshmallows (no hands, 1 min)

Most flavours of ice cream identified in one minute (blindfolded)

Germany's one-man record-breaking machine André Ortolf was able to correctly name 17 ice-cream varieties in a minute in Augsburg, Bavaria, on 11 Apr 2021.

The **most ice cream eaten in one minute** is 806 g (1 lb 12.43 oz) by a brain-frozen Isaac Harding-Davis (AUS). He gobbled just over two tubs of Ben & Jerry's Strawberry Cheesecake in Sydney, Australia, on 16 Jul 2017.

Longest line of...

• **Lollipops:** A team of 27 volunteers from the National Sea Rescue Institute of South Africa lined up 11,602 Stumbo lollies along the boardwalk in Durban on 6 Aug 2022. The attempt was filmed for *Stumbo Record Breakers (see above right)*.

• **Chocolate bars:** 5,130 Candyman Fantastik Chocobar XLs were laid out in Mumbai, India, on 5 Sep 2022. The 626.25-m-long (2,054-ft) line was organized by ITC Foods (IND) as a thank-you to schools on India's National Teachers' Day.

• **Pies:** USA Pears (USA), Emirates Culinary Guild and Jumeirah Creekside Hotel (both UAE) aligned 2,209 pear pies on 4 Jan 2021. After being counted, the tarts were donated to Sahem for Hope, who distributed them to families in need.

Largest bubblegum bubble blown

On 24 Apr 2004, at Double Springs High School (now Winston County High School) in Alabama, USA, Chad Fell (USA) blew a bubblegum bubble with a diameter of 1 ft 8 in (50.8 cm) – without using his hands to steady or stretch the bubble. The secret of his success was the combined strength of three pieces of Dubble Bubble gum.

It took Ali (*right*) and her team 3 hr to spin the cotton candy for the giant rabbit, which was eaten afterwards.

Largest candyfloss sculpture

A giant bunny weighing 16.78 kg (37 lb) was crafted from cotton candy by Ali Spagnola, Brian and Penny Brushwood, Matt Donnelly, Jacob Smith, Jason Murphy, Eli Carll, John Rael and Heather Tayte (all USA) in Austin, Texas, USA, on 8 Apr 2022. Two flavours of sugar were used – two cartons of pink vanilla and 12 of raspberry.

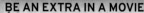

BE AN EXTRA IN A MOVIE

Extras can take a movie scene to a whole other level. Director Richard Attenborough (UK) certainly thought so. He assembled 300,000 people on 31 Jan 1981 – **the most film extras** – to record the funeral scene for *Gandhi* (UK/IND/USA/ZAF, 1982).

14.3-m-tall M&M's "spokescandy"...

LARGEST PIÑATA (VOLUME)

A six-storey piñata filled with around 8,000 lb (3,600 kg) of candy was unveiled by Carnival Cruises in Philadelphia, Pennsylvania, USA, on 2 Nov 2008. The 18.85-m-tall (61-ft 10.25-in) donkey was due to be hoisted by crane and smashed open with a wrecking ball, but the local police, worried about the safety of the thousands of spectators, insisted it be opened while on the ground.

The **largest standing piñata** overall (*right*) measured 20.9 m (68 ft 7 in) at its widest point. It was created by M&M's to celebrate the first birthday of their Pretzel Chocolate Candies. It was opened in New York, USA, on 4 Aug 2011 to reveal 1,500 lb (680 kg) of sweet treats.

...standing atop a 20.9-m-wide piñata birthday cake.

The prodigious piñata was opened by singer Cee Lo Green!

Largest suspended piñata

A 32-m-wide (105-ft) piñata filled with 800 kg (1,760 lb) of candies, chocolates and toys was hung from a crane by Vision Lightec (MEX) in the Plaza de Los Mártires in Toluca, Mexico, on 16 Dec 2015.

The Carnival Cruises burro was a scaled-up version of a commercially available piñata.

FITNESS WARRIORS

Most consecutive tandem push-ups
Hoping to inspire their children, George Kotsimpos and Apostolos Dervas (both GRC) performed 43 push-ups while resting their weight upon one another. They broke the record on 21 Dec 2022 at the Iron Body Gym in Heraklion, Greece.

The women's record is 21, by Kara Webb and Sammy Wood (both AUS) in Sydney, Australia, on 1 Feb 2017.

Longest time to hold the yoga womb pose
On 1 Oct 2022, Manish Katkar (IND) displayed his flexibility by maintaining this knotty pose for 1 hr 20 min 19 sec in Nashik, Maharashtra, India. He reclaimed the record after losing it six months earlier.

The longest time to hold the mermaid pose is 1 hr 15 min 5 sec, by Rooba Ganesan (IND) on 1 Jan 2023. *See more extreme yoga on p.90.*

Fastest 10-m rope climb
On 23 May 2022, fitness coach Micah Moses (USA) hauled himself up a 10-m (32-ft) rope in 20.51 sec in Lynden, Washington, USA. The 51-year-old ex-Marine developed his own training regimen specifically for this attempt. It was Micah's second GWR title, having set the fastest 5-m rope climb carrying a 40-lb pack – 7.99 sec – on 25 Mar 2022.

Fastest 100 m obstacle-course race (FISO)
The Fédération Internationale de Sports d'Obstacles oversees official obstacle-course racing (OCR). On 10 Apr 2022, Mark Julius Rodelas (PHL) completed a 100-m "ninja" course with 12 obstacles – including a rope swing, wall climb, monkey bars and hurdles – in 27.12 sec in Pasig City, Philippines.

The **women's** OCR record of 39.42 sec was also set on the same day in Pasig, by Kaizen Dela Serna (PHL).

Fastest explosive pull-up 4-m ascent (female)
On 15 Feb 2022, Astrid Sibon (NLD) used her immense upper-body strength to haul herself up a 4-m (13-ft) slotted rack using a horizontal bar in a mere 10.83 sec. She triumphed over a field of fellow Ninja Warriors on GWR's Italian TV series, *Lo Show dei Record*.

One of Astrid's competitors was Bethany Lodge (UK), who completed the **fastest 100 m forward rolls** in 42.64 sec on 8 Mar 2021 in Berinsfield, Oxfordshire, UK.

Most warped wall climbs in one minute (female)
On 31 Jan 2023, Immy Hales (UK) ran up eight steeply curved ramp walls in 60 sec on *Lo Show dei Record*. Each obstacle had to be at least 4 m (13 ft) tall to qualify.

Most squats in one minute (II)
Tom Enoch (UK) achieved 51 squats in 60 sec in Leamington Spa, Warwickshire, UK, on 19 Nov 2022. He has Down syndrome and set his record in GWR's intellectual impairment (II) category. Tom, who is studying to become a fitness coach, put on remote exercise classes for other people with Down syndrome during the COVID-19 lockdowns.

Fastest Concept2 SkiErg marathon (seated with full-core function, female)
On 1 May 2022, adaptive athlete Shana Coissard (FRA) skied 42.195 km (26.2 mi) in 4 hr 43 min 50 sec on a Concept2 training machine. The 20-year-old, who has a form of Ehlers-Danlos syndrome, ranked fourth in the world in her category at the 2022 CrossFit Open.

Longest single-event (continuous) triathlon
On 12–13 Aug 2022, Steven Green (UK) completed an epic 364.4-km (226.4-mi) triathlon around Redcar in North Yorkshire, UK. He was allowed breaks of no more than 5 min throughout his punishing effort, which involved a 12-hr bike ride, a 5-hr front-crawl swim across Ellerton Lake and an 11-hr run, all achieved on two of the hottest days of the year.

Most chin-ups in 24 hours
Gym manager Graham Morgan (UK) found a novel way to celebrate turning 60 – by completing 7,479 chin-ups on 19 Nov 2022 at Quinta do Lago in the Algarve, Portugal. He also used the event to raise money for the Save the Children charity.

The **most burpees in 24 hours** is 10,856, by Joe Reverdes (USA) in Johnston, Rhode Island, USA, on 10 Jul 2022.

The **most pull-ups in 24 hours** is 8,008, by Jaxon Italiano (AUS) in Sydney, Australia, on 12 Nov 2022.

Most...
- **Yo-yo vertical punches in one minute**: 138, by Naoshi Terasawa (JPN) in Iwakura, Aichi, Japan, on 13 Feb 2022.
- **Squats in one minute (male)**: 84, by Tourab Nesanah (SYR) in New York City, USA, on 9 Sep 2022.
- **Squats carrying a 20-lb pack in one minute (female)**: 65, by Vera Maier (DEU) in Dubai, UAE, on 6 Dec 2022.
- **Chest-to-ground burpees in one minute (male)**: 33, by Ieong Man Teng (CHN) in Macau, China, on 1 Aug 2022.
- **Backward somersault burpees in 30 seconds (female)**: 8, by Celeste Dixon (AUS) in Adelaide, Australia, on 7 Feb 2022.

Sam likes to compete in triathlons wearing a T-shirt with the slogan "Autism is my superpower".

First openly autistic person to compete at the IRONMAN® World Championship
On 6 Oct 2022, Sam Holness (UK) finished the iconic 140.6 triathlon at Kailua-Kona, Hawaii, USA, in 13 hr 5 min 44 sec. He had swum 2.4 mi (3.8 km), cycled 112 mi (180 km) and run 26.2 mi (42.1 km). Sam says that his neurodiversity gives him energy and focus – perfect for an endurance athlete.

GO HANG GLIDING
Fulfil that dream of flying like a bird by taking to the skies in a hang glider. You'll need a few lessons before attempting Chad Elchin's (USA) record for the **most consecutive loops with a hang glider** – he swooped head over heels 95 times in a row above Ridgely, Maryland, USA, on 16 Jul 2001.

NINJA WARRIORS

Australia's Ben Polson (*left*) and Olivia Vivian (*right*) are regulars on the popular obstacle-course TV show *Ninja Warriors*. In 2020, music producer Ben became the first contestant to win *Australian Ninja Warrior*, while Olivia – a former Olympic gymnast – is a gold-medal winner at the Ninja World Championships. Partners in real life, they also joined forces for Team Australia on *American Ninja Warrior: USA vs the World*.

In 2023, the pair got the chance to show off their skills on Italy's *Lo Show dei Record*. On 31 Jan, Ben achieved the **most mega walls climbed in one minute** – seven. A week later, Olivia completed the **most consecutive flying bar jumps** – 28. She also holds the GWR titles for the **farthest distance on monkey bars in one minute** – 54.5 m (178 ft 9 in) – and **three minutes** – 127.25 m (417 ft 5 in).

Another *Ninja Warrior* alumnus who has turned his hand to record breaking is Najee "The Phoenix" Richardson (USA, *below*). The Spider-Man-loving ex-gymnast has performed the **farthest lache cat leap (bar to wall)** – 4.9 m (16 ft 1 in) – and the **farthest backflip between hanging ropes** – 5.79 m (19 ft). In 2022, Najee invited Olivia, Ben and some other agile amigos to a very special record-themed celebration – *see below for more...*

Najee says he was a "frail kid" with asthma who "had to work a little harder to keep up with my friends".

On 15 Sep 2022, a small army of Ninja Warriors gathered at Movement Lab in Hainesport, New Jersey, USA, to celebrate Najee's wedding in the only way they knew how – by taking on a host of acrobatic GWR titles! And these high-flying heroes usually get what they aim for...

Discipline	Record	Name
Farthest lache (female)	4.29 m (14 ft 1 in)	Olivia Vivian (AUS)
Farthest distance on a cliff hanger in one minute (female)	30.28 m (99 ft 4 in)	Abby Clark (USA)
Farthest distance on a cliff hanger in one minute (male)	37.59 m (123 ft 3 in)	Joe Meissner (USA)
Farthest backflip between hanging ropes (female)	3.47 m (11 ft 4 in)	Madyson Howard (USA)
Most warped wall climbs in one minute (male)	4	Ben Polson (AUS)
Fastest 5-m rope climb (female)	6.25 sec	Isabella Wakeham (USA)
Fastest 5-m rope climb (male)	3.99 sec	Josiah Pippel (USA)

*All records correct as of 3 Mar 2023

SONNY MOLINA

1,043
Leather postcards, typically with text and images seared on using pyrography (literally "fire-writing").

Salacnib "Sonny" Molina (USA, b. PHL) has a dream: to collect more GWR collection records than anyone else on the planet. And he's off to a strong start, with a houseful of leather postcards, finger puppets, Pringles tubes, skull drinkware and seasoning sachets...

Sonny – a surgical nurse and orthopaedic team leader in McHenry, Illinois – dreamt of being a record-breaker as a child, after reading an edition of the *GWR* book. "I found out that there were records pertaining to running barefoot," he explains, "and I was always running around without shoes. But as a kid coming from the Philippines, it was almost impossible to apply, because I lived in a far-flung area with no internet connection."

Later, at the age of 20, a move to the USA suddenly opened up a world of possibilities for Sonny. By Sep 2016, he had achieved his ambition, bagging his first GWR record, for the **most half marathons completed in a month barefoot** (17, since broken by Sonny with 20). More athletic achievements followed, before his thoughts turned to collecting...

1,517
Finger puppets, ranging from vintage to contemporary; Sonny's favourite is a surgical nurse puppet.

When – and why – did you start building your record-breaking collections?
Growing up, I just liked collecting things, from marbles to stationery. These things all have sentimental value to me and remind me of my childhood: where I got them, or why, or the people who gave them to me. It's my dream to have the most "largest collections" records in the world, and house them in a museum where people – locals and tourists – can see them someday. And one day, I'd like to be a GWR Hall of Famer for my collections!

You've held 17 world records, for collecting but also for running vast distances barefooted... even on LEGO bricks! What motivates you to do this?
Having a GWR certificate means the world to me. Record-breaking is addictive! I like that feeling of excitement and fulfilment when I see my certificates – they remind me that nothing in life is impossible. Everyone can attain greatness and success if they work hard and believe in themselves.

395
Salt and pepper sachets, his most treasured being two intact packets from Kentucky Fried Chicken dating from the 1960s.

Do you have any advice for wannabe record breakers?
Always believe in yourself, even if no one else does. You and only you can prove to others that nothing is impossible if you put your mind and soul to it. And always be humble and kind.

What record do you want to break next?
My journey is just starting! I've got lots of other collecting records in the pipeline: lanyards, fortune-cookie fortunes, chopsticks, finger skateboards, teabags, pillow cases, paper cups, etc. And in the non-collecting categories, I'll be breaking more barefoot distance records! My goal is to be the Filipino-American with the most GWR titles!

307

And when you're not breaking records...?
I'm an ambassador for Soles4Souls, which collects and donates new and used shoes and footwear. If I'm not running or breaking records, I also organize medical missions abroad, especially in the Philippines, offering free dental, medical and surgical services.

Skull drinkware... As it sounds, mugs, cups and beakers shaped like – or printed with – human skulls!

On 1 May 2021, Sonny covered the **farthest distance walking barefoot on LEGO® bricks**: 8.89 km (5.5 mi)!

The saddle shape of a Pringle chip is known mathematically as a hyperbolic paraboloid.

LARGEST COLLECTION OF PRINGLES TUBES

At the last count, Sonny owned 256 Pringles tubes, which he stores in his basement "man cave" at home. He has a special affection for these stackable, saddle-shaped potato snacks because they remind him of his mother. "Growing up, she would buy me Pringles whenever I didn't feel good or was sick," he explained. "I seemed to get better every time she brought me them!"

"Pringle's Newfangled Potato Chips", as they were originally named, were launched in the USA in 1968 – 12 years after development work began on the product – and finally patented in 1976. Sonny's most precious tube is a yellow retro container for the "Rippled Style" of Pringles dating from the early 1980s; his favourite flavour is "anything cheese".

256

After his death in 2008, Pringles co-inventor Frederic Baur had his cremated remains buried in one of his tubes!

COLLECTIONS

AQUATIC COLLECTIONS

Here is a selection of record-breaking collections with a maritime flavour, in keeping with the nautical theme of this year's edition.

Marine biologist Aušra Šaltenytė (LTU) has 3,516 **dolphin-related** items, which she keeps at Mykolas Romeris University in Lithuania.

In 2016, by the age of 12, Will "Spike" Yocum (USA) had already amassed a total of 3,563 different **fishing lures**.

The unsinkable José Busto (USA) has **lifebelts** from 100 ships. They're displayed at the Museo del Mar in Puerto Rico.

The 726 items in New Yorker Laurie Koller's **mermaid-themed** collection include costumes for people and dogs.

Donald Dettloff's "**surfboard** fence" around his property in Haiku, Hawaii, USA, comprises 647 unique **surfboards**.

Lifelong DC Comics fan Brett Mitchell-Lutz (USA) has filled his home in Texas with 1,308 pieces of **Aquaman** memorabilia.

Inspired by her love of the children's series *Pingu*, Birgit Berends (DEU) cares for a colony of 11,062 **penguin-related** items.

College professor Charlotte Lee (USA) has a dedicated "duck room" for her 5,631 **rubber ducks**.

Scott Stoddard (USA) has gathered 840 **shark-related** items a safe distance from the sea in Salt Lake City, Utah, USA.

Educator Cynde McInnis (USA) owns 1,347 **whale-related** items, not including the "whalemobile" she takes on tours of schools.

No.1 singles
Dave Watson (UK) started collecting in 1988 after receiving the *Guinness Book of British Hit Singles* for Christmas. He has since acquired 1,258 tapes, CDs and vinyl records – a copy of every UK No.1 hit to have had a physical release.

Iron Man memorabilia
As ratified on 24 Apr 2021, Miguel Andrés Javier Hidalgo (PER) has 1,548 items related to the superhero Iron Man in Lima, Peru. His Marvel-ous collection includes action figures, comic books, costumes and movie posters.

Goofy memorabilia
As of 30 Jul 2022, diehard Disney devotee Shelley Jobe has 1,825 pieces depicting Mickey Mouse's friend Goofy at her home in Tacoma, Washington, USA. Close behind is Lora Petrak of Bull Valley, Illinois, who favours Mickey's other canine chum: she owned 1,516 items of **Pluto memorabilia** as of 29 Oct 2020.

Ladybug-related items
As a child, Sheri Cummings (USA) was given a ladybug tea-party set. Spotting her enthusiasm, friends and family donated more beetle-themed objects. As of 28 Feb 2022, Sheri's collection in Lake in the Hills, Illinois, runs to 6,047 items.

12,402

Largest collection of soft-drink cans (same brand)
On 19 Mar 2022, Italian Pepsi collector Christian Cavaletti was crowned king of the cans. His hoard of 12,402 unique Pepsi containers surpassed the ▶ **largest collection of Coca-Cola cans** – 11,308 – by Gary Feng (CAN; *below*) and verified on 15 Feb 2020. Christian's stock includes many items acquired by trading with international collectors.

11,308

32,809

Largest collection of Pokémon cards
Brothers Jens Ishøy Prehn and Per Ishøy Nielsen (both DNK) have taken the tagline "gotta catch 'em all" to heart. As of 13 Sep 2021, they have gathered not only cards for all 1,008 Pokémon, but also numerous variants and rarities for a total of 32,809 items.

Pin badges
Founded in 2010, the Busy Beaver Button Museum in Chicago, Illinois, USA, houses more than 9,000 unique badges. It's the work of siblings Christen and Joel Carter, who have long marvelled at how much these little pieces of decorative flair can express.

LEGO® Minifigures
As of 14 Apr 2022, Kyle Ugone of San Diego, California, USA, had 9,079 Minifigs. His plastic army includes examples of the very first Minifigures, released in 1978.

Kamen Rider memorabilia
Ratchaphon Rianchaivanich (THA) owns 15,550 pieces related to the Japanese vigilante superhero. The count was confirmed in Bangkok, Thailand, on 24 Nov 2022.

Largest collection of candy dispensers
With 5,548 items and rising, it's little wonder that Brian Trauman of Caldwell, New Jersey, USA, was voted 2020's PEZ Head of the Year. His houseful of PEZ started with a bag of 150 dispensers in 1999 – his mom's old collection – and a question about how many others there were. It has since grown to include complete sets of Disney and Nintendo characters, as well as rarities such as a limited-run Prince Harry and Meghan Markle set from 2018.

5,548

Deadpool was created by Rob Liefeld and Fabian Nicieza. He made his comic-book debut in 1991.

2,250

LARGEST COLLECTION OF DEADPOOL MEMORABILIA

Gareth Pahliney (IRL) has accumulated 2,250 unique items related to the sardonic Marvel superhero, as confirmed in Cloghan, Offaly, Ireland, on 19 Feb 2023. Among Gareth's favourite pieces are a high-spec model that shows Deadpool holding a rubber chicken – brought over specially for him from the USA by his aunt – and a life-size statue. He also owns a signed poster from the first *Deadpool* movie that he received after cosplaying as the "Merc with a Mouth" at the 2016 premiere.

PRITISH A R

From the moment he first picked up a pair of drumsticks at kindergarten, Pritish – from Sydney, New South Wales, Australia – knew that percussion and music were set to play a big part in his life. Starting with a beginner electronic kit, he took weekly lessons and practised every day, eventually moving on to an acoustic set. In Dec 2020, aged just 10, he passed his Grade 8 drumming exam at Trinity College London.

It was Pritish's mum who first mentioned the idea of combining his passion with a record attempt: "My mother asked if I'd like to try to break a record, and I liked the idea. I was always amazed watching fast drum rolls so I looked up the options and decided **most drumbeats in one minute** would be ideal."

Not surprisingly, becoming the world's "fastest drummer" was no easy feat. But on 16 Dec 2021, after many months of training and honing his technique, Pritish smashed it: 2,370 beats. This was 261 more than the previous record, held by an adult.

With his sights set on learning to play more instruments, winning talent contests and even trying out "fire drumming" (drumming with sticks ablaze!), nobody can accuse Pritish of not marching to the beat of his own drum.

When did you get into drumming?
I used to make sounds with my toys when I was little. My mum realized my natural attraction to music and signed me up to a programme at kindergarten which had a bus filled with musical instruments. The drum kit was very inviting and I went straight to it. That was the start of my journey with drums.

Any there other musicians in the family?
No. Music in my family history is limited to listening to music.

Which musicians inspire you?
Drummer Sridhar, my teacher – based in Chennai, India – and [composer] A R Rahman are two of my biggest musical inspirations. Generally, all my teachers are influencers and drive me to do hard but cool things with drums and other instruments.

How did you train for this attempt?
I started working on the technique in early 2021, and practised for almost seven months. With assistance from my teachers, I incorporated various methods that helped to improve my speed and muscle strength. I trained for one-minute intervals on a variety of surfaces including my snare and tom drums but also concrete and a cushion.

On the day of the attempt, did you think you were on track for the record?
Seeing the set-up and taking my seat to start the attempt, I had butterflies in my stomach. But once I started, I felt I was in a good flow and on track. When the minute was over, I was super-excited to hear I'd reached 2,370 beats – I had a huge smile on my face!

What did your friends say when they learned you'd set a world record?
They were super-surprised and they congratulated me. It was special when it was announced by my principal in assembly and published in the school newsletter.

1: The record attempt took place in a music studio to avoid background noise. This allowed all of the beats to be tracked with pinpoint precision by a Drumometer device.

2: Pritish with mum Aarthi, dad Rajesh and younger sister Shreya. Pritish said: "My parents played a huge supporting role in the preparation [for this record], by recording the number of beats for almost every practice attempt and doing analysis."

3: When not drumming, Pritish enjoys many other activities including cricket, martial arts, swimming and indoor climbing.

SOFIA TEPLA

A lot of people claim that they would bend over backwards to earn a place in the record books, but few take that quite as literally as Sofia Tepla... Having approached GWR about taking on a gymnastics record, the rising circus star from Ukraine was invited to appear on the Italian TV talent show *Lo Show dei Record* in 2022. Her skills proved to be as mind-boggling as they were bone-defying!

The then 11-year-old pushed her acrobatic abilities to the limits by rolling 20 m (65 ft) in 10.49 sec. This wasn't just any old tumble, though, but a contortion roll – a back-bending manoeuvre that requires the participant to start with their feet over their head (as demonstrated below), with soles flat on the ground, before arching back and propelling into a forward roll, then repeating.

Two weeks after claiming her first world record, events in Sofia's home country took a dark turn. But she's staying positive, and has vowed to continue honing her skills in anticipation of the day when she can once again represent Ukraine on a global stage.

1: Sofia with some of the 300 members of the Gratsia dance and circus school, set up by her mother in 2014.

2: The Ukrainian contortionist was "head over heels" to receive her GWR certificate for the fastest 20-m contortion roll.

3: A young Sofia pictured with her parents Maryna and Dmitry, and little brother Alexander.

4: Gymnastic skills clearly run in the family: Alexander also has an aptitude for acrobatics. The siblings often pair up to train and perform routines together.

Who inspired you to try contortionism?
When I was three, I used to watch TV talent shows and I liked to repeat some of the tricks. I would then put on concerts for my family. My parents decided to enrol me in a gymnastics/acrobatics class, but as we live in a small town, we didn't have a circus school nearby so my mum decided to start one!

Have you always been so bendy?
My body isn't naturally flexible. It's actually years of training – as well as good warm-ups. I have a lot of strength, but I developed flexibility gradually over a long time.

How proud were you to represent your country on a TV talent contest?
I'm happy I was the only one from Ukraine – it was an honour! But it was also bittersweet. I set this record in February, then as soon as I got home, the war started. There were many plans related to my achievement, but the focus quickly became just about surviving. It was very scary at first. On my first day back, a rocket flew into our town and people were killed. My family decided to stay at home, all together in Ukraine, even though it was difficult and dangerous. There are no hostilities in our area, but sometimes rockets fly in. I still train and want to be able to perform; in the future, I would love to show my skills to the whole world.

Any advice to other young people thinking of applying for a record?
You have to believe in yourself. And don't stop when things don't work out. Nothing in the world is impossible.

Any more records on the horizon?
Yes! That's my goal. There's a lot I can do, and I have some ideas. I'm good at doing push-ups in the contortion-roll pose*. I could also break the record for lifting flowers with my mouth while in a backward bend.

What else do you like to do for fun?
I like to make jewellery with beads, play board games with my family in the evenings and also to make pancakes.

*On 11 Mar 2023, Sofia successfully set the most contortion-roll push-ups in 30 seconds – 21!

Find out more about under-16s that made it into the record books at kids.guinnessworldrecords.com

BELLA J DARK

Many of us will spend our lives pondering whether or not we have a book in us. But Bella J Dark from Weymouth in Dorset, UK, didn't have to ponder for very long…
Her tale, *The Lost Cat* – which she both wrote and illustrated – was published by Ginger Fyre Press on 31 Jan 2022 when Bella (b. 4 Jul 2016) was aged just 5 years 211 days. This makes her the **youngest girl to publish a book**. (Incidentally, the **male** record holder was even younger: the UAE's Saeed Rashed AlMheiri was 4 years 218 days old when his book, *The Elephant Saeed and The Bear*, was released in 2023!)

According to her mum, Bella has always had a vivid imagination and started to pen short stories at just the age of three. It perhaps won't come as a surprise to hear that English and art are Bella's favourite subjects at school. So, what did her fellow pupils think on finding out she'd not just published her own book but also set a GWR title? "My teachers and my friends were very shocked and excited," she said.

1: Elder sister Lacie-May also drew one of the illustrations that appears in *The Lost Cat*. Here, the girls are snuggling with one of their pet cats, Minnie.

2: Bella with her sister, mum Chelsie and dad Myles. Chelsie told us how proud they are of their daughter: "It has been such an exciting journey so far, and her dad and I are over the moon she has been awarded this record as it's the least she deserves."

3: Published in early 2022, *The Lost Cat* has already gone on to sell more than 1,000 copies.

4: Asked what was the most difficult part about writing her book, Bella replied: "I didn't have a bad part – I enjoyed it all!"

Why did you write *The Lost Cat*?
I wanted to be an author, and I like drawing and writing. The idea started off as a picture. My daddy said I could make a book, and a story came from the picture.

How long did it take to complete?
About five days to write the story and a few months of sorting pictures and dealing with proof copies and things being changed.

Tell us the main premise of the story. Was it based on real life?
It's about a cat called Snowy who goes outside at night on her own and then gets lost. We do have two cats [Ginger and Minnie], but Snowy was entirely from my imagination. The moral of the story is to teach children not to go out on their own at night-time.

Any sequels on the horizon?
Yes! A second book about Snowy the cat will be out very soon. Also, I already have a third book in mind…

What are some of your favourite books? Which one did you last read?
Diary of a Wimpy Kid [by Jeff Kinney] was the last book I read. Some of my other favourites include *What the Ladybird Heard* [Julia Donaldson], *Splat the Cat* [Rob Scotton] and *The Runaway Pea* [Kjartan Poskitt].

What tips do you have for other young writers who'd like to publish a book?
Write a story that comes from you.

Would you like to be an author full-time when you're older?
Possibly – but I'm also thinking I'd like to be a doctor or a teacher as well.

When not writing, what else do you like to do in your free time?
Drawing, learning, playing "teachers", swimming and playing on my tablet.

REYANSH SURANI

There's a misconception that yoga is only for those in later life, but a *very* well-balanced youngster from Dubai, UAE, has made it his mission to flip that myth on its head.

Reyansh (b. 20 Dec 2011) was born in India and was inspired particularly by his grandmother to try out yoga when he was still just a toddler. He was a natural even then, according to his parents, and by the age of 9 years 219 days, he'd gained a qualification to teach the subject, making him the **youngest male certified yoga instructor**.

Now, he is guiding others – of all ages – on their yoga journeys and is out to extol the pastime's virtues: "Embracing yoga will be a game-changer in one's life. It's a lifestyle change that will enable you to keep your mind, body and inner-self balanced. My mission is to impart this ancient, beneficial practice to the Metaverse, as I believe Generation Alpha would love to connect through it."

Even someone as talented and wise beyond their years as Reyansh is the first to acknowledge there are still areas he has yet to master. "For me, the most challenging pose is the *Eka Pada Bakasana* ['Flying Crow']. Trust me, it's extremely difficult and, as I'm still growing, that core upper-body strength is tough!"

When did you start to practise yoga?
There are cute childhood videos of me doing *pranayama* [breathing techniques] when I hadn't even walked. My earliest memories of yoga were watching my grandparents and parents during their practice, and making them laugh as I tried to emulate their poses and toppling over!

How did you find the training process?
Honestly speaking, it was difficult! It included both physical and theoretical classes on different styles of yoga. Plus, I did my training in a remote rural area where there was no internet or all the luxuries I'm used to in Dubai. The routine was gruelling too: we'd start at seven in the morning and end at seven-thirty in the evening, with two meal breaks and an hour for rest/self-study.

What makes a good yoga teacher?
I think it's very important to be a yoga practitioner before teaching; one who has experienced it can explain it in a more philosophical way as yoga isn't only physical.

Is it tricky to balance yoga with other areas of your life?
Yes, it can be tiring. But because my mother is an excellent organizer, she balances my time, so that I can have fun while doing what I'm doing. And significantly my father, who is naturally a joyful person, ensures that we unwind in the evenings.

How does it feel to be in the *GWR* book?
I feel so proud and blessed. Everyone in the world has heard of Guinness World Records and actually being part of the book is a surreal experience. It took loads of hard work and teamwork. I'm very thankful to my teacher, Mr Anand Shekhar, my family and my school principal, Ms Nargish Khambatta.

Find out more about amazing younger record breakers at kids.guinnessworldrecords.com

1: Reyansh conducting a yoga class. He currently teaches only once a week, as most of his time is dedicated to studying.

2: In 2022, Reyansh completed another training course specializing in aerial yoga, in which you perform poses while suspended from a silk hammock.

3: Sports-mad Reyansh is a keen fan of skiing, SCUBA diving and parkour. He has also lent his support to a number of charitable causes; he donated the money from one of his yoga workshops to provide 40 blankets to the needy. If all that weren't enough, he even found time to write a book – *The Avid World of Reyansh* – which was published in 2022.

The Avid World of Reyansh

Reyansh Surani

SIMEON GRAHAM

When Simeon Graham (UK) had to stay home sick from school, he decided to fend off boredom by turning his hand to a new skill... Now, he's a teenage circus prodigy, destined for the big time in the big top!

Simeon was aged just seven when he took up his hobby, and within a few years he was confidently juggling five balls. Seeing his natural talent, his parents recruited a teacher to help hone technique and posture. Simeon went on to perform with the Circus Mash group and appeared as a guest artiste with Gandeys Circus. Having learned the basics from YouTube, he has now gone full circle and is giving tutorials on his own channel.

To underline his superlative skills, Simeon began practising for not one but two world records. On 25 Oct 2022, he achieved the **most juggling catches in one minute** with both **five balls** (423) and **six balls** (396). After even more training, on 4 Feb 2023 he added the **seven balls** record, racking up 378 catches in 60 sec. Now Simeon has a growing collection of GWR titles to juggle with – how many more will he go for?

#B2022

1: Beyond juggling, Simeon also loves to play videogames. He celebrated his 14th birthday in style at an amusement arcade.

2: Simeon with his mum and dad, Tracey and Tony, at the 2022 Commonwealth Games – where they watched a ball sport of a different kind: table tennis.

3: Simeon has been honing his skills with the Circus Mash performers school in his home city of Birmingham for six years.

4: One of Simeon's inspirations is Luca Pferdmenges (DEU), who has held several GWR titles of his own including currently the **most balls passed by a pair while juggling** – 16, set in tandem with Austrian juggler Daniel Ledel on 27 Jun 2020.

Find out more about amazing younger record breakers at kids.guinnessworldrecords.com

How did you first get into juggling?
I was sent home from school because I had chickenpox and I decided to learn how to juggle by watching YouTube videos. After I learned how to juggle three balls, I was hooked on learning more tricks.

How often do you practise?
In the summer, I practise outside for at least an hour a day. However, in the winter, I get less time because the weather is bad.

What makes a good juggler?
There are other qualities besides hand-eye coordination and dexterity that can help you become a good juggler: perseverance, determination and resilience.

Why did you attempt the five and six balls juggling records?
I thought they would be the "easiest" records to break because it helps to juggle low, and I spent six years learning to juggle inside under a low ceiling.

What's the most balls you can juggle at once? Do you think you could surpass Alex Barron's record 14-ball flash?
I've achieved an 11-ball flash on camera. I'm determined that one day I will be able to juggle 15. That would be a dream come true.

Do you also juggle other objects?
I can juggle three clubs but I'm focused on being the best ball juggler I can be.

What do your friends think of you being a circus performer?
They think that it's really cool that I can juggle 11 balls. One of my friends came to see me perform and he loved it!

Any words of wisdom for juggling beginners?
Never get angry when trying a trick; never give up; have fun!

MIA PETERSON

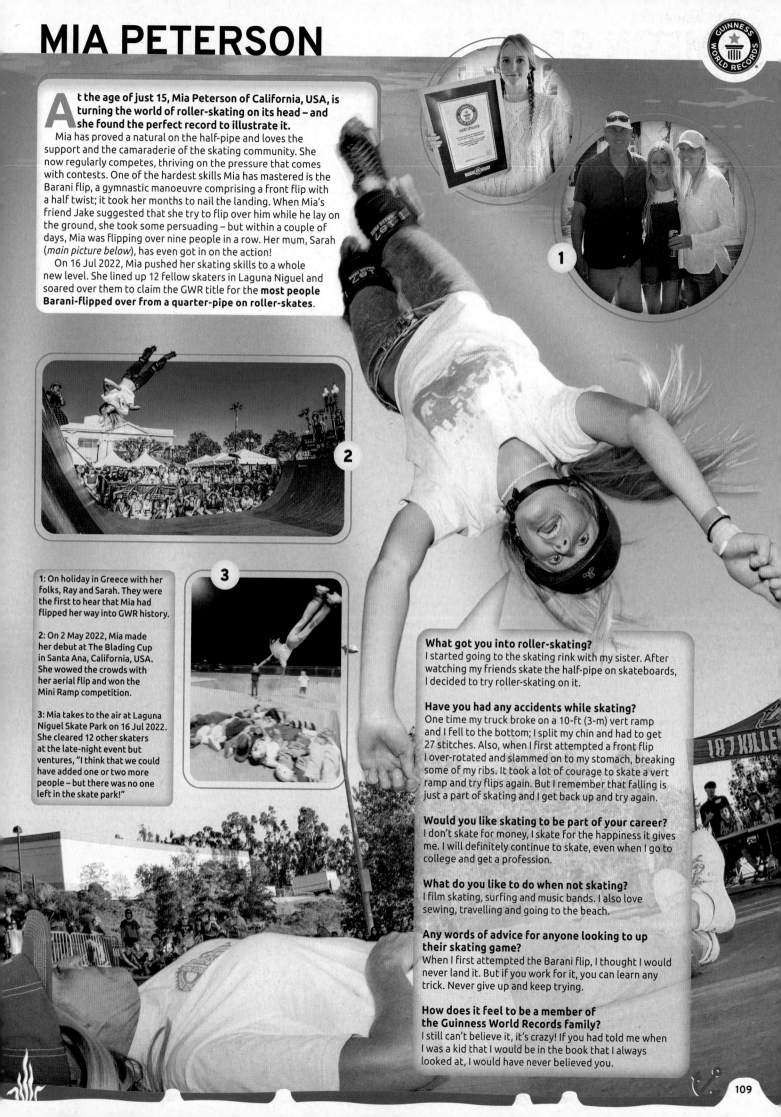

At the age of just 15, Mia Peterson of California, USA, is turning the world of roller-skating on its head – and she found the perfect record to illustrate it.

Mia has proved a natural on the half-pipe and loves the support and the camaraderie of the skating community. She now regularly competes, thriving on the pressure that comes with contests. One of the hardest skills Mia has mastered is the Barani flip, a gymnastic manoeuvre comprising a front flip with a half twist; it took her months to nail the landing. When Mia's friend Jake suggested that she try to flip over him while he lay on the ground, she took some persuading – but within a couple of days, Mia was flipping over nine people in a row. Her mum, Sarah (*main picture below*), has even got in on the action!

On 16 Jul 2022, Mia pushed her skating skills to a whole new level. She lined up 12 fellow skaters in Laguna Niguel and soared over them to claim the GWR title for the **most people Barani-flipped over from a quarter-pipe on roller-skates**.

1: On holiday in Greece with her folks, Ray and Sarah. They were the first to hear that Mia had flipped her way into GWR history.

2: On 2 May 2022, Mia made her debut at The Blading Cup in Santa Ana, California, USA. She wowed the crowds with her aerial flip and won the Mini Ramp competition.

3: Mia takes to the air at Laguna Niguel Skate Park on 16 Jul 2022. She cleared 12 other skaters at the late-night event but ventures, "I think that we could have added one or two more people – but there was no one left in the skate park!"

What got you into roller-skating?
I started going to the skating rink with my sister. After watching my friends skate the half-pipe on skateboards, I decided to try roller-skating on it.

Have you had any accidents while skating?
One time my truck broke on a 10-ft (3-m) vert ramp and I fell to the bottom; I split my chin and had to get 27 stitches. Also, when I first attempted a front flip I over-rotated and slammed on to my stomach, breaking some of my ribs. It took a lot of courage to skate a vert ramp and try flips again. But I remember that falling is just a part of skating and I get back up and try again.

Would you like skating to be part of your career?
I don't skate for money, I skate for the happiness it gives me. I will definitely continue to skate, even when I go to college and get a profession.

What do you like to do when not skating?
I film skating, surfing and music bands. I also love sewing, travelling and going to the beach.

Any words of advice for anyone looking to up their skating game?
When I first attempted the Barani flip, I thought I would never land it. But if you work for it, you can learn any trick. Never give up and keep trying.

How does it feel to be a member of the Guinness World Records family?
I still can't believe it, it's crazy! If you had told me when I was a kid that I would be in the book that I always looked at, I would have never believed you.

ROUND-UP

Largest water rocket
A 7.72-m-tall (25-ft 3.9-in) rocket powered by pressurized water blasted off from Hiroo in Hokkaidō, Japan, on 2 Aug 2022. Created by students from the Showa Gakuen school in Nakano, Tokyo, it soared to 16.78 m (55 ft).

Largest turban
On 26 Aug 2022 in Betul, Madhya Pradesh, India, Aditya Pacholi (IND) tied a traditional Rajputi Rajasthani *pagri* (or *pagdi*) using 345.25 m² (3,716.24 sq ft) of pink cotton. To wear it, your head would need to be 1.1 m (3 ft 7 in) wide.

Largest cup of coffee
Students at the University of Guanajuato in Mexico served up a 26,939.22-litre (5,925.8-gal) cuppa on 10 Dec 2022. The giant java – sponsored by Tonic World Center (MEX) – used 300 kg (660 lb) of beans.

▶ Largest pizza
American YouTuber Airrack (aka Eric Decker) worked with Pizza Hut and an army of volunteers to create a 1,296.72-m² (13,957.77-sq-ft) pizza in Los Angeles, California, USA, on 19 Jan 2023. It was 40.2 m (132 ft) wide – nearly 18,000 times larger than an average 12-in (30.4-cm) version.

Most inverts on a sit-down hydrofoil in three minutes
Seated hydrofoiling is a variant of water-skiing. On 21 Oct 2021, Geno Yauchler (USA, *above*) executed 72 flips while being pulled by a speedboat in Winter Haven, Florida, USA. Yauchler was declared the US Hydrofoil Association's Athlete of the Year for the fifth time in 2021. The women's award went to MJ Buckley (USA, *above right; see table*), for the 12th time.

MOST SIT-DOWN HYDROFOIL INVERTS IN...		
Duration	Total	Holder
One hour	826	Geno Yauchler
One minute	30	Geno Yauchler
Three minutes (Female)	55	MJ Buckley
One minute (female)	23	MJ Buckley

All figures correct as of 1 Mar 2023

Tallest *Calavera Catrina*
A 22.67-m-tall (74-ft 4.5-in) sculpture of an elegantly dressed female skeleton was the star of the Day of the Dead festival in Puerto Vallarta, Jalisco, Mexico, on 2 Nov 2022. The huge metal-and-fibreglass effigy was a public project overseen by local artist Alondra Muca (MEX).

Largest soap-bubble dome
Olga Buianovscaia (MDA) formed a 1.69-m-wide (5-ft 6-in) half bubble on a flat surface in Chişinău, Moldova, on 2 Dec 2022. The final dome had a volume of 1.23 m³ (43.4 cu ft).
   Other soap-bubble records that were burst in 2022 included:
• **Tallest bubble stack**: 27, by Pierre-Yves Fusier (FRA) in Massy, Essonne, France, on 1 Apr.
• **Longest hanging bubble chain**: 87, by Su Chung-Tai (CHN) in Taipei, Taiwan, China, on 7 Oct.
• **Longest bubble rally**: 27 passes, by father and daughter Eran and Paikea Backler (both UK) in Newport, Isle of Wight, UK, on 13 Nov.

Most Jenga blocks stacked on one vertical Jenga block
Auldin Maxwell (CAN) painstakingly balanced a remarkable 1,840 Jenga pieces on a single upright block in Salmon Arm, British Columbia, Canada, on 22 Jan 2023. The supreme stacker surpassed his own record, set on 27 Mar 2021, by 440 blocks.

▶ Longest underwater kiss
Engaged couple Beth Neale (ZAF) – a champion freediver – and Miles Cloutier (CAN) locked lips for 4 min 6 sec in a pool at LUX* South Ari Atoll in the Maldives on 4 Feb 2023. Former holders Michele Fucarino and Elisa Lazzarini had to kiss goodbye to their title after 13 years.

Most people dressed as astronauts
A 940-strong cosmic collective gathered on 25 Oct 2022 in a mission overseen by Repton Abu Dhabi (UAE). The school's students, teachers and staff from Year 2 to Year 7 all donned helmets and spacesuits at the Fry campus to commemorate the third anniversary of the *International Space Station* welcoming the UAE's first astronaut, Hazza Al Mansouri.

MILK A COW
Reconnect with nature, down on the farm. The **highest lifetime milk yield from a cow** is 216,891 kg (478,163 lb), as verified on 27 Feb 2012. The productive bovine was Smurf, a Holstein owned by La Ferme Gillette (CAN) in Embrun, Ontario, Canada.

Most expensive sports trading card sold at auction

A rare 1952 Topps Mickey Mantle card – graded 9.5/10 for its exceptional condition – realized $12.6 m (£10.7 m) at Heritage Auctions on 28 Aug 2022. It also claims the auction record for the **most expensive sports memorabilia** overall. The final hammer price is 252 times what the owner paid for the card in 1991.

Most candles extinguished with a single martial-arts strike

On 10 Nov 2022, Anthony Kelly (AUS) snuffed out 37 candles with a single stroke of his hand in Armidale, New South Wales, Australia.

Contrariwise, the **most matches lit with a nunchaku in one minute** is 41, by Yue Haichuan (CHN) in Jinan, Shandong, China, on 16 Mar 2022.

Longest no-hands motorcycle wheelie

Stunt rider Arūnas Gibieža (LTU) covered 580.81 m (1,905 ft 6 in) on just his rear wheel – *and* without holding on to the handlebars – in Vilnius, Lithuania, on 3 Sep 2022.

◗ Longest rail grind on skis

On 9 May 2022, Jesper Tjäder (SWE) skied 154.49 m (506 ft 10 in) along a railing at SkiStar Resort in Åre, Sweden. Tjäder is a pro skier and veteran of the last three Winter Olympics.

Longest time balancing an object on the nose

Christian Roberto López Rodríguez– one of Spain's most prolific record breakers – kept a broom on his nose for 2 hr 42 min 19 sec in Cabañas de la Sagra, Toledo, Spain, on 19 Jun 2022.

Longest time controlling a golf ball on two clubs

On 10 Nov 2022, Yujiro Ohata (JPN) kept a golf ball airborne for 1 hr 2 min 32 sec by bouncing it between two golf clubs in Fujieda, Shizuoka, Japan.

Youngest yoga instructor

Praanvi Gupta (IND, b. 15 Jun 2015) was certified to teach yoga aged 7 years 165 days in Dubai, UAE, on 27 Nov 2022. (*For the boy's record, see p.107.*)

Most stairs descended in a wheelchair in 12 hours

Haki Doku (ALB/ITA) negotiated all 1,150 steps of the 56-floor Montparnasse Tower in Paris, France, 10 times on 11 Sep 2021. He took an elevator back to the top after each descent, logging a total of 11,500 steps.

Longest hopscotch game

On 18 Sep 2022, Generation Wild (USA) created a 7.03-km-long (4.37-mi) hopscotch path at Chatfield State Park in Littleton, Colorado, USA. Three people completed the 21,871 squares in just 2.5 hr.

Most touches of a soccer ball with the soles in one minute (female)

Football freestyler Mélody Donchet (FRA) tapped a ball 227 times using just the bottom of her feet in Montpellier, France, on 12 Nov 2022.

On 8 Jul that year, fellow French freestyler Norman Habri executed the **most consecutive touches with two soccer balls** – 100.

3.5 times the length of a VW Beetle car

Largest candy dispenser

On 26 Jan 2023, PEZ Candy (USA) presented a 4.45-m-tall (14-ft 7.25-in) model of one of its singular vending machines at the firm's visitor centre in Orange, Connecticut, USA. The working replica is based on the Boy Blue Cap PEZ dispenser. Below, official company historian Shawn Peterson tries it out.

Farthest behind-the-back basketball shot

With his back to the board, Joshua Walker (USA) found the hoop from 14.63 m (48 ft) in Lake Charles, Louisiana, USA, on 22 Jul 2022. The trick-shot master netted several other records that day, including the **farthest bounce shot** (28.95 m; 95 ft), **hook shot** (24.38 m; 80 ft) and **basketball shot overall** (34.6 m; 113 ft 6 in) – greater than the full length of an NBA court!

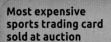

LEARN FRENCH

There are countless ways to attune your ear to a new lingo, thanks to online content. The **most subscribers for a French-language channel on YouTube** is 17.9 million, by Squeezie (aka Lucas Hauchard, FRA), as verified on 13 Mar 2023.

ERDEN ERUÇ

S ince first putting his hands to the oars on 9 Nov 2005, Turkish-American engineer Erden Eruç has spent a total of **2 years 354 days alone at sea**. In that time, he has covered the greatest distance rowed solo, sculling **26,705 nautical mi (49,457 km; 30,731 mi)**, and **completed the fastest solo circumnavigation under human power.**

The story of Erden's adventures begins not on the sea, but 3,917 m (12,851 ft) above it. In 1972, at the age of 11, Erden scaled Mount Erciyes in Türkiye with his mountaineer father – a trip that inspired a lifelong love of climbing. He kept up this hobby through university in Türkiye and two postgraduate degrees in the USA, eventually settling down in the shadow of the Cascade Mountains in Washington State.

The idea of a circumnavigation started as an office daydream, tracing his finger across a world map, traversing over Everest in the process. He called it "Around-n-Over". This might have gone no further had Erden not met Swedish adventurer Göran Kropp. In 1995–96, Kropp cycled from his home in Sweden to Everest base camp, before climbing it without oxygen – a feat similar to what Erden had been contemplating. Each time they spoke, Kropp would push Erden to follow through on his plan.

Tragically, in Sep 2002, Kropp was killed in a fall while he and Erden were climbing together in the Cascades. Two months later, on his way home from Kropp's funeral, Erden sketched a map of the world and traced a route across it. The name was already decided: "Around-n-Over". Circle the world under human power and climb the highest peak on every continent other than Antarctica in the process. Now, more than 20 years later, with one full circumnavigation done and three of the world's tallest peaks climbed, Erden's odyssey is still in progress.

Erden's longest solo row has now been surpassed by Jacob Adoram (USA), who spent 335 days crossing the Pacific in 2018–19.

1: When he's out at sea alone, Erden keeps his mind occupied by doing mental arithmetic, listening to audiobooks and, as a treat, music. The route of his first round-the-world trip (*below*) involved three massive ocean crossings, the longest of which saw him set what was then a record for the **longest time rowing solo at sea** (312 days).

2: In Feb 2016, Erden visited GWR's London office for a chat with Editor-in-Chief Craig Glenday. He was presented with as many GWR certificates as he could carry!

3: A curious red-footed booby lands on the 7.3-m (24-ft) rowboat *Around-n-Over*. Through his long voyages, Erden has become accustomed to close encounters with ocean life, including turtles that bump against the hull and fish that shelter in its shadow. His time in the midst of Earth's **largest biome** (*see p.21*) sharpened his attitudes towards the state of our planet, leading him to become an ambassador for the Ocean Recovery Alliance.

4: The "Around-n-Over" project started, not with an ocean crossing, but with a bike ride. On 1 Feb 2003, Erden cycled north from Seattle, aiming for the first of his "Six Summits", the 6,155-m (20,194-ft) peak of Denali in Alaska, which he reached on 29 May. On 10 Apr 2010, following his row across the Pacific, he climbed Kosciuszko (2,228 m; 7,310 ft) in Australia, the second of his peaks. Having crossed the Indian Ocean, he tackled the third, Kilimanjaro (5,895 m; 19,341 ft), in Jun 2011.

5: *Around-n-Over* has two watertight compartments at either end where food, water and navigation equipment are stored. Erden's circumnavigation was not the first record-breaking voyage made by *Around-n-Over*. In 2004, under the name *Calderdale*, the vessel was used by Sarah and Sally Kettle (both UK) to become the **first mother-daughter team to row an ocean**. Since acquiring the boat, Erden has travelled another 27,593 nautical mi (51,102 km; 31,753 mi), and will be putting many more miles on the clock before he's finished.

> Erden has three continent-topping peaks left to climb on his latest quest: Everest, Elbrus and Aconcagua.

Find out more about Erden in the Hall of Fame section at www.guinnessworldrecords.com/2024

ADVENTURES

Longest stage swim across the Red Sea
Between 11 and 26 Oct 2022, Lewis Pugh (UK) swam for 16 days – in 25 legs – across the Red Sea. Pugh, an endurance swimmer and UN Patron of the Oceans, departed from Tiran Island, Saudi Arabia, and ended in Hurghada, Egypt, having covered 123.4 km (76.7 mi) in a cumulative time of 46 hr 13 min 44 sec.

A passionate environmental activist, Pugh timed his swim to precede the COP27 conference, which took place in Egypt in Nov 2022. The Red Sea is home to some of the most biodiverse coral-reef ecosystems on the planet and his challenge was intended to raise awareness about the consequences of climate change in the region, where water temperatures have been known to reach a staggering 30°C (86°F).

The "Speedo Diplomat" has often used superlative swims to promote ocean conservation – and not always in such warm waters. On 23 Jan 2020, he became the **first person to swim beneath the Antarctic Ice Sheet** (*inset*), journeying *c.* 1 km (0.6 mi) in a subglacial river that was a bone-tingling 0.1°C (32.18°F). His goal was to draw attention to the plight of Earth's melting icescapes (*see pp.22–23*).

"If we continue to overheat our planet," Pugh said sombrely, "we are on course to lose 99% of all coral reefs."

DSV *LIMITING FACTOR*

A passion for exploration has seen Victor Vescovo (USA) rack up a string of GWR titles. He's best known for his many depth-defying dives into the oceans' uncharted reaches – adventures only made possible by a game-changing deep-submergence vehicle (DSV): *Limiting Factor.*

Manufactured by Triton Submarines and formally designated the Triton 36000/2, this is the first submersible designed to make repeated journeys to the greatest depths within the ocean. Its 90-mm-thick (3.5-in) titanium crew capsule can withstand the 8.5 tonnes (18,739 lb) of pressure per square inch at the ▷ **deepest point in the sea** – the Challenger Deep. In fact, it was engineered to cope with 25% greater pressure than it would ever experience.

Limiting Factor is supported by the scientific research ship *Pressure Drop* (*below*), and on many descents was accompanied by robotic landers (*opposite*). The sub has two banks of external batteries and another for internal power, enabling dives in excess of 16 hours. Three viewports sit at its base – one facing down, the others horizontally – while 10 LED lights (each a super-bright 20,000 lumens) provide essential illumination in the pitch-black benthic darkness.

As of Oct 2022, *Limiting Factor* had performed 126 descents, 18 of which were sub-10,900 m (35,760 ft). It has shone a light on the oceans' least-known sites – many for the first time – and also helped to discover the **deepest shipwreck** (see p.146), not once but twice. In late 2022, the entire operation was taken on by the marine-research organization Inkfish and *Limiting Factor* will embark on a new chapter of ultra-deep-sea science under the name *Bakunawa* (based on a mythological serpent-like dragon), under the stewardship of marine biologist Dr Alan Jamieson (see p.42). Truly, this sub's potential for exploration knows no limits.

Starboard modem

GPS beacon and strobe light

Titanium chassis

Sonar

Vertical tie bars

Oxygen cylinders

Multi-directional thrusters (10 in total) allow for precise manoeuvring

Lowering crane

PRESSURE DROP
MAJURO M.I.

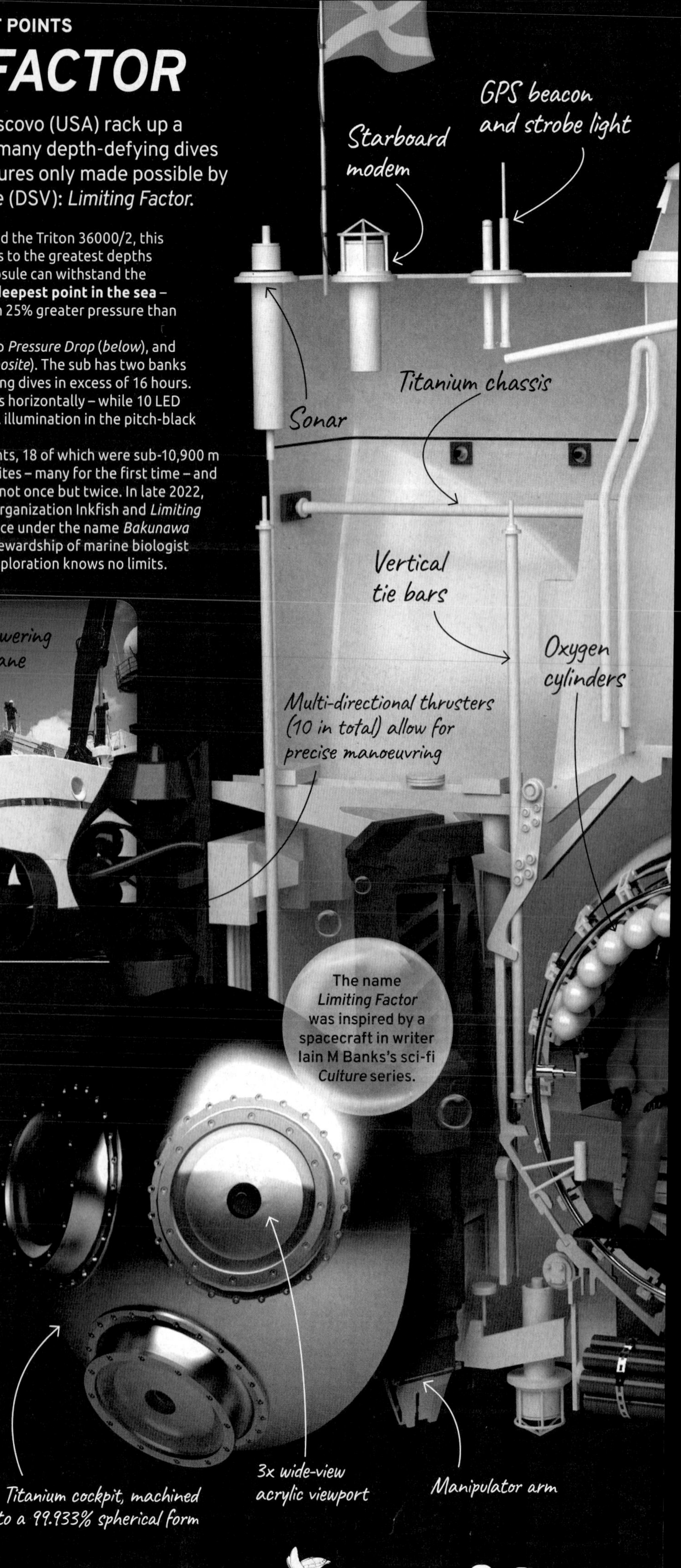

The name *Limiting Factor* was inspired by a spacecraft in writer Iain M Banks's sci-fi *Culture* series.

CREWED DIVES TO THE CHALLENGER DEEP

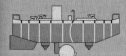

Trieste, 1960
Jacques Piccard (CHE) and Donald Walsh (USA) carried out the **first crewed descent** to the ocean's **deepest point** in a bathyscaphe on 23 Jan. They reached 10,911 m (35,797 ft).

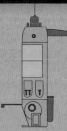

Deepsea Challenger, 2012
On 25 Mar, film director James Cameron (CAN) navigated to a depth of 10,908 m (35,787 ft) – the **first solo descent** into the Challenger Deep. He spent 2 hr 38 min on the seabed.

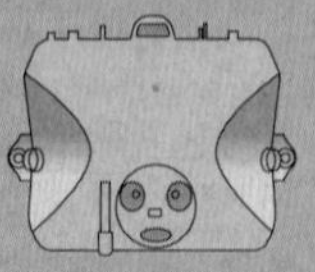

Limiting Factor, 2019–
Victor Vescovo first visited the Challenger Deep in 2019. A year later, he conducted the ▷ **deepest dive by a crewed vessel** – 10,935 m (35,875 ft). By Oct 2022, he'd plumbed this abyss a record-setting 15 times.

Fendouzhe, 2020–
Also reusable, this vessel descended into the Challenger Deep 13 times in Oct/Nov. The deepest dive, to 10,909 m (35,790 ft), was a new record for a Chinese submersible.

Titanium cockpit, machined to a 99.933% spherical form

3x wide-view acrylic viewport

Manipulator arm

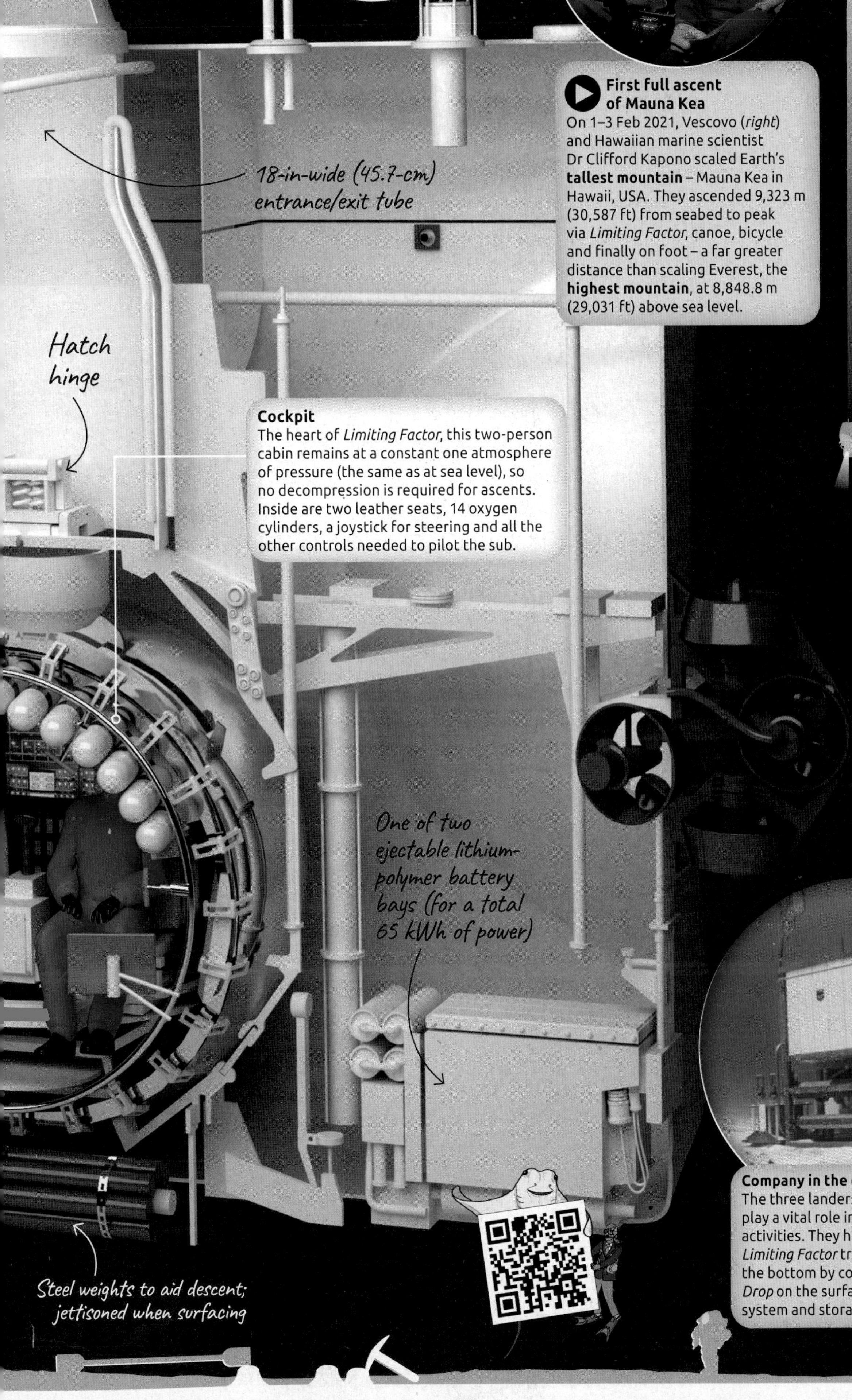

Exit trunk

For buoyancy, the sub is built with "syntactic foam" – epoxy resin permeated with air-filled glass beads.

18-in-wide (45.7-cm) entrance/exit tube

Hatch hinge

First full ascent of Mauna Kea

On 1–3 Feb 2021, Vescovo (*right*) and Hawaiian marine scientist Dr Clifford Kapono scaled Earth's **tallest mountain** – Mauna Kea in Hawaii, USA. They ascended 9,323 m (30,587 ft) from seabed to peak via *Limiting Factor*, canoe, bicycle and finally on foot – a far greater distance than scaling Everest, the **highest mountain**, at 8,848.8 m (29,031 ft) above sea level.

Cockpit

The heart of *Limiting Factor*, this two-person cabin remains at a constant one atmosphere of pressure (the same as at sea level), so no decompression is required for ascents. Inside are two leather seats, 14 oxygen cylinders, a joystick for steering and all the other controls needed to pilot the sub.

One of two ejectable lithium-polymer battery bays (for a total 65 kWh of power)

Steel weights to aid descent; jettisoned when surfacing

FIVE DEEPEST POINTS

Between 19 Dec 2018 and 24 Aug 2019, Vescovo – piloting *Limiting Factor* – became the first person to reach the lowest points of Earth's oceans. Their current maximum known depths are listed below.

Arctic Ocean: Molloy Deep – 5,550 m (18,208 ft)

Indian Ocean: Java Trench – 7,192 m (23,596 ft)

Southern Ocean: South Sandwich Trench – 7,434 m (24,390 ft)

Atlantic Ocean: Puerto Rico Trench – 8,374 m (27,474 ft)

Pacific Ocean: Challenger Deep, Mariana Trench – 10,935 m (35,875 ft)

Company in the depths

The three landers *Flere*, *Skaff* and *Closp* play a vital role in the sub's underwater activities. They have modems that help *Limiting Factor* triangulate its position on the bottom by communicating with *Pressure Drop* on the surface. Each also has a camera system and storage tubes for samples.

MOUNTAINEERING

RECLASSIFYING THE 8,000ERS

In May 2021, an article in *The New York Times* asked the question: "What is a summit?" The piece was one of the first in the mainstream media to discuss concerns raised by mountain chronicler Eberhard Jurgalski, who maintains the 8000ers.com website and is GWR's primary consultant for mountaineering superlatives.

Jurgalski and his team have spent the last 10 years re-investigating ascents of the 14 mountains over 8,000 m (26,247 ft). Their conclusion is that, with a number of peaks (particularly Annapurna I, Dhaulagiri I and Manaslu), the "true summits" had not been correctly identified for many years. This means that many climbers – usually through no fault of their own – had stopped before reaching the summit.

For any mountain climb to qualify for a record, it must now meet two key criteria:
1. The highest reachable point – aka the "true summit" – must be attained and proved.
2. Ascents must be made on foot, from base camp to the top and then back again; consideration will be given to helicopter descents from higher camps for medical emergencies.

As of Feb 2023, all relevant records affected by this new research have been archived as legacy climbs. The first and fastest "true summit" climb of all 8,000ers (and with no supplementary oxygen) is now 15 years 359 days, by Ed Viesturs (USA, *right*) between 18 May 1989 and 12 May 2005.

The fastest record (with bottled oxygen) is still held by "Nims" Purja (*right*), with a revised time of 2 years 168 days between 23 Apr 2019 and 8 Oct 2021. Nims continues to break records on the higher 8,000ers, often without bottled oxygen – *see p.124*.

For a full explanation of the reclassification, and a list of titles affected by the changes, visit guinnessworldrecords.com/2024

Most ascents of Everest
On 7 May 2022, Kami Rita Sherpa (NPL) ascended Everest (aka Sagarmāthā or Chomolungma) – the **highest mountain**, at 8,848.8 m (29,031 ft) – for the 26th time. He had first scaled it on 13 May 1994, aged 24 years. It was also his 36th climb of a mountain higher than 8,000 m (26,247 ft); in terms of "true summits", *see left*), this is the **most climbs over 8,000 m**.

The **most Everest ascents by a woman** is 10, by Nepal's Lhakpa Sherpa. She achieved her most recent summit on 12 May 2022 at 6:15 a.m. local time.

Fastest triple-header of the higher 8,000ers without bottled oxygen by a woman
In 2022, China's He Jing took just 69 days to scale Everest (14 May), Lhotse (20 May) and K2 (22 Jul). An experienced climber, she had previously made a "true summit" ascent of Annapurna I, also without supplementary oxygen.

The **fastest woman to climb Everest** is Ada, aka Tsang Yin Hung (CHN), who completed an ascent of Everest (with bottled oxygen) in just 25 hr 50 min. The Hong Kong-born marathon- and ultra-runner reached the top on 23 May 2021.

Most ascents of K2
Mingma "David" Gyabu Sherpa (NPL, *left*) topped the "Savage Mountain" five times – with bottled oxygen – between 2014 and 2022. He was also part of the 10-strong Nepalese team that made the **first winter ascent of K2** in Jan 2021 – an expedition that represents the **most winter ascents of an 8,000er**.

The **most ascents of K2 without bottled oxygen** is three, by Fazal Ali (PAK) in 2014, 2017 and 2018.

Fastest ascent of K2
On 28 Jul 2022, Chhiring Sherpa (NPL) climbed K2 from base camp to the top in an unprecedented time of 12 hr 20 min.

Most climbs of Makalu in one season
Lakpa Sherpa (NPL) made three ascents of the world's fifth-highest mountain during the 2022 season. His first was on 12 May to fix the ropes, with additional climbs on 20 and 28 May with clients. This is also the **fastest time to climb Makalu three times**.

On 27 Jul 2021, aged 19 years 138 days, Kashif became the **youngest person to climb K2** and **youngest to climb Everest and K2**.

First all-Black team to climb Everest
On 12 May 2022, seven Black climbers from the Full Circle team reached the top of Everest: Manoah Ainuu, Fred Campbell, Abby Dione, Demond Mullins, Rosemary Saal, Eddie Taylor (all USA) and James Kagambi (KEN). Prior to this, of the *c.* 10,000 Everest summits, only 10 had been by Black climbers. The aim of Full Circle is to "de-colonize" climbing, said organizer Phil Henderson, who led from base camp but did not make the final push to the summit. "It's about changing the narrative about Black people and the outdoors."

Youngest woman to climb the highest 8,000ers
Adriana Brownlee (UK, b. 8 Jan 2001) reached the summit of the world's second-highest point on 29 Jul 2022, aged 21 years 202 days. Achieved with Nepal's Gelje Sherpa, it was her ninth successful 8,000er. It also made her the **youngest woman to climb K2**, and the **youngest woman to climb Everest and K2**.

Youngest man to climb the higher 8,000ers
On 28 May 2022, Shehroze Kashif (PAK, b. 11 Mar 2002) topped Makalu (8,485 m; 27,837 ft) aged 20 years 78 days, completing his ascent of the world's five highest mountains. He aims to become the youngest person to climb the 8,000ers, and is well aware of the physical and mental demands required: "Mountaineering doesn't ask for compromise," he says. "Mountaineering asks for sacrifice."

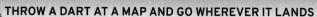

THROW A DART AT A MAP AND GO WHEREVER IT LANDS
With a bit of luck, you'll land in a tropical paradise or an alpine wonderland. So, let's hope you've got an aim as good as Paul Webber's (NZ). In Auckland on 17 Jul 2021, he achieved the **farthest distance to throw a bull's-eye in darts** – 7 m (23 ft)!

58

Fastest time to climb Everest and K2
Sheikha Asma Al Thani (QAT) topped Everest on 27 May 2022 and just 56 days later, on 22 Jul, made a successful climb of K2. Both ascents were made with bottled oxygen.

The **fastest without bottled oxygen** was Karl Unterkircher (ITA), who summitted Everest on 24 May 2004 and K2 on 26 Jul 2004 – a span of just 63 days.

FASTEST WOMAN TO CLIMB THE HIGHER 8,000ERS

In 2022, Kristin Harila (NOR) scaled the world's five highest mountains in just 69 days, with expeditions to Kangchenjunga (14 May), Everest and Lhotse (22 May, with just 9 hr 5 min between the two summits, the **fastest 8,000er double-header**), Makalu (27 May) and K2 (22 Jul).

Empowered by this, Harila decided that her next challenge would be to summit all 14 peaks over 8,000 m in six months. She duly broke the record for **most 8,000ers climbed in a year**, achieving 12 "true summits" in just 147 days.

Sadly, after topping her 12th – Manaslu (8,163 m; 26,781 ft) – on 22 Sep 2022, she was forced to put her plans on hold, as COVID restrictions in China meant that she was unable to secure permits to climb the final two mountains. She is, however, still on track to become the first woman to achieve this, and also to beat the absolute speed record.

The multi-talented Harila is also a former cross-country skiier and leads Arctic skiing expeditions.

GO ROCK CLIMBING

... but avoid the world's **hardest route climbed** –"Silence" – which has an unprecedented difficulty grade of 5.15d. The 45-m-long (147-ft) route, mostly inverted, is in the Hanshelleren Cave, near Flatanger, Norway. Only one person has completed it: Adam Ondra (CZE), on 3 Sep 2017.

57

OCEAN ODYSSEYS

First row across the Indian Ocean from Asia to Africa

On 20 Jun 2022, as part of a human-powered circumnavigation, Karlis Bardelis (LVA) arrived at Baraawe in Somalia, after rowing 6,265 km (3,383 nautical mi) from Kuala Perlis in Malaysia. Bardelis had earlier completed the **first row across the Pacific from South America to Asia** – a two-year trip between Callao in Peru and Pontian in Malaysia.

First team of three to row across the Atlantic east to west from mainland Europe to mainland South America

Between 25 Jan and 30 Mar 2022, Johnnie Ball, Stefan Vine (both UK) and Dirk Von Delft (ZAF) rowed *Wa'omoni* from Portimão in Portugal to Cayenne in French Guiana. They covered 5,704 km (3,080 nautical mi) in 63 days 19 hr 17 min.

First mixed team to row around Great Britain

James Scott (UK), Andrew Burns (UK), Mia Showell-Woodsmith (AUS) and Simone Talfourd (UK, *left to right*) rounded mainland Great Britain in 43 days 3 hr 5 min onboard *Emma*. They departed from Cowes on the Isle of Wight on 10 Jul 2021 and returned on 22 Aug. Two other rowers started the challenge but left before the finish.

Fastest circumnavigation of Antarctica by sailboat

Lisa Blair (AUS) piloted *Climate Action Now* around Antarctica in 92 days 18 hr 21 min 22 sec, from 21 Feb to 25 May 2022. She is only the third adventurer to have completed the gruelling journey, which starts and finishes at Albany, Western Australia. Blair shaved nearly 10 days off the previous record. The feat won her the Antarctica Cup Ocean Race, a 25,920-km (14,000-nautical-mi) round trip of the continent.

Fastest row of the Mid-Pacific east to west by a team of four (female)

Adrienne Smith, Brooke Downes, Libby Costello and Sophia Denison-Johnston (all USA) rowed from Sausalito, California, to Waikiki, Hawaii, USA, in 34 days 14 hr 20 min. Their 3,850-km (2,079-nautical-mi) journey in *American Spirit* began on 21 Jun 2022 and ended on 26 Jul 2022.

Oldest person to sail solo across the Pacific

Past-master yachtsman Kenichi Horie (JPN, b. 8 Sep 1938) was aged 83 years 269 days when he sailed *Suntory Mermaid III* into Cape Hinomisaki, Wakayama, Japan, on 4 Jun 2022. He had set out from San Francisco, California, USA, on 26 Mar, aged 83 years 199 days, and travelled nonstop for 70 days. (See also p.128.)

Fastest completion of the Fastnet original course

This 1,101-km (595-nautical-mi) yacht race began in 1925, and ran from Cowes on the Isle of Wight to Plymouth, UK, via the Fastnet Rock off the coast of south-west Ireland. A six-strong crew led by Giovanni Soldini (ITA) completed it in 23 hr 51 min 16 sec in the trimaran *Maserati Multi 70*, from 7 to 8 May 2021. In Aug 2021, the end point was changed to Cherbourg, France.

Fastest North Channel crossing by prone paddleboard

The North Channel is a UK waterway between north-east Northern Ireland and south-west Scotland. A recumbent Mark Walton (IRL) took 4 hr 55 min 15 sec to paddle his board across the stretch, from Donaghadee, County Down, to Portpatrick, Dumfries and Galloway, on 1 Jul 2022.

Samantha Rutt (UK) achieved the **stand-up paddleboard** record – 5 hr 2 min 35 sec – on the same day.

On 16 Sep 2022, Will Verling (UK) made the **fastest North Channel crossing by a windsurfer** in 1 hr 37 min 31 sec.

Youngest person to row any ocean

Bulgaria's Maxim Ivanov (b. 25 Aug 2003) was just 16 years 294 days old at the start of his row with his father Stefan across the Atlantic from Portimão in Portugal to Barbados. The journey, on board *Neverest*, lasted 114 days 9 hr 36 min, between 14 Jun and 6 Oct 2020, including a nine-day stopover in Lanzarote for repairs.

VISIT NEW ZEALAND
From its rich Māori culture to the stunning landscapes seen in *The Lord of the Rings* movies, the "Land of the Long White Cloud" has something for everyone. Emma Timmis (NZ) saw it all in 20 days 17 hr 15 min 57 sec, ending on 7 Jan 2022 – the **fastest crossing of New Zealand on foot by a woman**.

FIRST HUMAN-POWERED EXPEDITION IN THE SOUTHERN OCEAN

From 11 to 17 Jan 2023, Lisa Farthofer (AUT), Stefan Ivanov (BGR), Jamie Douglas-Hamilton (UK), Brian Krauskopf (USA) and their captain Fiann Paul (ISL) rowed from Antarctica's King George Island to Laurie Island in *Mrs Chippy*. The arduous 754-km (407-nautical-mi) crossing was the first row to be carried out entirely within this body of water; it also made Farthofer the **first woman to row on polar open waters**.

The adventure – dubbed "The Shackleton Mission" – was inspired by the journey made in 1916 by Anglo-Irish explorer Sir Ernest Shackleton. His ship, *Endurance*, had been crushed by pack ice in the Weddell Sea during an expedition to Antarctica, leaving him and his crew of 27 men stranded on an ice floe. Shackleton and five crewmates decided to sail in a small lifeboat from Elephant Island to South Georgia to seek help. Their mission was ultimately successful, and the entire crew was rescued. More than 100 years later, the row boat used by Paul and his team would be named in honour of *Endurance*'s cat, Mrs Chippy.

Cape Horn, Chile

Laurie Island

King George Island

Charles Point, Antarctica

*The multiple-record-breaking Shackleton Mission also saw Paul and Douglas-Hamilton become the **first people to row on the Southern Ocean in both directions**. Between 13 and 25 Dec 2019, they were part of a six-man crew that rowed north to south from Cape Horn in Chile to Charles Point in Antarctica, in Ohana. Their two traverses represent the **most rows on the Southern Ocean**.*

The 2023 journey is the **fastest polar row** and **fastest row on the Southern Ocean**, averaging 2.85 knots (5.2 km/h; 3.2 mph).

Left to right: Farthofer, Ivanov, Douglas-Hamilton, Krauskopf, Mike Matson (who became ill and had to quit the expedition before its completion) and Paul.

OUTDOOR SWIMMING

Longest tandem stage swim
Between 20 Jul and 13 Aug 2022, the USA's "Swim Brothers" (aka Joe and John Zemaitis) completed a marathon swim in each of the 50 US states. They logged a cumulative distance of 552.6 km (343.4 mi) in the water over the course of their 25-day swimathon, which began in Hawaii and ended in their home state of Arizona.

Longest journey open-water swimming
Martin Strel (SVN) swam the entire length of the Amazon River between 1 Feb and 8 Apr 2007 – a total distance of 5,268 km (3,273 mi). He covered as much as 127 km (79 mi) in a single day.

Strel also logged the **longest non-stop open-water swim** – 504.5 km (313.4 mi) along the Danube in Europe on 3–6 Jul 2001.

Longest continuous swim in a lake
On 7–9 Aug 2017, Sarah Thomas (USA) covered 168.3 km (104.6 mi) in Lake Champlain, on the state border between New York and Vermont, USA. In total, she spent 67 hr 16 min 12 sec in the water.

Thomas also swam the **fastest two-way North Channel crossing** on 9–10 Jul 2022. She went from Scotland to Northern Ireland, UK, and back – the first person to do so – in 21 hr 46 min 38 sec.

Farthest swim with a monofin
On 7 May 2022, Merle Liivand (EST) embarked on a 42.2-km (26.2-mi) marathon "mermaid swim" off Miami, Florida, USA. She propelled herself for 11 hr 54 min with dolphin kicks and didn't use her arms. An Estonian national team swimmer, Liivand uses her open-water feats to highlight the issue of marine pollution.

Most swims around Manhattan Island
Jaimie Monahan (USA, *see also p.124*) completed the 46-km (28.5-mi) loop around the heart of New York City 29 times in a decade between 2010 and 2020. This included a quadruple circumnavigation of the river island on 18–20 Sep 2020.

Fastest cumulative time to swim the Oceans Seven
Conceived by the World Open Water Swimming Association, the Oceans Seven challenge comprises crossing the Cook Strait, the Strait of Gibraltar and the North, English, Molokai, Catalina and Tsugaru channels. Atilla Mányoki (HUN) swam them all in 64 hr 35 min 49 sec, ending on 26 Aug 2019.

The **youngest Oceans Seven finisher** is Prabhat Koli (IND, b. 27 Jul 1999), aged 23 years 217 days when he crossed the Cook Strait on 1 Mar 2023.

Most swim crossings of the English Channel (consecutive decades)
Sally Minty-Gravett (UK) has swum between England and France for six decades in a row since her first crossing, at the age of 18, in 1975. Her latest swim was on 7 Aug 2022, aged 65.

Youngest person to swim the...
• **Tsugaru Channel (male):** Tariq Qazi (JPN/USA, b. 9 Nov 2005) was aged 16 years 253 days when he swam between the Japanese islands of Honshū and Hokkaidō on 20 Jul 2022. The crossing of the Sea of Japan took 11 hr 20 min 17 sec.
• **North Channel (female):** Australia's Fiona Cullinane (b. 9 Jan 2002) was 20 years 253 days old when she traversed from Northern Ireland to Scotland, UK, on 19 Sep 2022.

Farthest swim in handcuffs
Shehab Allam (EGY) swam 11.64 km (7.23 mi) while manacled in the Arabian Gulf off Dubai, UAE, on 5 Nov 2022. He smashed the previous record by 3 km (1.8 mi). In 2020, this swimming instructor and former monofin world champion became the first person to swim the 25-km (16-mi) Dubai Canal.

Fastest swim around Grand Cayman
On 17 May 2022, endurance swimmer Oliver Rush (UK) completed a 36-hr 59-min odyssey around the Caribbean island of Grand Cayman. He set out on the pioneering circumnavigation – a distance of 95.5 km (59.3 mi) – to raise awareness about plastic pollution in the ocean.

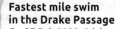

Fastest mile swim in the Drake Passage
On 27 Feb 2022, Bárbara Hernández Huerta (CHL) traversed 1 mi (1.6 km) of the wild stretch of ocean at the southern tip of South America in just 15 min 3 sec. The "Ice Mermaid", as she is known, made further headlines on 5 Feb 2023 when she covered 2.5 km (1.55 mi) in the waters off the subantarctic South Shetland Islands (*inset, Huerta meets some local gentoo penguins*). This was the **longest polar swim** in history, conducted in 2.23°C (36°F) water. Huerta was supported by the Chilean Navy and the feat was ratified by the IISA (*see opposite*).

TAKE ONE PHOTO A DAY FOR A YEAR
Compile a visual scrapbook of your life over 365 days, and perhaps share it on your Insta profile? The **first photo uploaded to Instagram** was taken by the company's co-founder Kevin Systrom (USA) and shared on 16 Jul 2010. It was a snap of a mystery golden retriever.

ICE SWIMMING

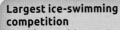

Largest ice-swimming competition

The fifth World Ice Swimming Championship took place in Samoëns, France, on 11–15 Jan 2023, with 467 swimmers from 41 different countries. The event is overseen by the International Ice Swimming Association (IISA), founded by open-water swimmer Ram Barkai (*left, and see below*). More than 20 world records (*see table*) were broken in milder-than-usual conditions at Samoëns – though the water was still a brisk 3.7°C (38.7°F)!

Farthest swim under ice on one breath (no fins, no diving suit)

On 5 Mar 2022, Amber Fillary (ZAF) swam 90 m (295 ft) in Kongsberg, Viken, Norway. This beat her own record by 20 m (65 ft). "The problem with setting records," Fillary mused, "is that you always want to push yourself further to see if you have what it takes to do more."

Most southerly ice swim

Male: Ram Barkai (ZAF, b. ISR) swam 1 km (0.6 mi) in Long Lake, Queen Maud Land, Antarctica, at a latitude of 70.76° S on 7 Feb 2008.

Female: Catherine Pendleton (UK) swam 1.6 km (1 mi) at 66.6° S in Hanusse Bay, off Graham Land, Antarctica, on 22 Feb 2020.

First man to complete the Ice Sevens Challenge

The "Ice 7s" are a septet of non-wetsuit mile-long swims in sub-5°C (41°F) water – one each in Europe, Oceania, Asia, Africa, North and South America, and a polar location. Ger Kennedy (IRL) completed the full set on 4 Oct 2019, ticking off his final ice mile in Laguna del Inca, Chile, in 36 min 55 sec. *For the **first person to swim the Ice 7s**, see the next page.*

ICE-SWIMMING RECORDS SHATTERED IN SAMOËNS

Fastest...	Time	Name & Nationality
1 km (male)	11 min 31.53 sec	Marcin Szarpak (POL)
1 km (female)	12 min 46.04 sec	Alisa Fatum (DEU)
1 km para (female)	16 min 45.12 sec	Nadja Joy Tønnesen (DNK)
500 m (male)	5 min 36.49 sec	Radostin Krastev (BGR)
500 m (female)	6 min 10.87 sec	Alisa Fatum
500 m para (male)	10 min 21.02 sec	Marc Boutin (FRA)
250 m (male)	2 min 36.99 sec	Marcin Szarpak
250 m para (female)	4 min 8.71 sec	Tina Deeken (DEU)
100 m freestyle (male)	55.69 sec	Keaton Jones (USA)
100 m freestyle (female)	1 min 4.42 sec	Ludivine Blanc (FRA)
100 m freestyle para (male)	1 min 29.51 sec	Marc Boutin
100 m freestyle para (female)	1 min 26.92 sec	Tina Deeken
100 m backstroke (male)	1 min 0.27 sec	Keaton Jones
100 m backstroke (female)	1 min 12.71 sec	Maja Olszewska (ISL)
100 m breaststroke (male)	1 min 11.33 sec	Michał Perl (POL)
100 m butterfly (male)	59.36 sec	Keaton Jones
100 m butterfly (female)	1 min 12.36 sec	Louise Bernard (FRA)
100 m individual medley (male)	1 min 3.55 sec	Sławomir Wilkowski (POL)
100 m individual medley (female)	1 min 15.38 sec	Marta Piasecka (ISL)
50 m freestyle (male)	25.22 sec	Keaton Jones
50 m freestyle (female)	28.85 sec	Ludivine Blanc
50 m freestyle para (female)	39.68 sec	Tina Deeken
50 m backstroke (male)	27.93 sec	Keaton Jones
50 m backstroke (female)	33.19 sec	Ludivine Blanc
50 m breaststroke (male)	31.83 sec	Michał Perl

*All records ratified by the IISA

Marcin Szarpak

Alisa Fatum

Keaton Jones

Tina Deeken

Farthest swim under ice on one breath (no fins, no diving suit, male)

David Vencl (CZE) swam 80.99 m (265 ft 8 in) beneath the frozen surface of a lake in a disused quarry in Lahošť, Czechia, on 23 Feb 2021. He spent around a minute and a half in the 3°C (37.4°F) water. Vencl had prepared for his attempt with regular winter lake swims; he practised holding his breath by fully submerging himself in a barrel of salt water on his balcony.

GRAND SLAMS

SEVEN SUMMITS

Climbers who wish to stand atop the highest mountain on each continent have a choice, depending on whether or not Australia is defined as a continent. The Bass list sends climbers to Kosciuszko in Australia, while those following the Messner list must scale Puncak Jaya on the Indonesian side of New Guinea.

1: ASIA: Everest
8,848.8 m (29,031 ft)

2: SOUTH AMERICA: Aconcagua
6,962 m (22,841 ft)

3: NORTH AMERICA: Denali (aka Mount McKinley)
6,194 m (20,321 ft)

4: AFRICA: Kilimanjaro
5,895 m (19,340 ft)

5: EUROPE: Elbrus
5,642 m (18,510 ft)

6: ANTARCTICA: Vinson Massif
4,892 m (16,049 ft)

=7: OCEANIA: Puncak Jaya (aka Carstensz Pyramid)
4,884 m (16,023 ft)

=7: AUSTRALIA: Kosciuszko
2,228 m (7,310 ft)

The two lists are named for the climbers who came up with them: Richard Bass (*see right*) and Reinhold Messner.

Youngest person to climb the Seven Volcanic Summits
Kuwaiti mountaineer Yousef Al Refaie (b. 25 Aug 1997) climbed the highest volcanic peak on each continent by topping out Antarctica's Mount Sidley on 22 Dec 2021, at the age of 24 years 119 days. He had started out six years earlier, on 30 Dec 2015, when he summitted Kilimanjaro in Tanzania.

Fastest Three Poles Challenge by a woman
Cecilie Skog (NOR) reached the three extreme points of Earth – Everest, the North Pole and the South Pole – in 1 year 336 days. She summitted Everest on 23 May 2004, arrived at the South Pole on 27 Dec 2005 and reached the North Pole on 24 Apr 2006 with Rolf Bae and Per Henry Borch. Her trip was the **fastest unsupported ski expedition to the North Pole by a woman** – 48 days 22 hr.

First person to climb the Seven Summits
On 30 Apr 1985, after two failed attempts, Richard Bass (CAN; *see left*) reached the summit of Everest to complete a globe-spanning adventure that had started two years earlier.
On 5 Aug the following year, Patrick Morrow (CAN) topped Puncak Jaya to become the **first person to climb the Messner Seven Summits**.

Youngest person to climb the Seven Summits and Seven Volcanic Summits
Satyarup Siddhanta (IND, b. 29 Apr 1983) completed this tough double-header aged 35 years 261 days. His last ascent was the 4,285-m (14,058-ft) Mount Sidley in Antarctica on 15 Jan 2019.

First person to complete the Adventurers' Grand Slam
David Hempleman-Adams (UK) was the first explorer to climb the Seven Summits and trek to the North and South poles. He began his quest in 1980 with Denali in Alaska, USA, and completed it 18 years later when, accompanied by Rune Gjeldnes, he arrived at the North Pole in 1998.

First person to complete the Ice Sevens Challenge
On 2 Jul 2017, ultramarathon and ice swimmer Jaimie Monahan (USA) swam for a mile in the Beagle Channel, near Ushuaia, Argentina, braving 4.7°C (40.5°F) waters. This completed a bone-chilling aquatic world tour that also saw her swim ice miles on five continents and in the Arctic Circle.

First woman to complete the...
• **Seven Summits**: Junko Tabei (JPN), by climbing Elbrus (5,642 m; 18,510 ft) on 28 Jul 1992. On 16 May 1975, she became the **first woman to ascend Everest**, despite an avalanche that knocked her unconscious for several minutes.
• **Three Poles Challenge**: Tina Sjögren (SWE) on 29 May 2002, by reaching the North Pole. The **first person** to achieve this feat was Erling Kagge (NOR), on 8 May 1994.
• **Peak to Pond Challenge**: Anna Brown (AND), by swimming the English Channel on 16 Sep 2021. The "peak" to that "pond" was Everest, which she climbed on 22 May 2018.

Fastest time to complete the Original Triple Crown
Martyn Webster (UK) swam across three major UK waterways in a cumulative time of 31 hr 57 min 30 sec. He traversed the North Channel (Northern Ireland–Scotland) on 13 Aug 2019, the English Channel (UK–France) on 16 Sep 2021 and the Bristol Channel (Devon–South Wales) on 19 Sep 2022.
The **fastest woman** to complete this feat is Siân Clement (UK), who finished the last leg (North Channel) on 10 Jul 2022. Her total time for all three swims was 39 hr 34 min 32 sec, despite choosing a path across the Bristol Channel that was 9 mi (14.4 km) longer than required.
The **oldest** is Pat Gallant-Charette (USA, b. 2 Feb 1951), who was aged 71 years 229 days when she swam the Bristol Channel on 19 Sep 2022.

Fastest ascent of the 8,000ers
Starting on 23 Apr 2019, adventurer Nirmal "Nims" Purja (UK, b. NPL) climbed all 14 mountains over 8,000 m (26,246 ft), finishing the slam in just 2 years 168 days (*see p.118*).
Nims's record breaking continues apace. On 15–16 May 2022, he logged the **fastest climb of Everest and Lhotse***, taking just 25 hr 1 min. He had earlier climbed Kangchenjunga (7 May), which meant that he also recorded the **fastest triple-header*** (9 days) and the **fastest to climb the higher 8,000ers twice** (4 years 345 days, starting with Everest on 27 May 2017). Additionally, his ascent of K2 on 22 Jul made him the **fastest to climb the three highest mountains***, achieved in just 76 days.
Without the use of bottled oxygen.

In 2022, Nims also recorded the **fastest time to climb Everest and Lhotse twice** (13 days 50 min); the first two ascents were without extra oxygen.

GO TO A MASQUERADE BALL
Dress to impress in a dazzling costume, concealing your true identity with a cunning disguise! When it comes to fancy-dress balls, Gerold Weschenmoser (DEU) is especially well prepared. He owns the **largest mask collection**, having taken over 60 years to amass, at the last count, 5,600 unique pieces.

FIRST WOMAN TO COMPLETE THE EXPLORERS' EXTREME TRIFECTA

Adventurers attempting this unique trio of feats must visit Earth's highest and deepest extremes and enter space. Vanessa O'Brien (UK/USA) topped Everest on 19 May 2012 and dived to the Challenger Deep on 12 Jun 2020 – making her the **first woman to reach Earth's highest and lowest points**. She then made a sub-orbital spaceflight on the sixth crewed flight (NS-22) of the Blue Origin New Shepard rocket on 4 Aug 2022. It took her 10 years 77 days to complete the trifecta.

O'Brien visited the Challenger Deep with US explorer Victor Vescovo in the submersible DSV *Limiting Factor* (*see pp.116–17*). On 4 Jun 2022, Vescovo became the **first person to complete the Explorers' Extreme Trifecta**, as part of Blue Origin's NS-21 mission.

On 4 Aug 2022, O'Brien joined five other adventurers on Blue Origin's NS-22 mission. At an altitude of 100 km (62 mi), they crossed the Kármán Line that marks the edge of the atmosphere, entering space and experiencing weightlessness. Not that they had long to enjoy it: after a duration of only 10 min 20 sec, they were back on Earth.

O'Brien was formerly a banker, but when the 2008 economic crisis hit, she underwent a fundamental reassessment of her priorities. A friend joked about her trying to climb Everest and O'Brien seized on it. Having summitted in 2012, she decided to attempt Denali. By the following year, she'd completed the Explorers' Grand Slam (Last Degree), having climbed all Seven Summits and visited both the North and South poles in 11 months.

CIRCUMNAVIGATIONS

First circumnavigation
Navigator Juan Sebastián de Elcano (ESP, "Elkano" in Basque) was a member of Ferdinand Magellan's 1519 expedition to sail around the world. Only 18 of the 237 original crew survived the journey; Magellan himself died. It was Elcano who guided his vessel *Victoria* back to Seville, Spain, on 8 Sep 1522.

Elcano's first round-the-world voyage took 1,082 days; the *International Space Station* orbits Earth every 90 min!

First circumnavigation (female)
Botanist Jeanne Baret (FRA) disguised herself as a man in order to travel with Louis Antoine de Bougainville's round-the-world expedition of 1766–69. A genus of Madagascan plant was named *Baretia* in Jeanne's honour, though it has since been renamed *Turraea*.

First circumnavigation by...
- **Aircraft**: US Army lieutenants Lowell Smith, Leslie Arnold, Erik Nelson and John Harding, flying the *Chicago* and *New Orleans* seaplanes, between 6 Apr and 28 Sep 1924.
- **Car**: racing driver Clärenore Stinnes (DEU) and Carl-Axel Söderström (SWE), from 25 May 1927 to 24 Jun 1929.
- **Walking**: David Kunst (USA), from 20 Jun 1970 to 5 Oct 1974.
- **Helicopter**: Ross Perot Jr and Jay Coburn (both USA), on 1–30 Sep 1982 in a Bell 206L-1 LongRanger II.

Fastest circumnavigation by tandem bicycle (mixed)
On 5 Jun 2022, Laura Massey-Pugh and Steven Pugh (both UK) arrived in Berlin, Germany, having cycled around the world in 179 days 12 hr 25 min. The married couple overcame illness, blizzards, border problems and a road-traffic accident to complete the epic journey *just* within their 180-day target.

Fastest circumnavigation by scheduled flights
On 8–9 Aug 2022, Umit Sabanci (UK) flew around the world in 46 hr 23 min 11 sec using public flights. He spent a month studying airline timetables before his Los Angeles-Doha-Brisbane-Los Angeles trek.

First circumnavigation by aircraft without refuelling
Between 14 and 23 Dec 1986, Dick Rutan and Jeana Yeager (both USA) flew 40,212 km (24,986 mi) around the world without landing or taking on fuel. Their lightweight aircraft, *Voyager*, was designed by Dick's brother, engineer Burt Rutan. Dick and Jeana spent 9 days 3 min 44 sec in the air, despite damaging the wings on take-off from Edwards Air Force Base in California, USA.

First circumnavigation by amphibious car
On 19 Jul 1950, Ben Carlin (AUS) and his wife Elinore set out from Halifax, Nova Scotia, Canada, on an eight-year adventure to drive around the world in a modified Ford GPA amphibious jeep called *Half-Safe*. An exasperated Elinore left the journey on arrival in India, but he continued on with a series of new crewmates. He made it back to Halifax on 8 May 1958, having navigated 62,765 km (39,000 mi) over land and 15,450 km (9,600 mi) by sea and river.

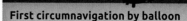

First circumnavigation by balloon
On 21 Mar 1999, the *Breitling Orbiter 3* touched down in the Egyptian desert after an epic 19-day 21-hr flight around the world. The balloon, piloted by aeronauts Bertrand Piccard (CHE, *inset right*) and Brian Jones (UK), had taken off from Château d'Oex in Switzerland and covered a total distance of 40,814 km (25,361 mi).

First solo voyage around the world by a double amputee (arm and leg)
Dustin Reynolds (USA), aka the "Single-handed Sailor", traversed the globe between 18 Jun 2014 and 4 Dec 2021, starting and ending in his home state of Hawaii, USA. Dustin, who had his left arm and leg amputated in 2008 after a road-traffic accident, was inspired to take on the maritime challenge despite having no ocean-sailing experience. He set out in a sloop named *Rudis*, which he exchanged in Thailand for a Bristol 35.5 sailboat called *Tiama*.

Fastest circumnavigation by car
The record for the **first and fastest man and woman to have circumnavigated the Earth by car** covering six continents under the rules applicable in 1989 and 1991 embracing more than an equator's length of driving (24,901 road miles; 40,075 km), is held by Saloo Choudhury and his wife Neena Choudhury (both IND). The journey took 69 days 19 hours 5 minutes from 9 September to 17 November 1989. The couple drove a 1989 Hindustan "Contessa Classic" starting and finishing in Delhi, India.

53

DANCE IN THE RAIN
When the heavens open, it's time to get your dancing shoes on. A fitting venue for your drenched disco might be the famously wet town of Cherrapunji in Meghalaya, India. It is here that a weather station recorded the **greatest monthly rainfall** – a total of 9,300 mm (366 in)!

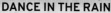

YOUNGEST PERSON TO CIRCUMNAVIGATE BY AIRCRAFT SOLO

Mack Rutherford (BEL, b. 21 Jun 2005) was aged 17 years 64 days when he completed his lone microlight flight around the world on 24 Aug 2022. The teen aeronaut – and younger brother of Zara (*see left*) – began his journey on 23 Mar 2022 in Sofia, Bulgaria. He flew over 52 countries and five continents, crossing the equator twice. Despite facing sandstorms in Sudan and monsoon rains in India, Mack said that his toughest moment was landing on an uninhabited Pacific island during an 11-hr flight between Japan and the USA.

Youngest person to circumnavigate by aircraft solo (female)

On 20 Jan 2022, Zara Rutherford (BEL, b. 5 Jul 2002) completed a 32,000-mi (51,500-km) airborne odyssey aged 19 years 199 days. Her journey, which started on 18 Aug 2021 at Kortrijk-Wevelgem airport in Belgium, was beset by weather delays, grounding Zara's microlight in Russia and Alaska, USA. She endured air temperatures of -20°C (-4°F) in Siberia, flew through wildfire smoke in California and experienced an earthquake in Mexico.

Mack gained his microlight pilot's licence aged 15, having already flown hundreds of hours with his father, a pilot.

ENJOY A NIGHT-TIME FIRE ON THE BEACH

There's no need to build your own pyre: just visit the Dutch seaside resort of Scheveningen. On New Year's Eve, a bumper bonfire is built on the beach; in 2015, they lit the **largest bonfire**, measuring 8,695 m³ (307,061 cu ft).

ECO TRAVEL

Longest-duration human-powered flight
Kanellos Kanellopoulos (GRC) used pedal power to keep his *Daedalus 88* aircraft aloft for 3 hr 54 min 59 sec on 23 Apr 1988. He flew the 115.11 km (71.52 mi) between Heraklion in Crete and the Greek island of Santorini, which was also the **farthest human-powered flight**.

On 3 Jul 2015, André Borschberg and Bertrand Piccard (both CHE) found a slightly less strenuous way to make fuelless-flight history: they piloted *Solar Impulse 2* for 4 days 21 hr 52 min from Japan to Hawaii, USA – the **longest solar-powered flight**.

Fastest human-powered speed on water
Pedalling the hydrofoil *Decavitator*, Mark Drela (USA) attained a speed of 18.5 knots (34.26 km/h; 21.28 mph) over a 100-m (328-ft) course on 27 Oct 1991. The foot-powered feat took place on the Charles River in Boston, Massachusetts, USA.

Highest altitude in an electric car
On 18 May 2022, Rainer Zietlow (DEU) drove a Volkswagen ID.4 GTX to 5,816 m (19,081 ft) above sea level on the Uturuncu volcano at Quetena Chico, Bolivia. He was supported by LG Energy Solution (KOR). In 2021, with Derek Collins (USA), he'd driven the **longest journey by electric vehicle (non-solar) in a single country** – 57,566.29 km (35,770.03 mi) in the USA – supported by Infineon (USA).

LONGEST JOURNEY BY ELECTRIC SKATEBOARD
Stefano Rotella (ITA, above) boarded 1,377.03 km (855.64 mi) between 10 Aug and 27 Aug 2021. He travelled from Trento in Italy to Budapest in Hungary, with seven swappable battery packs to power his board.

The women's record is 1,210 km (751.8 mi), by Stefanie Hasbauer (DEU, below). Stefanie started in Porto, Portugal, and finished in Seville, Spain, on 30 Jan 2020. Her eventful trip began with her board being stolen (it was soon recovered) and she had 10 flat tyres along the way!

Longest journey by electric bicycle in one week
Gordon Miller (UK) rode 1,706.85 km (1,060.58 mi) through Spain – from Cádiz in the south to Mallabia in the north – in seven days, finishing on 8 Oct 2021. He completed the journey on an Orbea Gain eBike. The route of his "Ride for Freedom" was chosen to highlight a documented human trafficking route.

Farthest flight by a paraglider
On 20 Jun 2021, Sebastien Kayrouz (USA) paraglided for 609.9 km (378.9 mi) using an Ozone Enzo 3 in Texas, USA.

A distance of 552.4 km (343.2 mi) won the **women's** record for Yael Margelisch (CHE) near Caicó, in Brazil, on 12 Oct 2019.

Longest journey by...
Solar-powered boat
On 27 Sep 2010, the *MS TÛRANOR* set out from Monaco on what was to be the **first solar-powered circumnavigation**. The crew, led by Raphaël Domjan (CHE), did not return to their home port until 4 May 2012, after 1 year 220 days at sea. The following year, between 26 Apr and 18 May, the *TÛRANOR* made the **fastest solar-powered crossing of the Atlantic**.

Wind-powered car
Dirk Gion and Stefan Simmerer (both DEU) travelled 5,000 km (3,106 mi) in their vehicle *Wind Explorer*, departing from Albany, Western Australia, on 26 Jan 2011 and arriving in Sydney, New South Wales, 18 days later. The car's wind turbine charged a lithium-ion battery pack to provide propulsion, and was augmented by a kite resembling a parasail.

Wave-powered boat
From 16 Mar to 4 Jul 2008, Kenichi Horie (JPN, b. 8 Sep 1938) undertook a 110-day voyage from Honolulu, Hawaii, USA, to Cape Hinomisaki, Japan. He travelled 3,702 nautical mi (6,856 km; 4,260 mi) in his catamaran *Suntory Mermaid II*, which generated propulsion via wave movements.

On 26 Mar 2022, the veteran adventurer left San Francisco, California, USA, in the monohull yacht *Suntory Mermaid III*. His latest adventure was a recreation of the journey he made in the original 2.8-m (9-ft 2-in) *Mermaid* back in 1989, which remains the **smallest boat to cross the Pacific**. He arrived at Cape Hinomisaki on 4 Jun 2022, becoming the **oldest person to sail the Pacific solo** at 83 years 269 days.

Fastest land yacht
Horonuku, piloted by Glenn Ashby (AUS), clocked 222.4 km/h (138.2 mph) at Lake Gairdner, South Australia, on 12 Dec 2022. The wind-powered vehicle was built by Emirates Team New Zealand using technology developed for their America's Cup-winning yacht (*see p.229*). *Horonuku* is a Maori word meaning "gliding swiftly across the land".

GO SNOWBOARDING
Glide, slide and flip over frozen expanses in a winter-sports wonderland, then retreat to a chair by the fire in a mountain chalet. That is unless you're like Bernhard Mair (AUT), who stayed out on the slopes for 180 hr 34 min – the **longest snowboarding marathon** – between 9 and 16 Jan 2004.

51

Jordan and Nicole created the 80-min documentary *Fly Monarca* from footage assembled on his journey.

LONGEST HIKE-AND-FLY JOURNEY BY PARAGLIDER

From 8 Apr to 4 Sep 2020, Benjamin Jordan (CAN) travelled 2,835 km (1,761 mi) across the USA between the Mexican and Canadian borders (*left*). His 150-day journey comprised 2,157 km (1,340 mi) via an unpowered paraglider and 678 km (421 mi) on foot. He carried his own food, shelter and supplies. Jordan's girlfriend, Lyndsay Nicole, documented most of the expedition.

Jordan's epic trek was inspired by the annual migration of the monarch butterfly (*Danaus plexippus*) between Canada and Mexico – the **longest journey by a butterfly**. Between Sep 1988 and Apr 1989, one tagged specimen flew a round-trip distance of at least 4,635 km (2,880 mi), an achievement that also represents the **longest insect migration**.

FINISH

CANADA

NOXVILLE, MT

MISSOULA, MT

NORTH FORK, ID

MONTANA

IDAHO

Pacific Coast Trail

Great Divide Trail

ARCO, ID

SALT LAKE CITY, UT

UTAH

ZION NATIONAL PARK, UT

FLAGSTAFF, AZ

ARIZONA

JORDAN'S ROUTE

FLYING 2157 KM

WALKING 678 KM

TOMBSTONE, AZ

START

SLACKLINING

INTERNATIONAL SLACKLINE ASSOCIATION

The International Slackline Association (ISA) aims to support and develop slackline communities of all sizes, including the urban-alpine activity as well as competitive sports. The ISA is devoted to increasing safety in all forms of slacklining through education and risk management. All records in this section have been approved by the ISA and were performed using a safety harness, unless stated otherwise.

In 2022, Switzerland became the first country to recognize slacklining as an official sport.

Multitasking slackliners
Some funambulists like to combine their performing skills. On 16 Apr 2022, Edgar Yudkevich (USA) covered the greatest distance on a slackline while juggling **three knives*** – 10.47 m (34 ft 4 in) – in Coronado, California, USA. The equivalent **three clubs** record is 45 m (148 ft), by Tijmen Van Dieren (NLD) in Almere, Netherlands.

Longest free solo highline (female)
On 7 Jul 2022, Lucia Bryn (USA) soloed 33 m (108 ft) without a safety harness on the Sierra Point highline in Yosemite National Park in California, USA. The line was 80 m (262 ft) above the ground. The previous women's free solo record of 25 m (82 ft), by Faith Dickey, had stood since 2012.

Longest longline without a harness
Lucas Giovanni Moreira (FRA) and Raphael Bacot (CHE) completed a 713-m (2,339-ft) walk along a slackline rigged across a field outside Lausanne, Switzerland, on 13 and 15 Nov 2021.

The **women's** record is 305 m (1,000 ft), by Annalisa Casiraghi (ITA) on 17 Aug 2019. Her longline was set up in a field in Schüpberg near Bern, Switzerland.

Highest free solo highline
Niklas Winter (DEU) crossed a 15-m-long (49-ft) highline tethered between two hot-air balloons flying at 1,400 m (4,590 ft) on 5 May 2017. He did not wear a safety harness and parachuted down from the line at the end. The daredevil feat occurred above Barcelona, Spain.

The **highest slackline walk** took place between two hot-air balloons at 1,901 m (6,236 ft) above Santa Catarina, Brazil. It was performed by Rafael Zugno Bridi (BRA) using a safety harness on 2 Dec 2021.

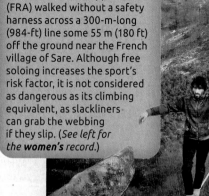

Longest free solo highline
On 6 Jan 2021, Philippe Soubies (FRA) walked without a safety harness across a 300-m-long (984-ft) line some 55 m (180 ft) off the ground near the French village of Sare. Although free soloing increases the sport's risk factor, it is not considered as dangerous as its climbing equivalent, as slackliners can grab the webbing if they slip. (*See left for the women's record.*)

Longest distance travelled on a slackline by unicycle
Circus artist Guillaume Fontaine (CAN) cycled 50 m (164 ft) along a line in Table Rock, New Hampshire, USA, on 30 Oct 2018. The line was 70 m (229 ft) long in total.

The **bicycle*** record is 10.05 m (32 ft 11 in), by Vittorio Brumotti (ITA) at Parco Leonardo in Rome, Italy, on 11 May 2014.

Longest slackline walk over an active volcano
The "LavaLine" team of Rafael Zugno Bridi and Alexander Schulz (DEU) battled acid rain, red-hot lava fountains and toxic fumes to walk 261 m (856 ft) over Mount Yasur on Tanna Island in Vanuatu on 15 Apr 2020. The line was 42 m (137 ft) above the volcano crater.

Longest slackline walk blindfolded
On 30 Dec 2021, Alexander Schulz walked 1,712 m (5,616 ft) with his eyes covered along a line over Cañón del Sumidero in Chiapas, Mexico. The slackline was positioned at a height of 800 m (2,624 ft).

First triple buttflip on a slackline
Gymnast Louis Boniface (FRA) performed a triple flip on a slackline – completing three rotations in a single jump from a seated position – on 28 Apr 2017. He followed that up with the **first triple butt backflip on a slackline**, on 8 Oct 2018 in Saint-Lambert, Yvelines, France.

*not ratified by the ISA

DID YOU KNOW?
A slackline is a synthetic fabric strap strung between two anchor points.

Modern slacklining originated with a group of American climbers in the early 1980s.

Styles include highlining, longlining, waterlining and slackline yoga.

Slackliner Andy Lewis performed with Madonna at the 2012 Super Bowl.

Longest slackline walk
On 3 Aug 2022, an eight-strong troupe of surefooted slackliners made an epic 2,710-m (8,891-ft) crossing along a line rigged between the Puy de l'Angle and Roc de Cuzeau peaks near Mont-Dore in France. The team consisted of Julien Roux, Augustin Moinat, Arthur Lefebvre, Benoît Brume, Joseph Premoselli, Tania Monier (all FRA), Mattis Reisner (DEU) and Mia Noblet (CAN).

50

SEE THE TAJ MAHAL
The marble mausoleum in Agra, Uttar Pradesh, India, was built on the orders of Mughal emperor Shah Jahan to house the tomb of his favourite wife, Mumtaz Mahal. It is the **most searched-for UNESCO World Heritage Site**, racking up 1.4 million online inquiries in Mar 2022 alone.

HIGHEST-ELEVATION HIGHLINE

On 7 Jul 2022, Federico Cantú, Alejo Roldan (both ARG) and Quirin Herterich (DEU) crossed a highline at an altitude of 5,882 m (19,298 ft) in the Central Andes in Argentina. The 24-m-long (79-ft) highline was 64 m (210 ft) above the ground. The drop in air pressure at such high altitudes makes it harder to ward off dizziness and maintain balance.

The **women's** record is held by Miriam Campoleoni (ITA, *inset*), who walked a highline at an altitude of 5,150 m (16,896 ft) over a frozen glacier on the Bolivian mountain of Chachacomani on 31 Aug 2021.

On 10 Oct 2021, Quirin Herterich made the **longest slackline walk between hot-air balloons** – 88 m (288 ft).

Deepest highline walk

On 13 Aug 2022, Gaël Fauroux (FRA, *above*) ventured across a highline rigged 1,038 m (3,405 ft) below ground in the Gouffre Berger cave near Grenoble, France. Fauroux traversed the full 75-m-long (246-ft) distance over a maximum height of 20 m (66 ft). It took a team of cavers (*inset*) four expeditions to rig the line.

ROUND-UP

Most joint climbs of Everest by twins
Brothers Mingma Tenje Sherpa and Mingma Dorchi Sherpa (both NPL) have climbed Everest (aka Sagarmāthā) together three times: on 19 May 2013, 19 May 2017 and most recently on 7 May 2021.

Fastest time to climb K2 then Everest
Sona Sherpa (NPL) made a winter ascent of K2 on 16 Jan 2021 followed by a summit of Everest on 11 May – a gap of just 115 days. The climbing season on K2 (Jun–Aug) starts later than it does on Everest (May), so to scale both mountains in this order, and in record time, necessitates a winter ascent of K2 – one of the most perilous challenges in alpinism.

Oldest woman to climb Everest and K2
Liliya Ianovskaia (CAN, b. BLR, 6 Aug 1959) reached the top of K2 on 22 Jul 2022 at the age of 62 years 350 days – also making her the **oldest woman to climb K2**. She had already summitted Everest two months earlier, on 14 May.

Oldest person to paddle the Mississippi River
"Greybeard Adventurer" Dale Sanders (USA, b. 14 Jun 1935) was aged 87 years 86 days after canoeing the USA's second-longest river from Minnesota to Louisiana, USA, on 8 Sep 2022. The Mississippi flows c. 3,770 km (2,340 mi) from Lake Itasca, around 200 km (124 mi) from the Canadian border, to the Gulf of Mexico.

Longest barefoot journey
From 8 May to 17 Oct 2021, Antonius Nootenboom (NLD) walked *sans* shoes for 3,019 km (1,875.9 mi) along Australia's east coast. The *sole*less hike raised funds and awareness for men's mental health.

Deepest scuba dive by a woman
On 27 Oct 2022, Karen Van Den Oever (ZAF) plunged 246.56 m (808 ft 11 in) into Boesmansgat Cave, a flooded sinkhole in Northern Cape, South Africa. It took just 15 min to descend but nearly 8 hr to ascend, to avoid decompression sickness.

Longest journey by pumpkin boat
Duane Hansen (USA) paddled 60.35 km (37.5 mi) up the Missouri River in a hollow gourd, as confirmed in Nebraska City, USA, on 27 Aug 2022. He'd grown the 846-lb (384-kg) pumpkin – dubbed the SS *Berta* – himself.

Oldest woman to cross the USA by bicycle (north to south)
Lynnea Salvo (USA, b. 21 Sep 1949) was 72 years 27 days old when she completed her transamerican journey in San Ysidro, California, on 18 Oct 2021. Despite arduous climbs and a wildfire that forced a route change, she relished the ride: "I loved facing and overcoming the challenges – heat, hill, headwinds, cold, rain."

Salvo had already set the same record **west to east**, riding from California to Delaware, aged 67 years 32 days on 23 Oct 2016.

On 19–30 Oct 2022, the septuagenarian cycled for 1,029.6 km (639.8 mi) in the shape of a peace symbol – the **largest GPS drawing by bicycle (individual)** – in Kansas, USA.

Potgieter embraced bungee jumping, along with skydiving, as a way of boosting her self-confidence.

Fastest high-altitude mile run (LA4)
It took Andrea Lanfri (ITA) just 9 min 48 sec to dash 1 mi (1.6 km) at Everest Base Camp in Nepal, on 1 Apr 2022. He ran at an altitude of 5,380 m (17,650 ft), where there is around 50% less oxygen than at sea level. A month later, the double-amputee athlete and explorer went on to summit the **highest mountain**.

Most outdoor bungee jumps in one hour (20-m cord)
On 15 Aug 2022, Linda Potgieter (ZAF) leapt fearlessly 23 times from Bloukrans Bridge in Western Cape, South Africa. This is the country's highest bridge, standing 216 m (708 ft) above Bloukrans River. She averaged one jump every 2 min 30 sec. The previous record – 19 jumps – had stood for over 19 years, until Potgieter took this challenge on as part of the *Stumbo Record Breakers* TV series.

Longest para ice swim (LA2)
Jonty Warneken (UK) swam 2.11 km (1.31 mi) in Lake Ellerton, North Yorkshire, UK, on 19 Jan 2014. The swim – performed in sub-5°C (41°F) water – lasted for 58 min 54 sec. Warneken underwent a below-knee amputation of his left leg following a car accident and also has osteoarthritis in his right ankle. (*For more ice-swimming records, see p.123.*)

DRIVE ROUTE 66
Running from Chicago to Santa Monica, this highway embodies America's love of the open road. Make time to see *Cadillac Ranch* in Amarillo, Texas – an artwork comprising 10 of the iconic US automobiles, buried nose-down in the ground. The **most Cadillac cars in a sculpture**, it was completed in 1974.

Longest solo unsupported one-way polar ski journey

British Army physio Preet Chandi skied 1,484.53 km (922.44 mi) across Antarctica from the Hercules Inlet to the Reedy Glacier between 13 Nov 2022 and 23 Jan 2023. "Polar Preet" had aimed to become the first woman to cross the continent coast to coast, but bad weather forced her to end slightly inland.

Fastest time to cycle the length of Japan (female)
Anna Endo (JPN) rode from Cape Sata, Kyūshū, to Cape Sōya, Hokkaidō, in 7 days 12 hr 18 min, between 22 and 29 Aug 2022.

The **male** record is 5 days 16 hr 30 min, by Yusuke Ochiai (JPN) from 15 to 20 Oct 2021.

Fastest completion of all trails on Mount Fuji
Battling heavy rain, Ruy Ueda (JPN) ran up all four paths that lead to the top of Japan's best-known peak in 9 hr 55 min 41 sec on 13 Jul 2022.

Most ski expeditions to the South Pole
Polar guide Devon McDiamid (CAN) reached the South Pole from the Antarctic coast for a sixth time on 9 Jan 2023, almost exactly 20 years after his first journey. This equals a record set by Hannah McKeand (UK) between 2004 and 2013. McDiarmid was travelling with the "Inspire 22" medical research expedition.

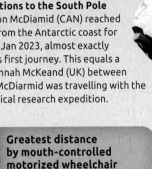

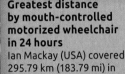

Greatest distance by mouth-controlled motorized wheelchair in 24 hours
Ian Mackay (USA) covered 295.79 km (183.79 mi) in his powered wheelchair in Portland, Oregon, USA, starting at 8 p.m. on 21 Jun 2022. A support team rode with him. "So often, as people with disabilities, we focus on what we can't do," Mackay said. "I have thrived by pushing that envelope and trying to see what else *is* possible."

Greatest distance by pocketbike in 24 hours
From 11 to 12 May 2021, Valerio Boni (ITA) rode a mini motorcycle for 751 km (466.6 mi) in Pavia, Italy. As well as wet road conditions, he had to cope with escalating knee pain – hardly surprising when your vehicle is just 30 cm (11 in) high! Exactly a year later, Boni covered 740.9 km (460.4 mi) in a day on a **motocross bike** to set another record in Bergamo, Italy.

Fastest time to cross all 10 Australian deserts on motorbike
On 8 Aug 2019, biker Benji Brundin (AUS) traversed the Tanami Desert in northern Australia – the last stop on a tour of his home nation's arid expanses. His charity trek took him 29 days 19 hr 38 min.

Fastest towed bicycle
On 22 May 2022, extreme cyclist Elias Schwärzler (AUT) hit 272.934 km/h (169.593 mph) while being pulled by a motorcycle. He rode on the Lausitzring track in Brandenburg, Germany. For a brief period, he was travelling almost as fast as a Porsche 911!

Greatest distance by trike in 12 hours (road)
Marshall Randall (USA) rode a three-wheeler for 334.34 km (207.75 mi) on 23 Sep 2022 in Michigan, USA. He maintained an average speed of 27.86 km/h (17.31 mph). Randall's day-long ride saw him notch up the **fastest 200 km** and **300 km** on a trike – 6 hr 47 min 43.3 sec and 10 hr 27 min 44.22 sec, respectively. All of these records were confirmed by the World Ultracycling Association.

Longest triathlon on ice
On 14 Mar 2022, Dirk Leonhardt (DEU) cycled, ran and skated for a cumulative 165.16 km (102.63 mi) on a frozen track at the Eissporthalle in Frankfurt, Germany.

Fastest row across the Black Sea (team)
Alex Dumbrava (ROM), Danny Longman, Gregg Botterman and Roland Burr (all UK) traversed the Black Sea in 9 days 18 hr 5 min between 11 and 20 Jun 2022. They travelled 1,200 km (745 mi) from Mangalia, Romania, to Batumi, Georgia, occasionally accompanied by curious dolphins or suspicious coastguards. The row raised funds for the International Committee of the Red Cross.

RIDE A CAMEL
Did you know that the **largest camel population in the wild** – numbering more than 1 million animals – lives not in Africa or Asia but Australia? These "ships of the desert" were once imported here for transport, but after motor vehicles replaced them, they were freed and thrived.

48

ELTON JOHN

O ver the course of a sparkling career that has spanned six decades, Elton John has secured his place in history as one of the most successful solo artists of all time. He has notched up 166 hits in the UK and US combined, sold more than 300 million records worldwide, and has nearly 4,000 concerts under his rhinestone-studded belt. It's hard to fathom the heights that this "Rocket Man" has reached.

The global megastar developed his love for music at a young age while learning to play his grandmother's piano. In his teens, he went on to form a band – Bluesology – in 1962. Though he parted ways with them five years on, he soon joined forces with lyricist Bernie Taupin, and theirs would prove to be one of the most indomitable partnerships in pop-music history. Indeed, "Candle in the Wind 1997", their tribute to Princess Diana, is the best-selling physical single since charts began, with 33 million sales worldwide.

Elton has racked up records from across the entertainment world thanks also to his movie and theatre scores. But just as noteworthy has been his philanthropic work. Founded in 1992, the Elton John AIDS Foundation – which has raised more than $565 m (£452 m) in the global fight against HIV/AIDS – was presented with the Global Impact prize at the 2020 British LGBT Awards.

His final gig was slated for summer 2023, but there's no sign of the "sun going down" on this pop legend. Indeed, in early 2023, it was confirmed that Elton's *Farewell Yellow Brick Road* had become the all-time highest-grossing music tour; between Sep 2018 and Jan 2023, it took over $818 m (£660 m).

VITAL STATISTICS

Name	Reginald Dwight (Elton Hercules John)
Birthplace	Pinner, Greater London, UK
Birth date	25 Mar 1947
Current GWR titles	Multiple, inc. best-selling physical single since charts began; best-selling single (UK); first album to debut at No.1 (USA)
Awards won	Ivor Novello:13
	Grammy:6
	BRIT:5
	Oscar:2
	Tony:1
No.1 chart singles	US:9
	UK:10
Billboard "Greatest of All Time Artists" rank	No.1 Solo Artist No.3 Overall

On 7 Jun 1975, Elton's *Captain Fantastic and the Brown Dirt Cowboy* became the first album to debut at No.1 on the Billboard 200.

With "Cold Heart (PNAU Remix)" reaching No.1 in 2021, Elton became the first solo artist to score a UK Top 10 hit single in six consecutive decades.

1: Elton began his musical journey by playing "The Skaters' Waltz" by ear at the age of three. Eight years later, he earned a junior scholarship to the Royal Academy of Music.

2: The Corvettes, later Bluesology, was set up in the early 1960s. His stage name is a tribute to two of his former bandmates: saxophonist Elton Dean and vocalist Long John Baldry.

3: Elton and David Furnish were among the first couples in the UK to enter into a civil partnership, in 2005. They married in 2014.

4: On 10 Nov 2021, the then-Prince Charles anointed Elton John a member of the Order of the Companions of Honour at Windsor Castle. He was knighted by the Queen in 1998 for his services to music and charities.

5: Taron Egerton played the lead role in the critically acclaimed 2019 biopic of Elton John's life, *Rocketman*. His performance earned him a Golden Globe.

6: Elton composed songs for Disney's *The Lion King* (USA, 1994), including now-classic hits such as "Circle of Life" and "Can You Feel the Love Tonight". He also worked on the music for the stage version, which has become the **highest-grossing musical theatre franchise,** having taken more than $9.1 bn (£7 bn) around the world to date.

As well as dressing in some of Elton's iconic outfits, Taron also had to learn to play piano for *Rocketman*.

Find out more about Elton John in the Hall of Fame section at www. guinnessworldrecords.com/2024

Largest wooden trebuchet

The fearsome Loup-de-Guerre – or "War Wolf" – siege engine was capable of launching a 120-kg (265-lb) projectile a distance of 200 m (655 ft). It has been estimated that the War Wolf was as tall as 90 m (295 ft) with its arm fully extended. The trebuchet was built in 1304 on the orders of King Edward I of England to end the siege of Stirling Castle, the last remaining stronghold of Scottish resistance to English rule.

You'll find more awe-inspiring creations and eye-opening facts throughout this section, as we open the annals to examine some of our favourite historical eras through GWR's superlative lens. From pyramids to pirates and phantasmagorical photographs, we're bringing the past to the present...

When released, the counterweight would drop, swinging this long wooden arm around and lofting the stone or metal ball, which was held in a leather-and-wood sling

Edward's army stripped the lead from the roofs of churches across central Scotland to add mass to this six-tonne counterweight

The winches that lifted the counterweight into position were powered by labourers walking inside these wheels

The garrison inside the castle reportedly tried to surrender the moment they saw War Wolf, but Edward insisted on demonstrating the weapon first!

Mystery Machine

No drawings of War Wolf survive, but a few key details about its capabilities and construction were noted in the records of Edward's army. This reconstruction was created by historical illustrator Bob Marshall in 2020, based on known medieval trebuchet designs.

TALLEST WOODEN PAGODA

ŚĀKYAMUNI PAGODA

One of China's most famous landmarks, the Śākyamuni Pagoda in Fogong Temple has stood strong for almost 1,000 years. It owes its survival – withstanding earthquakes, war and extreme weather – to the architectural secrets that lend surprising stability to its timber frame.

The Śākyamuni Pagoda was constructed in Shanxi Province in 1056, thought to be upon the orders of Emperor Daozong of Liao, on the site of his family home. Although the 67.31-m-tall (220-ft 10-in) Buddhist shrine has nine storeys, only five are visible from the exterior, with four mezzanine levels hidden from view. There are Buddhist statues on every main floor, with devotional artworks on the walls and ceiling, and sweeping views of the surrounding countryside through the windows. In China, it is known simply as *Muta* ("Timber Pagoda").

In the centuries since its construction, the pagoda has faced numerous structural challenges: it survived seven earthquakes in its first 50 years of existence alone, and came under direct gunfire during the Second Sino-Japanese War (1937–45). The secret to the shrine's longevity lies in its ingenious design and use of interlocking wooden brackets, known as *dougong*, to support the eaves and roof. It also owes a debt to the generations of local artisans who have mended damaged timbers; today, the shrine is maintained by the Pagoda Protection Institute.

The years of wear and tear have left their mark in one notable way, however – the building now slants slightly to one side, like the Leaning Tower of Pisa.

A feature of Chinese buildings since the Spring and Autumn period (770–476 BCE), *dougong* brackets are carved to lock together without nails or glue.

10-m-tall (32-ft) seven-piece finial cap

Glazed ceramic tiles

Main body made from 7,400 tonnes (8,150 tons) of larch

Hidden treasures
The Śākyamuni Buddha on the fourth level has a hollow space inside its torso that contains 160 relics. It is surrounded by the statues of eight *bodhisattvas* – attendants who have achieved spiritual enlightenment.

Central altar

Waico

Wooden columns

Stone veranda/platform

Each floor of the octagon-shaped pagoda is supported by 24 exterior and eight interior columns. These two series of columns create an outer aisle (*waicao*) running between them, while the shrine's statues are placed in the central area (*neicao*) inside the interior columns.

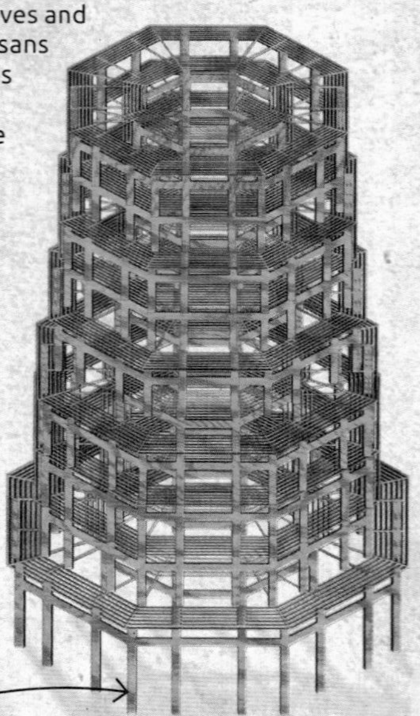

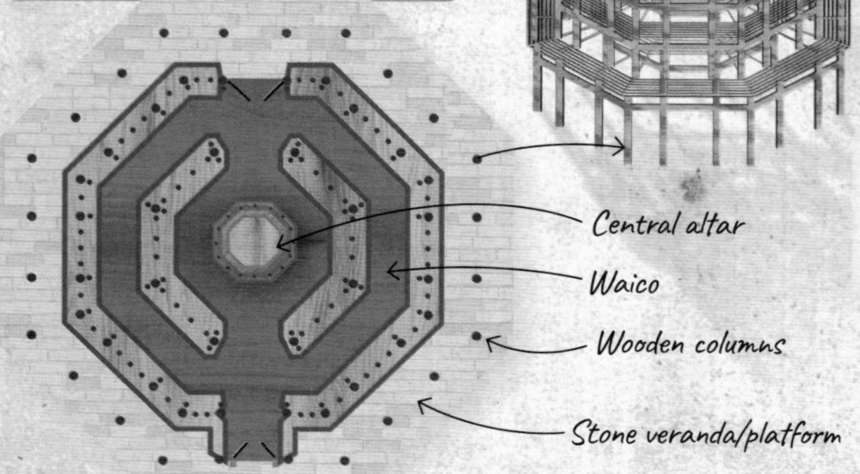

Mezzanine level

Object of worship
The ground level is dominated by an 11-m-tall (36-ft) statue of the Śākyamuni Buddha, sitting on a throne of lotus petals. Above its head is a *zaojing* – a decorative sunken panel on the ceiling, also known as a caisson.

Pagodas evolved from Indian stupas – monumental shrines for storing ancient relics and holy remains.

The *dougong* consists of a network of bow-shaped interlocking brackets (*gong*) that rest on a large wooden block (*dou*) placed on a column. The timbers flex and absorb forces acting on the building, such as strong winds, dissipating shocks throughout the structure.

Dou
Gong
Lu-tou

Stone platform

Śākyamuni Pagoda
67.31 m (220 ft)
The **tallest wooden pagoda** (*featured above*) is situated in China's Ying County, 85 km (53 mi) south of Datong.

Shwedagon Pagoda
99 m (324 ft)
Yangon in Myanmar is home to the **largest gilded building**; it is completely covered in gold. Legend has it that the temple was built 2,600 years ago, but scholars suggest it was between the 6th and 10th century CE.

Tianning Pagoda
153.79 m (504 ft)
Located in Changzhou, China, the world's **tallest pagoda** has 13 storeys and was completed in 2007. The structure has a steel frame and concrete foundation.

Shown here for comparison, the Statue of Liberty stands 46 m (151 ft) tall from the bottom of the plinth to the top of the torch. (Including her pedestal, Liberty is 93 m; 305 ft.)

Extraordinary Egyptians

First standardized measure

A "cubit" was a unit of length defined as the distance between a person's elbow and tip of the middle finger. As forearms vary, so too did the cubit. To rectify this, around 3000 BCE, a standard "royal cubit" was formalized, based on the arm of the reigning pharaoh. The royal cubit used to build the Great Pyramid (*see below*), for instance, was 52.4 cm (1 ft 8.5 in).

Oldest surviving papyrus document

The *Diary of Merer* is a logbook by a government official involved with the construction of the Great Pyramid. It dates to the end of Pharaoh Khufu's reign, *c.* 2570 BCE, and was found by French archaeologist Pierre Tallet in 2013.

Longest ancient Egyptian festival

The ancient Egyptian calendar was full of celebrations to commemorate special religious occasions. One of the most notable was the Festival of Opet, which honoured rebirth and fertility during the flooding season, known as Akhet. Starting as an 11-day event, festivities later went on for as long as 27 days at holy sites such as Karnak (*pictured; see right*).

Tallest pyramid

Giza's Great Pyramid of Khufu (*right*) rose 146.7 m (481 ft 3 in) above the desert when built *c.* 4,500 years ago. It was the world's **tallest structure** for around 3,780 years, though erosion and vandalism over millennia have now reduced its stature to 137.5 m (451 ft).

On the same site – just outside Cairo – lies the **largest monolithic sculpture**: the Great Sphinx (*left*). The limestone "lion man" is 73.5 m long and 20.2 m tall (241 ft 1 in x 66 ft 3 in).

At 136.4 m (448 ft), Khafre's Pyramid is the second-tallest in the world

General use of hieroglyphs was already on the wane in Egyptian society when the Romans took over in 30 BCE.

Largest ancient Egyptian temple site

Started *c.* 2000 BCE, the Karnak Temple Complex at Thebes (now Luxor), on the eastern shore of the River Nile, was added to by various dynasties over nearly two millennia. The site comprises numerous shrines, pylons (temple gateways) and even a sacred lake, spread across some 250 acres (101 ha). Karnak's most imposing structure is the Great Temple of Amun-Re. Its 5,000-m² (53,820-sq-ft) Hypostyle Hall retains its original 134 giant pillars (*inset left*); 12 of these, laid out in the centre of the hall, are the **tallest load-bearing stone columns** at 21 m (69 ft).

First deciphered hieroglyphs

The Rosetta Stone is a 1.14 x 0.7-m (3-ft 8-in x 2-ft 3-in) tablet unearthed in Rashid, Egypt, in Jul 1799. The *stele* is inscribed with a trilingual royal decree from 196 BCE, written in Greek, demotic (the cursive everyday script) and hieroglyphs. Armed with a "key" in the Greek text, and the knowledge that hieroglyphs, demotic and present-day Coptic (still used by Egypt's Orthodox Church) are the evolution of a single language, scholars were able to crack the code. French philologist Jean-François Champollion led the way in 1822 when he deciphered the names of Cleopatra and Ptolemy.

The Rosetta Stone has been housed at the British Museum since 1802, though there is now a petition for it – along with other items – to be repatriated to Egypt.

Hieroglyphs: the gods' words

Hieroglyphics ("holy carvings") is the pictogram-based writing system used in Egypt for almost 4,000 years. A complex mix of whole words, sound units (phonemes) and syllables, it took centuries to decode their meaning. The **earliest hieroglyphs** were on clay seal impressions and bone/ivory tags from Abydos dated to *c.* 3400–3200 BCE.

The **last hieroglyphs** appear in a religious inscription (*left*) etched by a priest named Nesmeterakhem in 394 CE. They are carved upon a wall in the Temple of Philae, on an island in the Nile near the city of Aswan.

Longest-reigning female pharaoh

Hatshepsut (*below*) ruled for some 21 years *c.* 1479–58 BCE in the Eighteenth Dynasty. Much of this was nominally as co-regent with her young stepson, Thutmose III.

The **longest-reigning pharaoh** overall was Pepi II Neferkare, with an alleged 94-year tenure *c.* 2278–2184 BCE… However, most scholars today favour a more conservative (albeit still unbeaten) span of 64–65 years.

Pink granite lid

Outer coffin 2.24 m (7 ft 4 in) long

Gilded wood with glass inlay

Pure-gold inner coffin weighs c. 110 kg (240 lb)

10.2-kg (25-lb 8-oz) gold mask

Body wrapped in linen strips, with amulets and trinkets

Cypress wood

Red quartzite sarcophagus c. 2.7 x 1.5 x 1.5 m (9 x 5 x 5 ft)

"GWR" in Egyptian hieroglyphs comprises a jar stand, a chick and a mouth

The Grand Egyptian Museum, due to open in 2023, hopes to display all 5,000+ items from King Tut's tomb.

Most extensive burial hoard for a pharaoh

The rediscovery of Tutankhamun's near-pristine burial chamber in Egypt's Valley of the Kings sparked an "Egyptomania" craze that left a lasting legacy on popular culture. It is now over a hundred years since British Egyptologist Howard Carter and his team (funded by Lord Carnarvon) first entered the hitherto-hidden tomb on 26 Nov 1922 – yet to this day, we're learning new things about this enigmatic ruler. He remains the only rediscovered pharaoh still in his final resting place.

The "Boy King" – who reigned between roughly the ages of nine and 19 – was sent to the afterlife very well prepared. Inclusive of his sarcophagus and nested coffins (*left*), 5,398 artefacts were packed into the grave. These included statues, weapons, games, clothing (along with the **oldest mannequin**), jewellery, paintings, instruments and even six chariots.

1. King Tut's iconic death mask contains two alloys of gold and is inlaid with glass paste and precious stones including lapis lazuli, carnelian and turquoise.
2. Howard Carter examines the Boy King's innermost gold coffin within his tomb.
3. Tutankhamun's remains were not in good condition. Resin used for preservation had essentially fused his body to the coffin and may have even contributed to spontaneous combustion!

Oldest mummified people
Preserving the dead by means of drying and embalming is synonymous with ancient Egypt, but this region was not the first to use mummification. South America's Chinchorro culture, which bordered the Atacama Desert (now in Peru/Chile), were exploiting local arid conditions to naturally desiccate their deceased as long ago as 7020 BCE. By 5050 BCE, Chinchorro mummification techniques had become more sophisticated: a corpse's innards were removed and replaced with plant matter and clay, with the skin then sewn back on and a layer of ash paste applied.

Egypt's oldest-known mummy, by comparison, is an adult male (dated to c. 3700–3500 BCE) now housed in Turin, Italy. Evidence of his embalming – pushing back the practice's origin in Egypt some 1,500 years – was unravelled in 2018.

Earliest named pet
Animals played a major role in both domestic and religious life in ancient Egypt. The oldest-known "pet name" is Beha. The curly-tailed hunting dog is depicted on a fragment of c. 2400 BCE funerary carving for a nobleman.

The **oldest pet cemetery**, dating to the 1st/2nd century CE, lies near the ancient port of Berenike on the Red Sea. The animal graveyard contained the remains of 536 cats, 32 dogs, several small monkeys and a young baboon.

Although King Tut's tomb was in remarkable condition, clues such as a repaired hole in the outer door indicate it was robbed – probably twice – soon after his death.

MEDIEVAL MAYHEM

Longest sword

Examples of Japanese ōdachi (*above, worn across the back*), Scottish claymores and German zweihänder more than 2 m (6 ft 6 in) long were all used in combat. Larger surviving swords were likely ceremonial or decorative.

would fight on their team. For the great tournament at Lagny-sur-Marne (*see opposite*), Henry the Young King of England arrived with 200 mounted knights in his entourage – a force whose daily wages would have added up to more than the annual tax revenue of some English counties.

Farthest shot by a catapult

The power of pre-gunpowder siege weapons has long been the subject of debate, as contemporary writers tended to exaggerate the feats of their patrons. In 1904, however, historian Frederick Wyn (UK) built a replica mangonel that launched a 10-lb (4.5-kg) projectile 320 m (1,049 ft).

Heaviest archery draw weight

In the Middle Ages, English longbowmen were some of the most feared soldiers in Europe. They trained from childhood in the use of 6-ft (1.83-m) yew bows. Examples from the wreck of the *Mary Rose* (*see p.147*) would have required a force of 185 lb (84 kg) to draw. On 15 Aug 2004, archer Mark Stretton (UK) showed that such a bow was usable by firing a 90-kg (198-lb) longbow in Somerset, UK.

Largest castle

The walls of Prague Castle enclose an area of 72,840 m² (784,040 sq ft) on an outcrop above the capital of Czechia. The earliest sections date from the 9th century, though it is likely that a fortification has existed there for longer.

The category of **smallest castle** is harder to define, but if a castle comprises a curtain wall enclosing a keep, then a strong candidate is Clitheroe Castle in Lancashire, UK. Built in the 12th century, the walls surround an area of just 882 m² (9,493 sq ft) - about the size of three tennis courts.

Longest siege

Although the siege of Ishiyama Hongan-ji (*see right*) was the longest campaign

against a small fortress or castle, fortified cities have been known to hold out much longer. According to Greek historian Herodotus, the city of Azotus (now Ashdod) in Israel resisted the forces of Pharaoh Psamtik of Egypt for 54 years between 664 and 610 BCE.

Largest knightly retinue

In their grandest form, medieval tournaments included a small-scale battle – or mêlée – fought purely for honour and prestige. Deliberate killing was discouraged, but accidental injuries and deaths were nonetheless common.

Each major participant would arrive at a tournament with a retinue of knights who

Longest castle siege

In 1570, as part of his campaign to unify Japan, the powerful *daimyo* (feudal lord) Oda Nobunaga laid siege to the fortified cathedral of Ishiyama Hongan-ji, stronghold of the Ikko-Ikki warrior monks. Although Nobunaga could surround the castle on land, allies of the monks were able to sneak supplies in by sea, allowing the garrison to hold out for 10 years before finally surrendering in Aug 1580. After its capture, the fortress was burned and replaced with Osaka Castle.

The armour's original owner was killed in a jousting accident in 1559

Helm

Visor

Gorget

Pauldron

Deadliest tournament

There were 60 deaths at an event in Neuss (now in Germany) in May 1241. Unusually hot weather was a key factor: a choking cloud of dust arose during the mêlée, making breathing difficult. This proved fatal for many knights fighting in full armour with padding and chainmail.

Most expensive armour

On 5 May 1983, the armour collection of Lord Gavin Astor went under the hammer at Sotheby's in London. The star lot was this suit of decorated parade armour made by Milanese master craftsman Giovanni Negroli in the early 1540s for King Henri II of France. It was purchased by American businessman Barry Trupin for £1,925,000 ($3,032,826). This armour dates from after the introduction of powerful firearms to the battlefields of Europe, a change that saw armour become more of a fashion statement than practical combat wear.

Couter

Breastplate

Fauld

Cuisse

Gauntlet

Nimble Knights

It is often assumed that a knight in full plate armour was so encumbered as to be almost immobile. In reality, fine plate armour weighed 20–30 kg (44–66 lb), which is about the same as the weight of gear carried by a modern soldier. Knights could run, jump and fight. On 21 Sep 2008, Danish re-enactor Peter Pedersen set out to prove this by completing the **fastest marathon in a suit of armour**, running 42.2 km (26.2 mi) in an impressive 6 hr 46 min 59 sec.

Every part of a suit of plate armour has a name

Largest medieval tournament

In Nov 1179, around 3,000 knights took part in the mêlée at Lagny-sur-Marne, France, which was held to celebrate the coronation of King Philip II. Its diplomatic significance drew nobles and tournament patrons from across Europe, including famous high-rollers such as Henry the Young King (*above right*) and Hugh of Burgundy.

Pirates

First "Jolly Roger" flag

French pirate Emanuel Wynn first raised this ominous banner during a battle in Jul 1700. At the time, pirates flew red or black flags: red meant "no quarter" (i.e, no mercy); black implied leniency. Sometimes the flags had a skull, but usually they were just plain colours. Below are the insignias of a few other notorious captains...

Stede Bonnet

Blackbeard

Christopher Moody

Edward Low

Largest pirate fleet

By 1809, the Guangdong Pirate Confederation, aka Red Fleet, in the South China Sea comprised about 1,800 junks and more than 70,000 crew. It was led by China's Zheng Yi Sao (b. Shi Yang, left), who assumed full command after her husband died in 1807.

First pirate queen

Queen Teuta was leader of the Ardiaei tribe in Illyria (on today's western Balkan Peninsula) in 231–227 BCE. She took part in raids on rival city-states and became known as the "Terror of the Adriatic". Teuta, who licensed ships to pillage on her behalf, only surrendered after Rome declared war against Illyria and sent a fleet of 200 ships against her armies. Her fate remains unknown.

First documented pirates

The earliest mention of piracy arises in Egyptian cuneiform tablets dated to the 14th century BCE. They refer to Lukkan pirates from the coast of Türkiye launching raids on nearby Cyprus.

First worldwide pirate hunt

Englishman Henry Avery, aka "Long Ben", became a pirate after working on a slave ship. In 1695, in an attack on 25 ships belonging to the Indian Mughal government, he captured a bounty of precious metals and jewels worth c. £600,000 (around £52 m or $62 m, today), making him the richest pirate at the time. As a result, a huge reward of £1,000 was offered for his capture by the UK Privy Council and the East India Company. "Long Ben" continued to evade arrest and all records of him cease after 1696.

Most ships robbed by a pirate

Bartholomew "Black Bart" Roberts, aka John Roberts, was a Welshman who plundered more than 400 ships between 1719 and 1722 – a higher hit rate than any other buccaneer. His attacks were focused off the Americas and the coast of West Africa.

Oldest pirate

Owing to many occupational hazards, most pirates only lived into their mid-30s. Captain William Kidd (c. 1645–1701), however, reached the grand age of 56. Born in Scotland, he became a privateer (i.e., a legally sanctioned pirate) in 1689 after a distinguished career at sea. Kidd was only charged with piracy in 1698 after he captured the Quedagh Merchant ship. Some historians argue his execution as a pirate was unjustified.

Highest-grossing pirate movie series

The five films in Disney's Pirates of the Caribbean (USA) franchise have hauled in $4.52 bn (£3.34 bn). They were inspired by the water-based theme park ride that opened at Disneyland in California, USA, in 1967. The second instalment, Dead Man's Chest (2006), is the highest-grossing swashbuckler, taking in $1.06 bn (£545.6 m) - that's a lot of pieces of eight!

Booty and other Whydah artefacts can be seen at a pirate museum in West Yarmouth, Massachusetts, USA.

Youngest pirate

On 9 Nov 1716, John King – c. 8–11 years old – and his mother were sailing on the *Bonetta* when it was raided by "Black Sam" (right). The *Bonetta's* captain later swore that King insisted on joining the pirate crew. Perhaps bearing this story out, when the wreck of another of Black Sam's ships was found, a small shoe, silk stocking and leg bone of a child of King's age were recovered.

Most profitable sea pirate

During the "Golden Age" of piracy (1650s–1730s), England's "Black Sam", aka Samuel Bellamy (right), accrued a fortune that would now be worth c. £120 m ($147 m). Remarkably, he did so in just two years: 1715–17. His biggest catch was the *Whydah Gally* (above), carrying more than £20,000 (£4.1 m; $5 m today) in gold and silver.

The vessel sank off Cape Cod on 26 Apr 1717, along with Black Sam and all but two of his crew. The ship's bell was retrieved on 30 Oct 1985 by Barry Clifford (USA), making the *Whydah* the <u>first known pirate shipwreck salvaged</u>.

Most adapted pirate story

First published in 1883, *Treasure Island* by Robert Louis Stevenson (UK) has been recreated on screen at least 41 times between 1917 and 2015. The Muppets (right) added their own distinctive spin on this classic in 1996.

TREASURE ISLAND

R. L. STEVENSON

SHIPWRECKS

Oldest shipwreck
The remains of an Early Bronze Age vessel dating to *c.* 2200 BCE were discovered off the Greek island of Dokos in 1975. All that remains of the vessel are two stone anchors and an array of clay pottery.

Deepest shipwreck
The USS *Samuel B Roberts* ("DE-413") was sunk by the Japanese Navy in Oct 1944 during the Battle off Samar in the Philippine Sea. The WWII destroyer escort was rediscovered on 22 Jun 2022 – at a depth of 6,865 m (22,523 ft) – by explorer Victor Vescovo and sonar expert Jérémie Morizet, diving in the DSV *Limiting Factor* (*see pp.116–17*). The *Sammy B* surpassed the 6,468.6-m-deep (21,222-ft) USS *Johnston* located in Mar 2021, also by Vescovo.

Most valuable shipwreck
Launched in 1698, the *San José* was part of the Spanish treasure fleet that transported precious metals and jewels back from South America. It sank on 8 Jun 1708 off Cartagena, Colombia, following a British attack. Its discovery was announced in 2015, though this is contested as part of an ongoing legal battle. Its cargo of gold and silver coins, emeralds and porcelain may be worth up to $20 bn (£16 bn).

DEADLIEST ICEBERG COLLISION
An estimated 1,517 people perished when the RMS *Titanic* struck an iceberg and sank in the North Atlantic on 14 Apr 1912. The iconic ocean liner was on her maiden voyage from the UK port of Southampton to New York City and had been declared "unsinkable". The *Titanic*'s wreck was located in 1985, 700 km (430 mi) off Newfoundland, Canada, and now has UNESCO protection.

MOST SHIPWRECKS IN A DESERT
There are at least 137 known shipwrecks on the "Skeleton Coast", a 1,600-km-long (1,000-mi) region of the Namib Desert in western Namibia that runs alongside the Atlantic Ocean. It is one of the most treacherous stretches of coastline in the world, plagued by fog, strong currents and heavy surf. Owing to the shifting desert sands, some of these wrecks appear to move inland over time.

Germany's Eduard Bohlen, grounded in 1909; now lies 400 m (1,300 ft) inland

Most southerly shipwreck
On 5 Mar 2022, HMS *Endurance* was located 3,000 m (9,800 ft) below the surface off Antarctica at 69°S 52°W. The three-masted barquentine had lain undiscovered since it sank during the Imperial Trans-Antarctic Expedition (1914–17), led by British explorer Ernest Shackleton. The *Endurance* became stuck in pack ice in the Weddell Sea in Jan 1915 and sank nine months later, leaving Shackleton and his men stranded. Incredibly, all 28 crew survived.

At 74°N 91°W, the British merchant supply ship HMS *Breadalbane* is the **most northerly shipwreck**. It sank off Devon Island in the Canadian Arctic after being punctured by an ice floe on 21 Aug 1853.

Most times for a submarine to sink
Launched in Jul 1863, the ill-fated CSS *H.L. Hunley* sank three times in seven months – killing a total of 21 crew. It was recovered for the final time from the seabed in 2000 and can now be seen at the former Charleston Navy Yard in South Carolina, USA.

MOST ARTEFACTS RETRIEVED FROM A SHIPWRECK

Approximately 350,000 pieces of near-pristine Chinese porcelain have been raised from the wreck of the *Tek Sing* ("*True Star*"), a junk that sank in the South China Sea on 6 Feb 1822 en route to the Dutch East Indies. It was rediscovered on 12 May 1999 by British treasure hunter Michael Hatcher. We've taken a look to see how this compares to the hauls salvaged from a few other famous shipwrecks...

Tek Sing: c. 350,000 pieces, including porcelain bowls, saucers and lidded pots

Titanic: c. 5,500, including letters, crockery and a violin

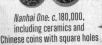

Nanhai One: c. 180,000, including ceramics and Chinese coins with square holes

Vasa: c. 25,000, including cannon, clothing, tools and Scandinavian coins

Mary Rose: c. 26,000, including weapons and a dog skeleton – named Hatch!

MOST EXPENSIVE SHIPWRECK MUSEUM

Opened on 20 Jul 2016, The Mary Rose Museum in Portsmouth, Hampshire, UK, took 10 years to build at an estimated cost of £39 m ($50 m). Its centrepiece is the wreck of the famous Tudor vessel that foundered on 19 Jul 1545 while fighting the French at the Battle of the Solent. The *Mary Rose* was raised from the seabed on 11 Oct 1982, watched by millions globally on TV. Visitors to the museum can now walk through reconstructed sections of the warship, as well as enjoy a wide range of its accompanying artefacts.

Ready for battle!

More than 8,300 pieces of ordnance – e.g., iron guns, pikes, longbows and arrows – have been salvaged from the *Mary Rose*: the **most medieval weaponry found on a shipwreck.**

Model displaying the *Vasa's* original vibrant colouring

Vasa's sister ship *Äpplet* was sunk in 1659 to defend Stockholm Harbour. Its wreck was located in Oct 2022.

MOST INTACT SAILING WARSHIP RESURFACED

The *Vasa* is a Swedish warship that sank in Stockholm Harbour on 10 Aug 1628, only 1.3 km (0.8 mi) into its maiden voyage. It was found in 1956 and raised on 24 Apr 1961. Around 98% of the *Vasa's* wooden structure has been preserved, including intricate sculptures and carved panels. The vessel is housed in Stockholm's Vasamuseet; with up to 1.5 million visitors a year, it is the **most visited shipwreck museum.**

OLDEST SUBMARINE WRECK

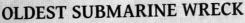

Brandtaucher ("Fire Diver") was an early submersible developed to attack enemy ships blockading Germany during the First Danish-German War (1848–51). On 1 Feb 1851, the submarine sank in Kiel Harbour as a result of instability caused by poor ballast control. It was rediscovered and raised intact on 5 Jul 1887. *Brandtaucher* is now on display at the Museum of Military-History in Dresden, Germany.

Propeller; top speed 3 knots (5.6 km/h; 3.5 mph)

Crew x2 turn the flywheel

Treadwheel to move the propeller

Steering control for third crew member

Viewing window

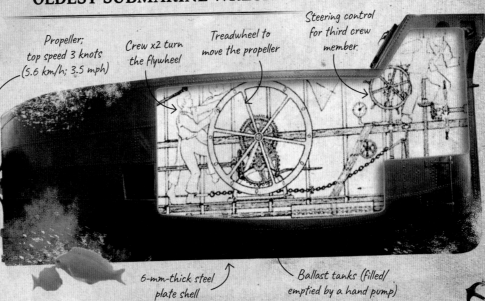

Lucky escape

Brandtaucher's crew of three, which included its inventor Wilhelm Bauer, were also the first sunken-submarine survivors!

6-mm-thick steel plate shell

Ballast tanks (filled/ emptied by a hand pump)

INCREDIBLE INVENTIONS

A CATALOGUE OF ENGINEERING MARVELS FOR YOUR EDIFICATION

First mobile phone call

On 3 Apr 1973, Motorola engineer Martin Cooper (USA) phoned his rival, Joel Engel of Bell Labs, while standing in the street in New York City. This historic call took place just over 97 years after the **first telephone call** was made by Alexander Graham Bell (UK) in Mar 1876. Cooper's phone was the prototype for what would become the **first commercially available mobile phone**, the Motorola DynaTAC (*pictured*), which was eventually released in Mar 1983.

IN STOCK NOW!

THE ELEPHANT IN THE ROOM

ENIAC's components were fitted into 40 panels, each 8 ft (2.4 m) tall. It took up three walls of a 1,500-sq-ft (139-m²) room and needed its own air-conditioning system to prevent overheating.

First...

Stone tools
Our capacity for invention is a key feature that distinguishes humans from other animals. The earliest evidence for this ingenuity dates back 3.3 million years, when our hominid ancestors first shaped rocks into sharpened axes. A range of stone flakes, cores and anvils from this period were discovered in 2011 near Lake Turkana in Kenya.

Musical instrument
Around 50,000 years ago, humans and Neanderthals started boring holes in bones to make simple flutes. These were able to play a sequence of notes similar to a pentatonic scale. One such flute, made from the femur of a cave bear, was found at the Divje Babe cave in Slovenia in 1995.

Paper money
In the Song Dynasty (960–1279), Chinese merchants used banknotes – with secret cyphers to foil counterfeiters – as currency.

Rockets
Ti'lao shu, or "ground rats", were simple rockets created in late 12th-century China, comprising a hollowed out bamboo stem filled with gunpowder. They could be attached to arrows or simply ignited and set off as fireworks, bouncing over the ground and generating lots of noise, flames and smoke.

Pendulum clock
Dutch scientist Christiaan Huygens conceived of a fully operational clock regulated by the action of a pendulum in late 1656. The following year, clockmaker Salomon Coster refined the idea into a working concept that was accurate to within a minute per day, and additional refinements soon reduced this to around 10 sec. By the end of the century, pendulum clocks were keeping time to within 0.5 sec per day – making them accurate enough to warrant the introduction of the first-ever second hand.

FIRST PROGRAMMABLE ELECTRONIC COMPUTER

The Electronic Numerical Integrator and Computer (ENIAC) at the University of Pennsylvania, USA, made its first calculations on 10 Dec 1945. Technicians rewired the connections between its many modules to create a "path" for data. ENIAC would then automatically run through the sequence (or program) that had been laid out.

FIRST REGULAR TELEVISION BROADCASTS

Experimental TV broadcasts were first made in the 1920s, but the television age as we know it debuted on 2 Nov 1936 in London, UK. At 3 p.m., the BBC began the transmission of its very first scheduled TV programme. Early adopters tuned in to see Adele Dixon herald the new era by singing the aptly titled "Magic Rays of Light".

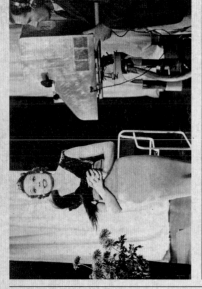

Oldest clock

Salisbury Cathedral in Wiltshire, UK, houses a faceless mechanical clock dating to c. 1386. Its chimes were designed to remind parishioners of church services. After some 498 years, and more than 500 million ticks, it was replaced and put aside. But in 1929 it was rediscovered, and in 1956 it was restored to full working order.

OLDEST SURVIVING PHOTOGRAPH

First public electricity power station

Built by the Edison Electric Light Company, the earliest power station built for public applications opened in Jan 1882. It stood at 57 Holborn Viaduct in London, UK. A Babcock & Wilcox boiler provided steam to power a 125-hp (93-kW) engine that drove a 27-ton (24.5-tonne) 110-V DC generator, known as "Jumbo". This supplied power to light the viaduct and local businesses, along with London's City Temple, the Old Bailey and General Post Office. It served as a template for Thomas Edison's later projects in New York.

Joseph Niépce (FRA) took the oldest known photograph (*above*) in 1827 with a camera obscura. It shows the view from his window. The **first photograph of a human** (*left*) was by France's Louis Daguerre, *c.* 1838. The long exposure needed for early photos meant that moving objects didn't register in his eerily empty Parisian street scene. But a static shoe-shiner and his customer did.

Steam locomotive on rails

On 21 Feb 1804, a locomotive built by English engineer Richard Trevithick hauled a train along a tramway at Penydarren Ironworks in Merthyr Tydfil, UK.

Electric Christmas tree lights

In 1882, Edison Electric Light Company investor Edward H Johnson (USA) hung the earliest-known incarnation of these festive favourites at his home in New York City, USA. They presented "a most picturesque and uncanny aspect", according to the *Detroit Post & Tribune* of 22 Dec that year.

FIRST INTERNAL COMBUSTION CAR

In late 1885, the Motorwagen – the earliest successful petrol-driven car – was put through its paces at Mannheim, Germany. Built by Karl Friedrich Benz (DEU) and patented on 29 Jan 1886, the three-wheeler weighed 254 kg (560 lb) and could reach 13–16 km/h (8–10 mph). The significance of Benz's invention was somewhat overlooked at the time: its first 1-km (0.6-mi) road test was reported in the local newspaper, the *Neue Badische Landeszeitung*, on 4 Jun 1886, under the heading "Miscellaneous".

Neu!

Praktisch!

Patentirt in allen Industriestaaten!

Patent-Motorwagen

mit Gasbetrieb durch Petroleum, Benzin, Naphta etc.

Immer sogleich betriebsfähig! — Bequem und absolut gefahrlos!

Lenken, Halten und Bremsen leichter und sicherer, als bei gewöhnlichen Fuhrwerken. — Keine besondere Bedienung nöthig. Sehr geringe Betriebskosten.

Patent-Motorwagen mit abnehmbarem Halbverdeck und Spritzleder.

Vollständiger Ersatz für Wagen mit Pferden. — Erspart den Kutscher, die theure Ausstattung, Wartung und Unterhaltung der Pferde.

BENZ & Co.

Rheinische Gasmotoren-Fabrik

MANNHEIM.

Neue Fabrik: Waldhofstrasse.

Oldest wheel

The Ljubljana Marshes Wheel has been dated to around 3150 BCE. It was discovered by archaeologists in Slovenia on 29 Mar 2002 within a Chalcolithic (or late Neolithic) settlement known as Stare Gmajne. The body of the wheel is formed from two thick planks of ash, jointed with a tongue and groove and cut into a circle. Its axle is fashioned from oak, and fits into a square hole in the wheel's centre. This combination of strong, hard-wearing ash and oak would remain a standard for wheelwrights across much of Europe until the early 20th century.

Powered flight

At 10:35 a.m. on 17 Dec 1903, Orville Wright flew the wood-and-canvas *Flyer I* for 120 ft (36.5 m) near Kitty Hawk, North Carolina, USA. As he was flying into a strong headwind, it had a ground speed of just 6.8 mph (10.9 km/h) and an altitude of 8–12 ft (2.4–3.6 m). Orville and his brother Wilbur (both USA) designed and built the *Flyer I* at their bicycle workshop in Dayton, Ohio, having used a home-made wind tunnel to test their theories.

Myths & Magic

Oldest depiction of a werewolf

Written in c. 430 BCE, the *Histories* of the ancient Greek geographer Herodotus claimed that once a year members of the Neuri tribe "become[s] a wolf for a few days" through a magical transformation. The Neuri are believed to have lived in the modern-day Western Balkans. There are earlier references to humans changing into wolves, e.g., in the *Epic of Gilgamesh* (c. 2150 BCE), but these transformations were permanent.

The word "werewolf" is an Old English term, "wer" meaning "man". Its earliest recorded usage was in the 11th-century *Ecclesiastical Ordinances of King Cnut*.

First-known stigmatic

Throughout the last 1,000 years, there have been numerous documented cases of the unexplained phenomenon of stigmata – mysterious bleeding wounds that seem to develop of their own accord, and which correspond to the crucifixion wounds of Jesus. The earliest-known stigmatic was St Francis of Assisi. It is said that, on 14 Sep 1224, he saw a fiery-winged seraph descending from heaven in the form of a crucified man; thereafter, he began to develop bleeding wounds in his hands, feet and side.

Largest outbreak of vampirism

The term "vampire" comes from the Serbian "vàmpir" – animated corpses, said to kill the living by drinking their blood or crushing them while they slept. Between 1725 and the 1750s, the so-called Great Vampire Epidemic in the Austrian Empire saw around 30 documented incidents where bodies of suspected blood-suckers were exhumed, staked and/or burned, to prevent their return from the dead. It is thought that the total number of cases was far higher.

Oldest coin tree

Since 1863, visitors have pressed coins into the bark of a prominent oak on the Scottish loch island of Maree. The tree stands beside a holy well, whose waters were believed to cure illness; initially, the pennies were left as thanks for a cure. Queen Victoria hammered in a coin during her visit in 1887, by which time the pennies were being used as wish tokens. The tradition is discouraged by modern conservationists, owing to the potential damage the practice can cause to forest ecosystems.

Oldest depiction of a witch on a broomstick

A 3-cm-high (1.1-in) illustration of a female heretic flying on a broom appears on a copy of Martin le Franc's long poem *Le Champion des Dames*. The manuscript was illuminated in 1451.

Oldest depiction of the "Night Parade of One Hundred Demons"

Painted in the first half of the 16th century, the Shinju-an scroll (below) is the first-known illustration of a Japanese folklore staple: a terrifying procession of yōkai (supernatural creatures) erupting into the world.

Most coins hammered into a wish tree

The Ingleton Money Tree in North Yorkshire, UK, has more than 48,000 coins inserted into its bark (above). Another focus for wishful thinking is the Pont des Arts (right) in Paris, France. In Jun 2015, it was stripped of more than 1 million love-locks – padlocks adorned with romantic inscriptions. This is the <u>most love-locks removed from a bridge</u>.

Many sitters wanted pictures with their departed children

A notable name to pose for one of William Mumler's spirit photographs was Mary Todd Lincoln, the widow of US president Abraham.

First "spirit photograph"
A picture of William Mumler (USA, centre), apparently showing him accompanied by the ghostly image of his dead cousin, was published in Nov 1862. Such "spirit photographs" were a popular phenomenon in the late 19th century. Today, they are understood to have been the result of various tricks, including multiple exposure and manually drawn images.

Most concealed shoes found in a house
In 2010, a total of 58 shoes and 189 shoe fragments dating to the 1870s–80s were discovered beneath the fireplace of Gelli Iago, a farmhouse in Eryri National Park, UK. Folklore records from the 19th century suggest that concealed shoes may have been considered a good-luck charm for Victorian households; there are also theories that they were hidden to protect the building from evil spirits, witches and demons.

Most witnesses of an apparition
On 13 Oct 1917, the "Miracle of Fátima" saw some 70,000 people in Fátima, Portugal, observe the Sun appearing to emit radiant colours and moving in dramatic and irregular patterns across the sky. The crowd had gathered as a result of a prophecy made by three local shepherd children, who claimed that the Virgin Mary would appear before them and perform miracles.

Oldest depiction of a ghost
A Babylonian clay tablet engraved some 2,500 years ago depicts the figure of an elderly male ghost being led back down into the Underworld by a female. The image and its cuneiform description forms part of a guide to exorcizing ghosts and was deciphered by Dr Irving Finkel, Curator in the Middle Eastern department at the British Museum.

Literary curses

Medieval scribes often wrote curses on their manuscripts in an attempt to deter would-be book pilferers. Thieves were threatened with blindness, drowning or even being ripped apart by pigs!

Largest cache of curse tablets
In Roman times, people entreated the gods to wreak misfortune upon their enemies on thin sheets of metal, which were then folded and left in holy places. Between 1977 and 1979, a hoard of 131 curse tablets was uncovered from the ruins of a temple of Mercury near the present-day village of Uley in Gloucestershire, UK.

ZION CLARK

Wrestling phenomenon Zion Clark has overcome daunting obstacles to excel both on and off the mat. A multiple record holder, he lives his life by the two-word mantra that he has tattooed upon his back: "No excuses".

Zion was born without legs on account of caudal regression syndrome, a rare condition that impairs the development of the lower half of the body. He spent his childhood moving from one foster carer to another, and endured periods of bullying and neglect. One place Zion felt at home was the wrestling mat, where he could exploit the upper-body strength that walking on his hands had given him. At high school, he developed a fierce training ethic and began to chalk up the wins. "I tired of being that bottom dog," he recalled. "I just put in the work, as much as I could, every day." Aged 16, Zion was adopted by Kimberlli Hawkins, who provided him with a loving family environment that only pushed him further to succeed. Not content with making the grade on the mat, Zion also became a two-time state champion at wheelchair racing.

When GWR challenged Zion to see if he could achieve a world record, he returned to his high school on 15 Feb 2021 and completed the ◑ **Fastest 20 m running on hands** in just 4.78 sec. He continues to push boundaries, aiming to represent the USA at both the Olympics and the Paralympics. And given what Zion has already achieved, who would bet against him?

VITAL STATISTICS

Name	Zion Clark
Birthplace	Columbus, Ohio, USA
Birth date	29 Sep 1997
Nickname	"Fastest Man on Two Hands"
Current GWR titles	• **Fastest 20 m running on hands** • **Most diamond push-ups in three minutes** • **Highest box jump with the hands**
Skills	Wrestling, music, wheelchair racing

Box jumps are one of Zion's favourite exercises, as they help him generate his explosive power.

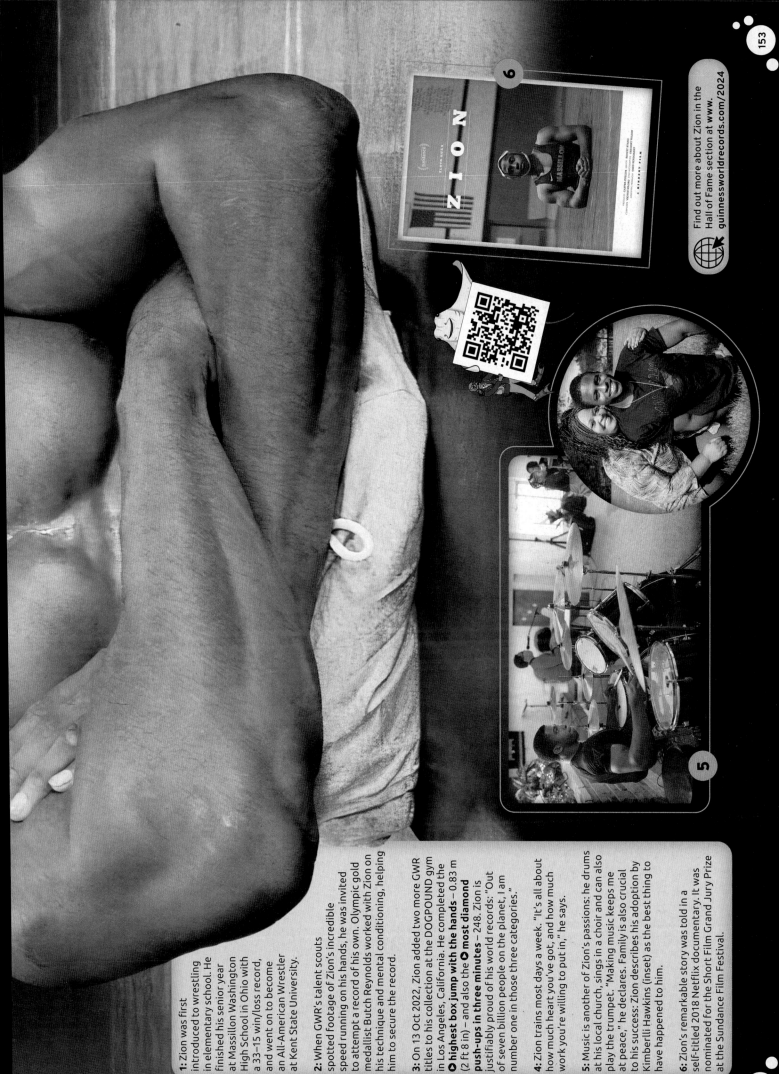

1: Zion was first introduced to wrestling in elementary school. He finished his senior year at Massillon Washington High School in Ohio with a 33–15 win/loss record, and went on to become an All-American Wrestler at Kent State University.

2: When GWR's talent scouts spotted footage of Zion's incredible speed running on his hands, he was invited to attempt a record of his own. Olympic gold medallist Butch Reynolds worked with Zion on his technique and mental conditioning, helping him to secure the record.

3: On 13 Oct 2022, Zion added two more GWR titles to his collection at the DOGPOUND gym in Los Angeles, California. He completed the ⊙ highest box jump with the hands – 0.83 m (2 ft 8 in) – and also the ⊙ most diamond push-ups in three minutes – 248. Zion is justifiably proud of his world records: "Out of seven billion people on the planet, I am number one in those three categories."

4: Zion trains most days a week. "It's all about how much heart you've got, and how much work you're willing to put in," he says.

5: Music is another of Zion's passions: he drums at his local church, sings in a choir and can also play the trumpet. "Making music keeps me at peace," he declares. Family is also crucial to his success: Zion describes his adoption by Kimberlii Hawkins (inset) as the best thing to have happened to him.

6: Zion's remarkable story was told in a self-titled 2018 Netflix documentary. It was nominated for the Short Film Grand Jury Prize at the Sundance Film Festival.

Find out more about Zion in the Hall of Fame section at www.guinnessworldrecords.com/2024

A 1:22.5-scale model was set up in Bergün. Even with a track just 4.5 cm (1.77 in) wide, the train was 80 m (262 ft) long!

Longest narrow-gauge passenger train

On 29 Oct 2022, Rhaetian Railway (CHE) ran a train between the villages of Preda and Bergün in Graubünden, Switzerland, that measured 1,906.3 m (6,254 ft) long. The 100-carriage train ran along a spectacular mountain route – part of a UNESCO World Heritage Site – which winds its way through spiral tunnels and viaducts as it descends around 700 m (2,300 ft) through the Albula Valley.

This train ran only once, to mark Rhaetian Railway's 175th anniversary. The **longest passenger train in scheduled service** is *The Ghan*, a weekly sleeper that runs between Adelaide and Darwin in Australia. A typical configuration consists of two locomotives and 30 carriages, giving an overall length of 774 m (2,539 ft).

300 SLR UHLENHAUT

On 5 May 2022, the hammer came down at a private auction organized by Sotheby's at the Mercedes-Benz Museum in Stuttgart, Germany. An anonymous collector won with a bid of €135 m ($142.3 m; £113.6 m) for the Mercedes-Benz 300 SLR "Uhlenhaut Coupé", making it the **most expensive car** ever sold.

COSTLY CARS

The vehicles that command the highest prices are road-legal racers from the 1950s and 1960s.

These cars were built in very small numbers and achieved worldwide fame.

The previous holder of this record was a 1963 Ferrari 250 GTO, which sold for $70 m (£52.7 m) in 2018.

Other cars that fetch prices in the tens of millions include the Jaguar D-Type, Alfa Romeo 33 Stradale and Ford GT40.

When it rolled out of the factory in 1955, the model 300 *Sport-Leicht Rennsport* ("sport light racing") was the fastest racing car in the world. Designed by engineer Rudolf Uhlenhaut for the Mercedes-Benz Silver Arrows racing team, it combined a lightweight body with the engine from the company's championship-winning W196 Formula One car.

The new car made an immediate impression, securing 1–2 finishes at prestigious races, and outpacing rivals from Ferrari and Jaguar. On 11 Jun 1955, however, the 300 SLR's run of success came to a tragic end. At the 24 Hours of Le Mans, one of the Mercedes entrants crashed into another car and went flying into a grandstand, killing not only the driver, Pierre Levegh, but also dozens of spectators.

Shocked and appalled by these events, Mercedes withdrew completely from motor racing. The remaining cars were put into storage, but Uhlenhaut kept one – a road-legal coupé intended for a road race the following year – as a personal company car.

It was this car that was put up for sale by Mercedes in 2022. The money raised at the auction was ploughed into an initiative called beVisioneers: The Mercedes-Benz Fellowship, which seeks to educate a new generation of gifted, environmentally focused engineers.

"Gullwing" doors
To allow the driver and passenger to climb in over the high-sided, stiffened racing chassis, the doors hinge upwards from the roof.

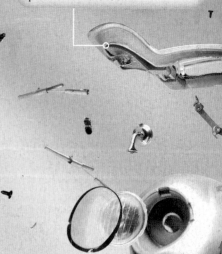

This exploded illustration was created by Swiss artist Fabian Oefner as part of his *Disintegrating* series.

Air intake manifold

Twin exhausts

Coolant tank

In its short racing career, the 300 SLR excelled in long-distance endurance events where its 290-km/h (180-mph) top speed gave it a decisive advantage. With racing legends such as Stirling Moss (*pictured*) and Juan Manuel Fangio behind the wheel, the 300 SLR recorded famous victories at the Targa Florio and Mille Miglia races in Italy.

Engine
The M196-S was an inline eight-cylinder engine that borrowed design innovations from the engines of WWII fighter planes. It generated 302 hp (225 kW), making it about 20% more powerful than its rivals.

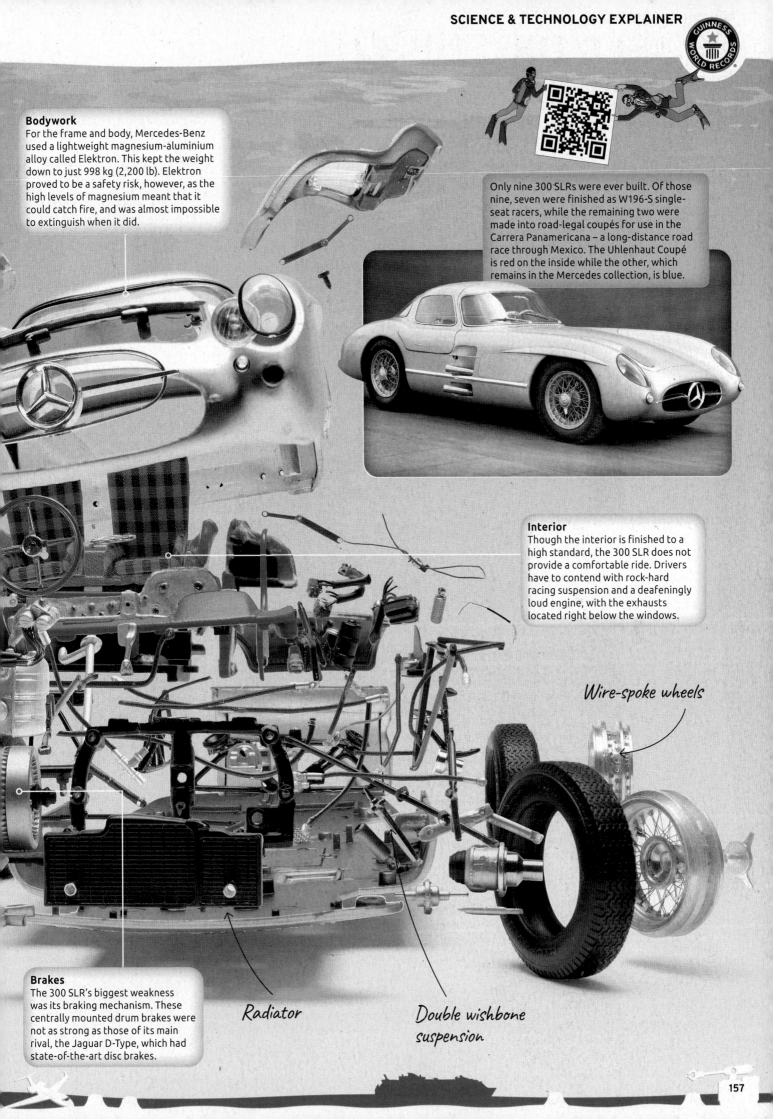

Bodywork
For the frame and body, Mercedes-Benz used a lightweight magnesium-aluminium alloy called Elektron. This kept the weight down to just 998 kg (2,200 lb). Elektron proved to be a safety risk, however, as the high levels of magnesium meant that it could catch fire, and was almost impossible to extinguish when it did.

Only nine 300 SLRs were ever built. Of those nine, seven were finished as W196-S single-seat racers, while the remaining two were made into road-legal coupés for use in the Carrera Panamericana – a long-distance road race through Mexico. The Uhlenhaut Coupé is red on the inside while the other, which remains in the Mercedes collection, is blue.

Interior
Though the interior is finished to a high standard, the 300 SLR does not provide a comfortable ride. Drivers have to contend with rock-hard racing suspension and a deafeningly loud engine, with the exhausts located right below the windows.

Wire-spoke wheels

Radiator

Double wishbone suspension

Brakes
The 300 SLR's biggest weakness was its braking mechanism. These centrally mounted drum brakes were not as strong as those of its main rival, the Jaguar D-Type, which had state-of-the-art disc brakes.

LIGHTHOUSES

Inside Bell Rock Lighthouse*
1. Lightroom/lantern
2. Library/living space
3. Sleeping quarters
4. Kitchen
5. Storage area
6. Provisions/winch room
7. Spiral staircase
8. Door (with ladder to jetty)
*1811 configuration

First lighthouse
The earliest lighthouse that can be verified is the Pharos of Alexandria. It stood on an island in the Nile Delta, near the Egyptian port city, and was completed c. 280 BCE. Heralded as one of the "Seven Wonders of the Ancient World", the fire-topped structure towered some 450 ft (137 m). It ultimately collapsed in Aug 1303 after a series of earthquakes.

The **oldest lighthouse still in use** is the Tower of Hercules at La Coruña in Galicia, Spain, built around the turn of the 2nd century CE, during the reign of the Roman Emperor Trajan. The 57-m-tall (187-ft) edifice was restored in the late 18th century, but some of the original structure still remains.

Oldest offshore lighthouse still in use
Cordouan Lighthouse in the Gironde Estuary of western France was constructed in 1584–1611 by Louis de Foix. Set 7 km (4.3 mi) off the coast, the 68-m (223-ft) tower sits on a small island in the tidal zone, where the sea level fluctuates. Cordouan was fitted with the **first Fresnel-lens light** on 25 Jul 1823, extending its beam to 20 mi (32 km).

The **first open-sea lighthouse** (i.e., constantly surrounded by water) was the original 1698 Eddystone Lighthouse, on a reef 19 km (12 mi) off Plymouth in Devon, UK. It was 80 ft (24 m) tall, built of wood and stone, and lit by 60 candles. A storm destroyed it in 1703, along with its creator, Henry Winstanley (UK). It has since been rebuilt three times.

Largest lens in a lighthouse (relative to size)
First lit on 1 Oct 1909, Makapu'u Point Lighthouse in O'ahu, Hawaii, USA, contains a hyper-radial lens that is 3.7 m (12 ft 1 in) tall with a diameter of 2.5 m (8 ft 2 in). The lens takes up more than 25% of the 14-m-tall (46-ft) structure's interior and is the largest in the USA.

First female lighthouse keeper
Entire families once conducted lighthouse-keeping duties, but the first female "principal keeper" was Hannah Thomas (USA). In 1776, she replaced her deceased husband, John, at Plymouth Lighthouse in Massachusetts, serving for 10 years.

The **most enduring lighthouse-keeping family** were the Knotts (UK). Five generations and eight members took on the role for a combined 278 years between 1730 and 1910, starting with William Knott and ending with Henry Thomas Knott.

Greatest distance to move a lighthouse
In order to save North America's tallest lighthouse – Cape Hatteras (*right*) in North Carolina, USA – from a receding shoreline, it was decided to relocate the entire structure. The complex operation, carried out by The International Chimney Corporation and Expert House Movers, took place between 17 Jun and 9 Jul 1999. Using hydraulic jacks and rollers, the structure was moved 883 m (2,900 ft) inland.

Oldest open-sea lighthouse still in use
Bell Rock Lighthouse, designed by Robert Stevenson (UK), became operational on 1 Feb 1811 and shines to this day. The beacon stands on an oft-storm-battered reef some 18 km (11 mi) off eastern Scotland, UK. Constructed from granite and sandstone, it is 35.3 m (116 ft) tall.

Highest-altitude lighthouse
First lit on 14 Oct 2010, the Rheinquelle Lighthouse stands 2,046 m (6,713 ft) above sea level. It is located in Sedrun in Switzerland's Oberalp Pass – the source of Europe's second-longest river, the Rhine. As a nod to this, the lofty lighthouse is modelled on one that formerly overlooked the terminus of the Rhine at the Hook of Holland, near Rotterdam, Netherlands.

Greatest range for a lighthouse lantern
Brazil's Abrolhos Lighthouse on Ilha de Santa Bárbara and Ilha Rasa Lighthouse, near Rio de Janeiro, have lights rated with a nominal range of 51 nautical miles (94.5 km; 58.7 mi). This does not account for Earth's curvature or bad weather, though.

Most northerly lighthouse
The Kapp Linné Light is located at a latitude of 78.06°N, on the southern side of the Isfjord in Spitsbergen, Svalbard, Norway. The 13-m-tall (43-ft) open metal tower topped by an enclosed section meets the International Association of Marine Aids to Navigation and Lighthouse Authorities' lighthouse definition.

The **most southerly** stands at 55.96°S on Chile's Isla Hornos, off the tip of mainland South America. It is part of a monument site for the many sailors who have perished in the Drake Passage. More southerly navigational beacons do exist.

Largest animal-shaped lighthouses
A pair of 12-m-tall (39-ft) "light-horses" sit on the Iho Hang breakwaters, west of Jeju City in South Korea. The concrete constructions were completed on 4 Feb 2009, their design inspired by the island's native Jeju horse. The red tower (*above*) is on the western breakwater; its white twin stands on the eastern counterpart.

GO WHALE WATCHING
What better way to appreciate the epic size of a full-grown blue whale (*Balaenoptera musculus*) – the **largest animal ever** – than from close-up? This majestic mammal averages 20–30 m (65–98 ft) long and c. 160 tonnes (176 tons) in weight, dwarfing any other creature in history.

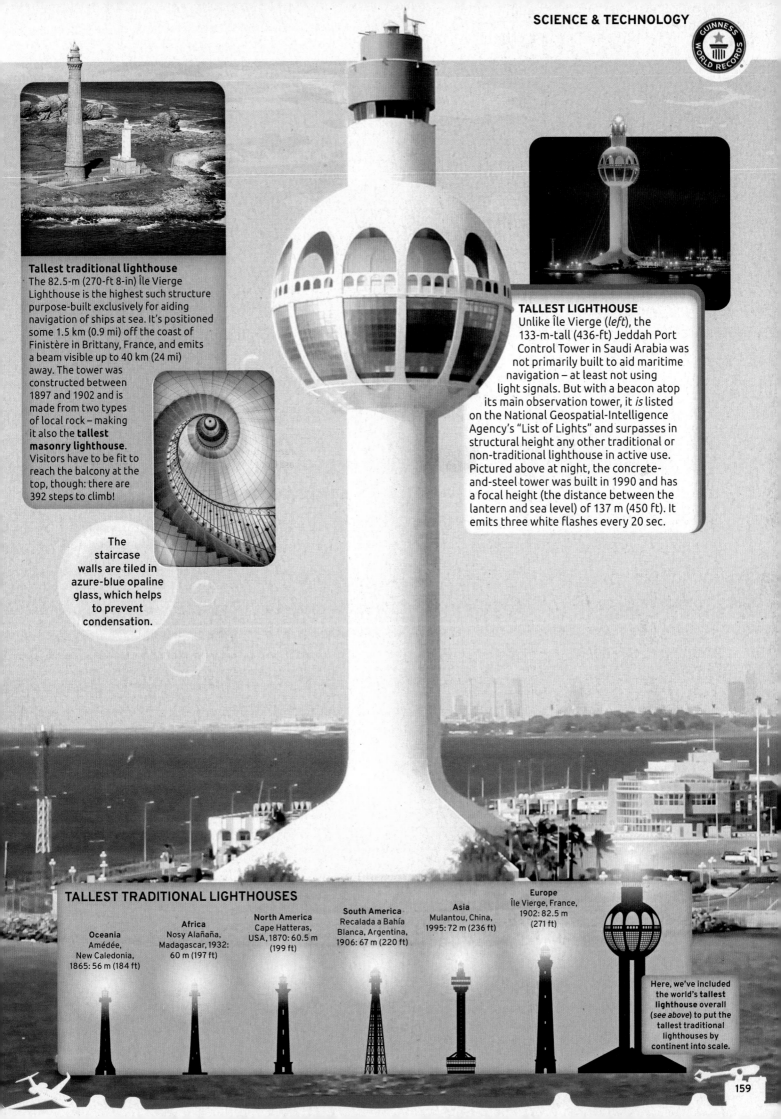

Tallest traditional lighthouse

The 82.5-m (270-ft 8-in) Île Vierge Lighthouse is the highest such structure purpose-built exclusively for aiding navigation of ships at sea. It's positioned some 1.5 km (0.9 mi) off the coast of Finistère in Brittany, France, and emits a beam visible up to 40 km (24 mi) away. The tower was constructed between 1897 and 1902 and is made from two types of local rock – making it also the **tallest masonry lighthouse**. Visitors have to be fit to reach the balcony at the top, though: there are 392 steps to climb!

The staircase walls are tiled in azure-blue opaline glass, which helps to prevent condensation.

TALLEST LIGHTHOUSE

Unlike Île Vierge (*left*), the 133-m-tall (436-ft) Jeddah Port Control Tower in Saudi Arabia was not primarily built to aid maritime navigation – at least not using light signals. But with a beacon atop its main observation tower, it *is* listed on the National Geospatial-Intelligence Agency's "List of Lights" and surpasses in structural height any other traditional or non-traditional lighthouse in active use. Pictured above at night, the concrete-and-steel tower was built in 1990 and has a focal height (the distance between the lantern and sea level) of 137 m (450 ft). It emits three white flashes every 20 sec.

TALLEST TRADITIONAL LIGHTHOUSES

Oceania
Amédée, New Caledonia, 1865: 56 m (184 ft)

Africa
Nosy Alañaña, Madagascar, 1932: 60 m (197 ft)

North America
Cape Hatteras, USA, 1870: 60.5 m (199 ft)

South America
Recalada a Bahía Blanca, Argentina, 1906: 67 m (220 ft)

Asia
Mulantou, China, 1995: 72 m (236 ft)

Europe
Île Vierge, France, 1902: 82.5 m (271 ft)

Here, we've included the world's **tallest lighthouse overall** (*see above*) to put the tallest traditional lighthouses by continent into scale.

CARS

Fastest car
On 15 Oct 1997, the jet-powered *Thrust SSC* set the official land-speed record of 1,227.985 km/h (763.035 mph) over 1 mi (1.6 km) in the Black Rock Desert, Nevada, USA. This speed translates to Mach 1.02, making driver Andy Green (UK) **the first person to break the sound barrier on land.**

Fastest rocket car
Blue Flame was driven by Gary Gabelich (USA) up to 1,016.086 km/h (631.367 mph) at Bonneville Salt Flats in Utah, USA, on 23 Oct 1970. It was powered by a liquid-natural-gas/hydrogen-peroxide rocket engine.

Fastest wheel-driven car
On 18 Oct 2001, the *Vesco Turbinator*, driven by Don Vesco (USA), was recorded at 737.794 km/h (458.444 mph) at Bonneville. Unlike jet-propelled cars, the *Turbinator*'s engine power was directed to the car's wheels.

Fastest piston-engined car
Challenger 2 achieved an average speed of 722.204 km/h (448.757 mph) over two flying-mile runs at Bonneville on 11–12 Aug 2018. Designer Danny Thompson (USA) was at the wheel.

Fastest electric car
Designed and built by engineering students at Ohio State University, the *Venturi Buckeye Bullet 3* hit an average of 549.211 km/h (341.264 mph) at Bonneville on 19 Sep 2016. It was driven by Roger Schroer (USA).

Fastest steam-powered car
On 25 Aug 2009, *Inspiration* reached 225.05 km/h (139.84 mph) at Edwards Air Force Base in California, USA. Designed by the British Steam Car Team, it was driven by Charles Burnett III (USA).

First car
The first passenger-carrying, self-propelled road vehicle was *Puffing Devil*, built by British engineer Richard Trevithick. This steam-powered car made its first test run carrying eight people through the streets of Cambourne in Cornwall on 24 Dec 1801. It was destroyed three days later when it caught fire while running unattended.

First electric car
It was not until the mid-1880s that compact steam, electric and internal-combustion powerplants made "horseless carriages" a practical proposition. French inventor Gustave Trouvé tested a battery-powered vehicle on the Rue Valois in central Paris in Apr 1881, and four years later Karl Benz in Germany debuted the **first internal-combustion car** (*see p.149*).

The **oldest surviving car**, *La Marquise*, also dates from this period. It was made by De Dion, Bouton et Trépardoux of France in 1884. Three years later, the car drove 30.5 km (19 mi) from Paris to Neuilly, at an average speed of 42 km/h (26 mph).

Longest car
American Dream is a 100-ft-long (30.51-m) super-stretched limousine that seats 75 passengers. Amenities on the 26-wheeler include a swimming pool, minigolf course and

First televised motor race
The Imperial Trophy Race, held on 9 Oct 1937 at the Crystal Palace Circuit in London, UK, was recorded using the BBC's new outside broadcast equipment and beamed live to viewers as far away as Manchester. The race was won by Prince Bira of Siam (now Thailand, *centre*), who would go on to drive in Formula One in 1950–54.

Fastest autonomous car
On 27 Apr 2022, a driverless AV-21 IndyCar racer took to the 4.7-km-long (2.9-mi) runway at the Kennedy Space Center in Florida, USA. Under the control of onboard computers programmed by the PoliMOVE Autonomous Racing Team (ITA), the car achieved a two-way average speed of 309.3 km/h (192.2 mph) over a flying kilometre. The AV-21 was developed by racecar builder Dallara.

helipad. Originally designed by Jay Ohrberg in the 1980s and restored by Michael Dezer, *American Dream* is currently on display at Dezerland Park in Orlando, Florida, USA.

The **lowest car** is *Mirai* ("Future"), which stood just 45.2 cm (1 ft 5.7 in) from the ground. Unveiled on 15 Nov 2010, it was the work of Okayama Sanyo High School in Asakuchi, Japan.

Greatest altitude change by an electric car
Between 27 and 30 Dec 2022, Qiao Jiao and his team (all CHN) drove an IM LS7 from Ayding Lake, 154 m (505 ft) below sea level, to the Tanggula Mountains in Tibet, China – a total climb of 5,389 m (17,682 ft). The stunt was organized by IM Motors (CHN) to celebrate the launch of its new electric SUV.

Fastest first-responder ambulance
On 29 Jan 2022, the Dubai Corporation for Ambulance Services unveiled its Hypersport Responder – a repurposed Lykan HyperSport with a top speed of 395 km/h (245.4 mph). Built at a cost of AED 13 m ($3.5 m; £2.6 m), the ambulance can accelerate from 0 to 100 km/h in 2.8 sec.

The same company also owns the **largest desert-rescue ambulance** – a heavily modified Mercedes Atego 1726 measuring 8.3 x 2.8 x 3.5 m (27 x 9 x 11 ft).

Shortest charging time to cross the USA in an electric vehicle
From 7 to 12 Nov 2021, Wayne Gerdes (USA, *inset*) drove a 2022 Porsche Taycan from Los Angeles to New York City with a cumulative charging time of just 2 hr 26 min 46 sec. Gerdes, a "professional long-distance traveller", stopped at 18 charge stations during his 2,834-mi (4,561-km) journey.

LEARN TO PLAY THE GUITAR
It's never too late to pick up a musical instrument. Although you might need to do some weight training before picking up the **largest acoustic guitar**, which measured 4.22 m (13 ft 10 in) long on 8 Sep 2018 and was created by Long Yunzhi (CHN) in Yunnan, China.

We spoke to Lennart Hessels, the leader of the Brunel team that will be competing at the Bridgestone World Solar Challenge in Sep 2023.

Tell us more about the Brunel Solar Team.
Our team was founded in 1998 and consists of students from Delft. The team members take more than a year out of their studies to build, develop and race a new solar car.

Are there any restrictions placed on the design of the cars?
The World Solar Challenge has a number of rules relating to the size of the car, battery and solar panel. These maintain an even playing field and further inspire innovation.

What's a race day like?
The alarm goes off at 5:00 a.m. and Race Management plan the day ahead. From 8:00 a.m. till 5:00 p.m., the race is on. Every day there is a control stop, where *Nuna* recharges in the sunlight for 30 min. At 5:00 p.m., a line is drawn on the road where *Nuna* needs to stop and camp is set up there. The support crew works through the night to make sure *Nuna* is ready to race.

How fast can solar-powered cars go?
The average speed of the car is 90 km/h [55 mph], with a maximum speed of around 120 km/h [74 mph].

How are preparations going for 2023?
After running hundreds of computer simulations to determine the ideal aerodynamic shape for the car, we have started hand-building it from carbon fibre. We are having to invent solutions for problems that have never been solved before. It's very exciting, but also challenging.

How has the car changed since the last race?
We are now driving on only three wheels for lower rolling resistance. The technology for solar panels, electric motors and batteries has also improved a lot. Our rivals have seen similar improvements, however, so we have to optimize everything to the millimetre.

The team preparing the car for maintenance at a control stop during the 2019 race

MOST WINS OF THE WORLD SOLAR CHALLENGE
First run in 1987, the World Solar Challenge is a biennial solar-powered car race across 3,020 km (1,876 mi) of the Australian Outback between Darwin and Adelaide. It has been won seven times by the Brunel (formerly Nuon) Solar Team from the Delft University of Technology in the Netherlands. The student team has constructed 11 different *Nuna* solar racers since its first iteration won the 2001 World Solar Challenge on debut. In 2005, *Nuna 3* (*left*) crossed the finish line after just 29 hr 11 min, recording the **fastest average speed at the World Solar Challenge** – 102.75 km/h (63.84 mph).

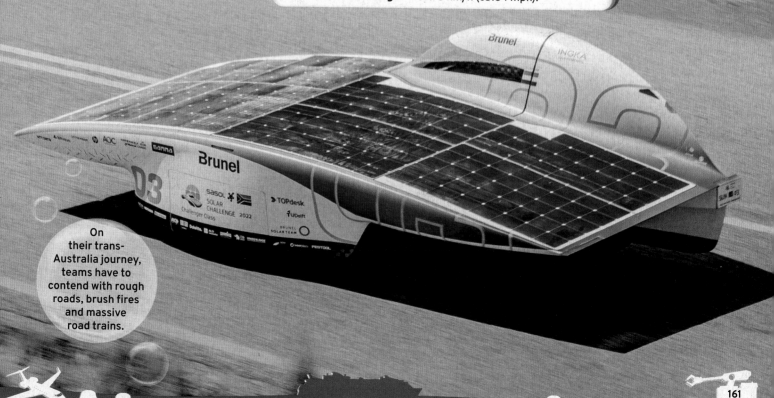

On their trans-Australia journey, teams have to contend with rough roads, brush fires and massive road trains.

SHIPS

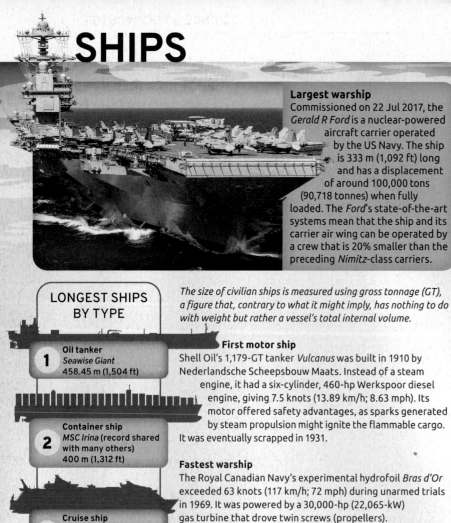

Largest warship
Commissioned on 22 Jul 2017, the *Gerald R Ford* is a nuclear-powered aircraft carrier operated by the US Navy. The ship is 333 m (1,092 ft) long and has a displacement of around 100,000 tons (90,718 tonnes) when fully loaded. The *Ford*'s state-of-the-art systems mean that the ship and its carrier air wing can be operated by a crew that is 20% smaller than the preceding *Nimitz*-class carriers.

Largest ship
At 403,342 GT, *Pioneering Spirit* is truly a ship of superlatives, being also the **largest catamaran, pipe-laying vessel** and **construction ship**. Built in 2011–14, it was designed for heavy-lift offshore building projects, including assembling and disassembling oil and gas platforms. It is operated by Allseas (CHE).

LONGEST SHIPS BY TYPE

1   **Oil tanker**
Seawise Giant
458.45 m (1,504 ft)

2   **Container ship**
MSC Irina (record shared with many others)
400 m (1,312 ft)

3   **Cruise ship**
Harmony of the Seas
362.12 m (1,188 ft)
(see also opposite)

4   **Ore carrier**
Vale-class
362 m (1,187 ft)

5   **Warship**
Gerald R Ford
333 m (1,092 ft)
(see above)

The size of civilian ships is measured using gross tonnage (GT), a figure that, contrary to what it might imply, has nothing to do with weight but rather a vessel's total internal volume.

First motor ship
Shell Oil's 1,179-GT tanker *Vulcanus* was built in 1910 by Nederlandsche Scheepsbouw Maats. Instead of a steam engine, it had a six-cylinder, 460-hp Werkspoor diesel engine, giving 7.5 knots (13.89 km/h; 8.63 mph). Its motor offered safety advantages, as sparks generated by steam propulsion might ignite the flammable cargo. It was eventually scrapped in 1931.

Fastest warship
The Royal Canadian Navy's experimental hydrofoil *Bras d'Or* exceeded 63 knots (117 km/h; 72 mph) during unarmed trials in 1969. It was powered by a 30,000-hp (22,065-kW) gas turbine that drove twin screws (propellers).

The **fastest warship with a displacement hull** (one that sits in the water, even at high speed) was the French destroyer *Le Terrible*. It reached 45.02 knots (83.38 km/h; 51.8 mph) in 1935.

First hydrogen-powered ferry
Norway's 2,699-GT *Hydra* was built for Norled AS by Westcon Yards, Florø, in Jul 2021 but was initially powered by conventional batteries. It was fitted with hydrogen fuel cells made by Ballard Power Systems (CAN) in Oct 2022, and underwent sea trials with the new powerplant the following month. Hydrogen systems are cleaner than other fuels as they only emit water vapour.

Largest superyacht
The 13,136-GT *Azzam* measures 180.6 x 20.8 m (592 ft 6 in x 68 ft 2 in). It can house 36 guests and up to 80 crew members, while its two gas turbines enable it to reach a speed of 33 knots (61.12 km/h; 37.98 mph). The ship was built in 2013 by Germany's Lürssen Yachts for Sheikh Khalifa bin Zayed al-Nahyan, who died in 2022.

Widest ships
The broadest monohull ships are the *Ramform Titan*-class survey ships, the lead ship of which was launched on 26 Apr 2013 by Mitsubishi Heavy Industries in Nagasaki, Japan. Their hulls are almost an equilateral triangle, measuring 70 m on the beam and 104 m from bow to stern (229 ft x 341 ft). These highly specialized vessels are designed to tow arrays of seismic sounders and microphones.

Largest semi-submersible heavy-lift ship
The 91,784-GT *BOKA Vanguard* was built by Hyundai Heavy Industries (KOR) in 2013. At 21,725 m² (233,845 sq ft), its deck is some 1.5 times larger than London's Trafalgar Square and can support a weight of 117,000 tonnes (128,970 tons). It is pictured in 2019 loading the cruise ship *Carnival Vista*, which it then transported to a shipyard for repairs.

BOKA Vanguard can partially submerge its hull to manoeuvre its deck under ships, before refloating to lift them up.

EXPERIENCE ZERO GRAVITY
Take the weight off your feet – literally – and say goodbye to gravity's pull for a while. Erin Finnegan and Noah Fulmor (both USA) liked the sensation so much they got married in the **first zero-g wedding** on board a "vomit comet" aircraft on 23 Jun 2009.

Pool deck

Water slides

Wonder Playscape
children's area

Ultimate Abyss

Wonder of the Seas is set to be surpassed by the 250,800-GT *Icon of the Seas* in early 2024.

Sports court

LARGEST CRUISE SHIP

The 235,600-GT luxury passenger liner *Wonder of the Seas* made its maiden voyage on 4 Mar 2022. The ship can accommodate around 7,000 passengers and 2,300 crew. Among its diverse attractions are an ice rink, an outdoor park with thousands of plants and the Bionic Bar (with robot bartenders). Thrill-seekers can ride the spiralling 70-ft-high (21.3-m) Ultimate Abyss slide between decks, or whiz along the 82-ft-long (25-m) zip wire, which is nine decks high.

Wonder of the Seas is the fifth of Royal Caribbean International's *Oasis*-class cruise liners, built by Chantiers de l'Atlantique in Saint-Nazaire, France. It is powered by six house-sized Wärtsilä diesel engines that generate a combined 100,140 kW (134,290 hp). They drive the propellers while also serving as the electrical power station for the whole ship.

AquaTheater

WONDER OF THE SEAS
NASSAU

TALL SHIPS

Sail Training International

Sail Training International is a charity that supports the development and education of young people through sail-training experiences. It began life as the Sail Training International Race Committee, which in 1956 organized the **first tall ships race** (*below*). A total of 20 vessels sailed from Torbay in Devon, UK, to the Portuguese capital Lisbon between 7 and 15 Jul. The race gave the fleet a new lease of life, and today Sail Training International's race series typically attracts 40–100 entrants. The main requirements are that 50% of the crew is aged 15–25 and that vessels have a waterline length of at least 9.14 m (29 ft 11 in). There are four classes of vessels: the largest is Class A, for square-rigged ships and sailing vessels of any rig with an overall length of 40 m (131 ft) or more.

Largest sailing ship ever
The *France II* measured 146.5 m (480 ft) in length and had a gross tonnage of 5,633. It was built at Chantiers et Ateliers de la Gironde in Bordeaux, France, and launched on 9 Nov 1912. Its two diesel engines were removed in 1919 as a cost-saving measure. The *France II* ran aground in a storm off the coast of New Caledonia in the South Pacific on 12 Jul 1922, having run for almost three years on sail power alone.

Largest wooden sailing ship ever
Launched on 15 Dec 1909, the *Wyoming* was a six-masted schooner measuring 137 m (450 ft) long and 15.3 m (50 ft) on the beam, with a gross tonnage of 3,730. It was constructed at a cost of $175,000 – equivalent to around $5.6 m (£4.5 m) in 2023 – and featured a hull built from yellow pine and a small steam engine that allowed its rigging to be operated by a crew of just 11. However, the *Wyoming*'s wooden hull hogged and sagged (flexed with the waves) in rough seas, causing leaks. On 11 Mar 1924, it foundered off Monomoy Island in Massachusetts, USA.

Most masts on a sailing ship
The only seven-masted sailing schooner ever built was the 114.4-m-long (375-ft) *Thomas W Lawson* (5,218 gross tons). Built at Quincy, Massachusetts, USA, in 1902, it was wrecked off the Isles of Scilly, UK, on 14 Dec 1907. All seven masts broke off and 16 crew were lost.

Most entrants in a tall-ships race
The Newcastle to Bergen leg of the Tall Ships Races 1993 had 122 vessels in competition. The UK–Norway race was won by *Frithjof II* (NOR), a Class B gaff cutter.
The **most tall-ships race leg wins** is 13, by the UK's *Jolie Brise*. The Class B gaff cutter, built in 1913 and operated by Dauntsey's School in Wiltshire, UK, has claimed the overall Tall Ships Races title five times (1980, 2008, 2011 and 2015–16).

DID YOU KNOW?
The winner of the 1956 Tall Ships Races, *Moyana*, sank on its voyage back to the UK.

Largest crew for a tall ship
The *Amerigo Vespucci* has a maximum complement of 415, including both professional crew and trainees. Built to resemble an early 18th-century wooden warship, it was constructed at the Castellammare di Stabia naval shipyard in Naples, Italy, and launched on 22 Feb 1931. Currently an Italian Navy training vessel, it carries 24 sails and can reach 12 knots (13.8 mph; 22.4 km/h).

Largest wooden sailing ship
The *Götheborg* measures 58 m (190 ft) from stern to bowsprit and has a gross tonnage of 788. It is a replica of a Swedish East India Company vessel that sank in 1735 near its home port of Gothenburg upon returning from China. The present-day *Götheborg* was built between 1995 and 2003 as an exact copy, based on the original plans.

Oldest tall ship
Built in 1874, *Far Barcelona* is a Spanish-owned Class B vessel that has taken part in the Tall Ships Races. It is a Norwegian *jakt*, originally named the *Anne Dorthea*, constructed in the Hardanger region to transport barrels of herring. Restored in Spain, it now serves as a floating classroom and has hosted 15,000 hours of training in shipbuilding and maintenance.

The *Amerigo Vespucci* was described as "the most beautiful ship in the world" by US Navy crews.

TRAVEL THE WORLD
Broaden your horizons by exploring new places and cultures. Between 1 Jun 2017 and 7 Dec 2018, Taylor Demonbreun (USA) went on a whistlestop tour of the world, achieving the **fastest time to visit all sovereign countries** in just 1 year 189 days.

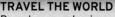

Trainees on board the *Statsraad Lehmkuhl* learn crucial mariner skills such as navigation and watchkeeping.

FASTEST TALL SHIP

Since 1964, Sail Training International has recorded the top speeds of all sailing vessels to have submitted fast passages for the annual "Boston Teapot Trophy". These records are calculated as an average across a 120-hr period, to counteract factors such as gusty winds that might provide short-lived peaks of speed. The *Statsraad Lehmkuhl* is an eight-time winner, with a highest recorded average speed of 12.49 knots (14.3 mph; 23.1 km/h) in 2016. The swift square-rigger was built in 1914 in Bremerhaven, Germany, and was acquired by Norwegian politician Kristofer Lehmkuhl in 1921. It has a crew of 150 and is run by a non-profit foundation.

SPACE

Fastest spacecraft speed
Orbiting the Sun, the Parker Solar Probe reached 586,800 km/h (364,620 mph) at 21:25:24 UTC* on 20 Nov 2021. The probe hit this speed at perihelion (the closest point in its elliptical solar orbit) after a gravity assist from a Venus flyby on 16 Oct.
      At the same moment, it achieved the **closest approach to the Sun by a spacecraft** – 8,541,744 km (5,307,594 mi). Both records will stand until after the probe's next encounter with Venus on 21 Aug 2023.

Longest career as a project scientist
At the time of his retirement in Oct 2022, American physicist Edward Stone had served as the project scientist for the Voyager missions for 50 years. He first assumed the role – taking responsibility for research operations – in 1972 during the planning stages, and became the public face of the Voyager program during its historic flybys of the outer planets. The *Voyager 1* probe that he saw launch in 1977 is now the **most remote human-made object**, cruising through interstellar space some 23.631 billion km (14.683 billion mi) from Earth.

FARTHEST FLIGHT ON MARS
On 8 Apr 2022, NASA's autonomous helicopter *Ingenuity* flew a distance of 704 m (2,309 ft) in the Jezero Crater. The flight was the longest leg of a 2-km-long (1.2-mi), six-stage journey across an area of soft, wind-blown sand called the Séítah, which is impassable to the heavy *Perseverance* rover. Shown below is the broken backshell of the descent module, discarded as the rover arrived on Mars in Feb 2021. It was later found in the Séítah and photographed by the helicopter.

DID YOU KNOW?
Ingenuity is a diminutive wonder, standing only 49 cm (1 ft 7 in) tall.

The helicopter recharges its battery cells with a 42 x 16-cm (16.5 x 6.3-in) solar panel.

It has a pair of two-bladed rotors that spin in opposite directions to keep it stable.

Ingenuity was only intended to make five test flights. As of 27 Jan 2023, it had made 41.

Longest time spent in space by a female astronaut
Between 2002 and 2017, Peggy Whitson (USA) spent a cumulative 665 days 22 hr 22 min in orbit. During her tenure, she became the **first woman to command the *International Space Station* (*ISS*)**. Although she retired from NASA in Jun 2018, the iconic astronaut is space-bound again in 2023, on private company Axiom's second flight to the *ISS*. She's shown here training with John Shoffner, who will be her co-pilot.

Longest-functioning Mars orbiter
NASA's *2001 Mars Odyssey* marked its 21st year in orbit around the Red Planet on 24 Oct 2022. It was launched on 7 Apr 2001 from Cape Canaveral Air Force Station in Florida, USA, and inserted into orbit around Mars on 24 Oct 2001 at 02:18.

Most launches in one year by a rocket model
Over the course of 2022, SpaceX Falcon 9 rockets made 60 successful launches, beating the record of 45 set by the Soviet Soyuz-U, which had stood since 1980. This total included six launches by core B1058, which ended the year with the **most launches by an orbital rocket stage** – 15 (a record equalled by B1060 on 3 Jan 2023).

Most powerful earthquake recorded on another planet
On 4 May 2022, the seismometer on NASA's Mars *InSight* lander recorded a magnitude-5 earthquake (or "Marsquake"), the largest ever detected on another world. As of 27 Oct 2022, *InSight* had recorded 1,318 quakes, most of them due to motions along fractures within Mars, but some caused by asteroid impacts.
      On 5 Sep 2021, *InSight* registered the **first asteroid impact ground quakes felt on another planet**. An asteroid exploded mid-air into at least three pieces that left impact craters on the ground. Earth is the only other planet where the ground-shaking and booms of an asteroid impact have been detected.

Largest space telescope
The long-awaited James Webb Space Telescope, with its massive 6.5-m (21-ft 3-in) primary mirror, returned its first calibrated images in Jul 2022. It has already captured a host of stunning celestial sights, including the Pillars of Creation (*right*) – towers of interstellar gas and dust where stars form. Excitingly, the very first deep-field image that it took (*above*) contains several potential candidates for the title of **most distant galaxy**, although we'll need further observations before we know for sure. Until then, watch this *space...*

All times and dates are in Coordinated Universal Time (UTC)

Greatest elevation gained by a space rover
Since landing on Mars on 6 Aug 2012, NASA's *Curiosity* rover has climbed more than 621 m (2,037 ft) above its landing site. *Curiosity* drove slightly downhill during the first year of its mission, so its exact elevation range had been 641.54 m (2,104 ft 9 in) as of sol 3606 – i.e., after 3,606 Martian days. This picture (taken by *Curiosity* on 9 Sep 2015) shows the rocky heights of the Vera Rubin Ridge. Circled in yellow, more than 3.5 km (2.1 mi) distant, is a *Curiosity*-sized boulder that the rover passed on 15 Jul 2022.

As of 6 Feb 2023, Curiosity was climbing the slope behind this ridge

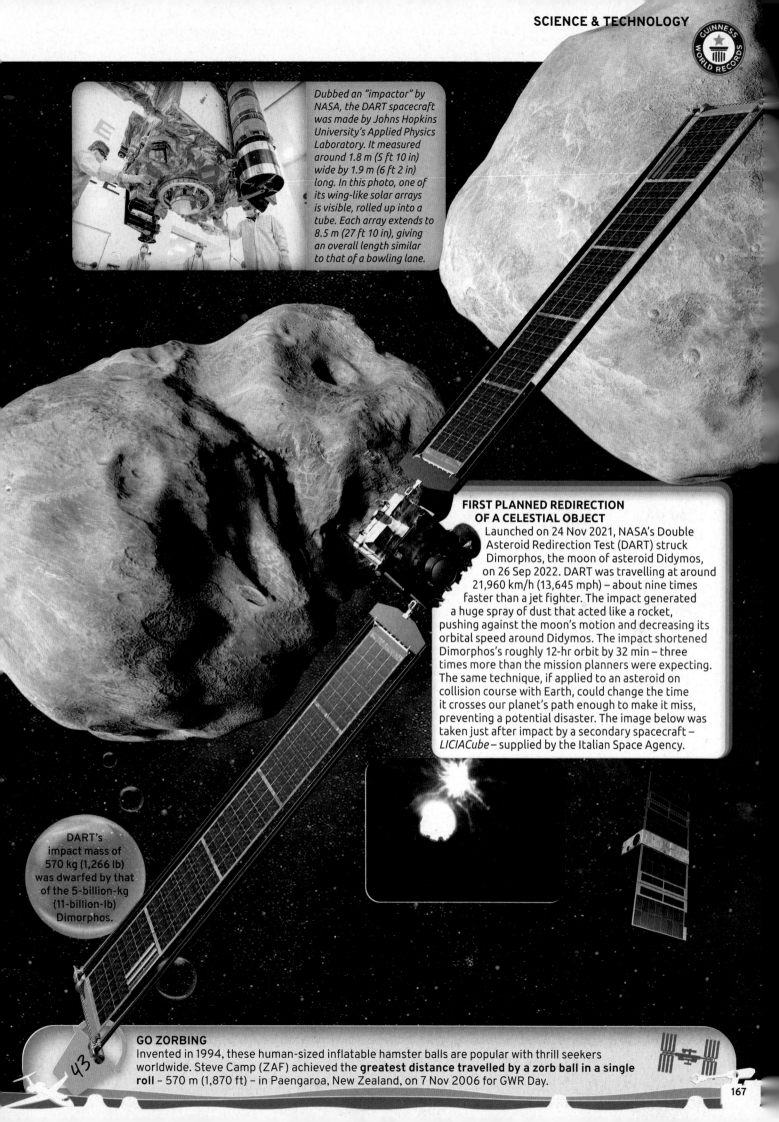

Dubbed an "impactor" by NASA, the DART spacecraft was made by Johns Hopkins University's Applied Physics Laboratory. It measured around 1.8 m (5 ft 10 in) wide by 1.9 m (6 ft 2 in) long. In this photo, one of its wing-like solar arrays is visible, rolled up into a tube. Each array extends to 8.5 m (27 ft 10 in), giving an overall length similar to that of a bowling lane.

FIRST PLANNED REDIRECTION OF A CELESTIAL OBJECT

Launched on 24 Nov 2021, NASA's Double Asteroid Redirection Test (DART) struck Dimorphos, the moon of asteroid Didymos, on 26 Sep 2022. DART was travelling at around 21,960 km/h (13,645 mph) – about nine times faster than a jet fighter. The impact generated a huge spray of dust that acted like a rocket, pushing against the moon's motion and decreasing its orbital speed around Didymos. The impact shortened Dimorphos's roughly 12-hr orbit by 32 min – three times more than the mission planners were expecting. The same technique, if applied to an asteroid on collision course with Earth, could change the time it crosses our planet's path enough to make it miss, preventing a potential disaster. The image below was taken just after impact by a secondary spacecraft – *LICIACube* – supplied by the Italian Space Agency.

DART's impact mass of 570 kg (1,266 lb) was dwarfed by that of the 5-billion-kg (11-billion-lb) Dimorphos.

GO ZORBING

Invented in 1994, these human-sized inflatable hamster balls are popular with thrill seekers worldwide. Steve Camp (ZAF) achieved the **greatest distance travelled by a zorb ball in a single roll** – 570 m (1,870 ft) – in Paengaroa, New Zealand, on 7 Nov 2006 for GWR Day.

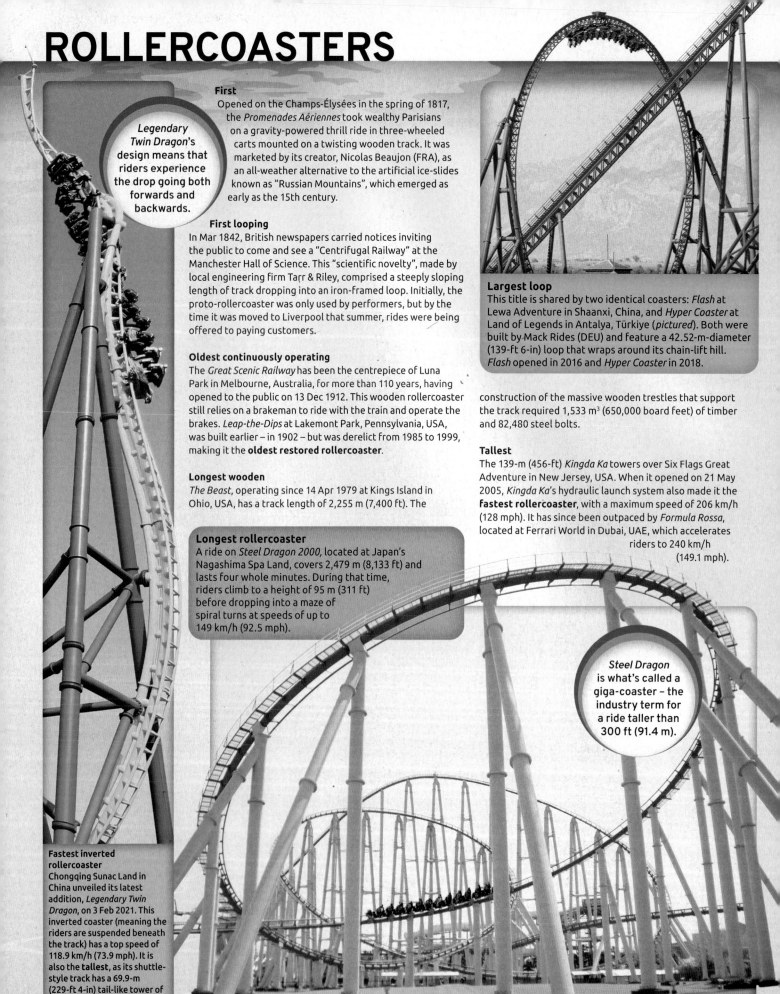

ROLLERCOASTERS

First
Opened on the Champs-Élysées in the spring of 1817, the *Promenades Aériennes* took wealthy Parisians on a gravity-powered thrill ride in three-wheeled carts mounted on a twisting wooden track. It was marketed by its creator, Nicolas Beaujon (FRA), as an all-weather alternative to the artificial ice-slides known as "Russian Mountains", which emerged as early as the 15th century.

First looping
In Mar 1842, British newspapers carried notices inviting the public to come and see a "Centrifugal Railway" at the Manchester Hall of Science. This "scientific novelty", made by local engineering firm Tarr & Riley, comprised a steeply sloping length of track dropping into an iron-framed loop. Initially, the proto-rollercoaster was only used by performers, but by the time it was moved to Liverpool that summer, rides were being offered to paying customers.

Oldest continuously operating
The *Great Scenic Railway* has been the centrepiece of Luna Park in Melbourne, Australia, for more than 110 years, having opened to the public on 13 Dec 1912. This wooden rollercoaster still relies on a brakeman to ride with the train and operate the brakes. *Leap-the-Dips* at Lakemont Park, Pennsylvania, USA, was built earlier – in 1902 – but was derelict from 1985 to 1999, making it the **oldest restored rollercoaster**.

Longest wooden
The Beast, operating since 14 Apr 1979 at Kings Island in Ohio, USA, has a track length of 2,255 m (7,400 ft). The construction of the massive wooden trestles that support the track required 1,533 m³ (650,000 board feet) of timber and 82,480 steel bolts.

Largest loop
This title is shared by two identical coasters: *Flash* at Lewa Adventure in Shaanxi, China, and *Hyper Coaster* at Land of Legends in Antalya, Türkiye (*pictured*). Both were built by Mack Rides (DEU) and feature a 42.52-m-diameter (139-ft 6-in) loop that wraps around its chain-lift hill. *Flash* opened in 2016 and *Hyper Coaster* in 2018.

Tallest
The 139-m (456-ft) *Kingda Ka* towers over Six Flags Great Adventure in New Jersey, USA. When it opened on 21 May 2005, *Kingda Ka*'s hydraulic launch system also made it the **fastest rollercoaster**, with a maximum speed of 206 km/h (128 mph). It has since been outpaced by *Formula Rossa*, located at Ferrari World in Dubai, UAE, which accelerates riders to 240 km/h (149.1 mph).

> *Legendary Twin Dragon*'s design means that riders experience the drop going both forwards and backwards.

Longest rollercoaster
A ride on *Steel Dragon 2000,* located at Japan's Nagashima Spa Land, covers 2,479 m (8,133 ft) and lasts four whole minutes. During that time, riders climb to a height of 95 m (311 ft) before dropping into a maze of spiral turns at speeds of up to 149 km/h (92.5 mph).

> *Steel Dragon* is what's called a giga-coaster – the industry term for a ride taller than 300 ft (91.4 m).

Fastest inverted rollercoaster
Chongqing Sunac Land in China unveiled its latest addition, *Legendary Twin Dragon*, on 3 Feb 2021. This inverted coaster (meaning the riders are suspended beneath the track) has a top speed of 118.9 km/h (73.9 mph). It is also the **tallest**, as its shuttle-style track has a 69.9-m (229-ft 4-in) tail-like tower of twisted track at each end.

VISIT GREECE
Travel to the heart of an ancient civilization, to the Acropolis of Athens, where millennia-old temples and civic buildings overlook the city. Among them is the **first permanent theatre**, the amphitheatre-style Theatre of Dionysus, built in *c.* 500 BCE. (*For more about Greek theatre, see p.184*).

MOST ROLLERCOASTERS IN A THEME PARK

With the opening of *Wonder Woman Flight of Courage* on 16 Jul 2022, Six Flags Magic Mountain in Valencia, California, USA, had a total of 20 active rollercoasters. This roster includes four current record holders (*see insets*), and several others which held records at the time of their construction.

Magic Mountain opened to the public in 1971 with just one full-size rollercoaster; it didn't become a major draw for coaster fans until 1976, with the debut of the *Great American Revolution* (now the *New Revolution*). This was the first modern rollercoaster to include a full vertical loop – a feature of early rollercoasters (*see opposite*) that had fallen out of favour for about 70 years owing to safety issues.

Tallest stand-up
Riddler's Revenge (1998)
47.5 m (156 ft)

Riders reach speeds of 93 km/h (58 mph)

Maximum height: 40 m (131 ft)

Wonder Woman Flight of Courage is the **tallest single-rail rollercoaster**, rising 40 m (131 ft) above the park.

This element is called an "overbanked cutback"

Tallest flying
Tatsu (2006)
52 m (170 ft)

Tallest shuttle
Superman: Escape from Krypton (1997)
126.5 m (415 ft)

87° initial drop

Airtime hills

Track length: 1 km (3,300 ft)

LEARN SIGN LANGUAGE

Brush up on your signing skills by watching *CODA* (FRA/CAN/USA, 2021). Actor Troy Kotsur (USA) became the **first deaf man to win an acting Oscar** thanks to his performance – his co-star, Marlee Matlin (USA), had become the **first Oscar-winning deaf actor** in 1987.

41

BIG SCIENCE

Most magnetic molecule
Engineered by an international team, the dilanthanide complex $(Cp^{iPr5})_2Tb_2I_3$ (*right*) has a coercive magnetic field of more than 25 tesla at -223°C (-369°F). This is more than 100 times greater than the most powerful iron-based magnets. It was made possible by joining two ions of a strongly magnetic rare-earth element (in grey) using a bridge of iodine and carbon (in teal and purple).

Fastest computer
In 2022, the Oak Ridge National Laboratory in Tennessee, USA, unveiled the first "exascale" computer, *Frontier*. In floating-point arithmetic tests (manipulating very large or small numbers), this 268-tonne (295-ton) supercomputer achieved a speed of 1.102 exaflops (just over a million billion floating-point operations per second). A typical desktop computer would take about six weeks to do what *Frontier* can do in one second!

Highest-resolution microscope image
Developed by a team led by David Muller of Cornell University (USA), electron ptychography can capture details just 20 picometres across. That's about one-fifth of the width of a hydrogen atom. An image made using this method was published in *Science* on 21 May 2021.

Largest plasma wind tunnel
To reproduce the conditions experienced during hypersonic flight – particularly during atmospheric re-entry – engineers use plasma wind tunnels. The largest example is the SCIROCCO facility at the Italian Aerospace Research Centre near Capua, Italy, which houses a 70-megawatt arc heater. It is capable of thrusting a 2-m-wide (6-ft 6-in) jet of superheated plasma through the test chamber at speeds of up to Mach 12.

Largest solar telescope
The Daniel K Inouye Solar Telescope (USA) has a primary mirror with a 4-m (13-ft) diameter. Declared complete on 22 Nov 2021, it is part of the Haleakalā High Altitude Observatory Site near the top of an inactive volcano on Maui, Hawaii. It can image the Sun multiple times a second, revealing features on the surface three times smaller than anything seen by previous solar observatories.

Longest-lasting bubble
PhD student Aymeric Roux and University of Lille (both FRA) produced a bubble that endured for 1 year 100 days in Lille, France. It contained a high concentration of glycerol, as well as plastic particles. The feat was verified on 18 Jan 2021.

A bubble is a thin layer of liquid enclosing a gas, such as air. By contrast, an "antibubble" is a thin layer of gas that encases a liquid, while immersed in liquid itself. The **longest-lasting antibubble** remained intact for some 13 hr in an experiment by a team of Chinese and Belgian scientists. The results were published in *Physical Review Fluids* on 27 Jun 2022.

Shortest measured day on Earth
According to the International Earth Rotation and Reference Systems Service, 29 Jun 2022 was 1.59 millisec shorter than typical. Earth's days have recently been growing incrementally shorter. This may be the result of shrinking glaciers and polar ice caps – relaxing the pressure on Earth's crust near the poles – or the periodic oscillation of the planet's magnetic poles.

Fallturm Bremen freefall drop tube
1. Release mechanism
2. Sled
3. Drop capsule
4. Drop shaft
5. Elevator
6. Hall
7. Deceleration chamber
8. Vacuum chamber
9. Hanger bars
10. Drop capsule
11. Base of chute
12. Acceleration shaft, housing catapult
13. Foundation

Longest drop-tube freefall time
What we call weightlessness is, in fact, a state of continuous freefall. This means that it is possible to replicate the behaviour of an object in orbit by simply dropping it into a vacuum tube. The problem with this technique is that unless the tube is extremely tall, the object only has a few seconds of freefall. The Fallturm drop tower at the University of Bremen, Germany, contains a 122-m-tall (400-ft) vacuum tube. To study objects in freefall, researchers load experiments into a capsule, which is then fired up the tower using a powerful catapult. The result is 9.3 sec of freefall, compared with only 4.74 sec if it were just dropped from the top.

Brightest X-ray source
The aptly named Extremely Brilliant Source (EBS) can generate an X-ray beam with an energy of 6 gigaelectronvolts. It can generate images 100 billion times brighter than hospital X-rays, enabling clinicians to view blood vessels a mere 5 micrometres wide. Located at the European Synchrotron Radiation Facility in Grenoble, France, this ring-shaped machine measures 268.6 m (881 ft) across. It has already made an invaluable contribution to University College London's online Human Organ Atlas, a detailed survey of body parts (*inset*).

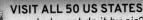

VISIT ALL 50 US STATES
... and why not do it by air? Treat yourself to a bird's-eye view of the geographic diversity – and mind-boggling scale – of the USA! The **fastest time to fly a hot-air balloon in all 50 US states** is 43 days 3 hr 11 min, by the UK's Andrew Holly, who completed his flight over Hawaii on 24 Mar 2016.

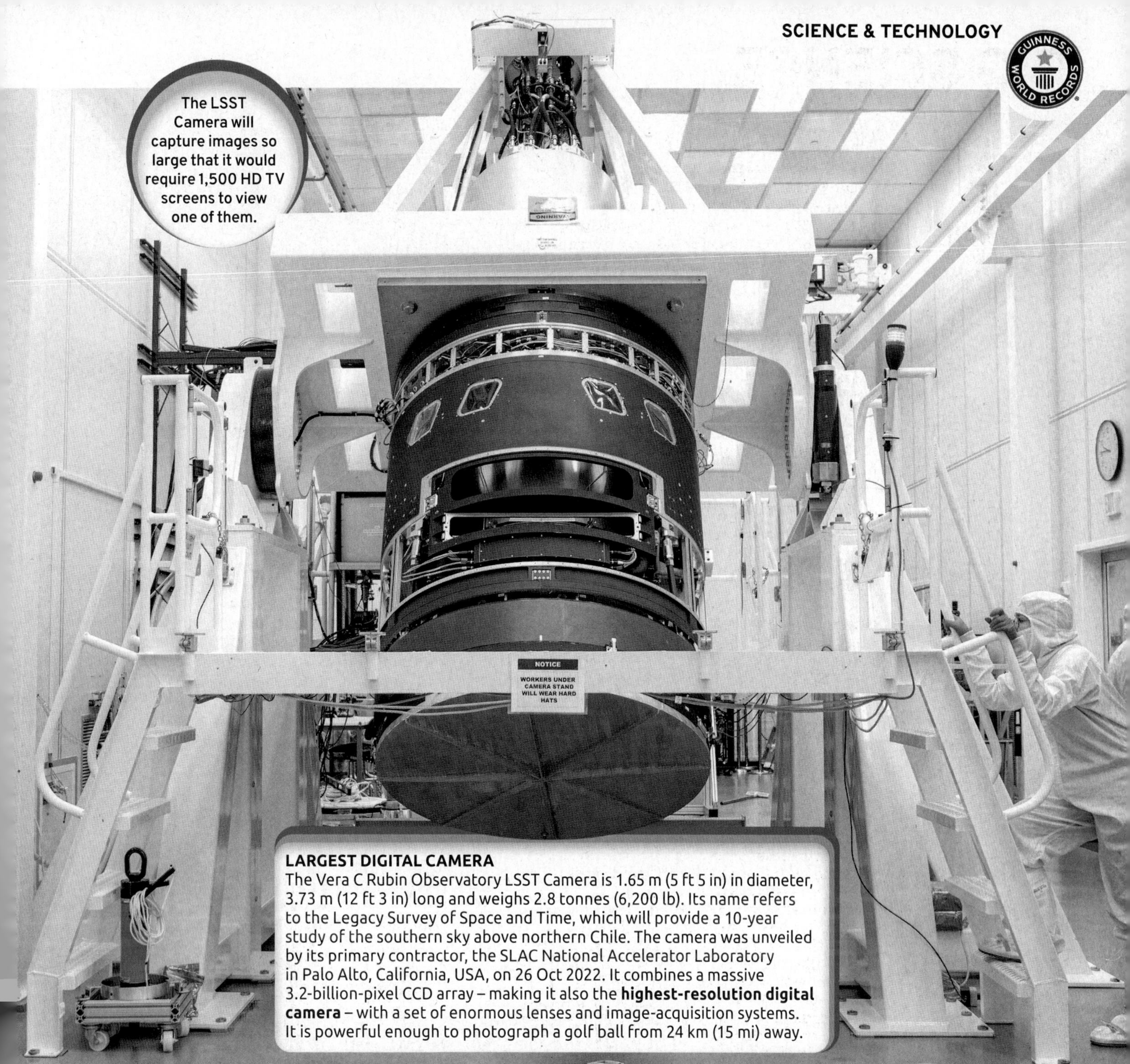

The LSST Camera will capture images so large that it would require 1,500 HD TV screens to view one of them.

NOTICE
WORKERS UNDER CAMERA STAND WILL WEAR HARD HATS

LARGEST DIGITAL CAMERA

The Vera C Rubin Observatory LSST Camera is 1.65 m (5 ft 5 in) in diameter, 3.73 m (12 ft 3 in) long and weighs 2.8 tonnes (6,200 lb). Its name refers to the Legacy Survey of Space and Time, which will provide a 10-year study of the southern sky above northern Chile. The camera was unveiled by its primary contractor, the SLAC National Accelerator Laboratory in Palo Alto, California, USA, on 26 Oct 2022. It combines a massive 3.2-billion-pixel CCD array – making it also the **highest-resolution digital camera** – with a set of enormous lenses and image-acquisition systems. It is powerful enough to photograph a golf ball from 24 km (15 mi) away.

The LSST Camera will record images from the Simonyi Survey Telescope. Both are housed in the Rubin Observatory – still under construction in Elqui Province, Chile. The telescope will photograph the night sky a few times a week.

The front part of the camera houses three lenses, filters and an automatic filter changer, as well as the CCD array. A utility trunk in the narrower part of the unit incorporates support electronics, vacuum pumps and cooling systems.

The L1-L2 lens assembly at the front of the camera houses the two carefully aligned primary lenses. The L1 lens, which is shown above, is 1.6 m (5 ft 2 in) in diameter. All lenses have broadband anti-reflection coatings.

GO TO THE AIRPORT AND TAKE THE NEXT RANDOM FLIGHT SOMEWHERE

Planning a trip can be stressful, so why not let fortune be your guide? Fate may land you at Dubai International Airport in the UAE, the **busiest airport for international passengers**. An estimated 88.8 million travellers passed through there in 2018.

39

ROBOTS

Deepest operational soft robot
Soft robots are made of flexible materials comparable to the materials found in living organisms, and their engineering often reflects the way that life forms operate. Researchers at Zhejiang University (CHN) deployed a soft robot at a depth of 10,900 m (35,761 ft) in the Mariana Trench; the results of the study were published on 3 Mar 2021. Its design is inspired by the **deepest fish**, the snailfish (*see p.43*).

Longest time inside a tropical cyclone by an uncrewed aircraft
On 28 Sep 2022, an ALTIUS-600 drone survived 102 min within the eye of category-4 storm Hurricane Ian. It was deployed into the storm north-west of the Florida Keys by a US National Oceanic and Atmospheric Administration (NOAA) hurricane hunter aircraft. The ALTIUS-600 is launched from a pneumatic tube, and has folding wings that extend to a span of 2.5 m (8 ft 4 in). Its guidance systems were fixed on the centre of the eye as it battled wind speeds of 188 knots (348 km/h; 216 mph) to return valuable weather data to NOAA scientists.

Fastest quadruped robot
Boston Dynamics' four-legged WildCat achieved a speed of 25 km/h (19 mph) during testing in Cambridge, Massachusetts, USA, in Oct 2013.

Though it was fast, WildCat's hydraulic actuators required a design that was heavy (154 kg; 339 lb) and extremely loud. Subsequent research has focused on

According to the International Federation of Robotics (IFR) *World Robotics 2022 Report*, the **most common type of domestic robots** are floor cleaners, such as mops and vacuums. There are an estimated 17 million such units active globally, with the true figure being likely significantly higher.

The next most common types are gardening and outdoor cleaning robots, each with around 1 million active units. Established in 1987, the IFR promotes the research, development and practical benefits of robots. The 2022 edition of its annual survey of the industry also revealed that South Korea has 1,000 robots per 10,000 employees – making it the **most automated economy** – while China has the **most active industrial robots** – around 1,224,000 units.

Most drones performing an aerial dance
On 5 Nov 2022, a swarm of 1,990 quadcopters lit up the night sky above Riyadh, Saudi Arabia. The performance was part of Noor Riyadh, an annual festival of light and art. The computer-controlled drones took part in two aerial displays under the title *the order of chaos: chaos in order*, choreographed by artist Marc Brickman.

using "reinforcement-learning" control systems to get better performance from all-electric designs such as the 9-kg (20-lb) MIT Mini Cheetah. In Mar 2022, a team at the Massachusetts Institute of Technology set a new **fastest electrically actuated speed** record of 14 km/h (8.7 mph) with one of these robots. This was beaten in Dec 2022 by a group from Zhejiang University, whose own Mini-Cheetah-based robot reached 18 km/h (11.18 mph).

Highest jump by a quadruped robot
On 4 Jul 2018, the MIT Mini Cheetah's larger sibling, the 45.3-kg (100-lb) Cheetah 3, cleared a height of 78.74 cm (2 ft 7 in) by launching with its rear legs alone, like a cat.

Largest robotic arm in space
Canadarm2, built by the Canadian Space Agency, is 17.5 m (57 ft 8 in) long and weighs 1,641 kg (3,618 lb). It was attached to the *International Space Station* (*ISS*) on 22 Apr 2001. The arm can detach from the station at either end and move like a caterpillar around the hull in order to handle construction and cargo on any part of the *ISS*.

Back on Earth, the **strongest robot arm** is the M-2000iA/2300 Super Heavy Payload Robot, released by the FANUC Corporation (JPN) in 2016. This six-axis mechanical arm can lift as much as 2,300 kg (5,070 lb).

DID YOU KNOW?

Renaissance polymath Leonardo da Vinci designed a human automaton in 1495.

The term "robot" derives from *robota*, a Czech word meaning "forced labour".

An "android" is a robot that has been designed with a human-like form.

There are some 3.5 million industrial robots active today, according to the IFR.

Most automated industry
According to the International Federation of Robotics' latest survey, published on 13 Oct 2022, car makers operate 31% of all industrial robots active today. The next most robot-heavy sector is electrical/electronics manufacturing, which employs 25% of the global total, followed by metal foundries at 11%.

NOAA's "hurricane" variant has a chopped-down sail for stability in high winds.

Highest wind speed recorded by an uncrewed surface vehicle
On 30 Sep 2021, Saildrone Explorer SD 1045 registered a wind speed of 125 knots (231 km/h; 143 mph) as it passed through the eyewall of the category-4 Hurricane Sam *c.* 750 km (466 mi) north-east of Puerto Rico. This 7-m-long (23-ft) autonomous research craft was designed by Saildrone (USA) in partnership with NOAA. Each of these vehicles is fitted with instruments to measure sea and air temperatures, wind speeds and ambient pressure.
Pictured right is the view from SD 1045's on-board camera during the storm.

VISIT HAWAII
Aloha! Welcome to the only US state that consists entirely of islands! Hawaii is also home to Mauna Kea, the **tallest mountain**. Measured from its submarine base in the Hawaiian Trough to its peak, it has a full height of *c.* 10,205 m (33,480 ft) – more than 1.3 km (0.8 mi) taller than Everest.

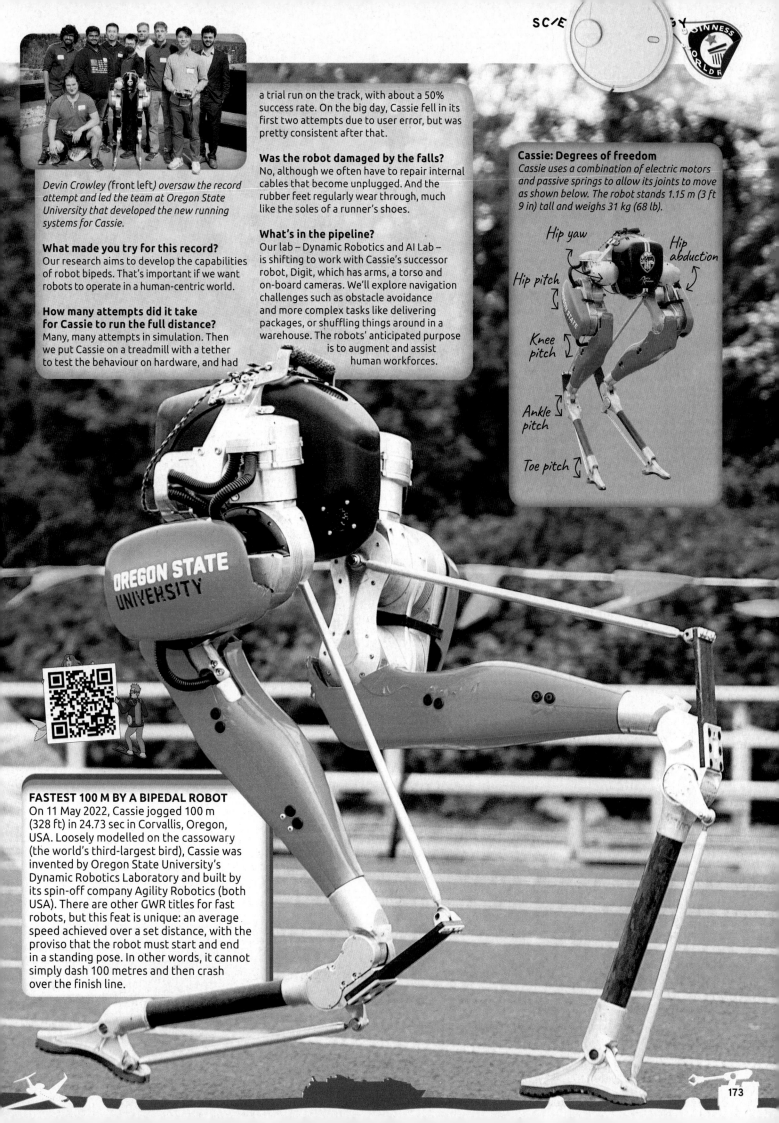

Devin Crowley (front left) oversaw the record attempt and led the team at Oregon State University that developed the new running systems for Cassie.

What made you try for this record?
Our research aims to develop the capabilities of robot bipeds. That's important if we want robots to operate in a human-centric world.

How many attempts did it take for Cassie to run the full distance?
Many, many attempts in simulation. Then we put Cassie on a treadmill with a tether to test the behaviour on hardware, and had a trial run on the track, with about a 50% success rate. On the big day, Cassie fell in its first two attempts due to user error, but was pretty consistent after that.

Was the robot damaged by the falls?
No, although we often have to repair internal cables that become unplugged. And the rubber feet regularly wear through, much like the soles of a runner's shoes.

What's in the pipeline?
Our lab – Dynamic Robotics and AI Lab – is shifting to work with Cassie's successor robot, Digit, which has arms, a torso and on-board cameras. We'll explore navigation challenges such as obstacle avoidance and more complex tasks like delivering packages, or shuffling things around in a warehouse. The robots' anticipated purpose is to augment and assist human workforces.

Cassie: Degrees of freedom
Cassie uses a combination of electric motors and passive springs to allow its joints to move as shown below. The robot stands 1.15 m (3 ft 9 in) tall and weighs 31 kg (68 lb).

Hip yaw
Hip abduction
Hip pitch
Knee pitch
Ankle pitch
Toe pitch

FASTEST 100 M BY A BIPEDAL ROBOT
On 11 May 2022, Cassie jogged 100 m (328 ft) in 24.73 sec in Corvallis, Oregon, USA. Loosely modelled on the cassowary (the world's third-largest bird), Cassie was invented by Oregon State University's Dynamic Robotics Laboratory and built by its spin-off company Agility Robotics (both USA). There are other GWR titles for fast robots, but this feat is unique: an average speed achieved over a set distance, with the proviso that the robot must start and end in a standing pose. In other words, it cannot simply dash 100 metres and then crash over the finish line.

ROUND-UP

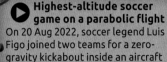

Highest-altitude soccer game on a parabolic flight
On 20 Aug 2022, soccer legend Luis Figo joined two teams for a zero-gravity kickabout inside an aircraft flying 20,230 ft (6,166 m) over Bordeaux, France. A referee and a GWR adjudicator were on board to ensure (f)air play at all times. The "Out-of-this-World Match" was organized by Mastercard.

Quietest room
The anechoic chamber at Orfield Laboratories in Minneapolis, Minnesota, USA, has produced a background noise reading of -13 dBA (decibels A-weighted). Zero on the decibel scale is the quietest sound a person can hear. The room, which is insulated with thick walls and fibreglass acoustic wedges, is used to test products' volume and sound quality.

First net-positive fusion reaction
On 13 Dec 2022, an important milestone was reached by researchers at the National Ignition Facility in California, USA. By focusing 192 laser beams on to a peppercorn-sized pellet of deuterium and tritium, the team triggered a nuclear-fusion reaction that created more energy than was required to initiate it.

Making electricity with this technology, however, will require continuous fusion reactions. So far, the **longest fusion reaction** is one that was sustained for 17 min 36 sec in a tokamak reactor at the Hefei Institute of Physical Science in China on 30 Dec 2021.

Greatest distance to sychronize two optical clocks
A pair of optical clocks 113 km (70.2 mi) apart in Xinjiang, China, were synchronized using a refined, high-powered laser by a team from the University of Science and Technology of China. The results were published in *Nature* on 5 Oct 2022. Optical clocks are capable of a higher degree of accuracy than current synchronization technology can support, meaning they can't be used for scientific standards. Making optical clock synchronization possible would enable technologies such as more accurate GPS.

Highest-capacity offshore wind farm
Hornsea Two is a 1,320-MW wind farm built by Danish firm Ørsted some 89 km (55.3 mi) off the coast of Yorkshire, UK. The facility's 165 turbines were declared operational on 31 Aug 2022. At maximum efficiency, the turbines can generate enough power for 1.4 million homes.

Farthest distance travelled by rubber-band-powered vehicle
On 20 Feb 2022, a construction-toy vehicle built by Micah Bartel (CAN) and powered by a twisted elastic band moved 32.93 m (108 ft) across a gymnasium in Winnipeg, Manitoba, Canada.

Highest wattage from a potato battery
On 16 Dec 2022, Brazilian pop star Anitta remixed her hit "Envolver" in a Los Angeles recording studio powered by a potato battery comprising 8,500 spuds that produced 67.76 Watt-hours of power. The musical "mash-up" was the result of a collaboration between ZyynLabs and potato-chip makers Frito-Lay North America (both USA).

Longest tin-can telephone
On 8 Oct 2022, two yoghurt pots joined by a wire carried voices 373.79 m (1,226 ft 4 in) along the seafront of Sidmouth in Devon, UK. The tin-can telephone was cooked up by John Hems and the Sidmouth Science Festival (both UK).

Most powerful rocket by thrust (current)
NASA's Space Launch System (SLS, *left*) generates 36,786 kN (8.27 million lbf) on launch. Its Block 1 model made its maiden launch on 16 Nov 2022 from the Kennedy Space Center in Florida, USA. With a payload capacity of 95,000 kg (209,439 lb), the SLS is also the **most powerful active rocket by lift capacity**.

The SLS has a heavyweight rival to its record: the SpaceX Starship (*right*), which was scheduled to launch in Apr 2023. The fully reusable rocket has a 30-engine first stage that is expected to generate 74,285 kN (16.7 million lbf). If successful, this will exceed both the SLS and the **most powerful rocket ever**, the ill-fated Soviet N1 (1969–72).

VISIT IRELAND
The Emerald Isle is renowned for its rich culture, warm hospitality and wild landscapes. If sport is your thing, head straight to Croke Park in Dublin, a historic arena and the **largest Gaelic football stadium**, with a capacity of 82,300.

Longest bridge span

The 1915 Çanakkale Bridge stretches 2,023 m (6,637 ft) across the Dardenelles Strait in Türkiye. Built over five years at a reported cost of around $2.8 bn (£2.1 bn), the steel suspension bridge opened on 18 Mar 2022. It is named for a famous Ottoman victory that took place nearby during World War I.

Strongest duct tape

In internationally standard tests performed on 6 Jul 2022 in Mentor, Ohio, USA, T-Rex Brute Force tape was found to have a tensile strength at break of 273.1 pounds per inch (30.8 Newtons per metre). The super-strong waterproof adhesive was made by Shurtape Technologies (USA).

First recorded volcanic eruption on Venus

In Feb 1991, NASA's *Magellan* probe scanned a Venusian mountain range called the Atla Regio. From orbit, it captured an image of a volcanic caldera near Maat Mons, an 8,000-m-high (26,250-ft) stratovolcano. When the probe returned to this area in Oct 1991, the caldera had changed size and shape, and a 69-km² (26-sq-mi) lava field had appeared on the slopes below. This eruption remained unnoticed until 2020, when geophysicist Robert Herrick (USA) took to comparing *Magellan* imagery during long work meetings on Zoom. The findings were published in *Science* on 15 Mar 2023.

Most emojis formed by UAVs in three minutes

On 19 Dec 2022, the night sky above Italy's Monza autodrome was lit up with a dazzling display of drone art, with 12 emojis depicted by Uncrewed Aerial Vehicles (UAVs) in 180 sec. The performance was filmed for *Lo Show dei Record* and produced by Nocturne Drone Shows and Jens Hillenkötter (both DEU).

Most powerful handheld laser

On 13 Jun 2022, a custom-made device built by Daniel Black (UK) achieved a peak power of 7.61 W in Melbourn, Cambridgeshire, UK. To qualify as a handheld laser, GWR guidelines stipulate that the laser and its power supply must fit into a case no more than 40 cm long and 5 cm wide (15.7 x 2 in).

Longest footbridge span

Opened on 13 May 2022, the Sky Bridge 721 stretches 721 m (2,365 ft) between two mountain ridges in Dolní Morava, Czechia. The design is inspired by traditional rope bridges, with the deck and suspension cables hanging down between the anchor points. Situated 1,125 m (3,690 ft) above sea level, it offers a bird's-eye view of the surrounding area, which is a haven for nature lovers and skiers.

Fastest monster truck

On 6 Aug 2022, Joe Sylvester (USA) drove his Jeep Gladiator monster truck *Bad Habit* to 101.84 mph (163.89 km/h) in front of a 40,000-strong crowd at the Summit MotorSports Park in Norwalk, Ohio, USA. Fan-favourite *Bad Habit* was brought out of retirement in 2019, having previously recorded the **longest monster-truck ramp jump** – 72.42 m (237 ft 7 in) – on 1 Sep 2013.

▶ Largest steam-powered tractor

Weighing 74,960 lb (34,000 kg) and measuring 25 ft (7.62 m) long, the *150 HP Case* has more pulling power than three semi-trucks. The titanic tractor – the life's work of steam enthusiast Kory Anderson (USA) – is modelled on a series of engines made by the Case Company in 1905. It was unveiled in 2018.

On 10 Sep 2022, the *150 HP Case* broke the record for the **most ploughs pulled** for the third time, dragging a 50-bottom John Deere plough near Andover, South Dakota.

GO SKINNY DIPPING
Ditch that bathing costume and take a daring dive as nature intended. On 9 Jun 2018, a total of 2,505 women braved the elements and swam naked in the Irish Sea for the "Strip and Dip" charity event in Wicklow, Ireland – the **largest skinny dip**.

36

HARLEM GLOBETROTTERS

The Harlem Globetrotters and GWR have a long history together. They made their debut appearance on these pages in our very first edition, 69 years ago, and have earned mentions almost every year since.

The history of the Globetrotters began in 1926, when a group of friends from Chicago started playing exhibition games at a local dance hall. Excluded from professional basketball leagues because they were Black, these players formed the Harlem Globetrotters, a barnstorming team that toured the USA playing (and usually beating) any team that dared face them.

Easy victories, however, aren't exciting for crowds, so the Globetrotters soon began peppering their court appearances with trick shots and joke plays, giving rise to the blend of athleticism and showmanship they're known for today.

In the near-century since their founding, the Globetrotters have become the **most travelled basketball team** (101 countries) and their 28-player squad makes hundreds of public appearances every year.

These days, the Harlem Globetrotters play games against their sister team, the Washington Generals.

VITAL STATISTICS

Name	Harlem Globetrotters
Birthplace	Chicago, Illinois, USA
Founded	1926
Countries played in	101
Largest audience	75,000 in 1951 (see below)
Current GWR titles	30 in total, including, in 2022, **most blindfolded slam dunks in one minute** (9) and **farthest under-the-legs shot** (19.43 m; 63 ft 8 in)

5

6

1: The Harlem Globetrotters in Italy during their 1951 European Tour. It was on this trip that the team earned their first GWR title: the 75,000 people who turned out to watch them play in Berlin, Germany, on 22 Aug represented what was then the **largest attendance for a basketball game.**

2: "Torch" George celebrates achieving the **most under-the-legs tumbles in one minute** (32) with adjudicator Hannah Ortman on GWR Day 2018.

3: For their 2021–22 Spread Game Tour, the Globetrotters swapped their traditional red, white and blue kits for their black and grey "new drip". Even Globie, the mascot who joined the team in 1993, got a new look.

4: The **First Female Globetrotter** was Lynette Woodard, who joined in 1985 after leading the US women's basketball team to a gold medal at the 1984 Los Angeles Olympics.

5: Joining the team in Dec 2017, "Hot Shot" Swanson is the **shortest Globetrotter**, at just 134 cm (4 ft 5 in). He and his younger brother, "X-Over" Tompkins, are the only current members of the team who hail from the Harlem neighbourhood of New York City.

6: NBA Hall-of-Famer Wilt Chamberlain became a Globetrotter for the 1958–59 season. He would go on to set many NBA records, including the **most points in a season** (4,029 in 1961–62), a record that still stands to this day.

Even at the height of his fame, Wilt Chamberlain would return to play with the Globetrotters in the off-season.

Find out more about the Harlem Globetrotters in the Hall of Fame section at www.guinnessworldrecords.com/2024

Highest-grossing movie series (average)

The two instalments of James Cameron's sci-fi odyssey *Avatar* had grossed an average of $2,607,691,829 (£2.1 bn) at the global box office as of 14 Mar 2023. This surpassed the *Avengers* franchise, whose four movies earned an average of $1.9 bn (£1.5 bn).

Released on 6 Dec 2022, *Avatar: The Way of Water* (USA) transported audiences back to Pandora, introducing an ocean-dwelling Na'vi clan called the Metkayina. The epic sequel continued the success of *Avatar* (USA/UK, 2009), which is the **highest-grossing movie** with takings of $2.9 bn (£2.4 bn). Three further sequels are planned, with *Avatar 5* set for release in 2028.

Left to right: *Actors Kate Winslet (Ronal), Zoe Saldaña (Neytiri; see also p.246), Cliff Curtis (Tonowari) and Sam Worthington (Jake) had their performances motion-captured underwater – a cinematic first. The surface of the water was covered with floating white balls to minimize light reflection. "It looks real because the motion was real," said director Cameron.*

To bring Pandora's oceans to life, the team behind Avatar: The Way of Water *had to adapt the motion-capture technology used in the original film so that it worked underwater. A pair of giant water tanks were constructed with cameras set up around them, and in order to perform their underwater scenes, the movie's stars learnt how to freedive. Kate Winslet (UK, right), who plays the Metkayina's Ronal, was reported to have held her breath for 7 min 15 sec. This is the* **longest breath-hold on screen (principal actor)**, *beating Tom Cruise's record of 6 min, which he set while filming 2015's* Mission: Impossible – Rogue Nation. *Across an 18-month period beginning in 2017,* The Way of Water's *cast and crew members logged more than 250,000 dives, making it the* **largest underwater motion-capture project**.

JURASSIC PARK SPINOSAURUS

The *Jurassic Park* movies are famous for their digital effects, but when actors need to get up close and personal with an ancient predator, they need something that is physically present. For 2001's *Jurassic Park III*, that meant making the **largest movie animatronic ever.**

Built by Stan Winston Studio, this full-size model of a *Spinosaurus*, which was the **largest carnivorous dinosaur**, was nearly 45 ft (13.7 m) long and weighed in at 25,000 lb (11.3 tonnes) – heavier than the real thing! The robotic giant moved and "roared" by means of a system of hydraulic pistons and electric motors, connected by a "nervous system" of electrical wiring to a team of eight puppeteers. The operator for its arms acted out their movements while wearing telemetry devices, which transmitted commands to a computer controlling the limbs' internal structures.

We're celebrating this astonishing feat of artistry and engineering to mark the 30-year anniversary of the first *Jurassic Park* film in 2023. Indeed, the two *Tyrannosaurus rex* animatronics created for that cinematic blockbuster provided much of the groundwork for the *Spinosaurus.*

The six *Jurassic Park* movies represent the **highest-grossing dinosaur franchise**, having taken $6.01 bn (£5.2 bn) to date. Of that, $1.67 bn (£1.09 bn) was earned by the fourth instalment, *Jurassic World* (USA, 2015), the **highest-grossing dinosaur movie.** Monster movies with monster records to match!

JURASSIC PARK

Special-effects teams working on the Jurassic Park films combined mechanical models with digital imagery to create jaw-droppingly realistic dinosaurs. Stan Winston observed that if you saw an entire dino, including legs, move on screen, it's probably digital. Otherwise, you're likely seeing an animatronic – especially in close-ups.

Sail built to flex as spine moves

Remotely controlled articulated tail

Initially, skilled technicians worked up maquettes of the Spinosaurus. These scaled-down, highly detailed models acted as a template for the final animatronics.

Hand-painted duplicates for each section in case of damage

Skinning a dinosaur

The *Spinosaurus*'s scaly hide was made out of foam rubber and painstakingly adjusted to stretch, sag or wrinkle as required. Bungee cords were attached to the inner frame to mimic the movements of tendons. It was then painted in a colour scheme approved by paleontology consultant Jack Horner.

The *Spinosaurus* was mounted on a motorized cart that ran along rails. And with 1,000 hp (745 kW) at its disposal, it could move frighteningly quickly!

From sketches to set

Nearly 80 of the studio's artists, engineers and designers worked on animatronics for *Jurassic Park III*. Of those, about 30 were devoted exclusively to the *Spinosaurus*, which took almost a year to complete.

Interior bladder simulates breathing movements

Eyes based on those of a crocodile

Slide levers enable full tongue mobility

Staring down a *Spinosaurus*

Below, Stan Winston (USA, 1946–2008) goes eye to eye with his studio's creation. Having started out as a Disney make-up artist, Stan went on to become one of Hollywood's premier effects artists. His studio's work has graced iconic movies such as *The Terminator* (1984), *Aliens* (1986) and *Avatar* (2009).

Not all of the studio's breathtaking puppets are mechanized. Real people were inside the raptors for 1993's *Jurassic Park*, for example. As "proof of concept" tests, life-size hollow foam mock-ups were created from maquettes (*below*). Special effects designers then slipped inside the dino suits and acted out a range of movements.

Steel rails to support the animatronic's massive weight

SCREEN STUNTS

WHO'S WHO IN MOVIE STUNTS

It takes a unique individual to thrive – not to mention *survive* – as a stunt actor. Below, we present three legends in the field, each with decades of blockbuster films to their name.

Roy Alon (UK) was the **most prolific stuntman**. A veteran of 1,000-plus TV, film and theatre projects, including several *Bond* movies, he's seen above in *Superman III* (USA, 1983).

The **most prolific film stuntman** is Vic Armstrong (UK). As stuntman, stunt coordinator and director, he has worked on some 250 movies, including the first three *Indiana Jones* films.

Rocky Taylor (UK, *left, doubling for Sean Connery*) debuted in *The Young Ones* (UK, 1961) and, 62 years later, worked on *Mission: Impossible – Dead Reckoning* (USA, 2023) – the **longest career as a stuntman**.

First professional film stuntman
Ex-US cavalryman Frank Hanaway (USA) secured a part in the 1903 crime movie *The Great Train Robbery* (USA) owing to his ability to fall from a horse without injuring himself.

The **first professional stuntwoman** was former Wild West performer Helen Gibson (USA, b. Rose August Wenger). She doubled for Helen Holmes in the serial *The Hazards of Helen* (USA, 1914–17), before taking over the title role in 1915.

Oldest stuntwoman
Aged 78 years 37 days, Jeannie Epper (USA, b. 27 Jan 1941) performed stunts in the TV show *The Rookie* (USA, 2019; "Manhunt", season 1, episode 15). After some 10 years in the movie industry, her breakthrough role came as stunt double for Lynda Carter in *Wonder Woman* (Warner Bros., 1975–79). She is also the **most prolific professional stuntwoman**, with 158 performances to date. Her first (uncredited) stunt work was for the John Ford movie *Cheyenne Autumn* (USA, 1964).

First woman to win an Emmy award for Outstanding Stunt Coordination
At the Emmy Awards on 8–9 Sep 2018, Shauna Duggins (USA, *inset, being lifted*) won for her stunt work on *GLOW* (Netflix, 2017–19) – a fictionalized account of the "Gorgeous Ladies of Wrestling", the wrestling circuit that debuted on US TV in 1986. She picked up the same award in 2019. In 2006, Duggins had been the **first female nominee** for this trophy, for *Alias* (ABC, 2001–06).

Highest-grossing stuntman/co-ordinator
The 36 movies on which Andy Gill (USA) has worked as stunt coordinator had grossed $12.2 bn (£10 bn) as of 13 Jan 2023. His resumé includes major blockbusters such as *Captain America: Civil War* (USA, 2016), *Black Panther* (USA, 2018) and the four most recent *Fast & Furious* movies, as well as the new *Fast X*. Pictured is Gill (*front*) in the aftermath of the "zombie car" pile-up in 2017's *The Fate of the Furious*, with second-unit director Spiro Razatos (*to his right*) and some of the 35 stunt actors who crashed about 40 cars for this one sequence.

Most stunts by an actor
Today, only a few movie stars have enough influence – and insurance cover – to perform their own stunts. Tom Cruise famously scaled the **tallest building** (*see p.63*), clung to a flying Airbus and motorcycled off a cliff edge. With 45 years' experience, however, the most prolific actor to take on the role of stuntman and coordinator is Jackie Chan (CHN), with more than 100 credits between *Fist of Fury* (CHN, 1972) and *Kung Fu Yoga* (CHN/IND, 2017).

Most Taurus World Stunt Awards won by a performer
Debbie Evans (USA) has won a prestigious Taurus World Stunt Award seven times, in 2002–11. A former motorcycle trials rider, her first movie stunt saw her leap a 30-ft (9-m) ravine for the sci-fi dystopia *Deathsport* (USA, 1978).

The **men's** record is five, an achievement shared by Troy Robinson and Jimmy N Roberts (both USA). *For more on this coveted stunt award, see right.*

Most wins of an Emmy award for Outstanding Stunts
Rowley Irlam (UK, *see below*) has picked up four trophies for stunt coordination on *Game of Thrones* (HBO, 2011–19). His big-screen projects include the Bond movies *Casino Royale* (UK/USA, 2006) and *Quantum of Solace* (UK/USA, 2008), the latter of which saw him nominated for a Taurus award.

Most full-body burns on screen
Stunt coordinator Rowley Irlam (*see above*) oversaw the breaking of two fire records in the HBO series *Game of Thrones*. In "The Spoils of War" (season 7, episode 4), Daenerys Targaryen ambushes the Lannister army with her fire-breathing dragon, Drogon – a **single sequence** in which a total of 73 stunt performers were set ablaze. Part of this scene (dubbed "The Loot Train") required 20 actors to burn simultaneously – a record for a **single take**. The whole sequence took three weeks to shoot.

Irlam and his team then broke the **single take** record while filming "The Bells" (s.8, e.5). The draconic annihilation of King's Landing featured a shot involving 22 simultaneous immolations.

MOST TAURUS WORLD STUNT AWARDS WON BY A MOVIE

Controversially, there are no Oscars awarded for stunt work, but the annual Taurus World Stunt Awards honour the "best and brightest stunt people for extraordinary performances". Three movies have each won a record five trophies: *No Time to Die* (UK/USA, 2021), *The Dark Knight* (USA/UK, 2008) and *The Fast and the Furious* (USA/DEU, 2001).

In *No Time to Die*, stuntman Dave Grant leapt 40 m (130 ft) from a bridge (*left, top*), winning Best High Work. Paul "Fast Eddy" Edmondson then jumped a motorcycle 12 m (40 ft) into the air on to a 20-m-tall (65-ft) wall (*left*), named Best Speciality Stunt. Fast Eddy also doubles for Bond actor Daniel Craig (*below*) in the motorbike chase that follows.

The Dark Knight
- **Best Fight:** Rob Cooper, Richard Hansen, Mark Mottram, Andy Pilgrim, Dominic Preece, Buster Reeves, Marvin Stewart-Campbell, Steen Young
- **Best High Work:** Mark Harper, Luke Kearney, Tom Lowell, Mark Mottram, Brian A Peters
- **Best Speciality Stunt:** Jim Wilkey
- **Best Work with a Vehicle:** Rick Avery, Richard Burden, George Cottle, Tobiasz Daszkiewicz, James Fierro, Jean-Pierre Goy, Terry Jackson, Tom Lowell, Rick Miller, Jim Wilkey
- **Best Stunt Coordinator/2nd Unit Director:** Paul Jennings, Rick LeFevour, Tom Struthers

No Time to Die
- **Best Stunt Coordinator/2nd Unit Director:** Lee Morrison, Olivier Schneider
- **Best Work with a Vehicle:** Evangelos Grecos, Mark Higgins, Martin Ivanov, Cristian Knight, Pascal Lavanchy
- **Best High Work:** Dave Grant (*top*)
- **Best Speciality Stunt:** Paul Edmondson (*above*)
- **Best Overall Stunt by a Woman:** Chelsea Mather, Christina Petrou, Charlotte Williams

The Fast and the Furious
- **Best Work with a Vehicle:** Jimmy N Roberts
- **Best Overall Stunt by a Woman:** Debbie Evans
- **Best Overall Stunt by a Man:** Tim Trella, Chris Tuck
- **Best Driving:** Debbie Evans, Matt Johnston, Mike Justus, Kevin Scott, Tim Trella, Chris Tuck
- **Best Stunt Coordinator/2nd Unit Director:** Mic Rodgers

The year 2023 marks the 70th anniversary of the publication of *Casino Royale*, Ian Fleming's first 007 novel.

PROPS

1. Most filmed sci-fi prop
Given the tongue-in-cheek nickname of "The Most Important Device in the Universe", the Modern Props "Dual Axis Generator" consists of a pair of clear tubes filled with flickering lights, supported by some industrial-looking fittings. It has appeared in more than 200 TV shows and films, including eight episodes of *Star Trek*. This piece of futuristic set dressing was built in 1977 by John Zabrucky (USA), founder of Modern Props, a properties rental house in Los Angeles, California, USA, which closed in 2020.

2. Most expensive car from a film
The properties manager is traditionally responsible for making or sourcing everything that isn't scenery or costumes, including large items such as cars. In Aug 2019, a modified 1965 Aston Martin DB5 sold for $6,385,000 (£5.2 m) at auction in Monterey, California, USA. This signature Bond car was one of two made for the fourth 007 movie, *Thunderball* (1965). In common with a DB5 seen in the previous year's *Goldfinger*, the vehicle was modified with a host of "Q branch" gadgets, including machine guns in the bumpers and a retractable, bulletproof rear screen.

3. First props managers
Craftsmen known as *skeuopoios* worked for the classical Greek theatre, which developed into the art form we'd recognize today in around 500 BCE. Their job was mainly to make masks, though they likely created or sourced other stage property.

4. Most expensive prop gun
A BlasTech DL-44 Heavy Blaster, made for the character of Han Solo in the original *Star Wars* trilogy, sold for $1,057,500 (£904,342) at Rock Island Auction in Illinois, USA, on 30 Aug 2022. The gun was the only survivor of the three originals made in 1976 by London props house Bapty & Co. for the first instalment, *A New Hope* (1977). It comprises a blank-firing Mauser C98, decorated with parts from a WWII machine gun, a 19th-century hunting rifle and a model aircraft kit.

5. Most expensive movie prop
On 21 Nov 2017, Robby the Robot sold for $5,375,000 (£4.06 m) at Bonhams New York. Robby, who memorably debuted in the 1956 sci-fi classic *Forbidden Planet,* was sold as a full system along with an alternative head, its control console and a motorized "jeep" that it used on screen. It reportedly cost more than $100,000 to build, equivalent to $1.1 m (£920,000) today.

6. Most screen appearances by a car model
As of 16 Jan 2023, the Ford Crown Victoria (1992–2012) has made 10,382 appearances in scripted live-action TV and film, according to the Internet Movie Cars Database. Its screen popularity is partly due to the fact that it was once one of the most common US police cars and was also widely adopted by urban taxi fleets throughout the country, in particular New York City's Yellow Cabs.

7. Most reused prop
The Recurring Newspaper has featured in more than 10,000 film and TV productions since its introduction in the 1960s. Its crisp pages look convincing from a distance, but a close-up would reveal that everything other than the headlines is gibberish. Filmmakers can order custom front pages to reflect the events of the story.

The newspaper is the work of the Earl Hays Press, which has provided printed props to Hollywood since 1917, making it the **oldest operating props house**. Its other products include the ubiquitous "Morley" brand cigarettes, which have appeared in everything from Alfred Hitchcock's *Psycho* (1960) to the TV sitcom *Friends* (1994–2004).

8. Oldest surviving theatre prop
A pair of Noh masks dating from the 14th century, which were used in traditional Japanese theatre, are the oldest extant theatrical props. Depicting

Terracotta replicas of masks from Greek theatre survive, but not the wood and stiffened fabric originals.

VISIT LAS VEGAS
Play small, win big! The **largest slot-machine payout** is $39,713,982.25 (£25.3 m), on 21 Mar 2003 at Vegas's Excalibur Hotel-Casino in Nevada, USA. The lucky winner was a 25-year-old software engineer from Los Angeles, who had put $100 (£64) into a Megabucks slot machine.

184

"Chichinojou" (a cheerful old man, *below*) and "Enmeikaja" (a young man) – standard characters in highly formalized Noh plays – they were used by the Konparu Troupe until the 1950s. Today, the masks are owned by the National Museum in Tokyo, Japan.

9. Most expensive hand prop

A hand prop is an object designed to be picked up and interacted with during a performance. On 25 Nov 2013, the namesake statuette from the 1941 film noir *The Maltese Falcon* sold at Bonhams New York for $4,085,000 (£2.5 m). The 1-ft-high (30-cm) cast-lead figure was one of several made for the film.

FALL IN LOVE

Poets have been waxing lyrical about their *amours* for millennia. The **oldest surviving love poem** is an anonymous work on a clay tablet from the time of the Sumerians, who invented writing in around 3500 BCE. Archaeologists gave it the distinctly unromantic title "Istanbul #2461".

TV

METACRITIC USERS' TOP TV OF 2022

At the end of 2022, for the 13th year running, review site Metacritic asked its users to vote for their favourite new TV shows of the last 12 months. Each participant nominated their top five shows; five points went to first-place listings and fifth-place series received only one point. Below are the results...

1 *Better Call Saul* (AMC, USA) 1,612

2 *Severance* (Apple TV+, USA) 1,164

3 *House of the Dragon* (HBO, USA) 657

4 *Andor* (Disney+, USA) 611

5 *The White Lotus* (HBO, USA) 608

6 *The Bear* (FX/Hulu, USA) 536

7 *Barry* (HBO, USA) 386

8 *Stranger Things* (Netflix, USA) 312

9 *The Rehearsal* (HBO, USA) 297

10 *Atlanta* (FX, USA) 278

Longest-serving TV news anchor duo
As of 24 Jan 2023, Rick Ardon and Susannah Carr (both AUS; Carr b. UK) had been co-presenting the latest headlines for *7NEWS Perth* in Australia for 38 years.

Longest career presenting a TV music series
Jorge Barón (COL) has been the face of *El Show de las Estrellas* (*The Show of the Stars*; Canal RCN, COL) since it debuted in 1969, giving him a tenure of 52 years 299 days by 19 Mar 2022.

The **oldest host of a music talent show** was Song Hae (KOR, b. 27 Apr 1927), who was still engaged with KBS's *National Singing Contest* (KOR) on 12 Apr 2022, aged 94 years 350 days. Sadly, he passed away two months later on 8 Jun.

Oldest TV director
"King of Action" Chalong Pakdeevijit (THA, b. 15 Apr 1932) directed his first TV series – *Raya* – in 1998. He was still on the job, working on *The Maekhong Connection* (Ch7HD, THA), at the age of 90 years 297 days on 6 Feb 2023. Pakdeevijit began in the business in 1950 and made his directorial debut with the 1968 film *Jao Insee* (*The Eagle*). He has produced and directed more than 60 films and TV shows in his 70-year-plus career.

Most in-demand rising star on TV
Kit Connor (UK) – Nick in *Heartstopper* (Netflix, UK) – was the most popular rising star of 2022–23, according to Parrot Analytics. His demand rating (*see opposite*) was 8.7 times greater than the average talent. This category is reserved for on-screen celebrities aged 25 and under who made the most impact in the previous year.

Most Emmy acting nominations in one year (show)
In Jul 2022, Season 3 of *Succession* (HBO, USA) received 14 nominations for its cast at the 74th Primetime Emmy Awards. It was also the most name-checked of the year with 25 nods, ahead of the 20 apiece received by *Ted Lasso* and *The White Lotus*. Matthew Macfadyen (who plays Tom Wambsgans) was the series' sole individual acting winner, picking up Outstanding Supporting Actor.

Longest-running TV cookery show
Clearly a recipe for success, *Kyou no Ryouri* (*Today's Cooking*; NHK, JPN) had been on Japanese TV screens for more than 65 years, as of Nov 2022. It premiered on 4 Nov 1957.

Most scripted jump scares in a TV episode
Netflix startled the audience a nerve-jangling 21 times in 58 min when premiering the debut instalment of its thriller *The Midnight Club* (USA) at New York Comic Con on 6 Oct 2022. The sinister series was conceived by Mike Flanagan (USA).

Most Emmy wins by an animated show in one year
Two series share this record, with six Emmy titles apiece. *LOVE DEATH + ROBOTS* (Netflix, USA), the multi-genre compilation of shorts featuring emotive stories and various automata, achieved the feat in 2021. It matched the veteran animated sitcom *The Simpsons* (Fox, USA), which bagged its sextet of trophies almost 30 years earlier in 1992.

Most National Television Awards (NTAs) for...
- **Best Factual Entertainment**: At the 27th NTAs on 13 Oct 2022, *Gogglebox* (Channel 4, UK) lifted its sixth trophy, having also won in 2015–18 and 2021.
- **Best Talent Show**: *Strictly Come Dancing* (BBC, UK) has waltzed off with this title 10 times to date: 2008, 2013–14 and 2016–22.
- **Best Serial Drama**: *EastEnders* (BBC, UK) has claimed 12 wins in this category. It is just ahead of the 10 wins by *Coronation Street* (ITV, UK) – the **longest-running TV soap opera**, debuting on 9 Dec 1960. *EastEnders*' all-time haul of 36 awards (up to 13 Oct 2022) also make it the **most decorated show at the NTAs**.

> Tim Burton – once lined up to direct the 1991 *Addams Family* movie – guest-directed four episodes of *Wednesday*.

Most viewed show on Netflix in one week
Wednesday (Netflix, USA) registered a *spook*-tacular 411,290,000 hr of viewing in the seven days ending 4 Dec 2022. More than 50 million households tuned in to the supernatural coming-of-age comedy – starring Jenna Ortega (*left*) in the title role – during its first week. This *Addams Family* spin-off, devised by Alfred Gough and Miles Millar, surpassed the peak of 335.01 million hr that was logged by Season 4 of *Stranger Things*.

VISIT ITALY
This southern European nation features the **most UNESCO World Heritage Sites** – 58 – making it a sightseers' paradise. They include Sicily's Mount Etna, producer of the **largest steam rings** at c. 200 m (650 ft) across, and the Orto Botanico in Padua, the **oldest botanical gardens**, dating back to 1545.

Parrot Analytics tracks more than 1.5 bn expressions of demand in 100+ languages from 200+ countries.

GUINNESS WORLD RECORDS®

PARROT
ANALYTICS

MOST IN-DEMAND TV SHOWS OF 2022

Parrot Analytics quantifies the global audience's engagement with TV shows using "Demand Expressions per capita", or DEx/c. This metric encompasses viewing figures and streaming numbers as well as coverage on social media. Each show is rated against that of the average programme – e.g., a score of 104.3 indicates that *Stranger Things* was 104.3 times more popular than the typical show. Here, in no particular order, is a selection of 2022's biggest small-screen hits…

1. Comedy / sitcom
The Big Bang Theory (CBS, USA)
45.9

2. Soap opera
Yeh Rishta Kya Kehlata hai
(StarPlus, IND); 28.8

3. Anime / animated show
Attack on Titan (MBS, JPN)
68.2

4. TV show debut*
House of the Dragon (HBO, USA)
114.9

5. Action & adventure / superhero
The Boys (Amazon Prime, USA)
55.3

6. Romantic drama
Bridgerton (Netflix, USA)
33.9

7. Reality show
RuPaul's Drag Race (VH1, USA)
22.1

8. TV show / sci-fi / digital original
Stranger Things (Netflix, USA)
104.3

9. Documentary
Formula 1: Drive to Survive
(Netflix, UK); 19.2

10. Children's show
SpongeBob SquarePants
(Nickelodeon, USA); 47.9

*Based on 30-day period after premiere

CHART-TOPPERS

Most streamed track on Spotify (current year)
"As It Was" by Harry Styles (UK) racked up more than 1.5 billion streams on Spotify in 2022. The single went on to win Song of the Year at the BRIT Awards on 11 Feb 2023 – one of four gongs claimed by the former 1D star.

Best-selling digital single
Released on 25 Apr 2020, "Spotlight" (aka "Light Spot", or "Made to Love") by Xiao Zhan (aka Sean Xiao, CHN) had shifted 54.31 million copies by 4 Jan 2023. It enjoyed 24.37 million download sales in the first 24 hr alone. The **best-selling physical single** remains "White Christmas" by Bing Crosby (USA), with an estimated 50 million copies purchased since 1942. (*For the best-selling physical single since charts began, see pp.134–35.*)

Most streamed act on YouTube (current year)
In 2022, Indian playback singer Alka Yagnik was YouTube's most watched artist worldwide, with 15.3 billion streams – an average of almost 420 million a day over the year. In a four-decade career, Kolkata-born Yagnik has recorded more than 20,000 songs for films and albums.

First No.1 hit on The Official MENA Chart
On 29 Nov 2022, "Calm Down" by Nigerian rapper Rema (b. Divine Ikubor) became the inaugural No.1 on The Official MENA Chart – the first authoritative pop-music ranking in the Middle East and North Africa (MENA). Its weekly Top 20 collects data from the major streaming platforms across 13 MENA countries, covering a population of more than 300 million.

TOP 10
STREAMING SERVICES (TOTAL TRACKS)

 1 SoundCloud (DEU) 300 million

 2 Napster (USA) 110 million

 =3 Amazon Music Unlimited (USA) 100 million

 =3 Apple Music (USA) 100 million

 =3 YouTube Music (USA) 100 million

 =6 Deezer (FRA) 90 million

 =6 KKBOX (CHN) 90 million

 =6 Qobuz (FRA) 90 million

 =6 TIDAL (NOR/USA) 90 million

 10 Spotify (SWE) 80 million

Longest gap between UK No.1 singles
Kate Bush's (UK) two British chart-toppers to date came 44 years 83 days apart. Her debut, "Wuthering Heights", spent its last week at No.1 on 1 Apr 1978. "Running Up that Hill (A Deal with God)" hit No.1 in the week ending 23 Jun 2022, after its inclusion in Season 4 of *Stranger Things* (*inset*). Bush was aged 63 years 342 days at the time – the **oldest female artist to have a UK No.1 single**.

Most cumulative weeks on the *Billboard* Hot 100 (one single)
On 22 Oct 2022, British indie-rock band Glass Animals spent their 91st week on the US *Billboard* Hot 100 with "Heat Waves". The track debuted at No.100 on 16 Jan 2021 before kicking off an unbroken 90-week run on 6 Feb 2021. It finally reached the top on 12 Mar 2022, after a 59-week journey – the **slowest climb to No.1 on the *Billboard* Hot 100**.

Highest-charting Spanish-language track on the *Billboard* Hot 100 (female)
"TQG", by Colombian vocalists KAROL G (b. Carolina Giraldo Navarro) and Shakira (b. Shakira Isabel Mebarak Ripoll), debuted at No.7 on the Hot 100 on 11 Mar 2023. "TQG" arrived just six weeks after Shakira debuted at No.9 with "BZRP Music Sessions Vol. 53" on 28 Jan 2023 – the **first female vocalist to debut in the Top 10 of the Hot 100 with a Spanish-language track**.

Most streamed on Spotify
- **Act**: Drake (b. Aubrey Drake Graham, CAN) – 75.56 billion combined streams, as of 16 Feb 2023.
- **Track**: "Blinding Lights", by The Weeknd (b. Abel Tesfaye, CAN) – 3.413 billion streams, as of 16 Feb 2023.
- **Album**: Ed Sheeran's (UK) ÷ (*Divide*), deluxe edition – 12.83 billion streams as of 16 Feb 2023.

First female K-pop group to reach No.1 on the US albums chart
On 1 Oct 2022, *Born Pink* – the second full-length studio album by BLACKPINK (KOR) – took the top spot on the US *Billboard* 200. In the same week, they became the **first female K-pop group to reach No.1 on the UK albums chart** with the same release.

FLY FIRST CLASS
Splash some cash and travel in style. Or perhaps you'd like the whole plane to yourself? The **largest private jet** is the Boeing Business Jet 747-8, with a maximum take-off weight of 447,700 kg (987,000 lb). Its list price was around $418 m (£360 m) as of 2022 – so you'd best get saving!

 31

IN THE *MIDNIGHTS* HOUR: SWIFT IN SUPERLATIVES

Taylor Swift set or extended a host of records after releasing *Midnights* on 21 Oct 2022. Here are just a few of them...

Record	Total
Most Top 10 hits on the US Hot 100 (female)	40
Most cumulative weeks at No.1 on the US albums chart (female)	60 weeks
Most debuts at No.1 on the US albums chart (female)	11
Most No.1s on the US Digital Song Sales chart	24
Most streamed act on Spotify in 24 hours	228 million (21 Oct 2022)
Most day-one streams of an album on Spotify (female)	184,695,609
Most streamed album on Spotify in one week	776,481,256 (21–27 Oct 2022)
Most streamed album on Amazon Music in 24 hours	7.97 million (21 Oct 2022)

Figures correct as of 15 Feb 2023

Boosted by *Midnights*, Swift is now Spotify's **most streamed female act**, with 41.13 billion plays by 16 Feb 2023.

Most American Music Awards (AMAs)

On 20 Nov 2022, Taylor Swift extended her haul of AMA gongs to 40. She picked up six statuettes from six nominations at the 50th annual ceremony, held in Los Angeles, California, USA. Michael Jackson (USA, 1958–2009) holds the **men's** title – 26.

Midnights

FIRST ACT TO DEBUT AT POSITIONS 1–10 SIMULTANEOUSLY ON THE US HOT 100

On 5 Nov 2022, Taylor Swift (USA) locked down the entire Top 10 of the *Billboard* Hot 100 with tracks from her No.1 album *Midnights*. Her feat surpassed rapper Drake's previous record of nine Top 10 new entries on 18 Sep 2021.

Midnights shot to No.1 on 5 Nov 2022, posting 1.140 million pure album sales – and 1.578 million album-equivalent units – across all formats. At the vanguard of a vinyl renaissance, *Midnights* is also the USA's **fastest-selling vinyl album in one week** – shifting 575,000 copies – since comprehensive tracking began in 1991.

Swift has also scored the **most million-selling weeks on the US albums chart** – five, each with a different album.

GLOBAL MUSIC

A WORLD OF FOLK

The online community database Rate Your Music (RYM) lists 26 genres – from ambient to spoken word – with a staggering 3,272 sub-genres combined. Classical (169 sub-genres), dance (267), electronic (327), folk (400), pop (159), regional (1,180) and rock (259) take up the lion's share. Below, we delve into RYM's folk portfolio to turn the spotlight on a few lesser-known regional variations from around the globe.

Freak folk: Offshoot of the "New Weird America" movement characterized by acoustic and eclectic instruments, peculiar vocal styles, romantic lyrics and a childlike atmosphere.

Ripsaw (aka rake 'n' scrape): Indigenous style of the Turks and Caicos Islands, which features a handsaw as the primary instrument.

White voice: Vocal style from Eastern Europe popularized by outdoor labourers. Singing technique with an open throat that has been likened to controlled screaming.

Baul gaan: Songs by the Bauls, a movement of mystic entertainers from Bangladesh and India who were influenced by diverse spiritual traditions.

Modinha: Popular in the 18th/19th centuries in Brazil. Characterized by works with amorous themes, poetic lyrics, acoustic instrumentation and operatic vocals.

DID YOU KNOW?

Inscribed on tablets dating to c.1400 BCE, "Hymn to Nikkal" is the **oldest notated song**, but fragments are missing…

The **oldest complete song** is the "Song of Seikilos", from a tombstone in Türkiye, dated to the 1st/2nd century CE.

First use of the term "world music"
Ethnomusicologist Robert "Bob" Brown (USA) is credited with coining the term "world music" in the early 1960s to denote popular music informed by non-Western musical traditions. In the 21st century, the term "global music" has gained traction; the Grammys renamed its Best World Music Album category as Best Global Music Album for the 63rd ceremony on 14 Mar 2021. Its first winner was Nigerian singer/songwriter and producer Burna Boy, with *Twice as Tall* (2020).

Best-selling world music album
The eponymous, Grammy-winning album from Cuban collective Buena Vista Social Club has sold more than 8 million copies. Encompassing the genres of son, bolero and danzón, the 1997 release brought together 20 of Cuba's finest musicians, including vocalist Ibrahim Ferrer, pianist Rubén González and vocalist/guitarist Compay Segundo.

First rock act to be UNESCO's Artist for Peace
On 25 Nov 2022, Mongolian folk-metal band The HU became the latest UNESCO Artist for Peace. They are the 37th recipient of this accolade, first awarded to Japanese violinist Eijin Nimura and Uruguayan double-bass player Milton Masciadri in 1998. Chosen creatives work with the organization to promote its core values and programmes.

Most nationalities in a pop group
Formed in 2017, Now United originally consisted of 14 members from 14 different countries: Brazil, Canada, China, Finland, Germany, India, Japan, Mexico, Philippines, Russia, Senegal, South Korea, the UK and the USA. The social-media-savvy collective picked up a Best Group nomination – alongside the likes of BLACKPINK, Little Mix and winners BTS – at the MTV Video Music Awards in 2020.

Longest-running annual international TV music competition
The *Eurovision Song Contest* has been staged every year since 1956 (except 2020). Formerly known as the Eurovision Grand Prix, the first competition featured seven European countries and was won by Switzerland's Lys Assia. In 2022, the event celebrated its 66th anniversary in Turin, Italy, where the winners were Ukraine's Kalush Orchestra (*above*) with "Stefania".

First winner of the Best Global Music Performance Grammy
Arooj Aftab (PAK/USA, b. SAU) won in this category – introduced at the 64th Annual Grammys in 2022 – for her 2021 song "Mohabbat". It attracted rave reviews and even appeared on ex-US president Barack Obama's summer playlist.

Best-selling *a cappella* group
Since 1960, Ladysmith Black Mambazo (ZAF) have sold 16.7 million albums and singles, and won five Grammys. The group's major breakthrough came with their mesmerizing vocal performances on Paul Simon's 1986 album *Graceland*.

Oldest folk musician
India's Thanga Darlong (b. 20 Jul 1920) was 98 years 319 days old when presented with the Padma Shri civilian award for his contribution to folk music on 4 Jun 2019. Born at Muruai village, in the state of Tripura, Darlong is celebrated as the last tribal musician to play the *rosem*, a flute-like instrument made from wood, bamboo and a traditional water pot.

All Africa Music Awards (AFRIMA)
• **Most awards:** eight, by Wizkid (b. Ayodeji Ibrahim Balogun, NGA). He also holds the **most Artist of the Year awards** – three, won in 2016–17 and 2021.

• **Most awards in a single year:** five, by Iba One (b. Ibrahim Mahamadou Fily Sissoko, MLI) at the seventh AFRIMA ceremony in Lagos, Nigeria, on 21 Nov 2021. These included Album of the Year (for *My Empire*) and Songwriter of the Year.

VISIT A DISNEY RESORT
Hanging out with Mickey Mouse and the gang is a sure-fire way to banish the blues! To uplift his mood while job hunting, Jeff Reitz (USA) visited the amusement park in California daily for 2,995 days from 2012 to 2020 – the **most consecutive visits to Disneyland**.

Most global music album Grammy awards
Angélique Kidjo (BEN, formerly Republic of Dahomey) has won Best Global Music Album at the Grammys four times: in 2015–16, 2020 and 2022, most recently for *Mother Nature* (2021). In 2008, she also won the short-lived Best Contemporary World Music Album. She's shown below on stage at WOMAD 2022.

LARGEST INTERNATIONAL MUSIC FESTIVAL

Since 1982, WOMAD (World of Music, Arts and Dance) has presented more than 300 festivals across six continents, featuring more than 10,000 artists and entertaining millions of festival-goers. It was co-founded by singer Peter Gabriel (*right*) to champion global musical diversity. Here, we picture highlights from the 40th-anniversary edition, held on 28–31 Jul 2022 at Charlton Park Estate in Wiltshire, UK, which attracted 40,000 music lovers.
1. Ghana and UK afro-rockers Osibisa perform on the Open Air Stage.
2. Crowds watch the festival's celebrated final-day procession.
3. Joji Hirota and the London Taiko Drummers.
4. ADG7 offer a contemporary take on traditional Korean folk music.
5. A member of Mariachi Las Adelitas, an all-female Mexican band.

"It was a simple idea, to create a festival out of all the brilliant music and art made all over the world," Peter Gabriel reminisced in 2015. *"Stuff made outside of the mainstream – music that wasn't getting on the radio and was even harder to find in record stores."*

SEND A MESSAGE IN A BOTTLE
Not the speediest of communiqués but certainly romantic. The **oldest message in a bottle** is 131 years 223 days old. Thrown overboard by the captain of the German barque *Paula* on 12 Jun 1886, it was found by Tonya and Kym Illman (both AUS) on Wedge Island, Australia, on 21 Jan 2018.

MANGA & ANIME

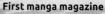

All nationalities JPN unless stated otherwise

First manga magazine
Tokyo Puck was founded in 1905 by Rakuten Kitazawa (1876–1955), Japan's first professional cartoonist and one of the founding fathers of modern manga. Aimed at adults, the comic featured mainly political and then satirical cartoons, and was published in Tokyo in 1905–15, 1919–23, 1928–41 and 1948.

Best-selling manga magazine
Weekly Shōnen Jump, published by Shueisha, had an average weekly circulation of 1.28 million copies during Jul–Sep 2022. The influential manga has sold more than 7.5 billion copies since it launched in 1968. Shueisha is the **largest manga publisher**, with annual sales of ¥195 bn ($1.3 bn; £1.15 bn) and 30% of the Japanese manga market as of 2021–22.

Most published volumes for a manga series
Golgo 13, which has been serialized in *Big Comic* since 1968, consisted of 206 collected (*tankōbon*) volumes as of Sep 2022. Published by Shogakukan, it follows a professional assassin also known by the pseudonym Duke Togo. The manga's original creator Takao Saitō passed away in 2021, but the series is being continued by the Saitō Production group in accordance with his wishes.

HIGHEST-GROSSING ANIME MOVIES
From the dreamlike fantasies of Studio Ghibli to *Mugen Train*'s demonic slaying, Japanese animations entrance audiences across the globe. This list of the genre's most successful movies includes the **first anime film to win an Oscar** – *Sen to Chihiro no kamikakushi* (*above*), which earned Best Animated Feature in 2003.

Movie	Gross
Kimetsu no Yaiba: Mugen Ressha-Hen (*Demon Slayer the Movie: Mugen Train*, 2020, below)	$506.5 m
Sen to Chihiro no kamikakushi (*Spirited Away*, 2001)	$383.8 m
Kimi no Na wa (*Your Name*, 2016)	$351.5 m
Hauru no ugoku shiro (*Howl's Moving Castle*, 2004)	$237.8 m
Gekijouban Jujutsu Kaisen 0 (*Jujutsu Kaisen 0: The Movie*, 2021)	$195.8 m

All figures as of 1 Jan 2023

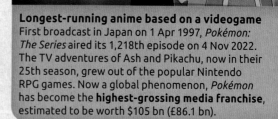

Longest-running anime based on a videogame
First broadcast in Japan on 1 Apr 1997, *Pokémon: The Series* aired its 1,218th episode on 4 Nov 2022. The TV adventures of Ash and Pikachu, now in their 25th season, grew out of the popular Nintendo RPG games. Now a global phenomenon, *Pokémon* has become the **highest-grossing media franchise**, estimated to be worth $105 bn (£86.1 bn).

Most wins of the Shogakukan Manga Award
Mangakas Naoki Urasawa and Akimi Yoshida have each won three competitive trophies at the most prestigious manga awards (inaugurated 1955): Urasawa for *Yawara!* (1989), *Monster* (2000) and *20th Century Boys* (2002); Yoshida for *Kisshō Tennyo* (1983), *Yasha* (2001) and *Umimachi Diary* (2015).

Largest fan convention
First held in Dec 1975 with 700 participants, the Comic Market or Comiket is now held twice a year at Tokyo's Big Sight arena. Attendance peaked in summer 2019, attracting *c.* 750,000 people. The event is devoted to *dōjin* goods – amateur and professional creators and "circles" (groups) sell everything from *dōjinshi* (fan-made comics) to anime- and manga-related memorabilia. The 100th Comiket took place in Aug 2022.

Most in-demand anime TV show
Shingeki no Kyojin (*Attack on Titan*; MBS) was the most popular TV anime in 2022, with a global demand measured at 68.2 times higher than that of the average TV show, according to data-monitoring firm Parrot Analytics.

Most expensive anime movie
Kaguya-hime no Monogatari (*The Tale of the Princess Kaguya*) was released by Studio Ghibli in 2013. Production on the largely hand-drawn animated film, based on the traditional story *Taketori Monogatari*, lasted eight years and cost ¥5.15 bn ($48.9 m; £29.6 m). The final film from Isao Takahata, it was nominated for Best Animated Feature at the Academy Awards in 2015.

Longest-running dedicated cosplay event
Debuting in Nagoya, Japan, in 2003, the annual World Cosplay Summit had been held 20 times, as of 5–7 Aug 2022. The event sees participants from all over the world dressing up as characters from Japanese videogames, manga, anime and *tokusatsu* ("special effects") media. Since 2005, the summit has climaxed with the World Cosplay Championship, in which teams representing different countries compete to be crowned Grand Champion in multiple cosplay divisions.

Tanjiro Kamado, hero of *Kimetsu no Yaiba: Mugen Ressha-Hen*.

Longest-running anime TV series
Sazae-san is a half-hour animated sitcom celebrating everyday life in the Japanese suburbs. It is based on the *yonkoma manga* (comic strip) created by Machiko Hasegawa, which was first published in 1946. The show made its debut on 5 Oct 1969, with 2,675 episodes as of 6 Nov 2022.

Sazae-San is also the **longest-running animated TV show** of any kind.

Masuo

Katsuo Isono

Tarao

Tama

Sazae

Namihei Isono

Fune Isono

Wakame Isono

GO PARASAILING
If you like the idea of parachuting but don't want to leap from a plane, then consider parasailing. And if you're *really* keen and want to aim for the **longest parasailing marathon**, the man to beat is Berne Persson (SWE): in Jul 2002, he stayed aloft for 24 hr 10 min on Sweden's Lake Graningesjön!

Largest collection of
***One Piece* memorabilia**
Treasure hunter Lam Siu Fung (CHN) had acquired 20,125 objects inspired by Eiichiro Oda's manga series in Hong Kong, China, as of 11 Apr 2021. He began his collection with *One Piece* Vol. 1, and his most beloved items are figurines from the *Portrait of Pirates* series.

MOST COPIES PUBLISHED FOR A SINGLE-AUTHOR COMIC-BOOK SERIES
A staggering 516.6 million copies of Eiichiro Oda's manga series *One Piece* were printed in 103 *tankōbon* volumes between Dec 1997 and Sep 2022. The ocean-going exploits of Monkey D Luffy, captain of the Straw Hat Pirates, are serialized in *Weekly Shōnen Jump* (*see opposite*). A special celebration was organized in 2015 by the magazine's Editor-in-Chief, Hiroyuki Nakano (*below, with certificate*), to mark *One Piece* sales passing the half-billion mark.

Eiichiro has said that the final *One Piece* chapter will be released in 2025.

ONE PIECE   RECORD ★ HOLDER
1人の作家が描いたコミック累計発行部数 世界No.1
ギネス世界記録®認定!!!

CIRCUS ARTS

Tallest rideable unicycle
The One Wheel Wonder (aka Wesley Williams, USA) teetered atop a 9.71-m-tall (31-ft 10-in) unicycle in Stuttgart, Germany, on 29 Dec 2022. As per GWR rules, he rode the vertiginous vehicle for a distance of at least 8.5 m (27 ft 10 in) unaided. Wesley topped his own record of 8.87 m (29 ft 1 in), set in 2020.

KING OF THE JUGGLE

Michael Ferreri (ESP), a fourth-generation circus performer, has his hands full with his ever-growing clutch of juggling records, shown here starting with the most recent…

 33

Most 360° body spins while juggling four objects in one minute in Balatonlelle, Hungary, on 20 Aug 2022.

 4

Most 360° body spins while juggling three objects in one minute in Debrecen, Hungary, on 20 Apr 2022.

 14

Most 360° body spins while juggling six objects with a one-handed pattern in one minute in Blackpool, Lancashire, UK, on 14 Jun 2021.

1,302

Most juggling catches in three minutes (four balls) in Jaén, Spain, on 7 Apr 2021.

1,208

Most juggling catches in three minutes (five balls) in Málaga, Spain, on 9 Feb 2021.

19

Most 360° body spins while juggling five objects in one minute in San Luis Obispo, California, USA, on 3 Jul 2018.

Tallest stilts
On 4 Jun 2022, Jordan Wolf (USA) walked 10 steps unsupported atop a 16.48-m-high (54-ft 1-in) pair of stilts in Marshfield, Wisconsin, USA. Breaking this record is a family tradition for the Wolfs; it has previously been held by Jordan's father, "Steady" Eddie, and his brother Travis.

Farthest axe kick
Sam Pollock (UK) eschewed tradition and used his foot to propel an axe into a target that was 14.2 m (46 ft 7 in) away in Bristol, UK, on 15 Jul 2021.

Farthest tightrope walk in high heels
On 16 May 2022, Ariana Wunderle (USA) teetered a total distance of 194.98 m (639 ft 8 in) along a tightrope in 4-in (10.2-cm) heels in Vermont, USA. She beat the previous record by 170 m (557 ft)!

Most aerial-hoop somersaults in one minute
Yammel Rodriguez (MEX) spun her body through a suspended ring 47 times in Las Vegas, Nevada, USA, on 8 Feb 2023. The aerial hoop was popularized by Cirque du Soleil in the 21st century. However, it first appeared in print on 12 Aug 1893 in an advert for artiste "Ceado the Marvel" in the *New York Clipper* trade newspaper.

Fastest time to walk 10 m on knives
Daredevil stunt artist Fakir Testa (aka Jaime Oms, ESP) crossed a 10-m-long (33-ft) boulevard of blades – barefooted – in just 1 min 5 sec on 24 Feb 2022 in Milan, Italy.

Fastest time to whip 10 targets using a Tasmanian cutback
In this technique, the performer swings a whip around their body and behind their back before cracking it forward. On 7 Nov 2022, April Choi (USA) knocked over 10 plastic cups using this method in just 5.56 sec in Titusville, Florida, USA. On the same day, Choi – a whip artist, fire breather and mechanical engineer – added to her GWR title tally with:
• **Highest throw and catch of a spinning fire knife**: 3.14 m (10 ft 3 in).
• **Most "shoot the moon" fire-eating transfers in one minute**: 30. In this trick, the performer orally extinguishes a flame from one torch, while concurrently lighting another torch held above the face, then repeats the process.
• **Most flowers crack-whipped from the hands in one minute**: 50, with assistance from her wife Bethany Byrnes (USA).

Highest-altitude aerial silks performance
On 27 Jun 2022, Daniela Dragan of Moldova staged a sky-high acrobatic exhibition 1,090 m (3,576 ft) above Manresa in Spain. She executed a 5-min routine while suspended from a hot-air balloon. Daniela is a qualified skydiver, and for the grand finale of her act, she let go and parachuted through the clouds back down to the ground.

MOST…

Swords balanced on the body in three minutes
Emily Quant (USA) supported 56 curved blades on her body in Salem, Massachusetts, USA, on 30 May 2022. Exactly a month earlier, she had set the **one minute** record, with 28.

Consecutive roll-ups on aerial straps while sword swallowing
Alex Magala (USA) ingested a steel sword then proceeded to perform 12 midair rolls with his arms entwined between two hanging straps in Milan, Italy, on 1 Mar 2022.

Concrete blocks broken on a bed of nails in one minute
On 10 Nov 2022 in Nellore, India, Prabhakar Reddy P sledgehammered 67 concrete slabs placed on the body of Vishal Singh Lakka, who was lying on a bed of nails. In Mar 2021, Prabhakar wielded a 68-cm (2-ft 3-in) sword to break his own record for **most watermelons chopped off the head in one minute**, halving 59 fruits placed on the crown of fearless partner Anil Paliwal (all IND).

Longest duration spinning in a Cyr wheel
Human gyroscope Daniel Craig (CAN) spent a dizzying 40 min 8 sec rocking, rolling and spinning a large metal ring in Winnipeg, Canada, on 10 Nov 2022. On 27 Oct 2021, Chen Yuantang (CHN) covered the **fastest 50 m in a Cyr wheel** – 12.17 sec – in Tianjin, China.

SEE THE GREAT WALL OF CHINA
First built *c.* 220 BCE, then extended and renovated up to the 17th century CE, this iconic feat of engineering comprises a total network of some 20,000 km (12,400 mi) of fortified defences. Time only renders the **longest wall** ever shorter, though, so don't put off your visit for too long!

27

MOST FIRE HOOPS SPUN SIMULTANEOUSLY
Grace Good (USA) claims that, "I'm not at all joking when I say that spinning fire hoops soothes my soul." The elite circus performer proved as much on 6 Dec 2022, by coolly spinning eight flaming hoops around herself for the required three complete rotations in Las Vegas, Nevada, USA.

Earlier the same day, she proved herself an equally accomplished equilibrist by executing the **most hula hoops spun simultaneously while balancing on a giant rolling globe** – 28 (*inset*).

Grace became hooked on hoops in 2011 after finishing high school. She's now a certified circus instructor.

JUST F😂R LAUGHS

MOST WINS OF FUNNIEST JOKE AT THE EDINBURGH FRINGE

British stand-ups Masai Graham (*above*) and Tim Vine (*below*) have each picked up the award for funniest quip at Edinburgh's world-famous Fringe festival twice. Graham's latest success was in 2022, while Vine's most recent triumph came in 2014. Here's the full list of killer one-liners:

2022 – Masai Graham
"I tried to steal spaghetti from the shop, but the female guard saw me and I couldn't get pasta."

2019 – Olaf Falafel
"I keep randomly shouting out 'Broccoli' and 'Cauliflower' – I think I might have Florets."

2018 – Adam Rowe
"Working at the job centre has to be a tense job: knowing that if you get fired, you still have to come in the next day."

2017 – Ken Cheng
"I'm not a fan of the new pound coin, but then again, I hate all change."

2016 – Masai Graham
"My dad has suggested that I register for a donor card. He's a man after my own heart."

2015 – Tommy Tiernan
"Two flies are playing football in a saucer. One says to the other: 'Make an effort, we're playing in the cup tomorrow.'"

2014 – Tim Vine
"I've decided to sell my Hoover... well, it was just collecting dust."

2013 – Rob Auton
"I heard a rumour that Cadbury is bringing out an oriental chocolate bar. Could be a Chinese Wispa."

2012 – Stewart Francis
"You know who really gives kids a bad name? Posh and Becks."

2011 – Nick Helm
"I needed a password eight characters long so I picked 'Snow White and the Seven Dwarfs'."

2010 – Tim Vine
"I've just been on a once-in-a-lifetime holiday. I'll tell you what, never again."

2009 – Dan Antopolski
"Hedgehogs – why can't they just share the hedge?"

Oldest joke
A Sumerian proverb warning new husbands about flatulent brides dates back to at least 1900 BCE, according to research led by Dr Paul McDonald of the University of Wolverhampton, UK. Found on a tablet from the Old Babylonian period, it reads: "Something which has never occurred since time immemorial: a young woman did not fart in her husband's lap."

Longest-running pun competition
The O Henry Museum in Austin, Texas, USA, has held an annual pun-off for 45 years, since 1978, with an online iteration in 2020 owing to COVID restrictions. It comprises "PunSlingers" (head-to-head improvised punning) and "Punniest of Show" (a 90-sec prepared performance). The contest is named after the pen name of wordplay-loving writer William Sydney Porter.

Most Primetime Emmy awards for a TV show
The satirical sketch show *Saturday Night Live* (NBC, USA) won 87 Emmys between 1976 and 2022 – or 93 including specials and short-form programmes. In 2009, it also recorded the **most nominations in one year for a variety show** – 13.

Most episodes for a sitcom
As of 2 Jul 2022, there had been 3,500 episodes of *Taarak Mehta Ka Ooltah Chashmah* (*Taarak Mehta's Inverted Spectacles*, SAB TV). The first instalment of the Hindi TV show aired on 28 Jul 2008.
The UK's *Last of the Summer Wine* (BBC) finished in 2010 after 37 years and 31 series – making it the **longest-running sitcom**. Every episode of the nostalgic show was written by Roy Clarke.

Highest-grossing comedy movie
Minions (USA, 2015) had taken $1,157,271,759 (£950.4 m) at the worldwide box office as of 1 Jan 2023. The titular diminutive yellow henchmen made their screen debut in *Despicable Me* (USA, 2010).
Ni Hao, Li Huan Ying (*Hi, Mom*; CHN, 2021) holds the **live-action** record, having earned $841,674,419 (£680.3 m), according to The Numbers.

The **most Emmy wins for a comedy series** is 37, for *Frasier* (NBC, USA, 1994–98), while the **most wins for a comedy in one season** is nine, by *Schitt's Creek* (Pop TV, CAN) in 2020.
The **most Emmy nominations in one year for a comedy debut** is 20, for *Ted Lasso* (Apple TV+/Doozer, USA) in 2021. It stars Jason Sudeikis as an American college football coach.

Most BAFTA children's awards for Best Comedy
Horrible Histories (UK; 2009–present) has won nine times at the British Academy Children's Award, a record six of which were for Best Comedy. The wins came in 2010–13, 2016 (for their *Sensational Shakespeare* special) and 2019.

Most tickets sold for a stand-up comedy tour
Jeff Dunham (USA) shifted 1,981,720 tickets for his global *Spark of Insanity* tour from 13 Sep 2007 to 21 Aug 2010.
Mario Barth (DEU) drew a crowd of 67,733 for his performance at the Olympiastadion in Berlin, Germany, on 12 Jul 2008, the **largest audience for a comedian**.

Most annual airings of a television comedy sketch
In 2022, the English-language comedy sketch "Dinner for One" notched up its 51st airing on German TV. The 18-min skit – about a butler (Freddie Frinton) who gets increasingly drunk while serving dinner to a nonagenarian (May Warden) – has been broadcast every New Year's Eve since 1972.

Most popular comedians on social media
• **TikTok** – Khabane Lame (ITA, b. SEN; @khaby.lame): 154.2 million followers watch as he reacts to overly complicated life hacks with a bemused shrug (*right*).
• **Twitter** – Ellen DeGeneres (USA; @EllenDeGeneres): Despite ending her chat show in May 2022, the comedian still has 76.8 million fans reading her tweets.
• **Instagram** – Kevin Hart (USA, @kevinhart4real): The actor and "comedic rockstar" keeps his 163 million Insta fans amused on a regular basis.
• **YouTube** – Whindersson Nunes Batista (BRA, @whinderssonnunes): The vlogger and stand-up comedian is enjoyed by 44 million subscribers.
As of 20 Jan 2022

GO ON SAFARI IN AFRICA
Take a ride on the wild side! The continent is home to cheetahs (*Acinonyx jubatus*) – the **fastest land animal over short distances**, capable of running at *c.* 100 km/h (62 mph). Perhaps easier to spot is the giraffe (*Giraffa camelopardalis*) – with adult males standing 15–18 ft (4.6–5.5 m), it is the **tallest animal**.

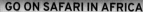

D'yan Forest

SEBASTIAN MANISCALCO

IMAAN HADCHITI

Jerry Seinfeld

A 40-hr 8-min set by The Midnight Swinger (aka David Scott, USA) in 2013 is still the longest stand-up comedy show by an individual.

1. Oldest female comedian: D'yan Forest, aka Diana Shulman (USA, b. 31 Jul 1934), performed her risqué stand-up routine live on *The Drew Barrymore Show* (CBS) on 30 Jan 2023 aged 88 years 183 days.

2. Highest-grossing stand-up comedian: Sebastian Maniscalco (USA) grossed $44,902,984 (£41.2 m) from 84 shows in the year ending 15 Sep 2022. He played to a total of 440,268 people, packing out venues such as Madison Square Garden Arena in New York City and TD Garden in Boston.

The **highest-grossing stand-up per show** for this same period was Dave Chappelle (USA), who took $21,499,305 (£18.6 m) from just 11 shows. This equates to $1,954,482 (£1.6 m) per appearance.

3. Shortest comedian (male): Imaan Hadchiti (LBN/AUS) stands 102.5 cm (3 ft 4 in) tall. He has been a regular performer on the comedy circuit in Australia and the UK since 2005. (*See also p.68.*)

4. Highest-earning comedian: Jerry Seinfeld (USA) reportedly netted $51 m (£36.1 m) in the 12 months to 1 Jun 2020, according to *Forbes*.

5/6. Most nominations for Best Show at the Edinburgh Comedy Awards: Two UK comedians have each received five nominations. Al Murray (*left*) gained his first nod in 1994 for *Harry Hill's Pub Internationale with Al Murray*, with four further nods in 1996–99, the last of which he won. Leftfield comic James Acaster (*right*) received his nominations in 2012–16.

RIDE A GONDOLA IN VENICE
Admire the beauty of the world's **most waterlogged city** from the comfort of a flat-bottomed boat, propelled by a pole-bearing gondolier. With water levels continuing to rise, and the city now flooding about 100 times a year, a gondola may soon be your only option for seeing the sights!

MAGIC

THE WORLD CHAMPIONSHIP OF MAGIC

Founded in 1948, the Fédération Internationale des Sociétés Magiques (FISM) includes 70,000 magicians from some 49 countries. Its World Championship is the **longest-running magic contest**. The **most wins of the FISM Grand Prix** – the most coveted prize – is three, by Fred Kaps (aka Abraham Pieter Adrianus Bongers, NLD; *above*) in 1950, 1955 and 1961. Kaps was most famous for a routine featuring a levitating cork. See below for the most recent world champions.

1 Laurent Piron (BEL) secured the FISM Grand Prix in the Stage category in Quebec City, Canada, in Jul 2022. For his winning trick – "Paper Ball" – scrunched-up paper appears to come to life.

2 At the same competition, Simon Coronel (USA) claimed the Close-Up Grand Prix. He created an "impossible object" by linking cut-out sections of playing cards with a ring from a spectator.

Oldest magic society

The Society of American Magicians was founded in Martinka's magic shop in New York City, USA, on 10 May 1902. From just 24 individuals initially, its membership has grown to c. 5,000 today. It expanded significantly in 1917–26, under the tenure of Harry Houdini (aka Erich Weisz; USA, b. HUN), who is widely regarded as one of the greatest illusionists of all time.

Houdini's automatic flowering rosebush was a mechanical stage prop from c. 1924. On 29 Oct 2022, it became the **most expensive magic trick sold**, fetching $324,000 (£279,970) at auctioneers Potter & Potter in Chicago, Illinois, USA.

Most live animals produced during a magic performance

Penn & Teller (both USA) summoned a swarm of more than 80,000 bees in their 1990 TV special *Don't Try this at Home*. The duo were seeking to represent every live animal ever conjured by a magician with a bee. After Penn was stung in the mouth during the routine, they opted to use flies going forward.

Longest online video chain of people performing a magic trick

On 20 May 2021, *Big Trick Energy* and truTV (both USA) brought together hundreds of amateur magicians to perform 274 tricks on TikTok. The #BigTrickTokChallenge videos were then edited into one take. Above is *Big Trick Energy*'s Chris Ramsay (*front*) with (*left to right*) fellow cast members Wes Barker, Alex Boyer and Eric Leclerc.

Most rabbits pulled out of a hat

Walter Rolfo and Jabba (aka Piero Ustignani, both ITA) conjured 300 bunnies from a single hat during the Magic Congress in Saint-Vincent, Aosta, Italy, on 17 May 2008.

Most playing cards thrown around a person in one minute

On 18 Oct 2022, Rick Smith Jr (USA) hurled 56 standard playing cards, which lodged in a target behind his assistant in Irvine, California, USA. Smith has also recorded the **farthest** and **highest** throws of a playing card – 65.96 m (216 ft 4 in) and 21.41 m (70 ft 3 in), respectively.

Farthest teleportation illusion

On 28 Aug 2018, Scott Tokar (USA) "teleported" an assistant 285.33 m (936 ft) between two tents in Boone, Iowa, USA. The assistant carried a card (chosen by a spectator) with a corner torn from it, to prove that it was the same person.

First person-sawn-in-half illusion staged

PT Selbit (b. Percy Tibbles, UK; *above*) debuted this classic body-splitting trick on 17 Jan 1921 at the Finsbury Park Empire in London, UK. His female assistant was entirely enclosed within the box. The more familiar version, with the head and feet visible, was first performed by US magician Horace Goldin on 3 Jun 1921 at the Hotel McAlpin in New York City, USA, with the help of a male "victim".

Most watched magic TV show

More than 50 million viewers tuned in for the first of Canadian magician Doug Henning's eight *World of Magic* 1-hr specials. The show aired live on NBC in the USA on 26 Dec 1975, and included a recreation of Harry Houdini's water-torture-cell trick. The performer is submerged upside down in a water-filled tank, with his legs locked in stocks, yet miraculously escapes.

The **largest audience at a magic performance** is 38,503, for a 3-hr set by the Ehrlich Brothers (DEU) at the Commerzbank-Arena (aka Waldstadion) in Frankfurt, Germany, on 11 Jun 2016.

Most copied stage illusion

Invented by Robert Harbin (ZAF) in 1965, the "Zig Zag Girl" features an assistant, standing in a cabinet, who is cut into three pieces and has their middle section pulled to one side. Harbin published a book in 1970 (limited to 500 copies) that allowed each purchaser to build one version of the prop. An estimated 15,000 such illusions have been built to date, meaning that some 14,500 are unauthorized copies!

David Copperfield

In the contemporary world of magic, no figure has achieved a higher profile than this US illusionist. Indeed, in 2000, FISM declared him to be the "Magician of the Millennium".

His CBS specials *The Magic of David Copperfield* have secured the **most Emmy Award wins** – 18 – and **nominations** – 36 – **for a magic TV series**. In 1991, he founded the International Museum and Library of the Conjuring Arts in Nevada, USA. With 150,000-plus props, books and other ephemera related to conjuring, it is the **largest collection of magic artefacts**.

HAVE CHILDREN

Bringing new life into the world is a unique experience – no matter how many times it happens… On 6 May 2021, Associated Press announced the delivery of nine children born to Halima Cissé (MLI) in Casablanca, Morocco – the **most children delivered at a single birth** (*see p.65*).

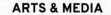
MARTIN "MAGIC MAN" REES

This British conjurer received his first magic set as a Christmas present aged just four. It sparked a lifelong love of illusion – and, in due course, a rack of GWR titles. On 26 Feb 2023, at Wonderville in London, UK, he accomplished in-a-minute records for the **most tricks** – 42 – and **most tricks blindfolded** – 36. Rees's riveting routines included vanishing, reappearing and levitating cards, changing the colour of roses, and making coins disappear.

Rees's previous records are proof positive that his multitasking game is as deft as his sleight of hand, as he has performed the **most magic tricks while...**

• **Underwater in three minutes**: 20 in 2020
• **In a wind tunnel in three minutes**: 8 in 2016
• **In a skydive**: 11 in 2016.

Rees also identified the **most cards in one minute** – 18. Each had been chosen by a stranger and returned to a deck, which was shuffled.

PUPPETRY

FIRST PUPPETS LISTED AS INTANGIBLE CULTURAL HERITAGES

In 2008, UNESCO introduced four historical puppetry forms to the list of what it terms "traditional, contemporary and living" heritage.

Ningyō Jōruri Bunraku puppet theatre (Japan, *above*): A blend of sung narrative, instrumental accompaniment and puppet drama.

Sicilian puppet theatre (Italy, *above*): Stories based on medieval chivalric literature and other sources, such as Renaissance poems.

Sbek Thom, Khmer shadow theatre (Cambodia): 2-m-tall (6-ft 6-in) puppets made of leather openwork and considered to be sacred.

Wayang puppet theatre (Indonesia, *above*): Used in rituals and ceremonies, and in the recounting of Javanese legends and Hindu epics.

Oldest puppet
During excavations for a sewerage system in 1981, a 28,000-year-old figurine was unearthed from a grave in Brno, Czechia. The 20-cm-tall (7.8-in) puppet or doll is considered to be a representation of a Palaeolithic shaman. It is carved from mammoth ivory and coloured with red ochre.

Oldest puppetry company
Compagnia Carlo Colla e Figli (ITA) is a family of puppeteers, still represented today by two companies. The probable date of the first (undocumented) public performance by the family's ancestor Gaspare Carlo Gioacchino Colla was 1815, while the first registered public performance took place on 6 Mar 1835 in a show in Piedmont.

Oldest international theatre organization
The Union Internationale de la Marionnette (UNIMA) was created in Prague, Czechia, in 1929, initially under the name of Union Internationale des Marionnettistes, with the goal of promoting puppetry arts. It adopted its current name in 1969. By 2022, there were around 100 national UNIMA centres, plus several countries with a UNIMA representative.

First puppet TV star
Muffin the Mule made his TV debut in *For the Children* (BBC, UK) on 20 Oct 1946, and continued to appear until 1955. The first puppet to headline its own show, the mischievous marionette from Muffinham danced on the top of a grand piano played by Annette Mills.

Greatest distance travelled by a full-body puppet
Little Amal is a 3.5-m-tall (11-ft 6-in) effigy of a nine-year-old Syrian refugee, operated by three puppeteers. From 27 Jul to 3 Nov 2021, she travelled 8,000 km (4,970 mi) from Gaziantep in Türkiye to Manchester in the UK. Amal means "Hope" in Arabic, and her epic trek was designed to shine a light on the refugee crisis.

Largest puppet in a theatre show
Global Creature Technology (AUS) created a 1.1-tonne (2,425-lb) ape for the musical *King Kong*, which opened in Melbourne, Australia, on 15 Jun 2013. Part marionette, part rod-puppet and part animatronic, the 6-m (20-ft) Kong had 45 axes of movement, from eyelids to elbows, and was worked by 35 on- and off-stage manipulators.

First puppeteer to win an Emmy Award
In 1949, Shirley Dinsdale (USA) picked up an Emmy for Outstanding Television Personality for *Judy Splinters*, in which she performed with her eponymous ventriloquist's dummy. Hers was the first Emmy to be presented at the inaugural Emmy Awards.

Sesame Street has won the **most Emmy awards for a puppet show**. As of 2021, its haul stood at 205 – including 193 Daytime awards. It has also garnered 11 Grammys.

In 1994, the show's singing, dancing, rollerskating superstar Big Bird (performed by Caroll Spinney) became the **first puppet honoured on the Hollywood Walk of Fame**. Sesame Street neighbour Kermit the Frog – who would later become the exasperated showrunner of *The Muppets* – was immortalized with a star of his own in 2002 (*see below*).

Longest dancing dragon
On 30 Sep 2012, more than 3,000 people danced through the streets of Markham in Ontario, Canada, bearing aloft a 5.56-km-long (3.45-mi) dragon. The traditional puppet was a cultural-exchange gift from the citizens of Zhongshan in China.

Highest-grossing puppet movie
Debuting on TV in the 1950s, the Muppets – created by American puppet pioneer Jim Henson – have had a long and successful career, including eight theatrical releases and two TV movies. Their biggest hit is Disney's *The Muppets* (USA, 2011), which grossed $160,971,922 (£101.2 m). *For more Muppetry, go to p.145.*

LEARN TO SURF
Picture yourself riding a cresting breaker, or gliding within the shimmering walls of a wave's tube! Maya Gabeira (BRA) achieved the **largest wave surfed by a woman** – 22.4 m (73 ft 6 in) – off the coast of Praia do Norte, Nazaré, Portugal, on 11 Feb 2020. *For the men's record, see pp.228–29.*

Asterion was the minotaur's birth name. According to Greek myth, the beast was imprisoned within a labyrinth on Crete.

You'll find Asterion at La Halle de la Machine in Toulouse. Up to 50 tourists at a time can ride in the temple on its back.

TALLEST MECHANICAL PUPPET

Asterion the Minotaur stands an intimidating 14 m (45 ft 11 in) tall. The half-man, half-bull first stalked the labyrinthine streets of Toulouse, France, on 1–4 Nov 2018, in a performance inspired by Greek myths.

The fire-breathing Dragon of Calais (*above*) is the **heaviest puppet**, at an incredible 65.3 tonnes (72 tons). A giant iguana-Komodo hybrid, it stretches for a nose-to-tail length of 25 m (82 ft) and is manipulated by up to 17 controllers.

Excluding mythological beasts, the **largest animal puppet** was the Sultan's Elephant (*top*), weighing in at 48.4 tonnes (53.3 tons). It reached a height of 11.2 m (36 ft 8 in), was 7.2 m (23 ft 7 in) wide and had a length – in full stride – of 22 m (72 ft).

All three puppets were designed by François Delarozière (FRA).

GO WHITE-WATER RAFTING

Slaloming through frisky currents and foam spray is an unmatchable thrill. But don't start off at Inga Falls in the Democratic Republic of the Congo. It's the **largest rapids by flow**, averaging around 42,400 m³/sec (1,500,000 cu ft/sec) – enough to fill London's Royal Albert Hall in around 2 sec!

COMMUNITIES

MOST DIGITAL DOGS PETTED

As of 12 Aug 2022, Tristan Cooper (USA) had befriended 269 canines in videogames. He has spent years searching for pattable pooches in titles ranging from *Fallout 4* to *Far Cry New Dawn*. The results are documented on Tristan's Twitter page, "Can You Pet the Dog?", which has more than half a million followers. He has also petted cats, crabs and capybaras, all in the name of research.

269

Hati the wolf is a Viking's best friend in *Assassin's Creed Valhalla* (Ubisoft, 2020).

Greeting Staub the greyhound in *Pentiment* (Obsidian Entertainment, 2022)

Kratos shows his softer side in *God of War* (Santa Monica Studio, 2018)

Square Enix's *Final Fantasy XVI* (2023) boasts a new canine cast member: Torgal.

Most players in an online FPS battle

On 5 Nov 2022, a total of 1,530 combatants squared off inside the epic MMO *PlanetSide 2* (2012). The enormous virtual showdown was sparked by a call to arms by developer Daybreak (USA), in the hope of breaking their 2015 record of 1,158 players. The new peak occurred on the Amerish map and Emerald server. Daybreak confirmed it would give all participants a special in-game title, tweeting: "Thank you for the madness."

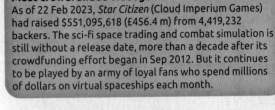

Largest *Minecraft* project

Started by YouTuber "PippenFTS" (USA) in Mar 2020, "Build the Earth" aims to recreate our entire planet, block by block, on a 1:1 scale. The project uses the Terra 1-to-1 mod to pull data from services such as Google Maps and automatically generate terrain. By the end of 2022, Build the Earth had 4,839 ongoing build projects, covering around 7,118 km² (2,748 sq mi).

Most money raised by a speedrunning event

Awesome Games Done Quick 2022 raised $3,416,729 (£2.7 m) for the Prevent Cancer Foundation between 9 and 16 Jan. The online-only event showcased 149 speedruns and received 49,482 donations from 28,073 people. The most high-profile run saw "Mitchriz" (USA) complete *Sekiro: Shadows Die Twice* (FromSoftware, 2019) in just over two hours – while blindfolded.

Most crowdfunded videogame

As of 22 Feb 2023, *Star Citizen* (Cloud Imperium Games) had raised $551,095,618 (£456.4 m) from 4,419,232 backers. The sci-fi space trading and combat simulation is still without a release date, more than a decade after its crowdfunding effort began in Sep 2012. But it continues to be played by an army of loyal fans who spend millions of dollars on virtual spaceships each month.

Most simultaneous users on Steam

A record 33,078,963 people were logged in to Valve's digital distribution service at the same time on 8 Jan 2023 – breaking the previous mark of 31 million set during the Thanksgiving holiday in 2022. The enormous concurrent user count was fuelled by Steam's winter sale and an influx of players that got new hardware (including Valve's portable Steam Deck) for Christmas.

Most watched videogame awards show

On 8 Dec 2022, a global audience of 103 million livestreamed The Game Awards 2022. The show, which took place in front of a live audience at the Microsoft Theater in Los Angeles, California, USA, was broadcast across more than 40 digital platforms and was also shown in IMAX cinemas.

Most viewed single-player game on Twitch

The launch of *Hogwarts Legacy* attracted a peak of 1,280,000 concurrent viewers on Twitch on 9 Feb 2023. The action RPG, developed by Avalanche Software (USA), transports gamers back to 1899, when a goblin rebellion threatens the Hogwarts School of Witchcraft and Wizardry.

Largest shiny Pokémon collecting online community event

On 3 Jun 2022, "Nomeyy" (aka Naomi Finnegan, IRL) and Jack Taylor (UK) led a team of 136 hunters in a quest to track down all shiny variants of the original 151 Pokémon, playing mainline *Pokémon* games and *Pokémon GO*. They completed their task in just 16 hr 23 min 12 sec – the **fastest time to collect all shiny variants of the original 151 Pokémon by an online community event** – and tracked down a total of 455 variants in 24 hr.

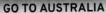

GO TO AUSTRALIA

Take a trip Down Under to sample the delights of the world's **smallest continent**, including the **longest reef** (*see p.44*). One must-see is Uluru, the **largest sandstone monolith**. The rock rises 348 m (1,141 ft) above the bush in Northern Territory and stretches 3.6 km (2.2 mi) in length.

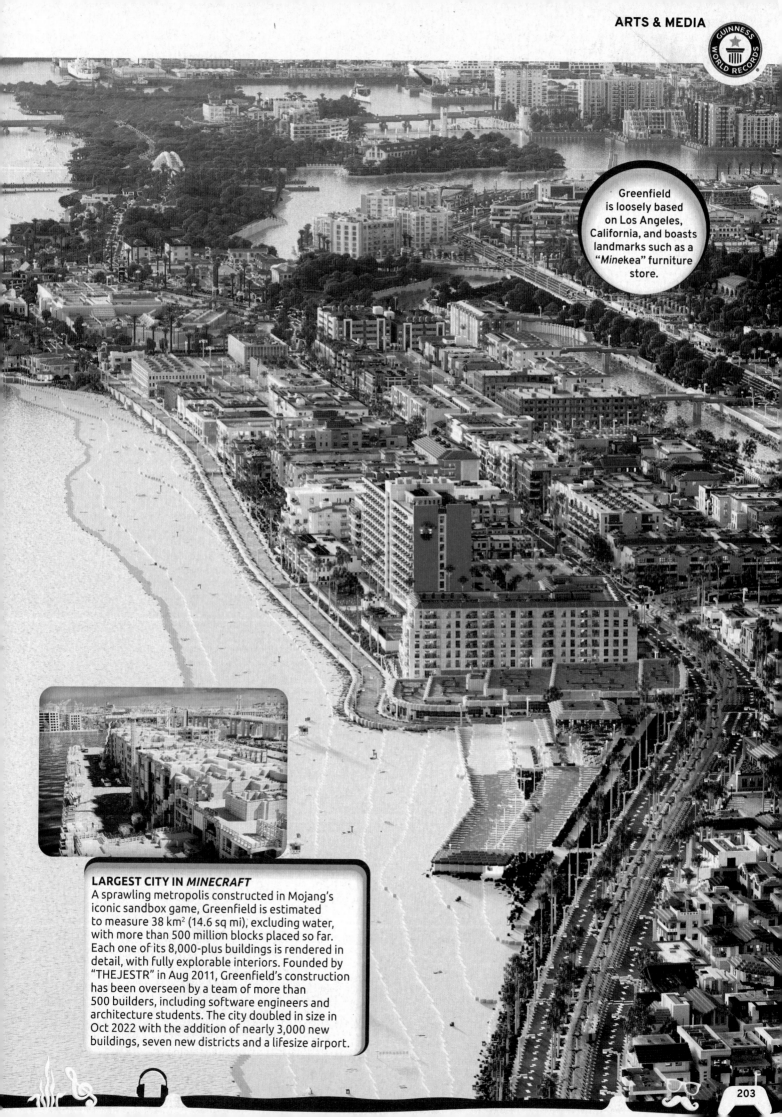

Greenfield is loosely based on Los Angeles, California, and boasts landmarks such as a *"Minekea"* furniture store.

LARGEST CITY IN *MINECRAFT*

A sprawling metropolis constructed in Mojang's iconic sandbox game, Greenfield is estimated to measure 38 km² (14.6 sq mi), excluding water, with more than 500 million blocks placed so far. Each one of its 8,000-plus buildings is rendered in detail, with fully explorable interiors. Founded by "THEJESTR" in Aug 2011, Greenfield's construction has been overseen by a team of more than 500 builders, including software engineers and architecture students. The city doubled in size in Oct 2022 with the addition of nearly 3,000 new buildings, seven new districts and a lifesize airport.

ESPORTS

Highest-earning esports team
Multinational Team Liquid had earned $43,011,651 (£34.9 m) from 2,395 tournaments, as of 3 Feb 2023. Based in the Netherlands, the organization competes in various games, and has chalked up notable victories at The International, playing *Dota 2*, and four consecutive *League of Legends* League Championship Series.

Longest-running esports tournament
Held annually in Dallas, Texas, USA, since 1996, QuakeCon is a celebration of fast-paced 1990s deathmatch shooters. The centerpiece is a tournament for players of the classic *Quake* and its sequels. Although COVID-19 restrictions forced the event to go digital, it is traditionally organized as an old-school LAN party, with each player bringing their own computer.

Highest-earning esports player
"N0tail" (aka Johan Sundstein, DNK) had earned $7,184,163 (£5.8 m) as of 3 Feb 2023, according to esportsearnings. The grandson of the former Faroese prime minister, N0tail began playing videogames at the age of two. He has made his fortune predominantly playing *Dota 2*, and is a two-time winner of The International (2018–19).

Largest esports team for people with disabilities
Permastunned Gaming, a global gaming collective exclusively for players with disabilities, had 33 members by Apr 2022. The brainchild of Belgium-based Alexander "Cristal" Nathan (b. NLD, *above*) and founded in 2019, the group specializes in *Dota 2*, *Call of Duty* and *Tekken*, among other games.

Most esports pro tournament wins (female)
Sasha "Scarlett" Hostyn (CAN) had racked up 43 tournament victories as of 3 Feb 2023. All came playing *StarCraft II*, in which Scarlett favours the alien Zerg faction. She started playing competitively in 2011, at the age of 17, and has gone on to earn $442,478 (£358,765) from 249 tournaments.

Highest-earning *Counter-Strike: Global Offensive* player
Peter "dupreeh" Rasmussen (DNK) had accrued $2,030,331 (£1.6 m) playing Valve's classic FPS as of 3 Feb 2023. Dupreeh overtook fellow Dane Andreas "Xyp9x" Højsleth when his Team Vitality won the ESL Pro League Season 16 in Malta on 2 Oct 2022. At the same time, he became the **first *CS: GO* player to earn $2 million**.

Most watched *Counter-Strike* tournament
The PGL Major Stockholm 2021 drew an audience of 2,748,850 viewers during Ukrainian team Natus Vincere's 2–0 grand final victory over G2 Esports on 7 Nov 2021. The battle took place at the Avicii Arena in Stockholm, Sweden.

Most tournament victories for a *Call of Duty* player
Ian "Crimsix" Porter (USA) is a 38-time champion playing Activision's all-conquering FPS. He has won a record-tying three world championship rings (in 2014, 2017 and 2020) and earned $1.4 m (£1.1 m). Crimsix stands seven tournament wins clear of his nearest rival, Seth "Scump" Abner.

TOP 5 ESPORTS GAMES
(ranked by prize money disbursed as of 16 Feb 2023)

1 *Dota 2* ($312.4 m; £258.6 m)

2 *Fortnite* ($150.2 m; £124.3 m)

3 *Counter-Strike: Global Offensive* ($147.1 m; £121.7 m)

4 *League of Legends* ($98.7 m; £81.7 m)

5 *Arena of Valor* ($70.3 m; £58.2 m)

Most esports tournament appearances
As of 3 Feb 2023, melee master Jason "Mew2King" Zimmerman (USA) had entered 618 gaming competitions. Mew2King – who boasts career earnings of $284,655 (£229,544) playing *Super Smash Bros. Melee* – was eight tournaments clear of *StarCraft II* specialist Kang "Solar" Min-soo.

Largest mobile-game prize pool
The *Honor of Kings* International Championship 2022 had prize money totalling $10 m (£8.3 m), with the eStar Pro (CHN) team walking away with the $3.5-m (£2.9-m) first prize. Tencent Games' 2015 MOBA is one of the most played games in the world, with an estimated 100 million daily players.

iDom has shown strong character loyalty to Brazilian jiu-jitsu star Laura, citing her high damage output.

Most watched *Street Fighter* tournament
The *Street Fighter V* tournament at the Evolution Championship Series 2022 in Las Vegas, Nevada, USA, hit a peak of 250,730 viewers on 7 Aug. The final showdown pitted the USA's Derek "iDom" Ruffin (*left*) against Japan's Masaki Kawano (*right*); it was the latter, playing as Kolin, who emerged victorious, roaring back to defeat iDom's Laura 3–2.

FLY A HOT-AIR BALLOON
The world's hot-air-balloon hot spot is Albuquerque in New Mexico, USA, which balloonists love for its predictable weather and stunning landscapes. The **greatest mass ascent** took place at the annual Balloon Fiesta here on 6 Oct 2019, when 524 "bags" took to the skies.

GUINNESS WORLD RECORDS

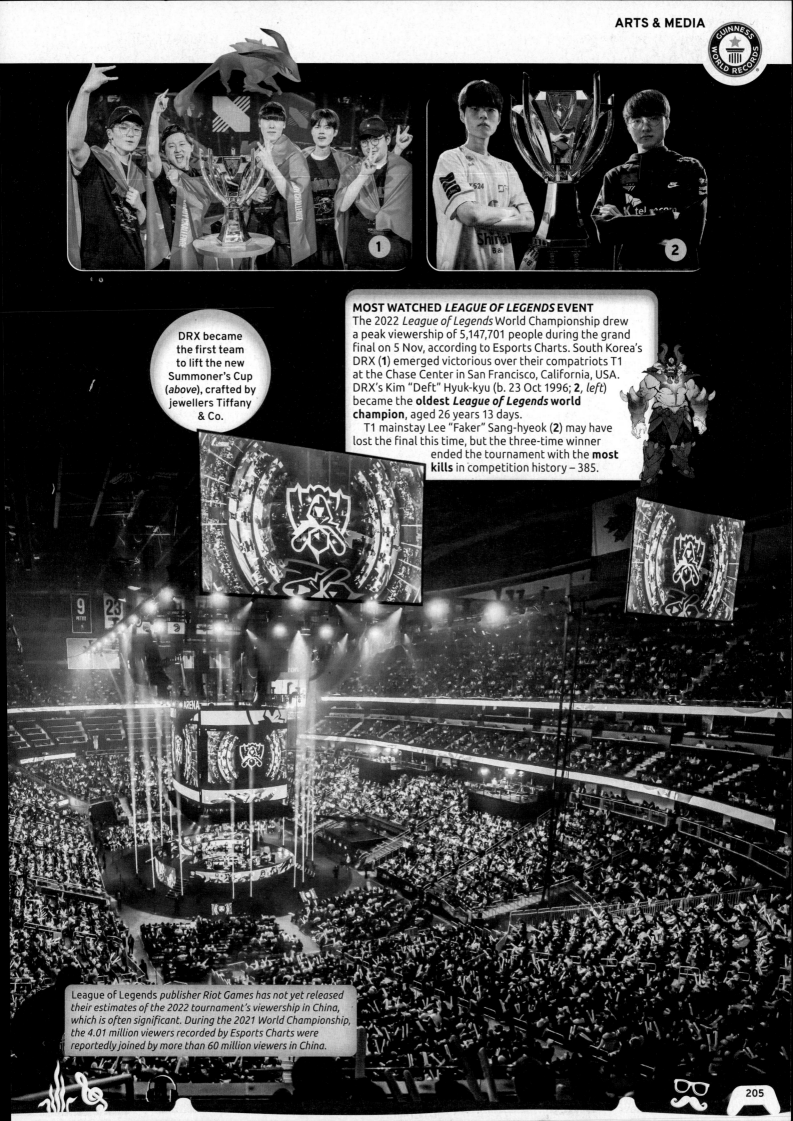

1

2

DRX became the first team to lift the new Summoner's Cup (*above*), crafted by jewellers Tiffany & Co.

MOST WATCHED *LEAGUE OF LEGENDS* EVENT
The 2022 *League of Legends* World Championship drew a peak viewership of 5,147,701 people during the grand final on 5 Nov, according to Esports Charts. South Korea's DRX (**1**) emerged victorious over their compatriots T1 at the Chase Center in San Francisco, California, USA. DRX's Kim "Deft" Hyuk-kyu (b. 23 Oct 1996; **2**, *left*) became the **oldest *League of Legends* world champion**, aged 26 years 13 days.

T1 mainstay Lee "Faker" Sang-hyeok (**2**) may have lost the final this time, but the three-time winner ended the tournament with the **most kills** in competition history – 385.

League of Legends *publisher Riot Games has not yet released their estimates of the 2022 tournament's viewership in China, which is often significant. During the 2021 World Championship, the 4.01 million viewers recorded by Esports Charts were reportedly joined by more than 60 million viewers in China.*

TOP 5 BEST-SELLING GAMES CONSOLES

1

Sony's PlayStation 2 shipped a total of 155 million units between its Japanese release on 4 Mar 2000 and 31 Mar 2012 – making it the **best-selling console**. Sony continued production even after releasing its next-gen PS3 in 2006.

2

The Nintendo DS is the **best-selling handheld console**, with worldwide sales of 154.02 million as of 30 Sep 2022. There have been four iterations of the DS since it launched on 21 Nov 2004.

3

The Nintendo Switch is the **fastest console to ship 100 million units**. The hybrid console reached the milestone on 31 Dec 2021, just 4 years 303 days after its release. It had shipped 122.55 million units as of 31 Dec 2022.

4

Although the Nintendo Game Boy received mixed reviews on its release on 21 Apr 1989, the 8-bit handheld became a cultural icon, shipping 118.69 million units. A Game Boy loaded with *Tetris* became the **first console in space** in 1993.

5

The PlayStation 4 has shipped 117.2 million units since its release in 2013, according to Sony financial reports from Mar 2022. The eighth-gen console, which also had "Slim" and "Pro" versions, allowed gaming to be streamed online.

Best-selling home console brand

As of 30 Sep 2022, a total of 833.58 million Nintendo consoles had been sold worldwide. This eclipsed its nearest rival, Sony's PlayStation, with 569.2 million units shipped. The first Nintendo console was released in Japan in 1983 as the Family Computer ("Famicom").

Most profitable arcade cabinet

The original 1980 *Pac-Man* arcade machines from Namco (JPN) had received an estimated $3.5 bn (£1.8 bn) in revenue by 1990, according to research conducted by *USGamer* in 2016. Its closest competitor was *Space Invaders* (1978), which generated $2.7 bn (£1.6 bn) in the four years to 1982.

First official adaptive controller

The Xbox Adaptive Controller enables gamers with limited mobility to connect external devices such as switches, buttons, mounts and joysticks, customizing gameplay to their specific requirements. It was released on 4 Sep 2018.

Smallest controller

On 12 Feb 2018, modder "Madmorda" (USA) unveiled a Nintendo GameCube controller measuring 63 mm wide, 45 mm high and 31 mm deep (2.4 x 1.7 x 1.2 in). It was fully functional, even down to the rumble feature. Using a GameCube controller keychain as the basis, Madmorda added 3D-printed parts for the L, R and Z buttons.

Smallest MAME cabinet

Phillip Burgess (USA) built a fully functional multiple arcade machine emulator cabinet measuring 67.2 mm tall, 33.6 mm wide and 35.8 mm deep (2.6 x 1.3 x 1.4 in), as verified on 14 Sep 2016. A Raspberry Pi computer runs games such as *Pac-Man* and *Donkey Kong* on a thumbnail-sized screen.

100%

Most unofficial videogame ports

Developed by id Software and released on the PC in 1993, *Doom* has been unofficially ported to at least 110 different platforms, according to research conducted by the *It Runs Doom* blog. The FPS was deliberately programmed to encourage modders to tinker with it, and a community of amateur developers built up around the game during the 1990s, developing extra levels and modifications. Modders have ported the game into a John Deere tractor, a Roomba robot vacuum, DJ deadmau5's enormous "Cube" stage set, and even a pregnancy test kit!

Modders squeeze every bit of performance from old mobile phones.

Doom has been made to run on the control computers for multi-million-dollar pieces of industrial machinery.

Anything with a simple computer and a screen – even a digital pregnancy test – can run some variant of Doom.

First videogame console

Released in the USA in 1972, the Magnavox Odyssey worked through a TV set and was powered by batteries. The console came with screen overlays and board-game accessories such as dice; the **first console peripheral**, a light gun, was sold separately. Despite poor sales, by 1975 the Odyssey was being distributed in Japan by Nintendo, helping to kickstart the gaming revolution.

Heaviest standard controller

Bundled with Nintendo's Wii U console upon its release on 18 Nov 2012, the Wii U GamePad weighed 500 g (1 lb 1.6 oz). Inspired by the successful Nintendo DS (*see left*), it included a 6.2-in (15.7-cm) secondary screen between the controls and a hefty battery pack. The GamePad's closest rival was the famously massive "Duke" controller for the original Xbox, which weighed in at 425 g (15 oz), despite being a conventional wired controller with no screen or battery.

Largest Xbox console

Michael Pick (USA) built an extra-large Xbox measuring 2.08 x 1.04 x 1.04 m (6 ft 9 in x 3 ft 4 in x 3 ft 4 in). It was verified on 9 Dec 2021 in Huntsville, Alabama, USA. Michael enclosed a standard Xbox Series X inside a supersized wooden frame. He said that the hardest challenge was recreating the glowing Xbox logo as a working push button.

At the opposite end of the spectrum, there is a community of hackers who push each other to make hardware mods of original console hardware. The Nintendo 64 (1996) is a popular target for these hackers, and the **smallest N64**, made by Gunnar Turnquist (USA), crams all the circuit boards, controls, screen and even speakers into a box just 11.8 cm (4.64 in) at its widest – less than half the size of the original.

DONATE BLOOD

Parting with your plasma is a small, selfless act with potentially life-saving consequences for others. Dale Faughn (USA, b. 8 Nov 1925) has never needed persuading. He had donated 36.5 gal (138.1 litres) of blood by 6 Feb 2023. Aged 97 years 90 days as of that date, he is the **oldest regular blood donor**.

Largest arcade machine
A 4.9-m-tall (16-ft) *Tetris* cabinet was unveiled by MadLab (ESP) at their leisure centre in Zaragoza, Spain, on 18 Dec 2021. The game operates as normal, although players have to climb steps to reach the controls and insert a giant coin in the slot to begin.

LARGEST GAME BOY

Engineering student Ilhan Ünal (BEL) created an upscaled version of Nintendo's classic handheld console measuring 1.01 m tall, 0.62 m wide and 0.2 m deep (3 ft 4 in x 2 ft x 7.8 in). The machine, which runs off a Raspberry Pi hidden in the external connector socket, was verified in Antwerp, Belgium, on 13 Nov 2016.

The **smallest Game Boy**, on the other hand, is just 54 mm (2.1 in) long and can be fitted on a keychain. It was created by Jeroen Domburg (NLD) in 2016.

How did you first come up with the idea to build a giant Game Boy?
My friend hosts festivals that play chiptune music, and we had the idea of having a giant Game Boy to draw people's attention to the gaming corner.

How long did it take to build?
The first version took me a week to design on a computer and one month of working in the laboratory. But then I had to implement some extra functions like cartridge reading, which meant I had to hack up an actual Game Boy. This took me about a year.

How many games can you play on it?
Every single original released Game Boy cartridge! But that's not the end of it.

I made it possible to play with a Raspberry Pi, so using emulation software you can play games from multiple different consoles.

Have you always been an inventor?
I could use a screwdriver at the age of four and I was interested in electronics, so I learned how to build computers. When I was 14 or 15, a friend invited me to the lab and that's where I started inventing cool things.

How does it feel to be recognized by Guinness World Records?
It's a huge achievement. It feels great to have a creation of mine acknowledged on a world scale. I want to make inventions that make people happy and that they love to interact with – that makes me happy too.

LEADERBOARDS

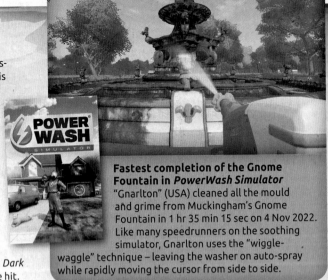

First completion of *Halo 2* "Legendary All Skulls On deathless"
Boasting harder enemies, sparser ammo and no heads-up display for Master Chief, *Halo 2* "LASO deathless" is considered by many to be the hardest challenge in all gaming. On 3 Aug 2022, "JerValiN" (USA) became the first player in history to complete it – before an audience of 12,000 Twitch viewers – in 6 hr 29 min 44 sec. He also earned a $20,000 (£16,375) bounty posted by YouTuber Charles "Cr1TiKal" White Jr.

Fastest Any% completion of *Super Mario Bros.*
On 7 Aug 2022, US speedrunner "Niftski" rescued Princess Peach from Bowser's clutches in just 4 min 54.798 sec. He broke his own Any% world record by just 83 milliseconds, using a keyboard to play an emulated version of the classic 1985 NES side-scroller. This is just 0.533 sec away from the pre-programmed tool-assisted (TAS) best possible run.

First no-hit completion of the seven-game "SoulsBorneKiroRing" run
On 13 Sep 2022, "BushidoYu" (ESP) conquered a challenge dubbed "The God Run 3" in a live Twitch broadcast. He had to complete a septet of the famously unforgiving FromSoftware-developed games – *Sekiro: Shadows Die Twice*, *Bloodborne*, *Demon's Souls*, *Dark Souls I*, *II* and *III*, and *Elden Ring* – without taking a single hit.

Fastest completion of the Gnome Fountain in *PowerWash Simulator*
"Gnarlton" (USA) cleaned all the mould and grime from Muckingham's Gnome Fountain in 1 hr 35 min 15 sec on 4 Nov 2022. Like many speedrunners on the soothing simulator, Gnarlton uses the "wiggle-waggle" technique – leaving the washer on auto-spray while rapidly moving the cursor from side to side.

DID YOU KNOW?
One of the earliest speedrunning leaderboards was for 1993 FPS *Doom*.

Today, speedrunning includes many different disciplines. Speedrun.com users have logged more than 2 million runs in 26,277 games.

In an Any% run, players skip huge chunks of the game in a dash to the end screen.

In a 100% run, the player completes everything there is to do in the game.

Longest overland journey in *No Man's Sky*
"Steam-bot" (USA) embarked on an epic trek across the surface of the planet Dudenbeaumodeme between 27 Aug and 11 Sep 2016, leaving his ship behind and travelling by foot and jetpack. He spent more than 40 hr circumnavigating the entire planet before returning to his ship, logging his journey on Reddit and Twitch.

Most PlayStation trophies
"ikemenzi" (aka Kenji Ito, JPN) had won 237,838 PS trophies as of 13 Jan 2023, as verified on PSNProfiles. He led the categories for the **most gold** (59,361), **silver** (51,763) and **bronze** (119,947). He had also won 6,767 platinum trophies.

The **most PlayStation platinum trophies** is 7,017, by "caro3c-gabber9" (FRA) as of the same date.

Fastest Any% completion of *Zelda: Ocarina of Time*
Link's N64 debut has provided one of gaming's most enduring challenges, with more than 9,000 runs logged on Speedrun.com as of 13 Jan 2023. Top of the tree is "Murph_E" (USA), who completed the game in 3 min 54 sec on 22 Oct 2022. Other classic Any% runs include:
- ***Minecraft: Java Edition* (Glitchless, set seed)**: 1 min 49 sec 160 ms (in-game time), by "EmpireKills702" (USA) on 11 Dec 2022.
- ***Celeste* (PC)**: 25 min 55 sec, by "secureaccount" (USA) on 7 Jan 2023.
- ***Super Metroid***: exactly 27 min (in-game time), by "zoast" (PLW) on 24 Oct 2022.

First 120-star blindfolded completion of *Super Mario 64*
On 8 May 2022, "Bubzia" (DEU) achieved 100% completion in Nintendo's seminal platformer using only audio cues and his encyclopaedic knowledge of the game. His run took 11 hr 22 min 43 sec and was streamed on Twitch. He had trained for more than 700 hr for the attempt.

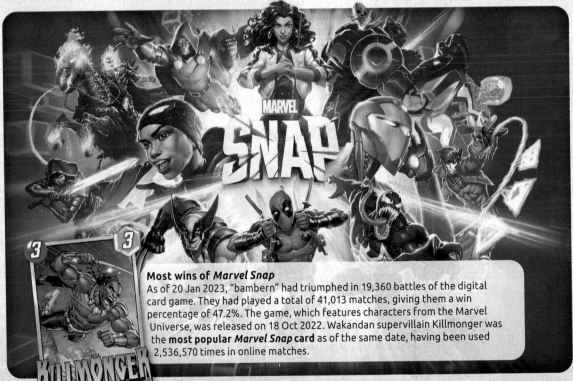

Most wins of *Marvel Snap*
As of 20 Jan 2023, "bambern" had triumphed in 19,360 battles of the digital card game. They had played a total of 41,013 matches, giving them a win percentage of 47.2%. The game, which features characters from the Marvel Universe, was released on 18 Oct 2022. Wakandan supervillain Killmonger was the **most popular *Marvel Snap* card** as of the same date, having been used 2,536,570 times in online matches.

GO TO PARIS
The world's capital of romance is a must-visit for connoisseurs of all things beautiful. Admire the city of love from the top of the Eiffel Tower. This 330-m (1,083-ft) landmark was the world's **tallest freestanding structure** from 1889 to 1930 and remains the **tallest iron structure**.

Elden Ring sold 12 million units in just two weeks following its release on 25 Feb 2022.

FASTEST ANY% UNRESTRICTED COMPLETION OF *ELDEN RING*

"HYP3RSOMNIAC" (USA) raced through FromSoftware's smash-hit action RPG on the PC in 3 min 56 sec on 15 Aug 2022. They made use of a warp glitch that enables players to cover huge distances and bypass entire chapters of the game. The **fastest Any%** run without the use of these warps is 19 min 49 sec, by "FirstTwoWeeks" (USA) on 17 Sep 2022.

One of 2022's more unlikely gaming superstars was "LetMeSoloHer" (USA), a cooking-pot-wearing volunteer helper on hand to assist players trying to take down Malenia, one of *Elden Ring*'s most feared bosses. Between 25 Feb and 10 May 2022, he recorded the **most times to defeat Malenia** – 1,000. The player was presented with a decorative sword by publisher Bandai Namco on 22 May to celebrate the milestone.

Dragonlord Placidusax, a legendary enemy located in Crumbling Farum Azula, is the **least-defeated boss in Elden Ring**. *As of 13 Dec 2022, its boss-battle trophy was the rarest achievement across the PS4 (26.1% of players), PS5 (26.6%), Xbox (38%) and PC (43%).*

Most overall wins in *Fall Guys*
Mediatonic's free-to-play "party royale" invites up to 60 players to outmanoeuvre the competition in a series of obstacle races. More than 50 million players have joined in the fun. "KawaiiNekoWaifu" (AUS) is currently top of the charts, having racked up 28,978 victories as of 5 Dec 2022.

Longest speech at The Game Awards
Christopher Judge (USA) gave thanks for an epic 7 min 59 sec upon receiving his Best Performance award on 8 Dec 2022. Judge, who was honoured for his work as Kratos in Sony's *God of War Ragnarök* (2022, *see opposite*), accepted his award from actor Al Pacino.

Fastest completion of *Amok Runner*
"Weegee" (USA) raced through Gamedeus's indie adventure in 25 min 32 sec on 10 Jan 2023. Interest in *Amok Runner* exploded when Twitch streamer "MoistCr1TiKaL" (aka Charles White Jr, USA) set up a $10,000 two-week speedrunning challenge for the previously little-known game.

First player to defeat every *Elden Ring* boss without taking a hit
"GinoMachino" (CAN) achieved the unthinkable on 25 Oct 2022, downing all 165 bosses in *Elden Ring* (FromSoftware, 2022) without receiving a single scratch in a gruelling 9-hr livestream. GinoMachino spent two months planning out the safest route through the world and left the training boss until the end, pulverizing it in one hit. He has also completed the game using only his bare fists.

Highest-grossing opening weekend for an animated film
Despite a lukewarm reception from film critics, *The Super Mario Bros. Movie* (USA/JPN, 2023) pulled in $375,579,730 (£302.2 m) at the global box office in its first weekend. This figure, confirmed on 10 Apr, put it more than $17 m (£13.6 m) ahead of *Frozen II* (USA/JPN, 2019).

Fastest 16-star completion of *Super Mario 64* with a drum kit
Cesar "CZR" Aguirre (USA) has mapped the buttons and analogue stick of a Nintendo 64 controller to his electric drum kit. So to run foward and jump, for example, he plays a drum roll on a rack tom, then hits the kick drum. He beat *Super Mario 64* (1996) with a 19-min 48-sec drum solo on 9 Dec 2022.

Most Role-Playing Game of the Year wins for a franchise at the DICE Awards
Final Fantasy XIV: Endwalker (Square Enix, 2021) claimed the series' fifth top prize at the DICE Awards on 24 Feb 2022. *Final Fantasy* titles have been nominated in this category an impressive 11 times since 1998.

The **most Game of the Year awards for a franchise** is two, and has been achieved by three titles: *Call of Duty* (Activision, in 2004 and 2008), *The Legend of Zelda* (Nintendo, in 1999 and 2018) and *God of War* (Sony, in 2006 and 2019).

▶ Largest *Sonic the Hedgehog* memorabilia collection
Barry Evans (USA) had amassed 3,050 items relating to Sega's spiky speedster as of 1 Mar 2022. He keeps his collection – which began with a Sonic bubblegum container – in his games room, which he has transformed into his childhood amusement arcade, "Yesterdays".

Most Racing Game of the Year wins for a franchise at the DICE Awards
The Xbox simcade series *Forza* has topped the podium seven times at the videogame industry's Oscars. At the 25th ceremony on 24 Feb 2022, *Forza Horizon 5* became the latest title in the franchise to speed off with the prize. The 2019 spin-off *Forza Street* is the only one of the 13 *Forza* titles not to be nominated in this category.

SEE ELEPHANTS IN THE WILD
With their long trunks and huge ears, these gentle giants of Africa and Asia have always made a big impression on us humans. The adult male African elephant (*Loxodonta africana*) is the **largest land-based animal**, typically weighing 4–7 tonnes (4.4–7.7 tons).

FROM THE EMMY-AWARD WINNING CREATOR OF *CHERNOBYL* AND THE CREATOR OF THE ACCLAIMED VIDEO GAME

HBO ORIGINAL

THE LAST OF US

WHEN YOU'RE LOST IN THE DARKNESS, LOOK FOR THE LIGHT.

NEW SERIES
STREAMING JAN 15

HBOmax

Most critically acclaimed TV videogame adaptation

HBO's post-apocalyptic drama *The Last of Us* (USA) was rated 84 out of 100 on review aggregator Metacritic upon its release on 15 Jan 2023. The show is based on Naughty Dog's 2013 survival-horror videogame, which follows smuggler Joel as he escorts 14-year-old Ellie across a monster-ravaged USA.

Most BAFTA nominations

God of War Ragnarök secured 14 nominations ahead of the 2023 BAFTA Games Awards on 30 Mar. The continued story of the Spartan warrior Kratos and his son Atreus received nods in all the categories it qualified for, as well as six for the cast (*see opposite*). The game's makers walked away with six gongs on the night, unexpectedly losing out on Game of the Year to indie shooter *Vampire Survivors* (Luca Galante, 2022).

First woman to qualify for a Call of Duty Challengers Elite tournament

Kelsie "Kels" Grieg (UK) made the cut for Activision's elite competition on 5 Jan 2023 playing *Call of Duty Modern Warfare II* (Infinity Ward, 2022). The 21-year-old was playing alongside her "Superstars" teammates James "Genesis" Smith, Conor "BBConor" Beale and Ewen "Disarray" Harmer. Call of Duty Challengers Elite is for amateur players in North America and Europe, with the best 12 teams competing for a grand prize.

Highest score in *Crossy Road*

On 8 Jan 2022, Joshua Beesley (UK) beat his own record for the fourth time, raising the score to 9,699 points in a mesmerizing 30-min run. Beesley dominates the leaderboards in Hipster Whale's 2014 road-crossing endless runner, which sees the player guide a chicken across an increasingly dangerous set of highway hazards.

First winner of the Grammy for game music

At the 65th Annual Grammy Awards on 5 Feb 2023, composer Stephanie Economou (USA) accepted the inaugural Grammy for Best Score Soundtrack For Video Games & Other Interactive Media. She was nominated for her score for 2022's *Dawn of Ragnarök* expansion to *Assassin's Creed Valhalla* (Ubisoft, 2020).

Level up!
50
Rewards

Style Rewards

Level 50 Jacket   Level 50 Jacket   Level 50 Jacket   Level 50 Jacket

First player to reach level 50 on *Pokémon GO*

At 3 a.m. on 26 Jan 2021, "FleeceKing" (aka Daniel Amos, AUS) attained *Pokémon GO*'s maximum level – watched by 5,000 Twitch viewers – just 16 min before fellow Australian "Lauren Lolly" (aka Lauren Bertoni) also hit level 50. FleeceKing had walked an incredible 20,614 km (12,808 mi) in pursuit of his goal, catching nearly 800,000 Pokémon. In Jan 2023, he reached 2 billion XP points on his account.

WRITE A BOOK
Get that idea from your head to the page and who knows where the story might end? Even with the benefit of divination lessons, it's unlikely that J. K. Rowling (UK) foresaw what magic lay in store for her. The *Harry Potter* creator was declared the **first billionaire author** by *Forbes* in 2004.

ROUND-UP

Largest published book
Based on the best-selling series *Ordinary People Change the World* by Brad Meltzer and Christopher Eliopoulos, *I Am Texas* is a 7.48-m² (80.51-sq-ft) compilation of Texas-themed stories and artwork by 1,000 students. Produced by iWRITE Literacy Organization and The Bryan Museum (both USA), it went on display in Houston, Texas, USA, on 5 Nov 2022.

Largest gathering of people dressed as vampires
On 26 May 2022, a group of 1,369 gothic-fiction fans flocked to Whitby Abbey in North Yorkshire, UK. The ghoulish gathering, convened by English Heritage (UK), marked the 125th anniversary of the publication of Bram Stoker's *Dracula* (1897), which was partly inspired by the abbey's ambience. In the novel, Dracula makes landfall at Whitby.

First leading actor with Down syndrome in an Oscar-winning film
Tom Berkeley and Ross White's dark comedy *An Irish Goodbye* (UK, 2022) – starring James Martin (UK, *second from left*) as Lorcan – won Best Live Action Short Film at the Academy Awards on 12 Mar 2023. The ceremony coincided with Martin's 31st birthday, and Hollywood's A-listers sang "Happy Birthday" as the Oscar was presented.

Oldest Oscar nominee
US composer/conductor John Williams (b. 8 Feb 1932) was aged 90 years 350 days when shortlisted for Best Original Score for his work on Steven Spielberg's *The Fabelmans* (USA, 2022) on 24 Jan 2023. It was the 53rd Oscar nod of his career – the **most Oscar nominations for a living person**; since 1968, he has been tipped 48 times for Best Original Score and five times for Best Original Song. He is just six shy of Walt Disney's (USA) **all-time Oscar nomination** haul.

Largest wire art
On 16 Feb 2022, Ali Alrawi (IRQ) presented a 203.76-m² (2,193.25-sq-ft) artwork made from copper wire in Al Ramadi, Iraq. It depicted a lamassu – a mythical Assyrian beast comprising a human head, a bull's body and an eagle's wings.

Most published copies of a *shōjo* manga series written by a single author
A total of 59,409,000 copies of *Hana Yori Dango* (*Boys Over Flowers*), created by Yoko Kamio (JPN), were printed and circulated from Oct 1992 to Nov 2022. The series follows the adventures of student Tsukushi Makino. (*See also pp.192–93.*)

Longest career in the same orchestra
Viola player Anne Miller (UK) has been a member of the Redhill Sinfonia for 71 years 194 days, as verified in Reigate, Surrey, UK, on 25 Jun 2022.

Youngest documentary presenter
Aneeshwar Kunchala (UK, b. 21 Jan 2015) was 7 years 288 days old when *COP27 – Six Ways to Save Our Planet* aired on 5 Nov 2022. This young conservationist, who counts David Attenborough among his heroes, has appeared regularly on screen, emphasizing the need to protect nature. He also received an award from the Scientific Exploration Society in late 2021.

Most Instagram followers
Footballer Cristiano Ronaldo (PRT; @cristiano) reigns with 565,143,282 followers – more than 50 times the population of his home nation.

In 2023, Selena Gomez (USA; @selenagomez) reclaimed the **women's** record: 403,011,388 fans.

BLACKPINK's Lisa (THA, b. Pranpriya Manobal; @lalalalisa_m) is the **most followed K-pop artist**, with 90,739,796 followers.

...**most liked image on Instagram** is a shot ...Messi (ARG; @leomessi) lifting the FIFA ...r Argentina won the final on 18 Dec ...e post has 75,471,946 "hearts".

...F 24 Mar 2023

Largest mechanical wings on a cosplay costume
Illustrator and committed cosplayer Arianna Palumbo (ITA) sported a pair of flappable wings that spanned 6.22 m (20 ft 4 in) in Santa Marinella, Italy, on 29 Jan 2022. Her show-stopping costume was based on the character Goddess Elizabeth, from the manga series *The Seven Deadly Sins* by Nakaba Suzuki.

Palumbo built her upscaled wings in just a month. She says the trickiest part was devising their electrical parts.

...UNGEE JUMP
A heart-pumping freefall followed by an exhilarating (and reassuring) rebound must be high on any adrenaline fiend's wish list. To take the pastime to new heights, visit the **highest commercial bungee-jump facility** – 370.25 m (1,214 ft 8 in) – on the Balinghe Bridge near Anshun in Guizhou, China.

Largest permanent cinema screen

The Traumpalast Leonberg (DEU) cinema is home to an 814.8-m² (8,770.4-sq-ft) IMAX screen – bigger than four tennis courts – as confirmed in Leonberg, Germany, on 6 Dec 2022. It opened with the James Bond thriller *No Time to Die* (UK/USA, 2021).

Largest Portuguese folk dance

On 17 Sep 2022, a group of 747 dancers joined in a "Vira Geral", courtesy of the Portuguese Cultural Centre of Mississauga (CAN) in Ontario, Canada.

The **largest *rueda de casino* dance** consisted of 1,585 people and was achieved by Retomando el Son (VEN) in Caracas, Venezuela, on 27 Nov 2022. This salsa-style group dance, which originated in Cuba, is performed in a circle.

Most selfies in three minutes

Bollywood megastar Akshay Kumar (IND) snapped 184 photos (more than one a second) with fans in Mumbai, Maharashtra, India, on 22 Feb 2023. Fittingly, the quickfire shoot was set up to celebrate his latest movie, *Selfiee* (IND, 2023).

Most streamed track on Spotify in one week

"Flowers" by Miley Cyrus (USA) amassed 115,156,896 worldwide streams on Spotify for the week ending 26 Jan 2023. This smashed the record she'd set a week earlier – 96,032,624 – with the same song, thereby surpassing "Easy on Me" by Adele, which was streamed 84,952,932 times in the week to 21 Oct 2021.

Most wins of the BET YoungStars Award

Marsai Martin (USA) collected her fourth consecutive YoungStars trophy at the 22nd Black Entertainment Television Awards in Los Angeles, California, USA, on 26 Jun 2022. The *black·ish* (ABC) sitcom actor first won this accolade in 2019, at the age of 14.

Most wins by a film at the Screen Actors Guild (SAG) Awards

Multiverse fantasy *Everything Everywhere All at Once* (USA, 2022) secured four gongs at the 29th SAG Awards on 26 Feb 2023: Michelle Yeoh (Lead Female, as Evelyn Wang), Jamie Lee Curtis and Ke Huy Quan (Supporting Female and Male, respectively) and Outstanding Performance by a Cast.

Two weeks later, at the 95th Academy Awards on 12 Mar 2023, Yeoh (MYS) would become the **first Asian to win a Best Actress Oscar**, for the same role.

First Marvel acting Oscar nomination

On 24 Jan 2023, American actress Angela Bassett received an Academy Award nod for her rousing performance as Queen Ramonda in *Black Panther: Wakanda Forever* (USA, 2022). The **first actor playing a comic-book character to win an Oscar** was Heath Ledger (AUS), who posthumously was named Best Supporting Actor for his portrayal of the Joker in *The Dark Knight* (USA/UK, 2008).

Most sequels nominated for Best Picture Oscar in one year

An unprecedented two sequels were in contention for the coveted Best Picture title at 2023's Academy Awards: *Top Gun: Maverick* (pictured) and *Avatar: The Way of Water* (*see pp.178–79*). The blockbusters were among 2022's highest-grossing releases. Having two films that took more than $1 bn at the box office among the Best Picture nominees is also unheard-of, perhaps indicating a shift towards more mass-market movies by the Academy.

There was speculation that the second *Black Panther* instalment might also be tipped, as the 2018 original was the **first superhero movie nominated for Best Picture**. However, *Wakanda Forever* had to make do with five other nods, including one that marked a milestone for Marvel (*see above*).

SEE THE PYRAMIDS IN EGYPT

Step back into ancient history and marvel at these awe-inspiring pharaonic tombs. The Pyramid of Khufu at Giza (*see p.140*) is the world's **tallest pyramid**. Originally clad in highly polished limestone, it stood 146.7 m (481 ft 3 in) high when constructed c. 4,500 years ago.

RECORD-BREAKING ROYAL

QUEEN ELIZABETH II

T he passing of Elizabeth II on 8 Sep 2022 evoked widespread sadness around the world. Her charm and selfless devotion to duty won her countless admirers, while her record-setting long reign made her a reassuring constant in tumultuous times.

Aged 25, she ascended to the throne on 6 Feb 1952, upon the death of her father, George VI. Her coronation the following year was televised live, prompting many British citizens to buy their first TV sets, and was watched by millions worldwide. Although the British Empire was by then in decline, it still had 70 overseas territories; by the close of her reign, the Queen presided over only around a quarter of those. But she remained a beloved presence at home and abroad. Testament to this were joyous celebrations of her four jubilees: Silver (1977), Golden (2002), Diamond (2012) and Platinum (2022), the latter marking her unprecedented 70 years as the British monarch.

Elizabeth II achieved numerous GWR titles, some of which survive her. She is history's ⦿ **longest-reigning queen**, having ruled non-stop for 70 years 214 days – surpassing her closest rival (and great-great-grandmother) Queen Victoria by around seven years. Elizabeth II also remains the **oldest queen ever**, passing while still in active duty at the age of 96 years 140 days.

During her lifetime, she toured nearly 120 countries and made 265 official overseas visits. In doing so, she travelled more than 1.6 million km (1 million mi), equivalent to more than 40 times around Earth. Ironically, she never needed a British passport: it bears the words "in the name of Her Majesty," so she would have been issuing one to herself! Her son and successor, King Charles III, has now inherited her title of **most countries to be head of state of simultaneously** – 15.

VITAL STATISTICS

Name	Elizabeth Alexandra Mary Windsor
Birthplace	London, UK
Birth date	21 Apr 1926
Coronation date	2 Jun 1953
Current GWR titles	Include longest-reigning queen and oldest-reigning queen
Sovereign states ruled over at death	15, including Australia, Canada, New Zealand, Belize and Jamaica
Estimated wealth	£365 m ($419 m)

This image of the Queen was taken in 2022 by long-serving GWR contributor Ranald Mackechnie.

1

2

The Queen visited GWR's London HQ in 2004 as part of British Enterprise Day celebrations.

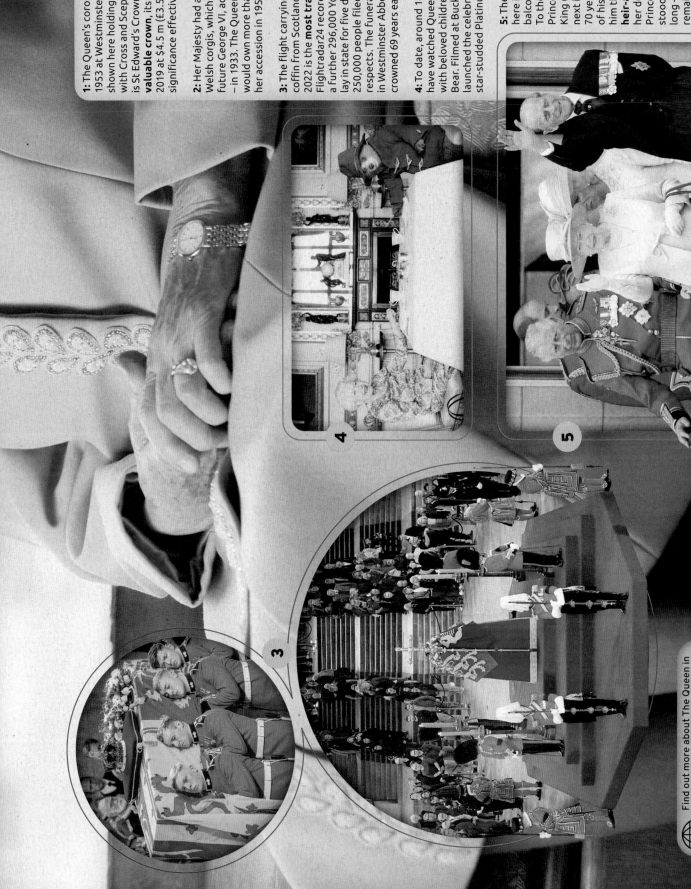

1: The Queen's coronation took place on 2 Jun 1953 at Westminster Abbey in London. She's shown here holding the ceremonial Sceptre with Cross and Sceptre with Dove. On her head is St Edward's Crown. Considered the **most valuable crown**, its worth was estimated in 2019 at $4.5 m (£3.5 m), although its historical significance effectively makes it priceless.

2: Her Majesty had a life-long love of Pembroke Welsh corgis, which began when her father, the future George VI, adopted one – called Dookie – in 1933. The Queen (*pictured here aged 10*) would own more than 30 of the dogs between her accession in 1952 and her death.

3: The flight carrying Queen Elizabeth II's coffin from Scotland back to London on 16 Sep 2022 is the **most tracked flight** in history. Flightradar24 recorded 4.79 million users, with a further 296,000 YouTube viewers. Her coffin lay in state for five days, during which some 250,000 people filed past to pay their final respects. The funeral took place on 19 Sep 2022 in Westminster Abbey, where she had been crowned 69 years earlier.

4: To date, around 14 million YouTube viewers have watched Queen Elizabeth II's tea party with beloved children's character Paddington Bear. Filmed at Buckingham Palace, the sketch launched the celebrations for Her Majesty's star-studded Platinum Jubilee.

5: The Royal Family are seen here in 2017 on the famous balcony at Buckingham Palace. To the Queen's right is her son Prince Charles (now His Majesty King Charles III), who had been next in line to the throne for 70 years 214 days at the time of his mother's death, making him the **longest-serving heir-apparent**. To her left is her devoted husband, the late Prince Philip (1921–2021), who stood at her side for almost as long – 69 years 62 days – and remains history's **longest-serving male consort**.

Find out more about The Queen in the Hall of Fame section at www. guinnessworldrecords.com/2024

SPORTS

Fastest long course 100 m freestyle swim
On 13 Aug 2022 in Rome, Italy, teenage sensation David Popovici (ROM) won the final of the men's 100 m freestyle at the European Aquatics Championships in 46.86 sec. The previous record had been set in 2009 during the "super-suit" era, when swimmers were briefly permitted to compete in low-friction non-textile suits.

Popovici is tipped to become the sport's next superstar – at the 2022 World Championships, the 17-year-old became only the second swimmer (after Jim Montgomery in 1973) to win both the 100 m and 200 m freestyle titles in the same year.

Popovici enjoyed a golden 2022, winning 11 titles at World, European and Junior championships.

BASKETBALL

NBA

Largest attendance at a regular-season game
On 13 Jan 2023, a 68,323-strong crowd packed out the Alamodome in San Antonio, Texas, to watch the San Antonio Spurs take on the Golden State Warriors. It was the Warriors who emerged victorious, by 144–113.

Most free-throw attempts by a team without missing
The Miami Heat converted all 40 of their free throws during their 112–111 victory over the Oklahoma City Thunder on 10 Jan 2023 in Miami, Florida. Jimmy Butler led the way with a perfect 23 for 23, hitting the final free throw with just 12 sec on the clock to surpass the previous record of 39, made by the Utah Jazz in 1982.

Most consecutive NBA games to score a three-point field goal
Stephen Curry of the Golden State Warriors had hit a three-pointer in 227 regular-season games in a row as of 1 Mar 2023. His streak from beyond the arc dated back to 1 Dec 2018. The deadly shooter also holds the NBA record for **most three-point field goals**, with 3,302.

Most games won by a coach
Gregg Popovich had masterminded 1,529 wins as head coach of the San Antonio Spurs as of 1 Mar 2023. This total included 170 postseason victories and the **most road wins by a coach** – 583. Popovich is the **longest-tenured NBA coach**, having spent 27 seasons with the Spurs. He has led them to all five of their championship titles (1999, 2003, 2005, 2007 and 2014).

Most teams played for
On 19 Oct 2022, Ish Smith appeared for his 13th NBA franchise when he took to the court for the Denver Nuggets. The veteran point guard first signed with the Houston Rockets in 2010, and recorded his longest spell – three seasons – with the Detroit Pistons. He had two stints at both the Philadelphia 76ers and the Washington Wizards.

All record holders are USA.

WNBA

Largest comeback in a regular-season game
On 21 Jun 2022, the Chicago Sky rallied from 28 points down to beat the Las Vegas Aces 104–95 at the Michelob Ultra Arena in Nevada. Chicago had trailed 51–23 in the second quarter.

On 20 Aug 2022, the Sky recorded the **largest margin of victory in a playoff game**. They beat the New York Liberty by 38 points, 100–62.

Most points scored in a playoff game
Breanna Stewart racked up 42 points for the Seattle Storm during Game 4 of their WNBA Semifinals against the Las Vegas Aces on 6 Sep 2022. Stewart equalled Angel McCoughtry's total for the Atlanta Dream on 7 Sep 2010.

Most NBA championships
Bill Russell won 11 titles in 13 years as a player with the Boston Celtics between 1957 and 1969. The 6-ft 10-in (2.08-m) centre, who recorded 21,620 career rebounds, played in the **most NBA Finals games** – 70. Russell died on 31 Jul 2022, at the age of 88.

Most NBA points scored
On 7 Feb 2023, LeBron James scored 38 points for the LA Lakers against the Oklahoma City Thunder to take his career total to 38,390. It took "King James" 1,410 NBA matches, at an average of 27.2 points per game, to surpass Kareem Abdul-Jabbar's tally of 38,387 – which had stood for 30 years.

Most WNBA games played
On 14 Aug 2022, Sue Bird played her 580th and final WNBA regular-season game, a 109–100 loss for her Seattle Storm against the Las Vegas Aces. Point guard Bird retired as one of the WNBA's greatest players, having won four titles and laid on the **most assists** – 3,234.

Most rebounds
Sylvia Fowles retired at the end of the 2022 WNBA season having claimed 4,006 rebounds across a 15-year career playing for the Minnesota Lynx and the Chicago Sky. She can also boast the **highest field goal percentage**, having made 2,531 of 4,228 – a success rate of 59.9%.

Most field goals in an All-Star Game
On 10 Jul 2022, Kelsey Plum converted 12 of 18 field goals for Team Wilson at the WNBA All-Star Game in Chicago. She also equalled the record for **most points** – 30 – set by Maya Moore in 2015.

VISIT EVERY CONTINENT
See the world in all its glory by stepping foot on all seven continents. If you want to do it in record time, you'll need to beat Sujoy Kumar Mitra and Dr Ali Irani (both IND), whose "world-wind" tour in Dec 2022 lasted 3 days 1 hr 5 min 4 sec – the **fastest time to travel to all seven continents.**

ICE HOCKEY

Most shootout wins by a goaltender
On 28 Jan 2023, Marc-André Fleury (CAN) won his 64th career shootout as the Minnesota Wild overcame the Buffalo Sabres 3–2, taking him three clear of Henrik Lundqvist's previous record. Fleury is one of only three goaltenders to have won more than 500 NHL games – his total of 540, as of 9 Mar 2023, was behind only Patrick Roy (551) and Martin Brodeur (691).

Longest goal-scoring streak by a defenseman from start of season
Rasmus Dahlin (SWE) of the Buffalo Sabres scored in his first five games of the 2022/23 NHL season. The final goal of his streak came against the Vancouver Canucks on 22 Oct 2022. Dahlin was a No.1 draft pick by the Sabres in 2018.

Most assists in a playoff series
Leon Draisaitl (DEU) laid on 15 goals for his Edmonton Oilers teammates during their Western Conference five-game series against the Calgary Flames on 18–26 May 2022. This total included the **postseason period** record of four assists, which Draisaitl produced during the second period of Edmonton's 4–1 win on 22 May. The Oilers went on to win the latest playoff instalment of the "Battle of Alberta" 4–1.

Most blocked shots
Defenseman Mark Giordano (CAN) had prevented 2,050 shots from reaching the goal as of 6 Mar 2023. He had become the category leader just eight days earlier while playing for the Toronto Maple Leafs, passing Kris Russell's mark of 2,044.

The **most blocked shots by a forward** is 1,058, by Joe Pavelski (USA). He spent 13 seasons at the San Jose Sharks and currently plays for the Dallas Stars.

Most overtime assists
Patrick Kane (USA) had set up 26 goals for his Chicago Blackhawks teammates in overtime as of 1 Mar 2023. The three-time Stanley Cup winner had also scored nine OT goals for a career total of 35 points – just six behind the record for the **most overtime points**, by Sidney Crosby (CAN; 19 goals and 22 assists).

Most faceoffs won
Patrice Bergeron (CAN) had won 14,614 faceoffs for the Boston Bruins as of 1 Mar 2023. As of 6 Mar, he was second for **most faceoffs taken**, behind the Pittsburgh Penguins' Sidney Crosby with 25,448. The NHL began officially tracking faceoff statistics in 2005/06.

The **highest faceoff winning percentage** is 62.86%, by centre Yanic Perreault (CAN) between 2005 and 2008. He won the puck 1,359 times in 2,162 career contests.

Most consecutive games played
Between 3 Nov 2009 and 1 Mar 2023, Phil Kessel (USA) recorded an unbroken ironman streak of 1,042 NHL games – that's more than 13 seasons without missing a single match. The 35-year-old winger became the first NHL player to reach the 1,000-game milestone on 17 Nov 2022, playing for the Vegas Golden Knights against the Arizona Coyotes.

Most hits
On 21 Nov 2022, Cal Clutterbuck (CAN) of the New York Islanders registered nine hits against the Toronto Maple Leafs to surpass Dustin Brown's career total of 3,632. As of 6 Mar 2023, right winger Clutterbuck had extended his record to 3,692.

Most games played by a defenseman
On 20 Sep 2022, Zdeno Chára (SVK) announced his retirement from professional hockey after 1,680 regular-season NHL games across 24 seasons. At 6 ft 9 in (2.06 m), "Big Z" was the **tallest NHL player ever**. He captained the Boston Bruins to three Stanley Cup Finals, winning in 2011.

All records are National Hockey League (NHL).

The Bruins opened their campaign with the **longest home winning streak from start of season** – 14.

Fewest games to reach 100 points
On 2 Mar 2023, the Boston Bruins defeated the Buffalo Sabres 7–1 to hit 100 points for the season in only their 61st game. The Bruins had won 48 of their matches, with eight losses and five overtime losses (for which they earned a point). They beat the previous record of the 1976/77 Montreal Canadiens by one game. The Canadiens went on to amass the **most points in an NHL season** – 132.

BASEBALL

Most franchises played for
Pitcher Edwin Jackson announced his retirement in Sep 2022 having appeared for 14 MLB teams since making his debut for the Los Angeles Dodgers in 2003.

Most postseason strikeouts
Justin Verlander has struck out 230 batters in 35 postseason appearances pitching for the Detroit Tigers and Houston Astros since 2005.

Most consecutive strikes to start a game
Seattle Mariners' pitcher George Kirby set an MLB record in his rookie season when he threw 24 straight strikes against the Washington Nationals on 24 Aug 2022. That's the most from the start of the first inning since pitch tracking was introduced in 1988.

Hardest-hit ball
Oneil Cruz (DOM) of the Pittsburgh Pirates ripped a 122.4-mph (196.9-km/h) single against the Atlanta Braves on 24 Aug 2022 – the hardest hit since MLB introduced Statcast tracking technology in 2015. Cruz has also produced the **fastest throw by an infielder** – 97.8 mph (157.3 km/h), in a game against the Miami Marlins on 14 Jul 2022.

Most pitchers to hit a home run off
Albert Pujols (DOM) went deep against 458 different pitchers in his career, moving past Barry Bonds' total of 449 on 29 Aug 2022. Pujols retired two months later having hit 703 home runs, the fourth most in MLB history. His favourite opponent was pitcher Ryan Dempster, whom he hit for eight dingers.

All records are Major League Baseball (MLB) and all record holders USA, unless indicated.

Most consecutive home runs in an inning
On 2 Jul 2022, the St Louis Cardinals' Nolan Arenado, Nolan Gorman, Juan Yepez (VEN) and Dylan Carlson became the 11th quartet to hit successive dingers in a single MLB inning. The streak occurred in the first inning of the Cardinals' 7–6 win over the Philadelphia Phillies.

Highest-paid player
Pitcher Max Scherzer signed a three-year deal with the New York Mets in Nov 2021 worth $130 m (£97 m), earning him an annual salary of $43.3 m (£32.4 m). The right-handed pitcher is a three-time winner of the Cy Young Award and has thrown the **most strikeouts in a match** (20) – an MLB record he shares with Roger Clemens and Kerry Wood.

Most wins for a pitcher-catcher battery
Starting pitcher Adam Wainwright and catcher Yadier Molina (PRI) combined for 213 victories while playing for the St Louis Cardinals from 2005 to 2022. The prolific pair surpassed the previous mark of 202, by Warren Spahn and catcher Del Crandall for the Boston and Milwaukee Braves between 1949 and 1963.

Slowest pitch to be hit for a home run
On 12 Jun 2022, first-baseman-turned-pitcher Frank Schwindel offered up a 35.1-mph (56.4-km/h) pitch that Kyle Higashioka homered on during the New York Yankees' 18–4 rout of the Chicago Cubs at Yankee Stadium. By way of comparison, the **fastest baseball pitch** is 105.8 mph (170.2 km/h), by the Cincinnati Reds' Aroldis Chapman (CUB) on 24 Sep 2010.

In Dec 2022, Judge signed a nine-year contract to stay with the Yankees worth $360 m (£298 m).

Most multi-home-run games in a season
Aaron Judge of the New York Yankees hit two or more home runs in the same game 11 times in 2022. The 6-ft 7-in-tall (2.01-m) slugger matched the feat of Hank Greenberg for the Detroit Tigers in 1938 and the Chicago Cubs' Sammy Sosa (DOM) in 1998. Judge set a new American League record for homers in 2022, hitting 62 to overtake Roger Maris's 1961 record – also for the Yankees – by one.

Fewest hits allowed in a World Series game
The Houston Astros gave up no hits during their 5–0 victory over the Philadelphia Phillies in Game 4 of the 2022 World Series on 2 Nov. Starter Cristian Javier (*centre*) pitched six innings, supported by (*from left*) relievers Rafael Montero, Bryan Abreu (all DOM), catcher Christian Vázquez (PRI) and reliever Ryan Pressly. The Astros matched the feat of the 1956 Yankees, for whom Don Larsen threw the **first perfect World Series game** – the only one to date by a single pitcher – on 8 Oct.

BUY A HOUSE
Put down some roots and make a house your home. The **largest private house** is a 27-storey personal skyscraper belonging to Mukesh Ambani in Mumbai, India. Every self-respecting billionaire business mogul needs three helipads, several swimming pools and a theatre!

AMERICAN FOOTBALL

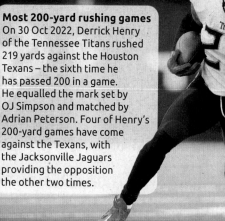

Most pass completions in a season
Tom Brady completed 490 passes for the Tampa Bay Buccaneers in 2022. The seven-time Super Bowl champion, who announced his retirement on 1 Feb 2023, added this achievement to his long list of quarterback records. He also extended his tally for the **most career pass completions** to 7,753 – 611 more than his nearest rival.

Most 200-yard rushing games
On 30 Oct 2022, Derrick Henry of the Tennessee Titans rushed 219 yards against the Houston Texans – the sixth time he has passed 200 in a game. He equalled the mark set by OJ Simpson and matched by Adrian Peterson. Four of Henry's 200-yard games have come against the Texans, with the Jacksonville Jaguars providing the opposition the other two times.

All records are National Football League (NFL) and all record holders USA, unless indicated.

Most 100-yard rushing games for a quarterback
Lamar Jackson of the Baltimore Ravens has completed 12 regular-season 100-yard rushing games since 2018. He surpassed Michael Vick's record of 10 with 119 yards against the Miami Dolphins on 18 Sep 2022; the following week, Jackson rushed for 107 yards against the New England Patriots.

Most rushing yards for a quarterback in a regular-season game
Chicago Bears QB Justin Fields rushed for 178 yards against the Miami Dolphins on 6 Nov 2022 at Soldier Field in Chicago, Illinois. He ran in a 61-yard touchdown and threw for three more, but couldn't prevent the Bears falling to a 35–32 loss.

The **postseason** record is 181, by Colin Kaepernick for the San Francisco 49ers against the Green Bay Packers during their 45–31 NFC Divisional Round playoff win on 12 Jan 2013.

Largest comeback
On 17 Dec 2022, the Minnesota Vikings turned a 33-point deficit into a 39–36 overtime victory against the Indianapolis Colts at US Bank Stadium in Minneapolis, Minnesota. Trailing 33–0 at halftime, the Vikings roared back to score five second-half touchdowns; in overtime, Greg Joseph (*above*) kicked a 40-yard field goal to seal the comeback.

Most game-winning drives by a quarterback
Tom Brady (*see above*) orchestrated 55 winning drives in the fourth quarter or overtime while playing quarterback for the New England Patriots and the Tampa Bay Buccaneers. He moved past Peyton Manning's total of 54 on 6 Nov 2022, throwing a 1-yard touchdown with just nine seconds left on the clock to earn the Bucs a 16–13 victory over the Los Angeles Rams.

Most kick-off returns for touchdowns
On 20 Nov 2022, Cordarrelle Patterson returned his ninth career kick-off return for a touchdown during the Atlanta Falcons' 27–24 win over the Chicago Bears. Nicknamed "Flash", he has played for five NFL teams since his debut season in 2013.

Patterson's tally includes the **longest kickoff return for a touchdown**, a 109-yard effort for the Minnesota Vikings against the Green Bay Packers on 27 Oct 2013.

Most 50-yard field goals
Matt Prater has kicked 71 field goals from 50 yards since 2007. They have come from 95 attempts, giving him a success rate of 74.7%.

Most 60-yard field goals
On 20 Nov 2022, Brett Maher of the Dallas Cowboys kicked a 60-yard field goal against the Minnesota Vikings – his fourth career success from that distance. He had to make his kick against Minnesota twice, as his first successful effort was chalked off after a play review. No other kicker in NFL history has converted more than two 60-yard field goals.

Most Grey Cup wins
The Toronto Argonauts won the Canadian Football League's Grey Cup for the 18th time on 20 Nov 2022. The East Division champions edged the Winnipeg Blue Bombers 24–23 in Regina, Saskatchewan. The Argonauts have played in 24 championship games since 1911.

Highest field goal percentage
Justin Tucker had converted 363 of 401 attempts for the Baltimore Ravens by the end of the 2022 season – a career field goal percentage of 90.52%. Among his successful kicks is the **longest field goal**, a 66-yard monster against the Detroit Lions on 26 Sep 2021. Tucker fell just short with a 67-yard attempt against the Jacksonville Jaguars on 27 Nov 2022.

Fewest games to reach 20,000 career passing yards
On 2 Oct 2022, quarterback Patrick Mahomes logged his 20,000th passing yard during his 67th regular-season game for the Kansas City Chiefs. He also holds the **10,000 passing yards** record, having reached that milestone in 34 games. Mahomes overcame an ankle injury to guide the Chiefs to a 38–35 win over the Philadelphia Eagles at Super Bowl LVII on 12 Feb 2023, securing his second championship in four years. He was voted league and Super Bowl MVP.

CRICKET

Most runs scored at the Men's T20 World Cup

Virat Kohli (IND) has hit 1,141 runs in 25 innings at the Men's T20 World Cup. He was top scorer at the 2022 edition with 296 runs as India reached the semi-finals.

The **most wickets taken** is 47, by Bangladeshi all-rounder Shakib Al Hasan (*inset*) since 2007. Al Hasan has appeared at all eight T20 World Cups to date, also weighing in with 742 runs.

Highest One-Day International (ODI) team score

On 17 Jun 2022, England's men piled up 498 runs for four wickets against the Netherlands at VRA Cricket Ground in Amstelveen. Their total eclipsed New Zealand Women's previous outright record of 491 for 4, which they recorded against Ireland on 8 Jun 2018. England compiled a staggering 300 runs from boundaries, including the **most sixes in an ODI innings** – 26.

Youngest player to score a double hundred in a men's ODI

On 18 Jan 2023, Shubman Gill (IND, b. 8 Sep 1999) made 208 against New Zealand, aged 23 years 132 days, at Hyderabad's Rajiv Gandhi International Stadium. Gill beat the record of his teammate Ishan Kishan, who was 24 years 145 days old when he hit 210 against Bangladesh in Chattogram on 10 Dec 2022. Kishan's rapid-fire effort came off just 126 balls – the **fastest ODI double hundred**.

Longest gap between ODI and Test debuts

On 8 Dec 2022, West Indies wicket-keeper Devon Thomas (ATG) took to the field against Australia at the Adelaide Oval, making his Test debut 13 years 133 days after his first ODI appearance. Thomas had first lined up on 28 Jul 2009 against Bangladesh in Roseau, Dominica.

Highest team score at the Women's T20 World Cup

On 21 Feb 2023, England smashed 213 for 5 against Pakistan in Cape Town, South Africa. However, it was Australia who went on to win the tournament for a sixth time – the **most Women's T20 World Cup titles**.

Most appearances in women's internationals

Mithali Raj (IND) announced her retirement from international cricket on 8 Jun 2022 having played 333 matches since 26 Jun 1999. Her career total of 10,868 runs is the **most runs in women's internationals**.

Most women's international wickets

Jhulan Goswami (IND) retired from international cricket on 24 Sep 2022 with 355 wickets to her name: 44 in Test matches, 56 in T20 Internationals and the **most wickets in women's One-Day Internationals** – 255. Goswami, a right-arm medium-pacer, made her debut for India in 2002.

Highest individual score in a List A match

Tamil Nadu opener Narayan Jagadeesan (IND) bludgeoned 277 off 141 balls in a Vijay Hazare Trophy match against Arunachal Pradesh in Bengaluru, India, on 21 Nov 2022. He surpassed Sripali Weerakkody's 15-year-old record of 271, for Kandyan Ladies Cricket Club in a domestic limited-overs tournament in Sri Lanka on 20 Aug 2007.

Lowest team score in a men's T20 match

On 26 Feb 2023, Isle of Man were skittled for just 10 runs by Spain at La Manga Club in Cartagena. Their duck-laden scorecard beat Sydney Thunder's 15 all out in their Big Bash League drubbing by Adelaide Strikers, in Sydney, on 16 Dec 2022.

Most consecutive men's T20 International wins

Malaysia were victorious in 13 matches in a row between 29 Jun and 19 Dec 2022. Their victims included Singapore, Qatar and Bhutan.

The **women's** record is 17, by Thailand from 12 Jul 2018 to 10 Aug 2019.

Most runs scored by a team on the first day of a Test match

England plundered 506 for 4 in just 75 overs on day one of the First Test against Pakistan at Rawalpindi Cricket Stadium on 1 Dec 2022 – overturning a 112-year-old opening-day record. Four players scored centuries, at a team run-rate of 6.74 per over. Under new coach Brendon McCullum and captain Ben Stokes (*left*), England's relentless attacking strategy – nicknamed "Bazball" – saw them romp to 10 wins in 12 Tests.

Highest individual score in blind cricket

On 14 Jun 2022, Steffan Nero (AUS) smashed 309 not out off just 140 balls during a One-Day International match against New Zealand in Brisbane, Australia. Nero's knock included 49 fours and a six, and is the first triple century recorded in blind cricket. The previous best was Masood Jan's 262 for Pakistan against South Africa at the Blind Cricket World Cup on 19 Nov 1998.

GO ZIPLINING
Strap yourself in and prepare for lift-off! Ultimate thrill-seekers should head for Jebel Jais Flight in Ras Al Khaimah, UAE, where you'll find the **longest zip wire**, stretching 2,831 m (9,290 ft) over mountain peaks and through ravines.

TENNIS

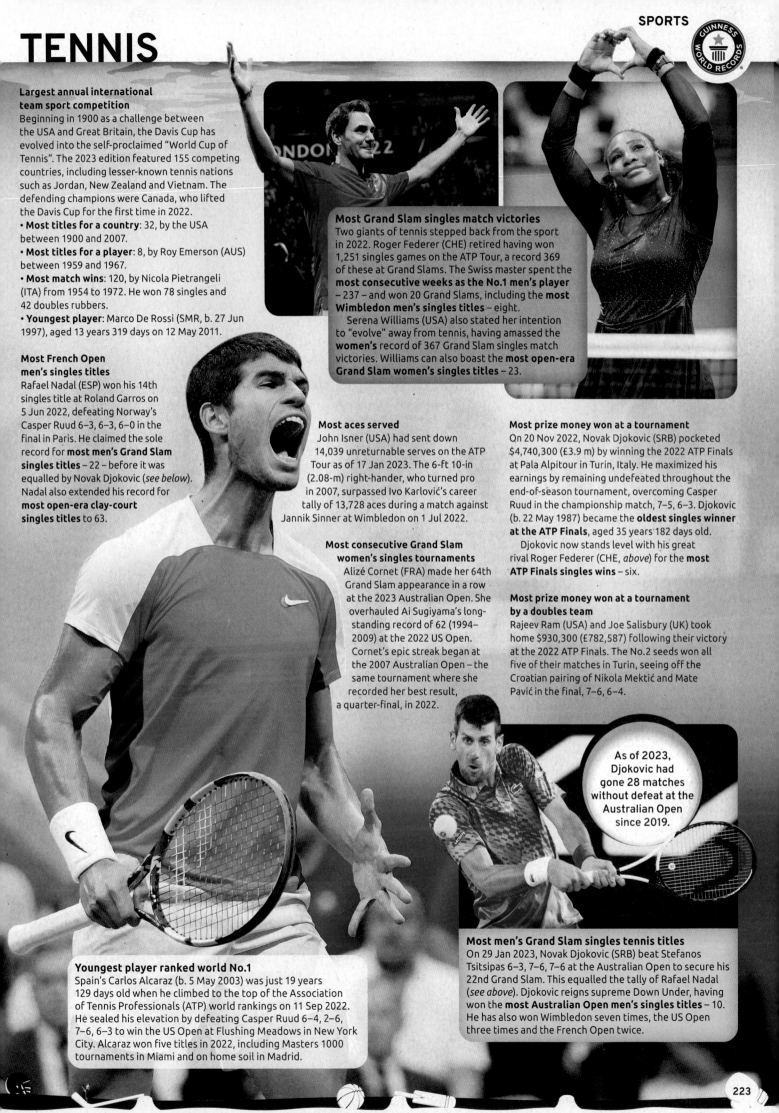

Largest annual international team sport competition

Beginning in 1900 as a challenge between the USA and Great Britain, the Davis Cup has evolved into the self-proclaimed "World Cup of Tennis". The 2023 edition featured 155 competing countries, including lesser-known tennis nations such as Jordan, New Zealand and Vietnam. The defending champions were Canada, who lifted the Davis Cup for the first time in 2022.

• **Most titles for a country**: 32, by the USA between 1900 and 2007.
• **Most titles for a player**: 8, by Roy Emerson (AUS) between 1959 and 1967.
• **Most match wins**: 120, by Nicola Pietrangeli (ITA) from 1954 to 1972. He won 78 singles and 42 doubles rubbers.
• **Youngest player**: Marco De Rossi (SMR, b. 27 Jun 1997), aged 13 years 319 days on 12 May 2011.

Most French Open men's singles titles

Rafael Nadal (ESP) won his 14th singles title at Roland Garros on 5 Jun 2022, defeating Norway's Casper Ruud 6–3, 6–3, 6–0 in the final in Paris. He claimed the sole record for **most men's Grand Slam singles titles** – 22 – before it was equalled by Novak Djokovic (*see below*). Nadal also extended his record for **most open-era clay-court singles titles** to 63.

Most Grand Slam singles match victories

Two giants of tennis stepped back from the sport in 2022. Roger Federer (CHE) retired having won 1,251 singles games on the ATP Tour, a record 369 of these at Grand Slams. The Swiss master spent the **most consecutive weeks as the No.1 men's player** – 237 – and won 20 Grand Slams, including the **most Wimbledon men's singles titles** – eight.

Serena Williams (USA) also stated her intention to "evolve" away from tennis, having amassed the **women's** record of 367 Grand Slam singles match victories. Williams can also boast the **most open-era Grand Slam women's singles titles** – 23.

Most aces served

John Isner (USA) had sent down 14,039 unreturnable serves on the ATP Tour as of 17 Jan 2023. The 6-ft 10-in (2.08-m) right-hander, who turned pro in 2007, surpassed Ivo Karlović's career tally of 13,728 aces during a match against Jannik Sinner at Wimbledon on 1 Jul 2022.

Most consecutive Grand Slam women's singles tournaments

Alizé Cornet (FRA) made her 64th Grand Slam appearance in a row at the 2023 Australian Open. She overhauled Ai Sugiyama's long-standing record of 62 (1994–2009) at the 2022 US Open. Cornet's epic streak began at the 2007 Australian Open – the same tournament where she recorded her best result, a quarter-final, in 2022.

Most prize money won at a tournament

On 20 Nov 2022, Novak Djokovic (SRB) pocketed $4,740,300 (£3.9 m) by winning the 2022 ATP Finals at Pala Alpitour in Turin, Italy. He maximized his earnings by remaining undefeated throughout the end-of-season tournament, overcoming Casper Ruud in the championship match, 7–5, 6–3. Djokovic (b. 22 May 1987) became the **oldest singles winner at the ATP Finals**, aged 35 years 182 days old.

Djokovic now stands level with his great rival Roger Federer (CHE, *above*) for the **most ATP Finals singles wins** – six.

Most prize money won at a tournament by a doubles team

Rajeev Ram (USA) and Joe Salisbury (UK) took home $930,300 (£782,587) following their victory at the 2022 ATP Finals. The No.2 seeds won all five of their matches in Turin, seeing off the Croatian pairing of Nikola Mektić and Mate Pavić in the final, 7–6, 6–4.

As of 2023, Djokovic had gone 28 matches without defeat at the Australian Open since 2019.

Youngest player ranked world No.1

Spain's Carlos Alcaraz (b. 5 May 2003) was just 19 years 129 days old when he climbed to the top of the Association of Tennis Professionals (ATP) world rankings on 11 Sep 2022. He sealed his elevation by defeating Casper Ruud 6–4, 2–6, 7–6, 6–3 to win the US Open at Flushing Meadows in New York City. Alcaraz won five titles in 2022, including Masters 1000 tournaments in Miami and on home soil in Madrid.

Most men's Grand Slam singles tennis titles

On 29 Jan 2023, Novak Djokovic (SRB) beat Stefanos Tsitsipas 6–3, 7–6, 7–6 at the Australian Open to secure his 22nd Grand Slam. This equalled the tally of Rafael Nadal (*see above*). Djokovic reigns supreme Down Under, having won the **most Australian Open men's singles titles** – 10. He has also won Wimbledon seven times, the US Open three times and the French Open twice.

CLUB SOCCER

Fastest UEFA Champions League hat-trick
On 12 Oct 2022, Liverpool's Mohamed Salah (EGY) scored three times in 6 min 12 sec against Rangers in Glasgow, UK. Salah came off the bench to hit a quickfire hat-trick as Liverpool romped to a 7–1 win.

Most consecutive La Liga appearances
On 29 Jan 2023, injury prevented Iñaki Williams (ESP) from playing in Athletic Bilbao's 1–0 defeat to Celta Vigo – breaking a streak of 251 Spanish top-flight matches across seven seasons.

Most English Premier League goals for one club
England captain Harry Kane had scored 204 league goals for Tottenham Hotspur as of 18 Mar 2023. Previous holders of this record include Thierry Henry, Wayne Rooney and Sergio Agüero.

Most goals in a UEFA Champions League game
On 14 Mar 2023, Erling Haaland (NOR, b. UK) struck five times for Manchester City during their 7–0 rout of RB Leipzig at the City of Manchester Stadium, UK. Haaland matched the single-game haul of Barcelona's Lionel Messi (ARG) on 7 Mar 2012, and Luiz Adriano (BRA) for Shakhtar Donetsk on 21 Oct 2014.

Most UEFA Women's Champions League appearances
Lyon's Wendie Renard (FRA) had played 110 times in the Champions League as of 30 Mar 2023. The centre-back is the only player to have made a century of appearances. Together with teammates Eugénie Le Sommer and Sarah Bouhaddi (both FRA), Renard has won the **most Champions League titles by a player** – eight.

Most Women's Super League appearances
Gilly Flaherty (UK) retired in Jan 2023 having played 177 top-flight English league games. The defender scored the first-ever WSL goal, on 13 Apr 2011.

Most consecutive women's national top-flight league titles
SFK 2000 Sarajevo won 20 editions of Bosnia and Herzegovina's Premijer Ženska Liga between 2003 and 2022.

Highest Major League Soccer attendance
On 5 Mar 2022, a total of 74,479 fans watched Charlotte FC's home debut at Bank of America Stadium in North Carolina, USA. Visitors LA Galaxy spoiled the party, beating Charlotte 1–0.

Most FIFA Club World Cup team appearances
On 1 Feb 2023, Auckland City (NZ) played in their 10th international club tournament, going down 3–0 to Egypt's Al Ahly in Morocco. Auckland's best finish in the competition is third, in 2014.
The eventual winners of the 2023 edition were Real Madrid (ESP), who extended their record for **most FIFA Club World Cup wins** to five.

Most goals by a player in a Copa Libertadores match
Julián Álvarez (ARG) struck six times during River Plate's 8–1 demolition of Alianza Lima on 25 May 2022 in Buenos Aires. He equalled the feat of Juan Carlos Sánchez (ARG), who hit Deportivo Italia for six while playing for Blooming on 7 Apr 1985.

Most Asian Football Confederation Champions League goals
Montenegrin striker Dejan Damjanović scored 42 times in Asia's premier club tournament between 2009 and 2022. He has played for four clubs in the competition: FC Seoul, Beijing Guoan, Suwon Samsung Bluewings and Kitchee.

Most wins of the UEFA Champions League
Spanish giants Real Madrid have won European club football's most prestigious prize 14 times – twice as many as their nearest rival, AC Milan. Madrid won six European Cups between 1956 and 1966, and eight Champions League titles after the competition's rebrand in 1992. Their latest triumph came on 28 May 2022, when they beat Liverpool 1–0 in the final.

VISIT THE GRAND CANYON
This 6-million-year-old chasm in Arizona, USA, is a natural wonder and UNESCO World Heritage Site. John Jepkema (USA, b. 8 Jun 1928) was aged 91 years 152 days when he became the **oldest person to cross the Grand Canyon rim-to-rim on foot** on 7 Nov 2019.

FIFA WORLD CUP

Most goals in a men's final

Kylian Mbappé (FRA) scored three times in the 2022 World Cup final on 18 Dec at Lusail Stadium in Qatar. His hat-trick included two penalties; he added another in the shoot-out, but couldn't save France from defeat. Mbappé matched the feat of Geoff Hurst, who scored three goals for England against West Germany in the 1966 final on 30 Jul.

Most goals in a tournament by a player

Just Fontaine (FRA) scored 13 times in only six matches at the 1958 World Cup in Sweden, including four in the third-place play-off against West Germany. This is just three short of the men's record for **most goals** – 16 – by Miroslav Klose (DEU, b. POL), in four tournaments from 2002 to 2014. Fontaine passed away on 1 Mar 2023.

Most goals in a tournament

A total of 172 goals were scored in 64 fixtures at the 22nd FIFA World Cup in Qatar, with all 32 countries finding the net at least once. Yet this pales into comparison with the 1954 tournament in Switzerland, where 140 goals were scored in just 26 games – the **highest goals-to-game ratio** of 5.38, compared with Qatar's 2.69.

First red card

Carlos Caszely was shown red by referee Doğan Babacan during Chile's 1–0 loss to West Germany on 14 Jun 1974. Red and yellow cards were brought in for the 1970 World Cup, although referees had been able to send players off before then.

Youngest player

Norman Whiteside (UK, b. 7 May 1965) was 17 years 41 days old when he lined up for Northern Ireland against Yugoslavia on 17 Jun 1982. The talented teen broke a record that had previously belonged to Pelé (*see below left*).

Most goals

Marta (b. Marta Vieira da Silva, BRA) scored 17 goals at the Women's World Cup between 2003 and 2019. She shares the record for **most women's tournaments scored in** – five – with Christine Sinclair (CAN). Both players were looking to add to their tallies at the 2023 FIFA Women's World Cup in Australia and New Zealand.

Most penalty shoot-out saves

Croatia's Dominik Livaković saved four spot kicks at the 2022 World Cup. He matched the total of West Germany's Harald Schumacher in 1982 and 1986, Argentina's Sergio Goycochea in 1990 and Livaković's fellow Croat Danijel Subašić in 2018.

MEN

Most wins by a team

The first Men's World Cup kicked off on 13 Jul 1930 in Montevideo, Uruguay. The quadrennial tournament has been won by Brazil five times – in 1958, 1962, 1970, 1994 and 2002 – on four different continents. The "Seleção" have also logged the **most matches played** – 114 – and the **most matches won** – 76.

Most men's matches played

Lionel Messi (ARG) featured in 26 matches across five World Cups between 2006 and 2022. He broke Lothar Matthäus's record of 25 in the final of the 2022 FIFA World Cup in Qatar – in which Messi completed a fairytale tournament by scoring twice during Argentina's 3–3 draw against France, before converting the first penalty to help them on their way to a 4–2 shoot-out win.

Most wins by a player

Pelé (b. Edson Arantes do Nascimento, 23 Oct 1940, BRA) earned World Cup winner's medals in 1958, 1962 and 1970. The legendary No.10, who died on 29 Dec 2022, was just 17 years 249 days old when Brazil beat Sweden 5–2 in the 1958 final, making him the **youngest winner**. Although injury forced Pelé out of the 1962 tournament, he was awarded a winner's medal by FIFA in 2007.

WOMEN

Most wins by a team

The USA have won four of the eight FIFA Women's World Cups to date. They lifted the trophy at the inaugural tournament in China in 1991, and were also victorious in 1999, 2015 and 2019.

Most tournaments played in

Formiga (b. Miraildes Maciel Mota, BRA) appeared in seven consecutive World Cups between 1995 and 2019. The defensive midfielder earned her nickname "Ant" for her unselfish workrate.

Most goals in a final

On 5 Jul 2015, Carli Lloyd (USA) hit a 13-min hat-trick during the USA's 5–2 win over Japan in Vancouver, British Columbia, Canada.

Most men's tournaments scored in

On 24 Nov 2022, Cristiano Ronaldo (PRT) made the scoresheet at his fifth World Cup, converting a penalty during Portugal's 3–2 win over Ghana in Doha, Qatar. Ronaldo hit eight World Cup goals in 22 games from 2006 to 2022; his most prolific tournament was 2018, when he scored four times.

Most men's high jump gold medals at the World Athletics Championships
On 18 Jul 2022, Mutaz Essa Barshim (QAT) sealed his third consecutive world title with a winning clearance of 2.37 m (7 ft 9 in) in Eugene, Oregon, USA. He is also the current Olympic champion, having memorably shared the 2020 gold with Italy's Gianmarco Tamberi.

MOST WORLD ATHLETICS CHAMPIONSHIPS...

Medals by an individual
Allyson Felix (USA) won 20 medals across eight championships between 2005 and 2022: 14 gold (the **most golds**), three silver and three bronze. Felix capped a sparkling career with two medals in her final tournament, the 2022 World Championships in Eugene, Oregon, USA. She won a bronze in the 4 x 400 m mixed relay and came out of retirement a week later to run in the heats of the women's 4 x 400 m, qualifying for a gold medal.

Medals by a country
The USA won 414 medals across 18 editions of the World Athletics Championships from 1983 to 2022: 183 gold, 126 silver and 105 bronze. On home soil in Eugene, the USA set a new single-championship record for the **most medals** – 33, including 13 gold. Their overall total was two more than that earned by East Germany in 1987.

Gold medals in the men's hammer throw
Paweł Fajdek (POL) secured his fifth hammer world title in a row with an 81.98-m (268-ft 11-in) effort on 16 Jul 2022. Together with Shelly-Ann Fraser-Pryce (*left*), Fajdek stands just one behind Sergey Bubka's (UKR) overall championship record for the **most consecutive individual gold medals** – six, which Bubka achieved in the men's pole vault between 1983 and 1997.

WORLD ATHLETICS CHAMPIONSHIPS

Fastest women's 400 m hurdles
Sydney McLaughlin-Levrone (USA) won gold at the World Athletics Championships in 50.68 sec on 22 Jul 2022. She has set new standards for the women's 400 m hurdles, clocking four world records in 13 months and lowering the fastest time by an incredible 1.48 sec.

Most World Athletics Championships women's individual gold medals
Sprint queen Shelly-Ann Fraser-Pryce (JAM) won her fifth world 100 m title on 17 Jul 2022, setting a championship record of 10.67 sec at the age of 35. Fraser-Pryce's 15th season of international racing was one of her most dominant yet – she recorded the fastest eight women's 100 m times of 2022.

Perković is the only athlete to have recorded two perfect Diamond League seasons – in 2013 and 2016.

Most Diamond League victories
Discus thrower Sandra Perković (HRV) has racked up 45 wins at the annual series of elite one-day athletics meets. She extended her record with victory at the Bislett Games in Oslo, Norway, on 16 Jun 2022. Perković has been crowned the overall Diamond League discus champion six times – the **most women's Diamond League titles**, a record she shares with shot-putter Valerie Adams (NZ) and jumper Caterine Ibargüen (COL).

VISIT NEW YORK CITY
Take a trip to the Big Apple, the USA's most populous city and home of the soaring skyscraper. The Chrysler Building, 40 Wall Street and the Empire State Building were all at one time the world's **tallest building**; the 472-m-high (1,548-ft) Central Park Tower is the **tallest residential building**.

FASTEST...

Men's 100 m (T47)
On 31 Mar 2022, Petrúcio Ferreira dos Santos (BRA) ran the quickest 100 m in para history, clocking 10.29 sec at the Brazilian Athletics Challenge event in São Paulo. The next day, dos Santos – who lost his lower left arm after an accident aged two – also ran the **fastest 200 m (T47)** in 20.83 sec.

Women's indoor 400 m
Femke Bol (NLD) broke one of the longest-standing records in athletics on 19 Feb 2023, running two laps of an indoor track in 49.26 sec at the Dutch Indoor Championships in Apeldoorn. The previous record had stood since 1982 – almost 18 years before Bol was even born.

Men's indoor 3,000 m*
On 15 Feb 2023, Lamecha Girma (ETH) won the 3,000 m in 7 min 23.81 sec at a World Athletics Indoor Tour meeting in Liévin, France. Girma broke Daniel Komen's 25-year-old record over the distance by more than a second.

Women's distance medley relay*
The distance medley relay is a rarely run event that consists of four legs measuring 1,200 m, 400 m, 800 m and 1,600 m. On 15 Apr 2022, the US quartet of Heather MacLean, Kendall Ellis, Roisin Willis and Elle Purrier St Pierre clocked a cumulative time of 10 min 33.85 sec at an indoor meeting in Boston, Massachusetts, USA.

FARTHEST...

Women's discus throw (F42)
On 4 Aug 2022, Goodness Nwachukwu (NGA) hurled the discus 36.56 m (119 ft 11 in) to win gold at the 2022 Commonwealth Games in Birmingham, UK. She broke her own world record with her first two throws of the competition.

Men's javelin throw (F40)
Ahmed Naas (IRQ) threw the javelin 39.08 m (128 ft 2 in) in Dubai, UAE, on 22 Mar 2022. Naas, who is short statured, bettered his own mark from the 2016 Paralympics.

Fastest women's 100 m (T63)
On 28 May 2022, Martina Caironi (ITA) ran 100 m in 14.02 sec at the Prefontaine Classic in Eugene, Oregon, USA. Caironi, who lost her left leg above the knee after a motorcycle accident in 2007, is a two-time Paralympic sprint champion. She has also logged the **farthest long jump** in her category – 5.46 m (17 ft 10 in) – in Paris, France, on 10 Jun 2022.

Most countries to win a gold medal at a World Athletics Championships
A total of 29 nations finished on top of the podium at the 2022 World Athletics Championships in Eugene, Oregon, USA, including three first-time winners: Peru, Kazakhstan and Nigeria. Peru earned two golds thanks to Kimberly García in the women's 20 km and 35 km walk (*right*), while Nigeria's Tobi Amusan (*above*) ran the **fastest women's 100 m hurdles** – 12.12 sec – in her semi-final, before going on to take the gold.

*pending ratification by World Athletics

Highest men's pole vault
On 24 Jul 2022, Armand Duplantis (SWE, b. USA) cleared 6.21 m (20 ft 4 in) at the World Athletics Championships. The pole-vaulting prodigy broke the world record three times in 2022. His 6.21-m effort in Eugene was the first time that the men's pole vault record had been broken outdoors since 1994 – five years before Duplantis was born. It was the 48th time that he had cleared 6 m (19 ft 8 in) in competition, also a new record. *See Stop Press (pp.246–47) for more "Mondo".*

WATER SPORTS

Most FINA Marathon Swim World Series women's titles
Ana Marcela Cunha (BRA) secured her sixth World Series title in 2022. Across four 10-km (6.2-mi) open-water races staged around the world, she won a bronze, silver and two golds – extending her career record for **most women's race wins** in the competition to 28.

Farthest freediving dynamic apnea
In dynamic apnea competitions, divers try to cover the maximum horizontal distance underwater on a single breath. Events take place in controlled environments such as swimming pools. All six categories monitored by freediving federation AIDA (International Association for the Development of Apnea) were broken in 2022:
• **with fins (men)**: 301 m (987 ft 6 in), by Guillaume Bourdila (FRA) on 24 Jun in Burgas, Bulgaria.
• **with fins (women)**: 277 m (908 ft 9 in), by Magdalena Solich-Talanda (POL) on 10 Apr in Łódź, Poland.
• **without fins (men)**: 250 m (820 ft 2 in), by Mateusz Malina (POL) on 1 May in Dębica, Poland.
• **without fins (women)**: 209 m (685 ft 8 in), by Julia Kozerska (POL) on 21 Jun in Burgas.
• **with bifins (men)**: 290 m (951 ft 5 in), by Mateusz Malina on 27 Mar in Łódź. (*See opposite for another of Malina's freediving feats.*)
• **with bifins (women)**: 243 m (797 ft 2 in), by Magdalena Solich-Talanda on 2 May in Dębica.

Fastest 2,000 m men's single sculls para-row (PR1)
On 17 Jun 2022, Giacomo Perini (ITA) rowed 2,000 m in 8 min 55.21 sec at the World Rowing Cup II regatta in Poznań, Poland. Perini, who had his right leg amputated after a tumour grew on his knee, set world-best times in the preliminary race and final of his first international meet.

PARA-ROWING BEST TIMES

Category	Time	Name & Nationality	Location	Date
PR1 men's single sculls	8:55.21	Giacomo Perini (ITA)	Poznań, Poland	17 Jun 2022
PR1 women's single sculls	9:50.39	Birgit Skarstein (NOR)	Poznań, Poland	17 Jun 2022
PR2 men's single sculls	8:20.61	Corné de Koning (NLD)	Poznań, Poland	18 Jun 2022
PR2 women's single sculls	9:14.65	Katie O'Brien (IRL)	Poznań, Poland	18 Jun 2022
PR2 mixed double sculls	8:06.21	Netherlands (Annika van der Meer and Corné de Koning)	Poznań, Poland	17 Jun 2017
PR3 men's coxless pair	6:52.08	France (Laurent Cadot and Jérôme Hamelin)	Poznań, Poland	18 Jun 2022
PR3 women's coxless pair	7:39.30	USA (Jaclyn Smith and Danielle Hansen)	Plovdiv, Bulgaria	15 Sep 2018
PR3 mixed double sculls	7:28.95	Brazil (Diana Barcelos de Oliveira and Jairo Klug)	Sarasota-Bradenton, USA	29 Sep 2017
PR3 mixed coxed four	6:48.34	Great Britain (Francesca Allen, Giedrė Rakauskaitė [b. LTU], Edward Fuller, Oliver Stanhope and Morgan Baynham-Williams)	Račice, Czechia	24 Sep 2022

Deepest freediving men's constant weight with bifins
Freedivers in the constant weight category must descend and ascend without altering their ballast, and can only touch the dive-line at the bottom in order to turn. On 9 Aug 2022, Arnaud Jerald (FRA) reached a depth of 120 m (393 ft 8 in) at the 2022 Vertical Blue freediving competition in The Bahamas.
The **women's** record is 97 m (318 ft 2 in), by Marianna Gillespie (FRA, b. RUS) on the Honduran island of Roatán on 17 Aug 2022.

Most World Surfing League women's world titles
On 16 Sep 2022, Stephanie Gilmore (AUS) won her eighth surfing world crown in style, battling through the top-five finals day at the Rip Curl WSL Finals to win the event and claim the overall women's title. Gilmore surpassed Layne Beachley, a seven-time champion on the ASP World Tour between 1998 and 2006.

▶ Largest wave surfed
Sebastian Steudtner (DEU) rode a 26.21-m-high (86-ft) wave off the coast of Praia do Norte in Nazaré, Portugal, on 29 Oct 2020. Steudtner, who left Germany for Hawaii at the age of 16 to pursue a career in surfing, is a three-time winner of the World Surf League Biggest Wave Award. Nazaré has become famous for its huge breakers, caused by an undersea canyon that channels the swell as it heads for shore. On 24 May 2022, Steudtner was given his official GWR certificate by the World Surf League's Francisco Spínola (*far right*) in Nazaré.

Steudtner beat Rodrigo Koxa's previous record by 6 ft (1.8 m). Both records were set in Nazaré.

RUN A MARATHON
Push your body by tackling the classic long-distance race... but why just do it on foot? Michelle Frost (UK) took the challenge to new heights at the 2018 London Marathon, completing the **fastest marathon on stilts** in 6 hr 37 min 38 sec.

Most individual gold medals at the ICF Canoe Slalom World Championship

Jessica Fox (AUS, b. FRA) claimed her ninth solo world championship title on 31 Jul 2022, winning the women's Extreme slalom in Augsburg, Germany. She has won three gold medals in the Kayak Single (K1) class, four in the Canoe Single (C1) and two in the Extreme slalom. Fox can also boast three titles in the women's C1 team competition.

Fastest 2,000 m women's lightweight single sculls

Imogen Grant (UK) won gold at the World Rowing Cup III regatta in 7 min 23.36 sec on 9 Jul 2022 – her first international race of the season. The competition was staged on the Rotsee lake in Lucerne, Switzerland. To qualify as lightweight, female rowers must weigh less than 59 kg (130 lb; 9 st 4 lb).

Longest women's waterski jump

On 31 Oct 2021, Jacinta Carroll (AUS) leapt 61.3 m (201 ft 1 in) on Lake Grew in Polk City, Florida, USA. That's about the same length as an NHL ice hockey rink. Carroll became the first female waterskier to break the 200-ft barrier at the 2021 Mastercraft Pro event. It was her fifth consecutive world record in the women's jump.

Deepest men's free immersion freedive

On 11 Aug 2022, Mateusz Malina (POL) dived 127 m (416 ft 8 in) at the Vertical Blue event at Dean's Blue Hole in The Bahamas. He was underwater for 4 min 32 sec. In the free immersion discipline, freedivers can use the dive-line for propulsion as they descend to – and ascend from – their targeted depth.

Most men's gold medals at the Sailing World Cup

Launched in 2008, the Sailing World Cup is run by World Sailing and comprises a series of regattas that take place around the globe. Australia's men had won 56 golds as of 2022 – along with 43 silvers and 39 bronze, for a total of 138.

Fastest women's windsurfing speed

On 25 Nov 2022, Heidi Ulrich (CHE) reached a speed of 47.06 knots (87.15 km/h; 54.15 mph) during the Lüderitz Speed Challenge in Namibia. It was the latest in a number of records set on a purpose-built trench in Lüderitz, which offers strong winds and flat water. Ulrich's achievement was verified by the World Sailing Speed Record Council.

Most women's water polo titles at the FINA World Championships

On 2 Jul 2022, the USA defeated hosts Hungary 9–7 in Budapest to seal their seventh water polo crown – and their fourth consecutively – at the aquatic championships. A superpower of the sport, the USA have also won the **most Olympic women's water polo titles** – three, in 2012, 2016 and the delayed 2020 Games in Tokyo, Japan.

Oldest international yacht race

The America's Cup was first contested on 22 Aug 1851, when the New York Yacht Club's *America* outraced 15 yachts around the Isle of Wight, UK. Since then, head-to-head match races have been staged every few years. The 36th America's Cup was held in 2021; it was won by the Emirates Team New Zealand and their monohull yacht *Te Rehutai* (*above left*).

Most wins of the Red Bull Cliff Diving World Series

Gary Hunt (FRA, b. UK) secured the coveted King Kahekili trophy for the 10th time in 2022. He sealed victory in dramatic fashion on 15 Oct, winning the title with his final dive of the season's final competition in Sydney, Australia.

Hunt is pictured inset with Rhiannan Iffland (AUS), who extended the **women's** record with her sixth consecutive Cliff Diving World Series title in 2022. Iffland has racked up 30 wins from just 37 events.

AWESOME ARENAS

1

Indianapolis Motor Speedway
Start your engines! Located in Speedway, Indiana, this 2.5-mi-long (4-km) oval racing circuit is the **highest-capacity stadium**, with an estimated 250,000 seats. It staged its first motorsport event on 14 Aug 1909; now fans flock to the "Brickyard" every Memorial Day weekend for the Indianapolis 500.

Fenway Park
The home of the Boston Red Sox is the **oldest Major League Baseball ground**. Its first official baseball game took place on 20 Apr 1912, when the Red Sox beat the New York Highlanders 7–6. Fenway's famous features include the "Green Monster" left-field wall and "Pesky's Pole" on the right-field foul line.

5

6

2

SoFi Stadium
With estimated construction costs of more than $5 bn (£4.2 bn), the **most expensive stadium** is home to Los Angeles' two NFL franchises: the Rams and the Chargers. The 70,000-seat state-of-the-art arena boasts a 110-m-long (360-ft) videoboard with 80 million pixels, a translucent canopy roof and 260 luxury suites.

St Andrews
Golf has been played at St Andrews Links in Fife, Scotland, since at least 1552 – making it the **oldest golf course**. Its famed Old Course was the first to make 18 holes the standard round, in 1764. Each of its 112 bunkers have names, such as Lion's Mouth, the Coffins and Hell.

3

Utah Olympic Oval
This high-altitude indoor arena is nicknamed the "Fastest Ice on Earth" on account of its low air resistance and hard, fast track. It was built for the 2002 Winter Olympics in Salt Lake City, where world records were set in eight of the 10 speed skating events. *For more on the records broken at the Oval in 2022, turn to pp.242–43.*

4

Maracanã Stadium
One of the world's most famous soccer grounds, the Maracanã in Rio de Janeiro holds the record for the **largest attendance at a FIFA World Cup match**. A total of 173,850 people saw Brazil's final game with Uruguay on 16 Jul 1950, which ended in heartbreak for the hosts as Uruguay produced one of the great World Cup upsets to win 2–1 and take the trophy.

GO SCUBA DIVING
Explore the watery world below the surface of the waves and swim among the amazing creatures that live there. Perhaps don't go quite as far as daredevil Ahmed Gabr (EGY), though, who plunged 332.35 m (1,090 ft) in the Red Sea off Dahab, Egypt, on 18 Sep 2014 – the **deepest scuba dive** (*see also p.132*).

Circuit de Monaco
Staged on a narrow street circuit with tight turns, the Monaco Grand Prix is one of the most challenging and glamorous races in Formula 1. At just 3.3 km (2 mi), it is also currently the **shortest F1 circuit**. Monaco is synonymous with driver Ayrton Senna, who won a record six times here between 1987 and 1993.

Beijing National Stadium
The 91,000-capacity "Bird's Nest" owes its nickname to its design – inspired by Chinese pottery – of cantilevered steel trusses. The stadium was built for the 2008 Olympics and in 2022 hosted the opening and closing ceremonies for the Winter Games, as Beijing became the **first city to hold Summer and Winter Olympics**.

Rally Finland
The so-called "Grand Prix on Gravel" is renowned for its blind crests, big jumps and blisteringly fast roads. Nine of the 10 fastest World Rally Championship (WRC) rallies have been clocked in the forests around Jyväskylä, Finland; in 2016, Kris Meeke (UK) set the **highest WRC average speed** of 126.62 km/h (78.67 mph).

Ellis Park Stadium
This Johannesburg venue staged its first rugby union Test in 1928 and was the site of South Africa's historic triumph at the 1995 Rugby World Cup. Ellis Park also hosts soccer – in 2010, it witnessed the **coldest FIFA World Cup match**. Temperatures plunged to -1°C (30°F) during the clash between Brazil and North Korea on 15 Jun.

Ryōgoku Kokugikan
Situated in the Yokoami neighbourhood of Tokyo, the **largest sumo stadium** can seat 11,908 spectators. Since opening in 1985, it has held three of the sport's six annual *honbasho* (tournaments). The walls are adorned with portraits of previous winners. The sumo hall has also opened its doors to WWE wrestling events.

Melbourne Cricket Ground
Built in 1853, the MCG staged the **first Test cricket match** on 15–19 Mar 1877, when an English touring party captained by James Lillywhite took on a Combined Australia XI. On 26 Dec 2013, it achieved the **highest attendance for a Test match day**, when 91,092 people packed in for day 1 of the Fourth Ashes Test against England. The MCG also plays host to Australian rules football, soccer and rugby league.

TARGET SPORTS

Highest score in women's 10 m air rifle standing (SH1)

Avani Lekhara (IND) scored 250.6 out of a possible 261.6 from 24 shots at the World Shooting Para Sport World Cup in Châteauroux, France, on 7 Jun 2022. Lekhara (*pictured at Tokyo 2020*) is India's first female Paralympic gold medallist; she competes in the SH1 class, for athletes with a lower-limb impairment.

Most Archery World Cup wins

Sara López (COL) claimed her seventh World Cup title in the women's compound on 15 Oct 2022, beating Ella Gibson 148–146 in Tlaxcala, Mexico. Compound bows use a levering system of pulleys and cables that makes them faster and more accurate than recurve bows, which have been used at the Olympics since 1972.

The most wins in the other Archery World Cup individual disciplines are:
• **Men's compound**: 4, by Mike Schloesser (NLD) in 2016, 2019 and 2021–22.
• **Women's recurve**: 3, by Ki Bo-bae (KOR) in 2012 and 2016–17.
• **Men's recurve**: 5, by Brady Ellison (USA) in 2010–11, 2014, 2016 and 2019.

Most Professional Bowlers Association major championships

On 19 Mar 2023, Jason Belmonte (AUS) beat E J Tackett 246–179 to claim the PBA Tournament of Champions – his 15th major bowling title. Belmonte is only the second bowler after Mike Aulby to complete the "Super Slam" of all five PBA major events.

> The "skip" is the captain of a curling team. They determine strategy and often throw the last two stones of the game.

Oldest player at the Mosconi Cup

An annual nine-ball pool tournament contested by two teams from the USA and Europe, the Mosconi Cup has been held 29 times since its inaugural edition in 1994. Earl Strickland (USA, b. 8 Jun 1961) was aged 61 years 175 days when he made his 15th cup appearance on 30 Nov 2022 in Las Vegas, Nevada, USA.

Most World Horseshoe Pitching Championships

Alan Francis (USA) secured his 26th National Horseshoe Pitchers Association world title in 2022. He recorded a pitch-perfect 15 wins from 15 matches in Monroe, Louisiana, USA.

Most Premier League Darts titles

On 13 Jun 2022, Michael van Gerwen (NLD) claimed his sixth Premier League Darts title after an 11–10 final victory over Joe Cullen in Berlin, Germany. The Dutch darts maestro – a previous Premier League winner in 2013 and 2016–19 – equalled the tally of Phil "The Power" Taylor (UK) between 2005 and 2012.

Most World Snooker Championship wins (modern era)

On 2 May 2022, Ronnie O'Sullivan (UK) beat Judd Trump by 18 frames to 13 to earn his seventh world title at the Crucible Theatre in Sheffield, South Yorkshire, UK. "The Rocket" equalled the mark set by Stephen Hendry (UK) between 1990 and 1999, pocketing yet another snooker superlative for his collection.

THE ROCKET'S RECORDS

Most...	Record	Years
Ranking titles	39	1993–2022
World Championships (modern era)	7 (shared)	2001, 2004, 2008, 2012–13, 2020, 2022
UK Championships	7	1993, 1997, 2001, 2007, 2014, 2017–18
Masters titles	7	1995, 2005, 2007, 2009, 2014, 2016–17
Centuries	1,196	1992–2022
147 maximum breaks	15	1997–2018

All figures correct as of 23 Feb 2023

Most gold medals at the World Women's Curling Championship

Alina Pätz and Carole Howald (both CHE) have been members of six title-winning Swiss teams since 2012 and 2014 respectively. Five of Howald's golds, and one of Pätz's, were earned playing as alternates. At the 2023 tournament in Sandviken, Sweden, both curlers were on the ice as Switzerland won all 12 of their round-robin matches, before going on to defeat Norway 6–3 in the final on 26 Mar.

Most gold medals won by a skip at the World Men's Curling Championship

Niklas Edin (SWE) won six world championship curling titles in 2013, 2015, 2018–19 and 2021–22. The Swedish skip guided his team to a fourth consecutive title at the 2022 World Men's Curling Championship in Las Vegas, Nevada, USA. Edin shares the overall **men's** record with teammate Oskar Eriksson, who has also won six golds, including one as an alternate (substitute) in 2013.

GET MARRIED

For many couples, the hope is that tying the knot will be a once-in-a-lifetime event... But that clearly wasn't the viewpoint of Baptist minister Glynn "Scotty" Wolfe (USA). He declared "I do" 29 times between 1927 and 1996 – the **most monogamous marriages**. He was believed to have fathered 41 children.

GOLF

First female winner on the DP World Tour
Linn Grant (SWE) made golfing history at the 2022 Volvo Car Scandinavian Mixed tournament at Halmstad Golf Club in Sweden. She shot a final-round 64 (8 under par) on 12 Jun to finish a massive nine shots clear of the field. The DP World Tour (formerly the PGA European Tour) event had a field of 78 men and 78 women, playing off different tees.

Most cuts made on the PGA Tour
Jay Haas (USA) survived the halfway cut at 592 PGA Tour events between 1976 and 2022. On 22 Apr 2022, Haas became the **oldest player to make the cut on the PGA Tour**, aged 68 years 141 days. He was playing at the Zurich Classic of New Orleans, paired with his son Bill.

Highest PGA Tour season's earnings by a rookie
Cameron Young (USA) earned $6,520,598 (£5.5 m) in 2021/22, his first season on the PGA Tour. He recorded five second-place finishes – including at the 2022 Open Championship – and came third at the PGA Championship. Young's prize-money total also broke Louis Oosthuizen's record for the **highest earnings in a PGA Tour season without a victory**.

Most wins of the FedEx Cup
First awarded in 2007, the FedEx Cup is the PGA Tour's championship trophy. Rory McIlroy (UK) claimed his third title with victory at the 2022 Tour Championship tournament on 25–28 Aug. He previously won the FedEx Cup in 2016 and 2019.

McIlroy capped a remarkable 2022 season by being crowned the champion golfer on the DP World Tour, lifting the Harry Vardon trophy for the fourth time. As of 23 Feb 2023, McIlroy had amassed the **highest DP World Tour career earnings** – €44,594,732 (£39.2 m; $47.4 m).

Lowest score in a round at the PGA Championship
Bubba Watson (USA) became the 17th player to shoot a round of 63 at the PGA Championship in 2022. During his second round at Southern Hills Country Club in Tulsa, Oklahoma, USA, the left-hander narrowly missed a putt on the 18th green that would have given him the tournament's first-ever round of 62.

Most wins on the PGA Tour Champions
On 19 Feb 2023, Bernhard Langer (DEU) registered his 45th victory on golf's over-50s tour at the Chubb Classic in Naples, Florida, USA. This equalled the total achieved by Hale Irwin (USA) between 1995 and 2007. Langer (b. 27 Aug 1957) also extended his record as the tour's **oldest winner**, aged 65 years 176 days. He has accrued the **highest PGA Tour Champions career earnings** – $34,057,198 (£28.1 m) – three times what he earned on the PGA Tour.

Highest earnings in a PGA Tour season
Scottie Scheffler (USA) accrued $14,046,910 (£11.9 m) in 2021/22. He recorded his first PGA Tour victory at the WM Phoenix Open on 13 Feb 2022, the beginning of an incredible run of four wins in six events – including a three-stroke victory at the Masters – that saw him rocket to No.1 in the world rankings.

Lowest score to par at The Open Championship
On 17 Jul 2022, Cameron Smith (AUS) lifted the claret jug at the 150th Open Championship at St Andrews after going through four rounds in 20 under par. Smith equalled Henrik Stenson's (SWE) winning total at Royal Troon in 2016. This is also the **lowest score to par in a men's major** – shared with Jason Day (AUS), who shot -20 at the 2015 PGA Championship, and Dustin Johnson (USA) at the 2020 Masters.

Lowest total score at the US Women's Open
Minjee Lee (AUS) carded a total score of 271 (67, 66, 67, 71; 13 under par) to claim victory at the 2022 US Women's Open. The event – held on 2–5 Jun in Southern Pines, North Carolina – boasted the **greatest prize money for a women's golf tournament**: $10 m (£8 m). Lee's win earned her a cool $1.8 m (£1.4 m).

Most birdies in a 72-hole PGA Tour event
On 6–9 Jan 2022, Jon Rahm (ESP) sank 32 birdies at the 2022 Sentry Tournament of Champions at the Kapalua Plantation Course in Maui, Hawaii, USA. He equalled the tour record of Mark Calcavecchia (USA) at the 2001 Phoenix Open and Paul Gow (AUS) at the 2001 BC Open. Rahm finished the tournament in second place behind Cameron Smith (AUS), who holed 31 birdies on his way to the **lowest score under par in a PGA Tour event**: -34.

SKIING

Most event wins at the FIS Ski Jumping World Cup
High-flyer Sara Takanashi (JPN) had claimed 63 World Cup wins as of 1 Mar 2023. She had recorded the **most podiums** – 115 – and the **most women's titles** – four. Takanashi also owns one Olympic and seven World Championship medals.

The **most men's Ski Jumping World Cup wins** is 53, by Gregor Schlierenzauer (AUT) from 2006 to 2014.

Most men's event wins at the FIS Freestyle World Cup
As of 1 Mar 2023, Mikaël Kingsbury (CAN) had racked up 78 victories: 52 in the moguls and 26 in the dual moguls. The **outright** freestyle record is 106, by Conny Kissling (CHE) between 1982 and 1992.

At the 2023 FIS Freestyle Ski World Championships in Georgia, Kingsbury extended his tournament record for **most gold medals** to eight.

Most event wins at an FIS World Cup
The International Ski and Snowboard Federation (FIS) stages annual competitions in ski jumping, snowboarding, Nordic combined, and Alpine, freestyle, speed and Telemark skiing. The most victories in any discipline is 163, by Amélie Wenger-Reymond (CHE) at the Telemark World Cup as of 2 Feb 2023. Her wins had come from just 222 starts, with a staggering 212 podiums.

Most event wins at the FIS Nordic Combined World Cup
Nordic combined events comprise a ski jump and a cross-country ski race; the World Cup has been held annually since the 1983/84 season. Jarl Magnus Riiber (NOR) has racked up 53 victories, winning four consecutive overall titles since the 2018/19 season.

Fastest speed at the FIS Alpine Ski World Cup
Johan Clarey (FRA) was clocked at 161.9 km/h (100.6 mph) on the Lauberhorn course at the Wengen downhill in Switzerland on 19 Jan 2013. At the 2022 Winter Games, Clarey (b. 8 Jan 1981) became the **oldest person to win an Olympic Alpine skiing medal**, taking silver in the men's downhill on 7 Feb at the age of 41 years 30 days.

Fastest speed skiing
Ivan Origone (ITA) hit 254.958 km/h (158.423 mph) on 26 Mar 2016 in Vars, France. The **women's** record of 247.083 km/h (153.530 mph) was also set at Vars on the same day, by Valentina Greggio (ITA).

Ivan's older brother Simone has registered the **most event wins at the FIS Speed Ski World Cup** – 54. The **women's** record is also held by Valentina Greggio, with 40 victories.

Most men's race wins in a season at the FIS Alpine Ski World Cup
Marco Odermatt (CHE) triumphed in 13 World Cup races in 2022/23. He became only the fourth male skier to reach that mark in a season, after Ingemar Stenmark (SWE) in 1978/79, Hermann Maier in 2000/01 and Marcel Hirscher (both AUT) in 2017/18.

Most Winter Olympic medals
Cross-country skier Marit Bjørgen (NOR) won 15 medals across five Winter Games between 2002 and 2018. Her haul comprised eight golds, four silvers and three bronze. Bjørgen also has the **most event wins at the FIS Cross-Country World Cup** – 114.

Most Tour de Ski stage wins
First held in 2006/07, the Tour de Ski is a Central European cross-country skiing event modelled on the classic French cycle race. Leading the way is Johannes Høsflot Klæbo (NOR), with 17 stage wins since 29 Dec 2018. Klæbo won his third overall crown in 2022/23; the **most Tour de Ski men's titles** is four, by Dario Cologna (CHE).

Most race wins at the FIS Alpine Ski World Cup
On 11 Mar 2023 – exactly 12 years after making her World Cup debut as a 15-year-old – Mikaela Shiffrin (USA) made skiing history by surpassing Ingemar Stenmark's record of 86 wins in the competition. Shiffrin ended her season on 88 victories: three downhill races, five super-G, 21 giant slalom, 53 slalom (the **most in an FIS World Cup discipline**), three city events, two parallel slalom and one combined.

MOST FIS ALPINE SKI WORLD CUP WINS

Men's discipline	Record	Name
Downhill	25	Franz Klammer (AUT)
Super-G	24	Hermann Maier (AUT)
Giant Slalom	46	Ingemar Stenmark (SWE)
Slalom	40	Ingemar Stenmark
Combined	11	Phil Mahre (USA) Pirmin Zurbriggen (CHE) Marc Girardelli (LUX, b. AUT)

Women's discipline	Record	Name
Downhill	43	Lindsey Vonn (USA)
Super-G	28	Lindsey Vonn
Giant Slalom	21	Mikaela Shiffrin (USA)
Slalom	53	Mikaela Shiffrin
Combined	8	Hanni Wenzel (LIE, b. DEU)

All figures correct as of 20 Mar 2023

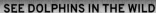

SEE DOLPHINS IN THE WILD
These charismatic mammals have captivated mariners since ancient times. Because they breathe air, they're usually found close to the surface – or even leaping above it! The **highest recorded jump by a dolphin** is 7.9 m (26 ft), logged by bottlenoses (*Tursiops truncatus*).

EXTREME SPORTS

Youngest snowboarding world champion
Mia Brookes (UK, b. 19 Jan 2007) was aged just 16 years 39 days when she won the women's slopestyle on 27 Feb 2023 at the FIS Freestyle Ski and Snowboarding World Championships in Bakuriani, Georgia. Brookes landed a CAB 1440 double grab on her second run to claim gold with a winning score of 91.38.

Most X Games gold medals
BMX legend Garrett Reynolds (USA) claimed his 15th X Games title on 22 Jul 2022, triumphing in the BMX Street event at the California Training Facility in Vista, USA. He tied with Shaun White (USA), who won 13 golds in snowboard events and two in skateboarding from 2003 to 2013.

Fastest men's speed skydiving (FAI-approved)
Marco Hepp (DEU) clocked an average vertical speed of 529.77 km/h (329.18 mph) across a three-second window of freefall on 22 Oct 2022. Hepp was competing at the 4th Fédération Aéronautique Internationale (FAI) World Speed Skydiving Championships in Eloy, Arizona, USA.
   Natisha Dingle (AUS) broke the **women's** record at the same event, averaging 491.99 km/h (305.70 mph) on 24 Oct.

Most Climbing World Cup gold medals
On 26 Sep 2022, Janja Garnbret (SVN) recorded her 37th victory at the International Federation of Sport Climbing World Cup, in Jakarta, Indonesia. Widely regarded as one of the greatest competitive climbers of all time, Garnbret has won 23 gold medals in lead climbing and 14 in bouldering.

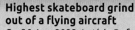

Fastest men's 15 m speed climb
On 8 Jul 2022, Indonesia's Kiromal Katibin scaled a 15-m (49-ft) climbing wall in exactly 5 sec at the IFSC World Cup in Chamonix, France. It was the fifth time that the 21-year-old had broken the world record in 2022.

Fastest timber sports men's underhand chop
Competitors in this event stand on a block and cut through a 32-cm-thick (1-ft) trunk from both sides with an axe. Brayden Meyer (AUS) recorded a time of 12.01 sec on 17 Sep 2022 at the Australian Pro Championship 2022 in Gold Coast, Queensland.

Most medals at the World Wheelchair Rugby Championships by a country
The USA won their eighth "murderball" world championship medal – a silver – at the 2022 edition in Denmark. They have medalled at every tournament to date, claiming the gold four times.

Highest skateboard grind out of a flying aircraft
On 30 Aug 2022, Letícia Bufoni (BRA) performed a spectacular feeble grind along a rail leading straight out of the back of an airborne C-130 Hercules plane. She then parachuted 2,750 m (9,022 ft) to the ground in Merced, California, USA. Skateboarder Bufoni holds multiple GWR titles, including the **most X Games medals in women's summer disciplines** – 12.

Most X Games medals in winter disciplines
Mark McMorris (CAN) has won 22 medals at the X Games since 2011: 11 golds, eight silvers and three bronze. On 29 Jan 2023, he claimed his seventh Snowboard Slopestyle title at X Games Aspen to break his overall tie with the **women's** record holder, snowboarder Jamie Anderson (USA). McMorris has also won four Snowboard Big Air events.

Fastest run at the Red Bull Monserrate Cerro Abajo
On 5 Feb 2022, Camilo Sánchez (COL) cycled the 2.4-km (1.4-mi) urban downhill course in 4 min 30.084 sec. First staged in 2012, this Red Bull race is an adrenaline-fuelled descent down the Monserrate mountain in the Colombian capital of Bogotá. Riders have to negotiate more than 1,600 steps.

RUGBY

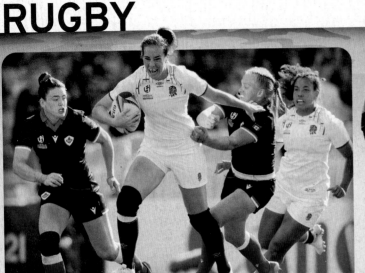

Most wins of the Men's Rugby World Cup Sevens
Fiji claimed their third Sevens World Cup title in 2022, defeating reigning champions New Zealand 29–12 in the 2022 Championship final on 11 Sep in Cape Town, South Africa. The Pacific Islanders – previous winners in 1997 and 2005 – equalled the All Blacks' record of three World Cups (2001, 2013 and 2018) in rugby union's seven-a-side variant.

Most consecutive wins in international rugby union
England Women won 30 games in a row between 9 Nov 2019 and 5 Nov 2022. The Red Roses surpassed the record of 24 wins, by Cyprus's men in 2008–14, with a 73–7 defeat of Wales on 14 Sep 2022. England's winning streak ended in crushing fashion in the final of the Women's Rugby World Cup (*see below*).

Most wins of the Women's Rugby World Cup
New Zealand Women secured their sixth World Cup title on home soil at the delayed 2021 tournament. The Black Ferns won a dramatic final against England 34–31 at Eden Park in Auckland on 12 Nov 2022. The game was witnessed by 42,579 spectators – the **largest attendance at a women's rugby union match**.

During New Zealand's 55–3 quarter-final win over Wales on 29 Oct 2022, winger Portia Woodman scored twice to set a new record for **most tries at the Women's Rugby World Cup** – 20. She surpassed the previous mark of 19, set by England's Sue Day between 1998 and 2006.

Most wins of the Men's Rugby League World Cup
Australia's men clinched a record-extending 12th World Cup title on 19 Nov 2022, overcoming Samoa 30–10 in Manchester, UK. In 16 editions of the tournament, they have never finished lower than third.

On the same day, Australia's women defeated arch-rivals New Zealand 54–4 to claim their third successive World Cup. The Jillaroos and the Kiwi Ferns are now tied for the **most Women's Rugby League World Cup wins**, with three victories apiece.

Most Six Nations Championship points
Irish fly-half Jonathan Sexton scored 566 points in rugby union's annual European competition between 2010 and 2023. He scored seven tries and kicked 106 penalties, three drop-goals and the **most conversions** – 102. Sexton overtook Ronan O'Gara's record of 557 points in his final Six Nations appearance – a 29–16 win over England on 18 Mar 2023.

Most international appearances in women's rugby union
On 25 Mar 2023, Sarah Hunter (UK) played her 141st and final game for England, a 58–7 win over Scotland. Hunter, a back-row forward, was a 10-time winner of the Women's Six Nations and lifted the World Cup in 2014.

As of the same date, Alun Wyn Jones (UK) had extended his **men's** record to 170, playing for Wales (158) and the British & Irish Lions (12).

Most World Rugby Sevens Series appearances
England winger Dan Norton retired from the World Rugby Sevens Series in Apr 2022, having featured in 470 matches between 2009 and 2022. He had scored the **most tries** in the competition – 358 – and a total of 1,804 points.

Most tries in a Super League match
On 15 Jul 2022, Bevan French (AUS) touched down seven times during Wigan Warriors' 60–0 demolition of Hull FC at the DW Stadium in Wigan, UK. The winger eclipsed Lesley Vainikolo's single-match record of six, which he set on 2 Sep 2005 for the Bradford Bulls – also against Hull.

Most tries at a Men's Rugby League World Cup
Josh Addo-Carr (AUS) scored 12 tries at the delayed 2021 Men's Rugby League World Cup, held in England on 15 Oct–19 Nov 2022. The jet-heeled winger – who has been clocked at 38.7 km/h (24 mph) in Australia's National Rugby League – equalled the tournament record of his teammate Valentine Holmes from 2017. Addo-Carr's haul included five tries in Australia's quarter-final win over Lebanon (*see left for more*).

Addo-Carr has scored 13 international tries in just seven appearances for Australia.

GO ON A CRUISE
Leave your cares behind on dry land and head out to sea in the most luxurious of surroundings. On 4 Mar 2022, the *Wonder of the Seas* made its maiden voyage – with a gross tonnage of 235,600, it is the **largest cruise ship** (*turn to p.163 to see more on this superlative liner*).

SWIMMING

Most World Aquatics Championships women's swimming medals

Katie Ledecky (USA) has won 22 world championship medals since 2013: three silvers and the **most women's golds** – 19. At the 2022 edition in Budapest, Hungary, Ledecky claimed four titles, including her fifth 800 m freestyle in a row – the **most consecutive golds in the same long course world championship event**.

FASTEST...

Men's 50 m backstroke

Hunter Armstrong (USA) swam a single length of the pool in 23.71 sec on 28 Apr 2022. He was competing at the US International Team Trials in Greensboro, North Carolina, USA.

Women's 50 m breaststroke (SB2)

On 12 Jun 2022, Ellie Challis (UK) won gold at the World Para Swimming Championships in Funchal, Madeira, Portugal, in a time of 1 min 4.33 sec. It was one of four medals in Funchal for the 18-year-old, who had both legs amputated below the knee, and both arms below the elbow, after contracting meningitis as a baby.

Men's 100 m breaststroke (SB7)

On 31 Mar 2022, Carlos Serrano Zárate (COL) touched home in 1 min 11.18 sec at the Para Swimming World Series event in Berlin, Germany. Zárate, who is short-statured, also set new men's world records for the **50 m breaststroke (SB7)** – 32.23 sec – and the **100 m butterfly (S7)** – 1 min 6.89 sec – at the same meet.

Men's 100 m backstroke

On 20 Jun 2022, Thomas Ceccon (ITA) won the final of the 100 m backstroke in 51.60 sec at the 2022 FINA World Championships in Budapest. He beat Ryan Murphy's six-year-old record.

Ceccon was also part of the Italian team who swam the **fastest men's short course 4 x 100 m freestyle relay** – 3 min 2.75 sec – at the 16th FINA World Swimming Championships (25 m) on 13 Dec 2022 in Melbourne, Australia. His teammates were Alessandro Miressi, Paolo Conte Bonin and Leonardo Deplano.

Men's 200 m butterfly

Kristóf Milák (HUN) delighted the home crowd at the 2022 World Championships by winning gold in 1 min 50.34 sec on 21 Jun. To date, Milák has recorded seven of the 10 fastest swims in the history of the men's 200 m butterfly.

Fastest men's 100 m backstroke (S9)

On 17 Jun 2022, Simone Barlaam (ITA) won gold at the World Para Swimming Championships in 59.72 sec in Funchal, Madeira, Portugal. It was one of six titles at the event for Barlaam, who also set men's S9 records for the **100 m freestyle** – 52.23 sec – and **50 m freestyle** – equalling his own mark of exactly 24 sec.

Oldest world champion

Nicholas Santos (BRA, b. 14 Feb 1980) was aged 42 years 303 days when he won the men's 50 m butterfly at the FINA World Swimming Championships (25 m) in Melbourne, Australia, on 14 Dec 2022. He saw off the field in a time of 21.78 sec – just 0.03 sec off the **fastest men's short course 50 m butterfly** record of 21.75 sec that he shares with Szebasztián Szabó (HUN, b. DEU). Santos announced his retirement from the sport after his victory.

Women's 400 m freestyle

Ariarne Titmus (AUS) triumphed at the Australian Swimming Championships in 3 min 56.40 sec in Adelaide, South Australia, on 22 May 2022. She shaved 0.06 sec off Katie Ledecky's previous fastest time from the 2016 Rio Olympics.

Another world record to fall in Adelaide was the **fastest men's 200 m breaststroke** – 2 min 5.95 sec – to Zac Stubblety-Cook on 19 May. He became the sixth Australian to hold the world record in the event.

Women's short course 800 m freestyle

On 5 Nov 2022, Katie Ledecky (USA) completed 16 laps of a 25-m pool in 7 min 57.42 sec at the FINA World Cup in Indianapolis, Indiana, USA. In her first appearance over the distance in a short course meet, Ledecky smashed Mireia Belmonte's record of 7 min 59.34 sec, which had stood since 2013.

Seven days earlier, Ledecky had destroyed the **women's short course 1,500 m freestyle** record by almost 10 sec at another World Cup meet in Toronto, Ottawa, Canada. She came home in 15 min 8.24 sec – also in her first short course race at this distance.

all records long course (i.e., set in a 50-m pool) unless otherwise stated. FINA was officially renamed World Aquatics in Jan 2023.

Fastest women's 4 x 200 m freestyle relay

On 31 Jul 2022 in Birmingham, UK, the Australian team of Madison Wilson, Kiah Melverton, Mollie O'Callaghan and Ariarne Titmus claimed gold at the 2022 Commonwealth Games in 7 min 39.29 sec. The quicksilver quartet destroyed the field, finishing more than 12 sec ahead of second-placed Canada. Swimming the anchor leg, Titmus (*above*) recorded the fastest-ever split in the history of the women's 4 x 200 m freestyle: 1 min 52.82 sec.

AUTO SPORTS

Most NASCAR race victories
On 3 Mar 2023, Kyle Busch (USA) extended his record for wins in the three tiers of US stock-car racing to 226. Busch has triumphed in 61 races in the top-tier NASCAR Cup Series, and has also recorded the **most Xfinity Series wins** (102) and the **most Truck Series wins** (63).

Most Formula One starts
Fernando Alonso (ESP) had taken part in 357 F1 Grands Prix as of 19 Mar 2023, driving for six different teams. He made his debut in Australia in 2001 and went on to win 32 races, claiming the world championship with Renault in 2005 and 2006. Alonso surpassed Kimi Räikkönen's previous record of 349 starts at the Singapore Grand Prix on 2 Oct 2022.

Youngest World Rally Championship title winner
Kalle Rovanperä (FIN, b. 1 Oct 2000) was crowned world champion at the 2022 Rally New Zealand a day after his 22nd birthday. Rovanperä, son of former WRC driver Harri, won six out of 13 rallies for Toyota Gazoo Racing alongside co-driver Jonne Halttunen.

Most NHRA wins by a woman
Angelle Sampey (USA) has won 46 National Hot Rod Association events in the Pro Stock Motorcycle (PSM) class since 1996. Her most recent victory – which came on 26 Jun 2022 in Norwalk, Ohio, USA – took her to third outright on the all-time PSM list, behind only Andrew Hines (56) and Eddie Krawiec (49).

Fastest speed in an NHRA Top Fuel race
On 11 Nov 2022, Brittany Force (USA) hit 338.94 mph (545.47 km/h) during qualifying at the NHRA Finals in Pomona, California, USA. She beat her own record of 338.48 mph (544.73 km/h), set a month earlier at the Midwest Nationals. Top Fuel dragsters are the fastest in the NHRA, capable of covering the 1,000-ft (304-m) track in around 3.5 sec.

Fastest Indianapolis 500 pole position run
Scott Dixon (NZ) completed four qualifying laps for the 2022 Indy 500 at an average speed of 234.04 mph (376.65 km/h) on 22 May. It was the fifth time Dixon had qualified fastest at the Indianapolis Motor Speedway – only one behind the record for **most pole positions**, set by Rick Mears (USA) between 1979 and 1991.

The **fastest Indy 500 qualifying run** outright was set by Arie Luyendyk (NLD) on 12 May 1996. His four-lap average of 236.986 mph (381.391 km/h) was recorded on the second day of time trials and was not eligible for pole – he qualified in 21st place.

Youngest driver to finish the 24 Hours of Le Mans
In 2022, Josh Pierson (USA, b. 14 Feb 2006) became the youngest driver in 99 years of the classic French endurance race. Aged just 16 years 118 days, Pierson and teammates Alex Lynn and Oliver Jarvis steered their #23 ORECA 07 to a 10th-place overall finish.

Fastest Supersport lap at the Isle of Man TT races
On 6 Jun 2022, Michael Dunlop (UK) completed the final lap of his 600-cc Supersport-class race in 17 min 29.070 sec. He drove his Yamaha YZF-R6 at an average speed of 129.475 mph (208.370 km/h).

By the end of the 2022 Isle of Man TT, Dunlop stood just five victories away from his uncle Joey Dunlop's (UK) record for the **most race wins** – 26.

Fastest completion of the Goodwood hillclimb course
On 26 Jun 2022, ex-F1 driver Max Chilton (UK) took just 39.08 sec to complete the 1.16-mi-long (1.8-km) classic track in Chichester, West Sussex, UK. He was behind the wheel of the innovative McMurtry Spéirling fan car, an all-electric single-seater with a fan capable of deploying 2,000 kg (4,410 lb) of downforce. Chilton broke the previous record – set by Nick Heidfeld in an F1 car in 1999 – by 2.52 sec; he even went quicker than the 2019 practice run of 39.9 sec by Romain Dumas in the *Volkswagen ID.R*.

Most Grand Prix wins in a Formula One season
Max Verstappen (NLD) reigned supreme during the 2022 F1 season, winning 15 of 22 races for Red Bull Racing to secure his second world championship in a row. Verstappen also notched two further podium finishes, seven pole positions and five fastest laps.

Most Formula E Grand Prix starts
Lucas di Grassi (BRA) had lined up for 104 races in the electric car championship as of 11 Feb 2023. He became the first driver to make 100 starts at the Seoul E-Prix on 14 Aug 2022. Di Grassi, winner of Formula E's first-ever race on 13 Sep 2014, shares the record for **most wins** – 13 – with Sébastien Buemi (CHE).

GET A TATTOO
Transform your skin into your own personal canvas. In 2017, Charlotte Guttenberg of Florida, USA, was verified as the **most tattooed woman ever** with 98.75% ink coverage. Proving it's never too late, the senior citizen only got her first tat in her 50s!

COMBAT SPORTS

Highest annual earnings for a boxer
Saúl "Canelo" Álvarez (MEX) took home $90 m (£71.5 m) in the 12 months up to 1 May 2022, according to *Forbes*. An estimated 94% of this came from his super-middleweight bouts against Billy Joe Saunders and Caleb Plant in 2021.

Youngest UFC fight winner
On 10 Dec 2022, Raul Rosas Jr (MEX, b. 8 Oct 2004) defeated Jay Perrin at UFC 282 in Las Vegas, Nevada, USA, aged 18 years 63 days. Rosas Jr – nicknamed "El Niño Problema" – submitted Perrin in the first round of his first fight in the promotion. The high-school senior had already recorded six MMA victories before being signed up by UFC.

Most gold medals at the International Brazilian Jiu-Jitsu Federation World Championship (female)
Beatriz Mesquita (BRA) has accrued 10 golds at the Mundials – eight lightweight (-64 kg) world titles between 2012 and 2021, and two in the absolute class (2013 and 2014).
   The **men's** record is 13, by Marcus Almeida (BRA) between 2012 and 2019.

Youngest ONE Championship world champion
Smilla Sundell (SWE, b. 12 Nov 2004) claimed the ONE Women's Strawweight Muay Thai World Title aged 17 years 161 days on 22 Apr 2022. She defeated Jackie Buntan at ONE 156 by unanimous decision – her 33rd professional victory. Sundell, known as "The Hurricane", took up Muay Thai after her family moved from Sweden to Thailand.

Most UFC finishes
On 8 May 2022, Charles Oliveira (BRA) won his 19th Ultimate Fighting Championship bout inside the distance. The ex-lightweight champion – who has overcome bone rheumatism and a heart murmur – made Justin Gaethje tap out at UFC 274 to extend his record for the **most UFC submissions** to 16.

UFC STAT LEADERS

Most men's...	Record	Name
Fights	41	Jim Miller (USA)
Wins	24	Jim Miller
Finishes	19	Charles Oliveira (BRA)
KOs/TKOs	13	Derrick Lewis (USA)
Submissions	16	Charles Oliveira
Decisions	13	Neil Magny (USA)
Most women's...	**Record**	**Name**
Fights	23	Jéssica Andrade (BRA)
Wins	15	Amanda Nunes (BRA)
		Jéssica Andrade
Finishes	10	Amanda Nunes
KO/TKOs	7	Amanda Nunes
Submissions	6	Gillian Robertson (CAN)
Decisions	11	Katlyn Chookagian (USA)

* Figures correct as of 24 Mar 2023

Most wins of the mixed team event at the World Judo Championships
Japan has won all five editions to date of the World Judo Championships' mixed team competition. They kept alive their 100% record with a 4–2 defeat of France on 13 Oct 2022 in Tashkent, Uzbekistan – avenging their defeat in the Olympic final the previous year.

Most medals at the World Judo Masters
First staged in 2010, the IJF World Judo Masters is an invite-only annual competition. At the 2022 edition on 20–22 Dec in Jerusalem, Israel, Miku Takaichi (née Tashiro, JPN) won gold at half-middleweight to take her career tally to six medals. Both Takaichi and Kosovan half-lightweight Distria Krasniqi equalled the event record for **most golds** – four – matching Dorjsürengiin Sumiyaa (MNG), Kim Polling (NLD) and Teddy Riner (FRA).

Most medals in the Karate 1 Premier League
Sandra Sánchez (ESP) announced her retirement in 2022, following a golden career in which she claimed a record 37 Karate 1 Premier League medals in the women's kata. Her total included the **most golds** – 19 – a record she shared with Ryo Kiyuna (JPN). Sánchez also won two world championship titles and Olympic gold.

> Taylor had previously defeated Serrano's sister, Cindy, by unanimous decision on 20 Oct 2018.

First women's boxing match to headline Madison Square Garden
On 30 Apr 2022, the lightweight title clash between Katie Taylor (IRL) and Amanda Serrano (PRI) topped the bill at the iconic boxing venue in New York City, USA. Taylor defended her WBA, IBF, WBO and WBC belts via a split decision to take her pro record to 21 wins from 21 fights.

CYCLING

Fastest women's 500 m time trial (C3)
On 20 Oct 2022, Aniek van den Aarssen (NLD) clocked 39.093 sec in the final of the women's C3 500 m time trial at the UCI Para-cycling Track World Championships. Van den Aarssen hit 46 km/h (28 mph) as she sped to both the gold medal and the world record in the French town of Saint-Quentin-en-Yvelines.

Farthest women's track distance in one hour
On 23 May 2022, Ellen van Dijk (NLD) cycled 49.254 km (30.605 mi) in 60 min at the Velodrome Suisse in Grenchen, Switzerland. Van Dijk surpassed the UK's Joss Lowden's previous hour record by 849 m (2,785 ft), maintaining an average speed of more than 48 km/h (29 mph) throughout her attempt.

Fastest men's 200 m flying time trial (C2)
On 20 Oct 2022, Alexandre Léauté (FRA) crossed the line in 11.212 sec at the UCI Para-cycling Track World Championships in Saint-Quentin-en-Yvelines, France. He was competing in the multi-discipline omnium event. Léauté won four golds and a silver on home soil, setting further C2 world records in the **1 km time trial** – 1 min 8.365 sec – and the **3 km individual pursuit** – 3 min 31.082 sec.

The omnium saw new **fastest women's 200 m flying time trials** in the following classifications:
• **C1**: 15.606 sec, by Katie Toft (UK).
• **C3**: 12.666 sec, by Mel Pemble (CAN).
• **C5**: 11.605 sec, by Marie Patouillet (FRA).

Fastest women's 750 m team sprint
Germany (Pauline Grabosch, Lea Friedrich and Emma Hinze) cycled three laps of the track in 45.967 sec at the UCI Track Cycling World Championships in France on 12 Oct 2022. They defeated China in the final to claim the gold.

Fastest men's 4 km individual pursuit
On 14 Oct 2022, Filippo Ganna (ITA) won the final of the men's 4 km in 3 min 59.636 sec at the 2022 UCI Track Cycling World Championships in Saint-Quentin-en-Yvelines, France. He became the first rider to break the four-minute barrier at sea level. It completed an historic week for Ganna, who on 8 Oct cycled the **farthest men's track distance in one hour**. He rode 56.792 km (35.288 mi) in 60 min in Grenchen, Switzerland.

Fastest average speed at the Paris–Roubaix race
Known as the "Hell of the North", Paris–Roubaix is a one-day classic famed for its treacherous cobbled streets. It runs for *c.* 257 km (159 mi) between the French capital and the Belgian border. Mathieu van der Poel (NLD) won the 2023 edition on 9 Apr with an average speed of 46.841 km/h (29.105 mph).

Most stage wins of the Giro d'Italia Donne
Marianne Vos (NLD) won 32 stages of the elite women's race – formerly known as the Giro Rosa – between 8 Jul 2007 and 6 Jul 2022. This is 14 more than her closest rival, Petra Rossner.

Most women's cross-country titles at the UCI Mountain Bike World Championships
Pauline Ferrand-Prévot (FRA) won her fourth cross-country world championship on 28 Aug 2022 at Les Gets in France, having previously triumphed in 2015 and 2019–20. She equalled the record of Gunn-Rita Dahle Flesjå (NOR) in 2002 and 2004–06.

Most men's cross-country titles at the UCI Mountain Bike World Championships
Nino Schurter (CHE) secured his 10th cross-country crown on 28 Aug 2022 at Les Gets in France. He has also won four team golds. A week later, Schurter followed up by claiming the outright record for the **most UCI Mountain Bike World Cup men's cross-country titles**, winning his eighth.

Pogačar won three stages of the 2022 Tour de France, taking his career total to nine at the age of just 23.

Most wins of the Tour de France's young rider classification
Since 1975, the *maillot blanc* ("white jersey") has been awarded to the leading rider in the Tour de France's overall standings aged 25 or under. Tadej Pogačar (SVN) won the young rider classification for the third consecutive year in 2022 – equalling Jan Ullrich (DEU) in 1996–98 and Andy Schleck (LUX) in 2008–10. Pogačar finished the 2022 Tour in second place in the general classification, having won the race the previous two years.

SKYDIVE
Experience the ultimate adrenaline rush, leaping into the clouds. And don't forget to ask Grandma if she'd like to join you. Four generations of the McNabb family (USA) parachuted from a plane at the same time on 26 Jun 2021 – the **most generations of one family to skydive simultaneously**.

ENDURANCE

Fastest-run men's marathon
Eliud Kipchoge (KEN) won the Berlin Marathon in Germany in 2 hr 1 min 9 sec on 25 Sep 2022. He beat his own world record – also set in Berlin, in 2018 – by 30 sec. Kipchoge equalled Haile Gebrselassie's (ETH) record for the **most men's Berlin Marathon wins** – four. It was his 15th win from 17 races over the distance.

Fastest-run debut men's marathon
Kelvin Kiptum (KEN) enjoyed a remarkable victory at the Valencia Marathon in Spain on 4 Dec 2022, winning in 2 hr 1 min 53 sec – the fourth-fastest time ever recorded over the distance.

Letesenbet Gidey (ETH) set the **women's** record at the same event, finishing in 2 hr 16 min 49 sec. The track star had run the **fastest women's half marathon** – 1 hr 2 min 52 sec – in Valencia the previous year, also her first race over that distance.

Most marathon appearances at the World Athletics Championships
Mongolian distance runner Bat-Ochiryn Ser-Od competed in his 10th consecutive world championships on 17 Jul 2022. Aged 40, he finished 26th in 2 hr 11 min 39 sec in Eugene, Oregon, USA.

Most consecutive days to run a marathon distance (LA2, female)
Jacky Hunt-Broersma (USA) ran 26.2 mi (42.1 km) for 104 days in a row in Arizona, USA, from 17 Jan to 30 Apr 2022. Jacky lost her lower left leg in 2001 after contracting Ewing sarcoma, a rare form of cancer that impacts tissue around the bones.

Fastest-run men's 100 km
On 23 Apr 2022, Aleksandr Sorokin (LTU) took just 6 hr 5 min 41 sec to run 100 km (62 mi) at the Centurion Running Track 100 Mile event in Bedford, UK. His average pace was 3 min 39 sec per km. During the same race, Sorokin also broke Donald Ritchie's 43-year-old record from Oct 1978 for the **farthest distance run in 6 hours**, covering 98.496 km (61.202 mi).

Sorokin continues to push the limits of the possible in ultra-running. On 7 Jan 2022, he completed the **fastest-run 100 miles** – 10 hr 51 min 39 sec – and the **farthest distance run in 12 hours** – 177.410 km (110.237 mi). Sorokin was competing at the Spartanion 12-Hour race in Tel Aviv, Israel. All times and distances were ratified by the International Association of Ultrarunners (IAU).

Hug broke a 12-year-old course record in Chicago, registering his third career victory in the race.

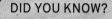

Fastest Chicago Marathon (men's wheelchair)
Marcel Hug (CHE) powered to victory in 1 hr 25 min 20 sec in Illinois, USA, on 9 Oct 2022. The "Silver Bullet" was untouchable in 2022, completing the **fastest London Wheelchair Marathon** – 1 hr 24 min 38 sec, on 2 Oct – and also in **New York** – 1 hr 25 min 26 sec, on 6 Nov.

Fastest IRONMAN® women's triathlon
On 5 Jun 2022, Laura Philipp (DEU) finished in 8 hr 18 min 20 sec at the IRONMAN European Championship in Hamburg, Germany. Philipp swam 2.4 mi (3.8 km) in 54 min 39 sec; cycled 112 mi (180 km) in 4 hr 31 min 14 sec; and completed a 26.2-mi (42.1-km) marathon in 2 hr 45 min 39 sec.

Fastest time to bag all Wainwrights
On 2–7 May 2022, John Kelly (USA) climbed all 214 peaks of the Lake District National Park in Cumbria, UK, in 5 days 12 hr 14 min 43 sec. The route measured around 515 km (320 mi) and involved a total ascent of 36,000 m (118,110 ft) – more than four times the height of Everest.

Most laps completed in a backyard ultramarathon
Competitors in this idiosyncratic event have to complete a single lap of 4.167 mi (6.706 km) every hour – adding up to exactly 100 mi over 24 hr – until only one runner remains. At the 2022 Backyard Ultra – World Team Championships on 15–19 Oct, Merijn Geerts and Ivo Steyaert (both BEL) completed 101 loops in Belgium before agreeing to end the race in a gesture of solidarity. They each ran a total of 420.867 mi (677.319 km) over 4 days 5 hr. Despite setting a world record, both runners were listed as "Did Not Finish", as backyard ultra rules state that the final runner must complete a single solo lap to be declared as a finisher.

Fastest Hardrock Hundred Mile Endurance Run
Starting and ending in the town of Silverton, Colorado, USA, the Hardrock 100 is a punishing 102.5-mi (164.9-km) trek through the steep dirt trails of the San Juan Mountains. On 15–16 Jul 2022, Kilian Jornet (ESP) secured his fifth Hardrock victory in 21 hr 36 min 24 sec.

The **women's** course record was also broken in 2022, by Courtney Dauwalter (USA, *inset*) in 26 hr 44 min 36 sec.

DID YOU KNOW?
The Hardrock 100 was first held in 1992, with 18 finishers inside the 48-hr limit.

The course is run clockwise and anti-clockwise on alternating years.

The high point is 14,058 ft (4,284 m) – the summit of Handies Peak.

Finishers have to "kiss the Hardrock" – a painted image of a ram's head.

ROUND-UP

Most wins of the FIBA 3x3 Men's World Cup
On 26 Jun 2022, Serbia secured their fifth men's 3x3 World Cup title with a 21–16 win over Lithuania in Antwerp, Belgium. Strahinja Stojačić, the No.1-ranked player, top scored with nine points. This three-a-side variation of basketball is played on a half-court; the winners are the first to 21 points, or the highest scorers after 10 min of play.

First quadruple axel in figure skating
On 14 Sep 2022, 17-year-old Ilia Malinin (USA) successfully landed a quad axel jump at the US International Classic in Lake Placid, New York. The axel is the only figure-skating jump with a forward take-off, meaning that its quad has an extra half-revolution on top of the standard four.

Fastest speed in MotoGP
Jorge Martín (ESP) hit 363.6 km/h (225.9 mph) on his second lap of the 2022 Italian Grand Prix, held on 29 May at the Mugello Circuit in Scarperia e San Piero. Martín, who was riding a Pramac Ducati, beat the previous record of 362.4 km/h (225.1 mph), shared by Johann Zarco and Brad Binder.

Fastest Berlin Inline Skating Marathon
The long-distance race in the German capital is one of the highlights of the inline skating calendar. Bart Swings (BEL) won the 2022 edition in 56 min 45 sec on 25 Sep, beating his own course record from 2015 by 4 sec. Swings extended his event record for **most wins** to eight, having also triumphed in 2013–18 and 2021.

Fastest men's finswimming surface 100 m
On 24 Apr 2022, Max Poschart (DEU) swam a 100-m relay leg in 33.71 sec at a CMAS Finswimming World Cup meet in Leipzig, Germany. Competitors in this category race across the surface of the water using a mask, snorkel and monofin.

Another finswimming record to fall during the 2022 CMAS World Cup was the **fastest men's surface 800 m**, to Nándor Kiss (HUN). He recorded a time of 6 min 13.53 sec on 26 Feb 2022 in Eger, Hungary. This was also a world junior record.

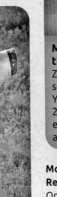

Most consecutive gold medals at the World Orienteering Championships
Tove Alexandersson (SWE) won 11 straight world orienteering titles between 2018 and 2022. Her winning streak, across four competitions, included golds in every event category: middle, long, relay, sprint, knockout sprint and mixed sprint relay.

Most mixed doubles gold medals at the Badminton World Championships
Zheng Siwei and Huang Yaqiong (both CHN) secured their third title on 28 Aug 2022, beating Yuta Watanabe and Arisa Higashino 21–13, 21–16 in Tokyo, Japan. The victorious pair equalled the feat of compatriots Zhang Nan and Zhao Yunlei, winners in 2011 and 2014–15.

Most women's singles titles at the Real Tennis World Championship
On 17 Apr 2022, Claire Fahey (UK) defeated Lea Van Der Zwalmen 6–0, 6–2 at the Chateâu de Fontainebleau in France to secure her sixth consecutive world championship. This equalled the feat of Penny Lumley (UK) between 1989 and 2003. On the same day, Fahey teamed up with her sister Sarah Shuckburgh (UK) to extend their **most women's doubles titles** to five.

Youngest London Marathon women's winner
Yalemzerf Yehualaw (ETH, b. 3 Aug 1999) was aged 23 years 60 days when she won the 42nd London Marathon on 2 Oct 2022. Yehualaw battled back after a fall with six miles to go to cross the line in 2 hr 17 min 26 sec – the third-fastest time in the history of the elite women's race.

Kerry are also tied with Cork for the most All-Ireland Senior Ladies' Football Championships – 11.

Most wins of the All-Ireland Senior Football Championship
First held in 1887, Gaelic football's premier competition has been won 38 times by Kerry. The county lifted the Sam Maguire Cup for the first time since 2014 on 24 Jul 2022, following a 0–20 to 0–16 victory over Galway at Croke Park, Dublin. Kerry's David Clifford led the way for "The Kingdom", scoring eight points.

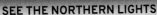

SEE THE NORTHERN LIGHTS
And finally, top of the world's collective bucket list is nature's most dazzling light show. The aurora borealis is the result of Earth's magnetic field redirecting energized particles from the Sun. The **highest atmospheric phenomenon**, it shimmers 400 km (248 mi) above our planet's surface.

Heaviest men's weightlifting total (89 kg)
Antonino Pizzolato (ITA) lifted a cumulative 392 kg (864 lb 3 oz) across two disciplines at the European Weightlifting Championships in Tirana, Albania, on 2 Jun 2022. Pizzolato completed successful lifts of 175 kg (385 lb 12 oz) in the snatch and 217 kg (478 lb 6 oz) in the clean & jerk.

Heaviest men's para powerlift (-97 kg)
On 17 Dec 2022, Abdelkareem Khattab (JOR) lifted 255 kg (562 lb 2 oz) at the 12th Fazza Dubai Para Powerlifting World Cup in the UAE. He recorded three record lifts in succession in Dubai to smash the previous best at -97 kg. Khattab became a record holder at two different weights, having lifted 250 kg (551 lb 2 oz) at **-88 kg** on 4 Dec 2021 in Tbilisi, Georgia.

The **men's -107 kg** world record also fell in Dubai on 17 Dec, to Aliakbar Gharibshahi (IRN) with a lift of 254 kg (559 lb 15 oz).

Most wins of the IIHF Ice Hockey Women's World Championship
Canada became women's ice hockey world champions for the 12th time on 4 Sep 2022, edging the USA 2–1 in the final in Herning, Denmark. The two North American arch-rivals have contested all 21 finals in the tournament's history – bar 2019, when Finland lost out to the USA in a shootout.

Most women's team wins at the World Table Tennis Championships
On 8 Oct 2022, China's women claimed the Corbillon Cup for the 22nd time with a 3–0 final victory over Japan in Chengdu, China. The team maintained a perfect record throughout the tournament, winning every match.

The next day, China extended the **men's** record by defeating Germany 3–0 to lift the Swaythling Cup for the 22nd time. That's 10 more than their closest rivals, Hungary.

Fastest winning time at the IRONMAN® World Championship
On 9 Oct 2022, Gustav Iden (NOR) made a record-breaking championship debut at Kailua-Kona in Hawaii, USA, winning in 7 hr 40 min 24 sec. Iden powered to victory on the final run section of the triathlon, completing the 26.2-mi (42.2-km) marathon in a course record of 2 hr 36 min 15 sec. The first four male finishers in 2022 all came in under the previous championship-best time.

Most wins of the World Lacrosse Women's World Championship
On 9 Jul 2022, the USA recorded an 11–8 victory over Canada in Towson, Maryland, USA, to secure their ninth world championship (previously known as the Women's Lacrosse World Cup). The only other country to have won the event since it began in 1982 is Australia, in 1986 and 2005.

Most Superbike World Championship race wins
Jonathan Rea (UK) won six races during the 2022 Superbike season to take his career tally to 118. This was exactly twice as many victories as Rea's closest rival, Carl Fogarty.

Most wins of the FIH Hockey Women's World Cup
The Netherlands have triumphed at field hockey's quadrennial tournament nine times since 1974 – seven more than any other nation. On 17 Jul 2022, the Dutch overcame Argentina 3–1 in the final of the latest World Cup to secure title No.9 in Terrassa, Spain. They won all six of their matches, scoring 17 goals and conceding just five.

Fastest women's 1,000 m short track speed skating
On 4 Nov 2022, Suzanne Schulting (NLD) skated 1,000 m in 1 min 25.958 sec at the Utah Olympic Oval in Salt Lake City, USA (*see p.230*). Schulting broke her own world record over the distance at the ISU Short Track Speed Skating World Cup.

On the same day in Salt Lake City, the **women's 500 m** record fell to Schulting's compatriot Xandra Velzeboer, who finished in 41.416 sec.

Most Trials World Championships
Toni Bou (ESP) is the undisputed king of motorcycle trials, having won an astonishing 32 consecutive indoor and outdoor world championships since 2007. In 2022, he extended his records for **most wins of the FIM X-Trials** and the **FIM Trial World Championship** to 16 apiece. By the end of the latter, Bou had increased his number of event wins to 205 (73 indoor and 132 outdoor). His lowest finish in championship events in 2022 was second place.

SHINGO KUNIEDA

VITAL STATISTICS

Name	Shingo Kunieda
Birthplace	Tokyo, Japan
Birth date	21 Feb 1984
Grand Slam titles	Singles: 28 Doubles: 22
Paralympic medals	Gold: 4 Bronze: 2
Current GWR titles	8, including most Grand Slam wheelchair singles tennis titles (male)
Highest rank	No.1
Preferred surface	Hard court

With a record-smashing 50 Grand Slams to his name, Japanese tennis icon Shingo Kunieda hung up his racquet in Jan 2023, announcing his retirement.

Shingo has used a wheelchair since recovering from a spinal tumour at the age of nine. Having initially taken an interest in basketball, at 11 years old he was introduced to wheelchair tennis by his mother. Within a decade, he had come to dominate the sport, rising up the rankings to world No.1.

The shelves of his trophy cabinet were soon groaning, but one prize eluded him: a singles title at Wimbledon. That changed on 10 Jul 2022, at the age of 38, after a three-set thriller against the UK's Alfie Hewett. His *50th* major represents the **most Grand Slam tennis titles won** – by any player. Having already triumphed at other events, he also became the **first male wheelchair-tennis player to earn a Career Grand Slam, Golden Slam** and **Super Slam** in singles (*see 1*).

Inscribed on all Shingo's racquets are the words "I'm the strongest". With such unprecedented success, it was clearly a conviction only surpassed by innate talent on the court.

Between 2008 and 2010, Shingo won 106 matches in a row: the longest winning streak for a male tennis player.

1: In 2022, Shingo celebrated his record-breaking "Career Slams", including a Super Slam in singles: that's winning all four Grand Slams (Australian Open, US Open, French Open and Wimbledon), Paralympic gold and the end-of-year Masters title. Diede de Groot (*below*) achieved this in 2021.

2: At the most recent Paralympic Games, Shingo earned his third singles gold medal. Succeeding on home soil clearly meant a lot to him: "It's a dream because after Rio [2016] I had an injury and I thought many times of retiring," he revealed. "So I can't believe it."

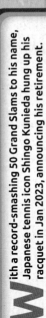

DIEDE DE GROOT

At just 25, Diede de Groot has already laid claim to a feat achieved by no solo tennis player before her: winning all four Grand Slams for two years back to back – in 2021 and 2022. To top that off, with success at the Tokyo Games in 2021, she also became the first woman since trailblazer Steffi Graf in 1988 to claim a same-year "Golden Slam" in singles.

A prosthetic leg has been part of Diede's life for as long as she can remember. Doctors diagnosed that her legs would not develop equally just a few months after she was born.

When she first took up tennis aged seven, physiotherapists advised she play in a wheelchair. Although at the time she had little experience of using one, it was a recommendation that she embraced and a tennis star was born.

After turning pro at 17, Diede rapidly went on to stamp her name in the annals of the sport. Clinching her first Grand Slams in 2017, she has since added 31 more to her tally (16 singles and 15 doubles), as well as countless other titles and trophies. With so much achieved so quickly, you wonder what ambitions Diede has left? "My dream is to become the best wheelchair tennis player I can be," she said.

Diede was nominated as the Laureus Sportsperson of the Year with a Disability in 2019, 2020 and 2022.

1: Diede on the training courts with her GWR certificates. She attributes part of her huge success to her friends, who she says always treated her the same as everyone else.

2: Diede and doubles partner Aniek van Koot celebrate victory for the Netherlands at the 2021 Paralympics – the day after Diede also won gold in the singles. They smashed their British opponents 6–0, 6–1. Reflecting on the win, Diede said: "Even though I was really tired, it was a good match... Today, we were in control. We were getting that title, and we did that."

Find out more about Shingo and Diede in the Hall of Fame section at www.guinnessworldrecords.com/2024

STOP PRESS

Largest slime-making lesson
On 19 Jun 2022, a total of 491 students were taught the finer points of gunk generation at the Montréal Science Centre in Quebec, Canada. The lesson was led by "local slime star" Yannick Bergeron and coincided with the *Science of Guinness World Records* exhibition at the institution.

Largest disco dance
On 30 Jul 2022, Sophie Ellis-Bextor led 598 disco divas in cutting some shapes on the dancefloor at the Camp Bestival music festival held at Lulworth Castle in Dorset, UK. The record attempt raised money for the Ellen MacArthur Cancer Trust.

Longest sawdust carpet
A decorative walkway created for the annual pilgrimage of the image of the Virgen de la Caridad through Huamantla in Tlaxcala, Mexico, stretched 3.94 km (2.45 mi) on 14 Aug 2022. That's longer than the National Mall in Washington, DC. Laid by 240 artisans and overseen by the Secretaría de Turismo de Tlaxcala (MEX), it required 80 tons (72 tonnes) of multicoloured sawdust.

Largest cornhole tournament
The Iowa State Fair in Des Moines, USA, staged a bean-bag-throwing competition on 20 Aug 2022 for a record 730 players.

Most par-three golf holes completed in three minutes by a women's team
On 23 Aug 2022, the trio of Jennifer Kupcho, Alison Lee (both USA) and A Lim Kim (KOR) completed the 17th hole of the Ottawa Hunt & Golf Club in par or better six times in 180 sec in Ontario, Canada. They won a head-to-head challenge organized by Golf Canada with Pauline Roussin (FRA), Megan Khang (USA) and Rebecca Lee-Bentham (CAN).

Largest game of Red Light, Green Light
On 21 Sep 2022, a total of 1,415 students played statues at the University of California, Irvine, USA. School mascot Peter the Anteater joined in the fun as the traffic light.

Fastest 0–100 km/h acceleration by an electric car
E0711-11 EVO took just 1.461 sec to reach 100 km/h (62 mph) from stationary on 23 Sep 2022 on a test track at Robert Bosch Campus in Renningen, Germany. The car was designed and produced by GreenTeam Uni Stuttgart, who reclaimed a record that they had previously held in 2015.

Largest parade of kitesurfers
On 25 Sep 2022, the skies above Cumbuco beach in Ceará, Brazil, were filled with colourful canopies as 884 kitesurfers took to the waves. More than 31 nationalities took part in the 1-hr 45-min display, orchestrated by Winds for Future (BRA).

Most models in a fashion show
A total of 430 models paraded down the catwalk at the "Ribbons Rock the Runway" fashion show in New Orleans, Louisiana, USA, on 1 Oct 2022. Many of the participants were cancer survivors and wore outfits in colours representing cancer ribbons. The event was organized by You Night Events, Positive Image Modeling and Chic Nouvelle Worldwide Model Management (all USA).

Largest doughnut wall
Attendees of the "Bridging the Gap" conference in Rochester, Minnesota, USA, were rewarded with a wall bearing 3,000 hanging ring doughnuts. The sugary spectacle was created with the aid of Convoy of Hope (USA) on 1 Oct 2022.

Most dogs attending a film screening
On 15 Oct 2022, a *paw*-dience of 199 pooches and their owners watched *A Dog's Way Home* (CHN/USA, 2019) at the Litchfield Skyview Drive-In, located on Route 66 in Illinois, USA. The outdoor movie screening was put on by KeepRoute66Kickin.com and Mobil 1 (both USA).

Largest display of monster-truck toys
To celebrate the 30th anniversary of Monster Jam (USA), Spin Master (CAN) delivered 10,005 toy trucks to an event in Orlando, Florida, USA, on 29 Oct 2022. The entire fleet of "mini monsters" was then released down a 40-ft (12-m) ramp and subsequently donated to charity.

Most glass bottles collected for recycling in one hour
On 5 Nov 2022, recyclable receptacles weighing a total of 9,519.78 kg (20,987 lb 8 oz) were collected by Imagination Station in Toledo, Ohio, USA. The science museum, located in the heart of the "Glass City", was hosting the *Science of Guinness World Records* exhibition.

Greatest jackpot in a national lottery
A Powerball draw with a $2.05-bn (£1.79-bn) jackpot was held on 8 Nov 2022. It was won by Edwin Castro (USA), courtesy of a $2 (£1.75) ticket he had bought at a Californian convenience store. Castro chose to receive his winnings as a single reduced sum of $997.6 m (£872.8 m). According to Powerball, the odds of winning were around 1 in 292.2 million.

Most nationalities at a dance party
On 16 Nov 2022, a total of 84 countries were represented by dancers from the Erasmus Student Network (ESN) Sweden. The international students were sailing between Stockholm and Tallinn in Estonia onboard the MS *Baltic Queen* at the time. On the same journey, they also achieved the **most nationalities at a coffee party** – 75 – and in **a simultaneous pop-music sing-along** – 85.

Largest prayer wheel
A prayer wheel at Samten Hills in Dalat, Vietnam, stood 37.22 m (122 ft) tall – almost double the height of the White House – and had a 16.53-m (54-ft) diameter, as verified on 11 Dec 2022. The 181-tonne (200-ton) cylindrical structure is coated in 24-karat gold; it contains holy Buddhist relics and more than 1 billion mantras.

Fastest women's short course 100 m butterfly swim
On 18 Dec 2022, Maggie Mac Neil (CAN, b. CHN) swam four laps of a 25-m (82-ft) pool in 54.05 sec. She was competing at the 16th FINA World Swimming Championships in Melbourne, Australia.
Two days previously at the same event, Mac Neil had broken the **women's 50 m backstroke** record with a time of 25.25 sec.

Most people in soap bubbles in 30 seconds
Professional bubble artist Eran Backler (UK; *see also p.110*) formed soap bubbles over 15 volunteers in Ipoh, Malaysia, on 20 Dec 2022.

Most people to take a penalty kick in 12 hours
On 10 Jan 2023, Manjeri Football Stadium in Malappuram, Kerala, India, saw 4,470 people try to score a goal from the penalty spot. The event was arranged by Kerala's Department of Sports & Youth Affairs and AAK International (both IND).

Largest wearable cake dress (supported)
Natasha Lee Fokas (CHE) cooked up a 131.15-kg (289-lb 2-oz) wedding dress made from sponge cake and fondant icing, as unveiled on 15 Jan 2023 at the Swiss Wedding World fair in Bern. The model wearing the edible outfit had to walk 5 m (16 ft) without it falling apart. Fokas is the founder of baking firm SweetyCakes.

Highest between-the-legs slam dunk
On 20 Jan 2023, Piotr "Grabo" Grabowski (POL) pulled off a spectacular dunk through a basket set 3.2 m (10 ft 5 in) above the ground – 15 cm (5.9 in) higher than a standard NBA hoop. The Dunk Elite athlete was performing at a promotion for the HONOR Magic5 Series smartphone at Crystal Palace National Sports Centre in London, UK.

Longest table-tennis serve
On 22 Jan 2023, Álvaro Martín Mendieta (ESP) unleashed a legal table-tennis serve 16.28 m (53 ft 4 in) from the table in Madrid, Spain. The stunt reclaimed Mendieta a record that he had previously held in 2020.

Largest wedding bouquet
To celebrate their parents' 25th wedding anniversary, Roshan Samuel and Angelina Sky (both IND) presented Prem Kumar and Ceceliya Prem with a single bouquet of 9,400 flowers on 22 Jan 2023 in Bengaluru, Karnataka, India.

Most awards won by a short film
ON/OFF (ARG, 2020) had been presented with 1,125 awards as of 24 Jan 2023. The animated 7-min film, created by Nicolás Pedro Villarreal and Red Clover Studios (both ARG), tackles the impact of social media on people's day-to-day lives.

Most films to surpass $2 billion at the global box office by an actress
Zoe Saldaña (USA) had appeared in four of the six movies to have grossed $2 bn (£1.6 bn) as of 25 Jan 2023: *Avatar* (USA/UK, 2009), *Avengers: Infinity War* (USA, 2018) *Avengers: Endgame* (USA, 2019) and *Avatar: The Way of Water* (USA, 2022).

Heaviest pomelo
Kazuki Maeda (JPN) grew a specimen of the Asian citrus fruit weighing 5.528 kg (12 lb 2.9 oz) in Yatsushiro, Kumamoto, Japan, as verified on 27 Jan 2023. The 26-cm-wide (10-in) pomelo broke Maeda's own previous record by 142 g (5 oz).

Oldest wombat in captivity ever
A common wombat (*Vombatus ursinus*) named Wain had his age verified at a minimum of 33 years 86 days on 31 Jan 2023. Wain, who was rescued from the wild in Australia, was born *c.* Jan 1989 and now lives at Satsukiyama Zoo in Osaka, Japan.

Most consecutive football touches while balancing a football on the head in one minute
On 1 Feb 2023, Chinonso Eche (NGA) juggled a soccer ball 133 times while keeping another on his head. He was performing on *Lo Show dei Record* in Milan, Italy.

Smallest floating golf green
Golf Saudi unveiled a 1-m² (10.7-sq-ft) circular green in the middle of a lake in King Abdullah Economic City, Saudi Arabia, on 1 Feb 2023.

Fastest swim crossing of Kuwait Bay (male)
On 2 Feb 2023, Yousef Alshatti (KWT) took 9 hr 44 min to swim 17.3 km (10.7 mi) across Kuwait Bay. The Kuwaiti Navy Special Forces officer spent three months training for this attempt.

Most handstand push-ups in one minute (male)
On 4 Feb 2023, calisthenics coach Feras Alahmad (SYR) completed 66 handstand push-ups in 60 sec in Doha, Qatar. His record attempt was carried out in association with Qatar's National Service Academy to mark World Cancer Day.

Most T-shirts worn during a half marathon
David Eliuk (CAN) wrapped up warmly for the Edmonton Hypothermic Half Marathon on 5 Feb 2023 by running in 120 tops. He had to complete the race in Alberta, Canada, in under 3 hr to qualify for the record. It took David and his helpers 15 min to remove and count his T-shirts after the race.

Largest gathering of people wearing capes
On 6 Feb 2023, a total of 2,854 superheroes attended a home game of the Raptors 905, an NBA minor-league team in Toronto, Ontario, Canada. It was the seventh edition of the "Capes for Kids" fundraising programme by the Holland Bloorview Kids Rehabilitation Hospital Foundation (CAN).

Largest *wai kru* muay Thai dance
Before bouts, Thai boxers perform a traditional demonstration to show their respect and gratitude to their teachers. On 6 Feb 2023, the Tourism Authority of Thailand arranged a display with 3,660 participants in Prachuap Khiri Khan, Thailand.

Most neck ties worn at once
On 9 Feb 2023, David Araújo (BRA) modelled 330 ties during a photoshoot for *Dazed* magazine in Paris, France. It was part of a feature devoted to record-breaking fashion, which also included the **largest trousers** – measuring 13.07 m (42 ft 11 in) long with a 9.22-m (30-ft 3-in) waist, made by Anh Quynh Duong (USA) – and the **most hair clips on the head** – 1,415, by Alicia Farida Daïf (FRA).

Most people simultaneously performing the yoga plough pose
On 11 Feb 2023, a group of 560 nimble *yogis* lay down and bent their backs over their heads in Bengaluru, Karnataka, India. The record was a collaboration between the Akshar Yoga Research and Development Centre, Shree Mahaprabhu Jagannath Sangha and Himalaya Yoga Ashrama (all IND).

Heaviest weight lifted by kettlebell swing in one minute (male)
On 11 Feb 2023, Stefan Schwitter (CHE) lifted 2,184 kg (4,814 lb) in Zurich, Switzerland. Stefan, a former pro wrestler and Zen practitioner, made 39 reps lifting a 56-kg kettlebell in the allotted time.

Fastest time to solve a Square-1 cube
Michał Krasowski (POL) unscrambled a Square-1 cube in just 3.87 sec at the Olsztyn Squared 2023 event in Poland on 11 Feb 2023. He smashed the previous world record by 0.41 sec, completing the first sub-4-sec solve.

Largest decorated Easter egg
For the Easter festival in Pomerode, Santa Catarina, Brazil, on 18 Feb 2023, Associação Visite Pomerode (BRA) created an egg measuring 16.72 m (54 ft 10 in) tall and 10.88 m (35 ft 8 in) in diameter. Designed by a local artist, it was painted in the style of Kashubian folk art.

Largest teapot
On 18 Feb 2023, Khadeer Tea (SAU) unveiled a towering teapot standing 4.19 m (13 ft 8 in) high – taller than two adult men – and with a diameter of 2.81 m (9 ft 2 in) in Riyadh, Saudi Arabia. They broke a record that had stood since 2016.

Highest men's pole vault
Armand Duplantis (SWE, b. USA) broke the pole vault world record for a sixth time on 25 Feb 2023, clearing the bar at 6.22 m (20 ft 4 in) at an indoor meeting in Clermont-Ferrand, France.

Most points in a women's indoor pentathlon
On 3 Mar 2023, Nafissatou Thiam (BEL) won pentathlon gold with a score of 5,055 at the European Athletics Indoor Championships in Istanbul, Türkiye. She crossed the line in the final event – the 800 m – just seconds after her rival Adrianna Sułek had posted a winning score of 5,014, surpassing Nataliya Dobrynska's world record from 2012 by a single point.

Youngest gold medallist at the World Single Distances Speed Skating Championships
Jordan Stolz (USA, b. 21 May 2004) was aged 18 years 286 days when he won the men's 500 m in Heerenveen, Netherlands, on 3 Mar 2023. Stolz went on to add the 1,000 m and 1,500 m titles – the most gold medals by a man at a single edition of the championships.

Most family members to complete the World Marathon Majors
On 5 Mar 2023, the "Wolfpack" (aka Rodrigo Lobo Puccio and his five sons – Tomás, Rodrigo, Santiago, Raimundo and Agustín Lobo van Wersch) from Chile completed the Tokyo Marathon in Japan – the last of six World Marathon Majors they had run as a family unit since 2016. The other races are held in Boston, London, Berlin, Chicago and New York City.

The Wolfpack were among a total of 3,049 runners in Tokyo to complete the World Marathon Majors – the **most people to earn a Six Star Medal at a single marathon**.

Fastest swim crossing of the Cook Strait
Andrew Donaldson (UK) traversed the 23-km-wide (14.3-mi) channel between New Zealand's North and South Islands in 4 hr 33 min 50 sec on 7–8 Mar 2023. His swim was ratified by the New Zealand Open Water Swimming Association.

First female vocalist to reach No.1 on the *Billboard* 200 with an all-Spanish-language album
On 11 Mar 2023, KAROL G (COL, b. Carolina Giraldo Navarro) debuted at No.1 with her fourth studio effort, *MAÑANA SERÁ BONITO* ("*Tomorrow Will Be Pretty*"). The album knocked SZA's *SOS* off the top after generating 94,000 album-equivalent units.

MAÑANA SERÁ BONITO also helped KAROL G to set new records for the **most simultaneous entries on the US singles chart by a female Latin artist** – 11, also on 11 Mar – and the **most streamed Latin album on Spotify in 24 hours (female)**. Its 17 tracks attracted in excess of 32 million plays on 24 Feb 2023.

Fastest average time to solve a 3x3x3 rotating puzzle cube
Yiheng Wang (CHN) cracked five puzzle cubes in an average time of 4.69 sec on 12 Mar 2023 at the Yong Jun KL Speedcubing event in Kuala Lumpur, Malaysia. His fastest and slowest solves – 3.90 and 6.16 sec – were excluded from the average, as is standard. Yiheng beat the previous record of 4.86 sec, which had been shared by Max Park and Tymon Kolasiński (*see p.86*.)

Farthest ice swim
On 12 Mar 2023, Krzysztof Gajewski (POL) swam 5 km (3.1 mi) in a lake at Kopalnia Wrocław near Paniowice, Poland. His icy dip in sub-5°C (41°F) water lasted 1 hr 24 min 43 sec. On the same day, Krzysztof's compatriot Marcin Szarpak (*see also p.123*) completed the **fastest one-mile ice swim**: 19 min 57 sec, in Kąpielisko Skałka, Świętochłowice, Poland. Both records were ratified by the International Ice Swimming Association.

Most diamonds set on a pendant
Shiv Narayan Jewellers (IND) fashioned a miniature sculpture of Lord Ganesha embellished with 11,472 diamonds in Hyderabad, Telangana, India. It also boasts ruby and emerald florets. The lavish piece of jewellery was assessed on 13 Mar 2023.

Longest lanyard
On 17 Mar 2023, a lanyard measuring 3.78 km (2.34 mi) was unfurled at Anfield Stadium in Liverpool, UK. It was produced by the Hidden Disabilities Sunflower scheme (UK) as part of their mission to improve awareness of disabilities that may not always be visible. Their lanyard – which was long enough to wrap around the arena 10 times – broke a record by the Hong Kong Girl Guides' Association that had stood for 23 years.

Longest career as administrative assistant to the same person
Maureen Chant had been working for Jim Pattison (both CAN) of The Jim Pattison Group for 59 years 193 days, as of 15 Mar 2023. Maureen started working as a switchboard operator before Jim saw her practising his speeches and hired her as an administrative assistant. Fifty-nine years later, and they are still working together.

INDEX

CONSULTANTS

Each year, we collaborate with dozens of experts who intimately know their specialist subjects. New recruits who worked on *GWR 2024* excel in everything from mermaids, tall ships, siege warfare and pirates to manga and anime, theatrical props, comedy and miniature golf, to name just a few. For a full list, visit www.guinnessworldrecords.com/records/partners.

David Fischer has been GWR's senior US sports consultant since 2006. He has written for *The New York Times* and *Sports Illustrated for Kids*, and has worked at *Sports Illustrated*, *The National Sports Daily* and NBC Sports. David has authored *Tom Brady: A Celebration of Greatness on the Gridiron* (2021), *The New York Yankees of the 1950s: Mantle, Stengel, Berra, and a Decade of Dominance* (2019) and *The Super Bowl: The First Fifty Years of America's Greatest Game* (2015).

Monica Hanna is an Egyptologist and currently an associate professor and acting dean of the College of Archaeology and Cultural Heritage at the Arab Academy for Science, Technology and Maritime Transport in Aswan, Egypt. There, she has founded a BA programme specializing in Archaeology and Cultural Heritage. Her recent research focuses on decolonizing archaeology, repatriation, public accessibility to archaeology and digital humanities.

Tom Beckerlegge is an award-winning writer whose books have been translated around the world. He is also GWR's lead sports consultant, updating hundreds of new records every year across athletic disciplines and liaising with sporting federations to keep abreast of the latest stories. This year has seen him learning more about Canadian football, Telemark skiing and the curious nature of the 1950 FIFA World Cup.

Richard Gottfried has played minigolf since he was a child and from 2006 has blogged about his travels (with his wife, Emily) to more than 900 minigolf courses. He has won multiple titles as a player on the UK tournament circuit and has competed in international championships in Finland, Sweden and the USA. An avid collector of minigolf items and ephemera, he has built up a large archive and collection in the Crazy Golf Museum. Learn more at **hamandeggerfiles.blogspot.com.**

Vanessa Heggie is an Associate Professor in the History of Science and Medicine at the Institute of Applied Health Research at the University of Birmingham, specializing in the period 1800–2000. She has published articles on nursing, public health and medical advances in sport and adventure. Her books include *A History of British Sports Medicine* (2011) and *Higher and Colder: A History of Extreme Physiology and Exploration* (2019).

Bruce Dessau is a comedy journalist and arts critic, and the chief comedy critic of London's *Evening Standard*. He is the editor of the comedy website Beyond the Joke, co-editor of *The Best British Stand-up and Comedy Routines*, and author of *Beyond a Joke: Inside the Dark World of Stand-Up Comedy* (2011) and *The Bluffer's Guide to Stand-Up Comedy* (2014). He has also written biographies of major comedic figures such as Rowan Atkinson.

R G Grant is a historian who has published some 20 books for adults, as well as writing numerous children's history titles and contributing to many multi-author works. His best-sellers include *Flight: 100 Years of Aviation* and *World War I: The Definitive Visual Guide*. His most recent work was the highly praised *Sentinels of the Sea*, an illustrated history of lighthouses, which came in useful for the pharological feature in this edition.

Andrea Horbinski holds a PhD in modern Japanese history with a designated emphasis in new media. Her book manuscript, *Manga's Global Century*, is a history of Japanese comics from 1905 to 1989. She has discussed anime, manga, fandom and Japanese history at conventions and conferences and has published many articles on these topics. She currently serves as the submissions editor for *Mechademia: Second Arc* and on the board of *The Journal of Anime and Manga Studies*.

Jay Duckworth has over 40 years' experience in Broadway and Off-Broadway shows as a props artisan and designer. His resumé includes *Hamilton, Fun Home, Road Show, Here Lies Love, Latin History for Morons, For Colored Girls Who Have Considered Suicide/When the Rainbow is Enuf* and NYC's *Shakespeare in the Park* from his decade-long residency at The Public Theater. Jay teaches at Colorado State University and Pace University. Learn more about him at **proptologist.com.**

Ambrose Greenway, an independent member of the House of Lords since 1975, specializes in maritime affairs and is currently joint chairman of the All-Party Parliamentary Ports & Maritime Group. He is an Elder Brother of Trinity House, and past appointments have included President of Cruise Europe and The World Ship Society, and Chairman of The Marine Society and The World Ship Trust. Publications include works on ferries, cargo liners and Soviet merchant ships.

Ceri Houlbrook is a Folklore and History Lecturer at the University of Hertfordshire, UK, having attained her doctorate in Archaeology on the (rather niche) subject of British and Irish coin-trees. She is a committee member of the Folklore Society and is a published author on popular beliefs and ritual practices, past and present. Ceri loves teaching the curious, trying new foods in the name of folklore, and diving deep into the research rabbit-hole.

To help investigate and verify records across a broad spectrum of disciplines, GWR also works with clubs, institutions and federations. A few that assisted with this edition are included here. For a full list, visit www.guinnessworldrecords.com/records/partners.

8000ers.com
Eberhard Jurgalski has developed the system of "Elevation Equality", a method of classifying mountain ranges and peaks. His website has become the main source of altitude statistics for the Himalayas and Karakoram ranges.

American Coaster Enthusiasts
Founded in 1978, ACE is a non-profit, volunteer organization dedicated to the preservation and appreciation of rollercoasters. ACE's 7,000 worldwide members receive exclusive park benefits, newsletters and the opportunity to attend tours at parks. ACE hosts more than 75 national and regional coaster events across North America every year.

Behind the Stunts
Behind the Stunts is an audio and video archive of Q&As and deep-dives into action on film and TV compiled by movie-stunts historian Jon Auty, host of the podcast and YouTube channel *Behind the Stunts*. He is the author of the book *Jump Rocky Jump* (2019), about the life and times of legendary stuntman Rocky Taylor. Auty has also penned the soon-to-be-released *Stunts, Bond Stunts* – the definitive history of stunts in the *James Bond* film franchise.

European Coaster Club
The ECC was founded by GWR's chief rollercoaster consultant Justin Garvanovic in 1996, initially drawing its members from the readership of his *First Drop* magazine. It has grown to become a popular social club for fans of coasters and theme parks, with thousands of members and many corporate partners.

Fédération Internationale des Sociétés Magiques
FISM was created in 1948 and today consists of 112 magic societies that represent over 80,000 magicians from more than 49 countries. Headquartered in Lausanne, Switzerland, the board (President Andréa Baioni and two Vice Presidents, Peter Din and Satoru Yamamoto) supervises six continental championships and manages the triannual FISM World Championship of Magic, at which the best 150 magicians compete to become the World Champion of Magic.

Gerontology Research Group
Established in 1990, the GRG's mission is to slow and ultimately reverse ageing via the application and sharing of scientific knowledge. It also keeps the largest database of supercentenarians (i.e., people aged over 110), which is managed by GWR's senior gerontology consultant Robert Young.

International Federation of Robotics
The IFR is the voice of robotics in the world, founded as a non-profit by robotics organizations from over 20 countries in 1987 at the 17th International Symposium on Robotics. The IFR's purpose is to promote and strengthen the robotics industry worldwide, and to raise public awareness about robotics technologies.

International Ice Swimming Association
Founded by Ram Barkai, the IISA was established in 2009 with a vision to formalize swimming in icy water – i.e., below a threshold of 5°C (41°F). It has put in place rules to allow for maximum safety measures, and to regulate swim integrity in terms of distance, time and conditions. The IISA also oversees the International Ice Swimming Championships.

International Slackline Association
The mission of the ISA is to support and develop slackline communities of all sizes, as well as providing governance for slacklining as a competitive sport.

Ocean Rowing Society International
The ORSI was established in 1983 by Kenneth F Crutchlow and Peter Bird, later joined by Tom Lynch and Tatiana Rezvaya-Crutchlow. The organization documents all attempts to row the world's oceans and major bodies of water, and classifies, verifies and adjudicates ocean-rowing achievements.

Parrot Analytics
Parrot Analytics is the leading global content demand analytics company for the modern multi-platform TV business. It tracks more than 1.5 billion daily expressions of demand in over 100 languages and 200 countries.

Polar Expeditions Classification Scheme
PECS is a grading and labelling system for extended, unmotorized polar journeys that is overseen by a committee of polar-expedition specialists, managed by Eric Philips. Polar regions, modes of travel, routes and forms of aid are defined under the scheme, giving expeditioners guidance on how to classify, promote and immortalize their journeys.

Sail Training International
Sail Training International is the organizer of The Tall Ships Races and a registered charity established to develop and educate young people – regardless of nationality, culture, religion, gender or social background – through sail-training experience. Sail Training International works with the world's sail-training Tall Ships and National Sail Training Organisations to help young people grow in self-confidence, develop effective communication and learn new life skills. They are also the world's leading provider of Tall Ships events.

The Malacological Society of London
This UK-based institution is dedicated to the advancement of research and education on molluscs. It is an international organization and welcomes as members all who are interested in the scientific study of molluscs. The Society was founded in 1893, with the objectives "to advance education, research and learning for the public benefit in the study of Mollusca from both pure and applied aspects". It also publishes the *Journal of Molluscan Studies*. The Society's current president is Jon Ablett.

Union Internationale de la Marionnette
UNIMA is a UNESCO-affiliated NGO and the oldest international theatre organization, created in 1929. Its global members contribute to the development of the puppetry arts. Present in more than 90 countries, UNIMA is a platform for exchange and collaboration between people who practise puppetry, work in the field, or who are passionate about the art form. UNIMA supports meetings, conferences, festivals, exchanges and collaborations, provides opportunities to co-operate with people in all areas of puppetry, and supports collecting and distributing information and publications about research, courses and workshops.

World Cube Association
The WCA governs competitions for mechanical puzzles that are operated by twisting groups of pieces, such as the Rubik's Cube. Its mission is to have more competitions in more countries, all participating under fair and equal conditions.

World Flying Disc Federation
The WFDF is the international sports federation responsible for governance of flying-disc (Frisbee) sports, including Ultimate, Beach Ultimate, Disc Golf, Freestyle, Guts and individual events. It comprises 103 member associations, which represent flying-disc sports and their athletes in more than 100 countries.

World Minigolf Sport Federation
The WMF is the umbrella organization of minigolf sport associations worldwide, with continental federations on five continents. Founded in 1980, WMF is a member of GAISF (Global Association of International Sports Federations) and AIMS (Alliance of Independent Recognized Members of Sport), representing 65 national associations and more than 38,000 registered players. WMF members organize 1,500+ tournaments annually.

World Meteorological Organization
Based in Geneva, Switzerland, this UN body is the global authority on weather, climatology and hydrology, for both the purposes of science and advising policy. Dr Randall Cerveny is a President's Professor in Geographical Sciences who specializes in weather and climate. He has held the position of Rapporteur of Weather and Climate Extremes for the WMO since 2007.

World Ultracycling Association
WUCA is a non-profit organization dedicated to supporting ultracycling across the world. It holds the largest repository of cycling records for all bike types, and certifies successful rides for its members.

Alan Jamieson is the founding Director of the Minderoo-UWA Deep Sea Research Centre at The University of Western Australia. He has over 22 years' experience in deep-sea science, technology and exploration. A global authority on the hadal zone, he has published more than 125 scientific papers, participated in nearly 70 expeditions, and pioneered the design of full-ocean-depth landers that have been deployed in excess of 500 times in the world's deepest trenches.

Aimee Schofield is an independent researcher and teacher. She gained a PhD from the University of Manchester in 2014 in Classics and Ancient History, focusing on ancient Greek catapult technology. She was an Honorary Visiting Fellow at the University of Leicester until 2020. Her research centres on ancient siege warfare, with particular interests in ancient military technology as well as the role that women played in Greek and Roman warfare.

Colin Stuart is a multi-award-winning astronomy author, writer and speaker. His 20 books have sold over 400,000 copies worldwide and have been translated into 23 languages. He's also written more than 250 popular-science articles for publications including *The Guardian*, *New Scientist* and *The Wall Street Journal*, as well as for the European Space Agency. In recognition of his efforts to popularize astronomy, the asteroid 15347 Colinstuart is named after him.

Emily Lakdawalla is a science communicator, author and educator who specializes in planetary science and space exploration. She has contributed to Planetary Society publications since 2002, and is an associate editor for *Sky & Telescope*. Her 2018 book, *The Design and Engineering of Curiosity*, is due to be followed up by the companion volume, *Curiosity and Its Science Mission: A Mars Rover Goes to Work*. Emily also has an asteroid named after her: 274860 Emilylakdawalla.

Karl P N Shuker has a PhD in Zoology and Comparative Physiology from the University of Birmingham, UK, and is a Scientific Fellow of the Zoological Society of London, a Fellow of the Royal Entomological Society and a Member of The Society of Authors. He has penned 25 books as well as hundreds of articles covering many aspects of natural history. Karl's work has an emphasis on anomalous animals, including new, rediscovered and unrecognized species.

Matthew White is GWR's music, cricket and tennis consultant. Additionally, between 2009 and 2023, he pored over more than 60,000 published records as proofreader for the world's **best-selling annual**. After training as a journalist, Matthew landed his dream job as a member of the team that produced the final four editions of the *Guinness Book of British Hit Singles & Albums*, and he has also worked on projects for the likes of EMI, Universal Music Group and the Official UK Charts Company.

Sarah Peverley is an academic, writer and broadcaster. She is Professor of English at the University of Liverpool, where her research focuses on medieval culture, early books, and the history of mermaids in literature, art and world mythologies. As an expert on the Middle Ages and mythical creatures, Sarah regularly contributes to TV and radio broadcasts and writes for the press. She is one of BBC Radio 3's New Generation Thinkers and a Fellow of the Royal Historical Society.

Rebecca Simon is a historian of early modern piracy, Colonial America, the Atlantic World and maritime history. Rebecca has written numerous articles and two books: *Why We Love Pirates: The Hunt for Captain Kidd and How He Changed Piracy Forever* (2020) and *Pirate Queens: The Lives of Anne Bonny and Mary Read* (2022). She has also shared her expertise on numerous podcasts, such as *You're Dead to Me*, and pirate documentaries for Netflix and the History Channel.

Sam Willis is one of the UK's best-known historians. He has made more than 10 television series for the BBC and National Geographic, and has penned more than 15 books, many of them centring on maritime and naval history. Sam is also the presenter of two chart-topping history podcasts: *Histories of the Unexpected* and, for those interested in the history of the sea, *The Mariner's Mirror Podcast*.

Mara Reed is a graduate student in the Department of Earth and Planetary Science at the University of California, Berkeley, USA. As a teenager, she became hooked on "geyser gazing" and now channels that curiosity towards research. Her studies focus on the factors that influence changes in geyser eruption intervals that often integrate observations from the geyser enthusiast community. Mara also serves as a scientific advisor for **geysertimes.org**.

Chris Stokes is a former President of the British Branch of the International Glaciological Society and now is a professor at Durham University, UK. His expertise lies in glaciers and their response to climate change, and his research spans from monitoring small mountain glaciers over the last few decades to large-scale reconstructions of continental ice sheets over millennia. In the last 20 years, Chris has published more than 140 scientific papers and contributed to several books.

Wesley Yin-Poole is a veteran journalist who has worked on a long list of videogame websites that includes Eurogamer, Digital Foundry and VideoGamer.com. He plays *FIFA*, *Call of Duty* and almost all the games BioWare and Bethesda release. But his real love is fighting games, especially Capcom's *Street Fighter* and NetherRealm's *Mortal Kombat*. When not playing *Ultimate Team* or *Warzone*, he can be found furiously practising frame-perfect combos with his favourite fighter-game character, Guile!

Thanks also to...
American Coaster Enthusiasts (Derek Perry, Elizabeth Ringas); American Numismatic Society (Jesse Kraft); Mark Aston; Iain Baird; Victoria Bartels; Beard Team USA (Bryan Nelson); beforesandafters (Ian Failes); Bellrock.org.uk (David Taylor); Benetech (Michael Johnson, Charles LaPierre); Meg Bernstein; Sabina Berretta; Brickset (Huw Millington); British Stunt Register (Kelly Fletcher); Rosalind Brown-Grant; Bucketlist.net (Miika Hakala); Melissa Chadderton; Andy Chipling; Ben Clark; Cole Conway; Mildred Cookson; Kate Corry; Cosmic Shambles Network (Trent Burton); Martyn Davis; Dawbell (Jordan Shepley); Nicolai Lynge Drost; Wade Eastwood; Edinburgh Festival Fringe (Niki Boyle); Mohammed Ezkat; Aleatha Ezra; Basil Fairston; Steve Feltham; Peter Finer; Florida Atlantic University (Chelsea Bennice); Stephen Follows; Ghost Club (Alan Murdie, Rosie O'Carroll); Victoria Grimsell; Thaneswar Guragai; Carolyn Harris; Carsten Heer; Sven Herrmann; Hop King (Ben Hopkinson); Howard League for Penal Reform (Rob Preece); Robin Ince; International Climbing and Mountaineering Federation, UIAA (Rafael Jensen, Stephanie Stettbacher); MJ Johnson; Doug Jones; Anna King; Christy Kreisa (GRACE - LA, on behalf of Taurus World Stunt Awards); Matt Lodder; Monty Lord; Adam Lucas; Gabriel Margolis; Alessandro Mariani; Rick Mayston; Jonathan McDowell; Heather McFarland; Stuart McKie; Alejandro Mirabal; Mullet Fest (Melinda Murray); Dacian Muntean; Alan Murray; NASA (Fred Calef, Hallie Gengl, Andrew Good, Tammy Lee Long); National Cave and Karst Research Institute (George Veni); National Geospatial-Intelligence Agency: List of Lights, Radio Aids and Fog Signals (Robbin H Brooks); National Motor Museum (Patrick Collins, Jon Murden, Anna-Marie O'Connor); NBC Universal (Shannon Lee); Laura Neves; NOAA (Monica Allen, Laura Chaibongsai, Joe Cione, Emily Crum, Aurora Elmore, Gregory Foltz, Jenn Virskus); Octonation (Warren Carlyle); Optical Oceanography Laboratory, University of South Florida (Chuanmin Hu); Mark O'Shea; Caroline Overy; Merav Ozair; Schwan, Miki and Max Park; Richard Parks; Parrot Analytics (Samuel Stadler); Ellen Peltz; Antoine Potten; Propstore (Brandon Allinger, Felicity Beardshaw, Tim Lawes); Isis Prummel; Anders Rhodin; Sam Roberts; Anna Rolls; Royal Armouries (Maeve Anderson, Eleanor Wilkinson-Keys); Royal Caribbean International (Miriam Mortimer); Juan Sanchez; Joel Saunders; Dan Schreiber; Michael Scott (aka Props to History); Nancy Segal; Will Shortz; Roland Sigrist; Tina Smart; Stanley Stepanic; The Broadway League (Scalla Jakso); The IRONMAN® Group (Colby Gornewicz); The Jim Henson Company (Karen Falk, Nicole Goldman); The Numbers (Bruce Nash); Chris Thompson; Roger Tomlin; Allen Tran; Ken Trethewey; UK & International Timing Adjudication (Trevor Duckworth, Malcolm Pitwood); UK Handlebar Club (Rod Littlewood); UNIMA (Steve Abrams, Richard Bradshaw, Kathy Foley, Karen Smith, Nancy Staub); University of Bologna (Jo Hilaire Agnes De Waele); University of Bristol (Dr Ben Moon); University of Lund (Eric Warrant); University of Reading (Paul Williams); Karin Rabe Vance; Richard Vranch; Georg Wessels; Kieran Wilson; Wonderville (Dickson Cossar, Bailey Harris-Kelly, Sean Sweeney); Greg Woolf; World Freestyle Football Association (Daniel Wood); World Jigsaw Puzzle Federation (Alfonso Alvarez-Ossorio); World Sailing Speed Record Council (John Reed); World Sport Stacking Association (Lisa Berman); Xpogo (Will Weiner); John Zabrucky

ACKNOWLEDGEMENTS

SVP Global Publishing
Nadine Causey

Editor-in-Chief
Craig Glenday

Managing Editor
Adam Millward

Senior Editor
Ben Hollingum

Junior Editor
Aishwarya Khokle

Layout Editors
Tom Beckerlegge, Rob Dimery

**Proofreading
& Fact-Checking**
Matthew White

Picture Editors
Alice Jessop, Abby Taylor

**Director of Publishing
& Book Production**
Jane Boatfield

**Production & Distribution
Director**
Patricia Magill

**Production & Distribution
Manager**
Thomas McCurdy

Talent Researcher
Charlie Anderson

Design
Paul Wylie-Deacon,
Rob Wilson at 55design.co.uk

Cover Design
Rod Hunt

Indexer
Marie Lorimer

**Head of Commissioned
Content**
Michael Whitty

Original Photography
Brien Adams, Mustapha Azab,
Abdellah Azizi, Ken Blaze,
Ian Bowkett, Jon Enoch,
Brittany Hirst, Paul Michael
Hughes, Erik Isakson,
Adam Kenna, Manuel
Orts Lloris, Scott Lloyd,
Zach Machen, Alexandre
Montesinos, Abigail Mook,
Tony Noel, Wade Payne,
Rod Penn, Cameron Spooner,
Sammy Tillery

Original Artwork
Joanna Butler, Alex Pang,
The Maltings Partnership

Production Consultants
Karolina Kelc, Kevin Sarney,
Maximilian Schonlau

Printing & Binding
MOHN Media Mohndruck
GmbH, Gütersloh, Germany

Global Marketing Director
Nicholas Brookes

**Head of Publishing & Brand
Communications
(UK & International)**
Amber-Georgina Maskell

**PR Manager
(UK & International)**
Madalyn Bielfeld

**PR Executive
(UK & International)**
Alina Polianskaya

**Marketing Executive
(UK & International)**
Nicole Dyer-Rainford

**Senior Content Manager
(UK & International)**
Eleonora Pilastro

**Senior PR Manager
(USA & Canada)**
Amanda Marcus

Senior PR Manager (LATAM)
Alice Pagán

PR Executive (Americas)
Kylie Galloway

**Content Manager
(USA & Canada)**
Aliciamarie Rodriguez

Content Manager (LATAM)
Luisa Sánchez

Global Sales Director
Joel Smith

Senior Key Account Manager
Mavis Sarfo

International Sales Manager
Aliona Ladus

Reprographics
Resmiye Kahraman and Louise
Pinnock at Born Group

British Library Cataloguing-in-publication data: a catalogue
record for this book is available from the British Library

UK: 978-1-913484-38-5
US: 978-1-913484-37-8
CAN: 978-1-913484-42-2
US PB: 978-1-913484-43-9
Middle East: 978-1-913484-39-2
Australia: 978-1-913484-40-8

Records are made to be broken – indeed, it is one of the key
criteria for a record category – so if you find a record that you
think you can beat, tell us about it by making a record claim.
Always contact us before making a record attempt.

Sustainability
At Guinness World Records, we continue to run our business
in the most sustainable, environmentally conscious way we
can. As part of that commitment, the pages of this book are
printed on a fully recycled paper, made of 100% reclaimed
paper and post-consumer de-inked pulp.
No chlorine bleaching is used in the
paper production process. It has been
awarded the Blue Angel and EU Ecolabel
recognition.

This paper is produced at the Steinbeis
Papier mill in Germany, which is one of
the most energy-efficient and low-emission
paper mills in Europe. The mill is focused on ecological
balance throughout the production process – from the
regional procurement of reclaimed paper as a raw material,
to production with an almost entirely
closed energy and water cycle.

GWR is committed to ethical and
responsible sourcing of paper, as well
as ink. We also work to ensure that all
our supply-chain partners meet the
highest international standards for
sustainable production and energy
management. For more information,
please contact us.

Thanks to innovative use of combined heat and power
technology, up to 52% less CO_2 was emitted in printing this
product when compared with conventional energy use.

GWR has a very thorough accreditation system for records
verification. However, while every effort is made to ensure
accuracy, GWR cannot be held responsible for any errors
contained in this work. Feedback from our readers on any
point of accuracy is always welcomed.

GWR uses metric and imperial measurements. Exceptions are
made for some scientific data where metric measurements
are universally accepted, and some sports data. Where a
specific date is given, the exchange rate is calculated
according to the currency values at the time. Where only
a year date is given, the exchange rate is calculated from
31 Dec of that year.

Appropriate advice should always be taken when attempting
to break or set records. Participants undertake records
entirely at their own risk. GWR has complete discretion
over whether or not to include any record attempt in any of its
publications. Being a GWR record holder does not guarantee
you a place in any Guinness World Records publication.

Printed in Germany

Registered address: Ground Floor,
The Rookery, 2 Dyott Street,
London, WC1A 1DE

**OFFICIALLY
AMAZING**

Global President
Alistair Richards

Governance
Alison Ozanne

Global Finance: Elizabeth Bishop,
Jess Blake, Arianna Cracco, Lisa Gibbs,
Kimberley Jones, Jacob Moss, Bhavik
Patel, Ysanne Rogers, Andrew Wood

**Business Partnering & Product
Marketing:** Sara Kali, Maryana Lovell,
Aled Mann, Blair Rankin, Lorenzo Di
Sciullo, Scott Shore

Global Legal: Mathew Alderson,
Greyson Huang, Matthew Knight,
Raymond Marshall, Maria Popo,
Jiayi Teng

IT & Operations (Global)
Rob Howe

Digital Technology & IT: Mike Emmott,
Adeyinka Folorunso, Diogo Coito
Gomes, Veronica Irons, Sohail Malik,
Benjamin McLean, Ajoke Oritu, Cenk
Selim, Roelien Viljoen, Alex Waldu

Central Records Services
Mark McKinley

Record Content Support: Lewis
Blakeman, Amelis Escalante, Clea
Lime, Will Munford, Mariana Sinotti,
Dave Wilson, Melissa Wooton

Records Curation Team: Nana Asante,
Olly de Boer, Megan Bruce, Dominic
Heater, Hadiqa Javed, Esther Mann,
Will Sinden, Luke Wakeham

Global People & Culture
Stephanie Lunn

London: Jackie Angus, Isabelle
Fanshawe, Gurpreet Kaur, Monika Tilani

Americas: Rachel Gluck,
Jennifer Olson

China: Crystal Xu, Nina Zhou

Japan: Emiko Yamamoto

UAE: Monisha Bimal

Brand & Digital
Katie Forde

**Brand Strategy, Communications
& Design:** Momoko Cunneen,
Juliet Dawson, Rebecca Fisher,
Lucy Hunter, Doug Male

Social Media: Josephine Boye,
Lisha Howen, Dominic Punt,
Dan Thorne

Website Content: Sanj Atwal,
Vassi Bakogianni, Vicki Newman

GWR Studios: Karen Gilchrist,
Kathryn Hubbard

**Content Production
& Licensing:** Jesse Hargrave,
Aisheshek Magauina, Fran
Morales, Matthew Musson,
Joseph O'Neil, Catherine Pearce,
Spoorthy Prakash, Emma Salt,
Michael Whitty

Global Consultancies
Marco Frigatti

Event Production: Paul O'Neill,
Alan Pixsley

Global Demand Generation:
Angelique Begarin, Melissa Brown

Beijing Consultancy
Charles Wharton

Content Licensing: Chloe Liu

Editorial: Angela Wu

Brand Communications: Echo Zhan,
Yvonne Zhang

Commercial Account Services:
Catherine Gao, Xiaona Liu, Tina
Ran, Amelia Wang, Elaine Wang,
Paige Wu

Commercial Marketing: Theresa Gao,
Lorraine Lin

Events Production: Fay Jiang

Records Management: Ted Li,
Vanessa Tao, Alicia Zhao, Sibyl Zou

Dubai Consultancy
Talal Omar

Commercial Account Services: Sara
Abu-Saad, Naser Batat, Mohammad
Kiswani, Kamel Yassin

Commercial Marketing: Shaddy Gaad

Brand & Content Marketing:
Mohamad Kaddoura, Alaa Omari

Event Production: Daniel Hickson

PR: Hassan Alibrahim

Records Management: Sarah Alkholb,
Hani Gharamah, Reem Al Ghussain,
Karen Hamzeh

London Consultancy
Sam Prosser

Commercial Account Services:
Nick Adams, Monika Drobina, Sirali
Gandhi, Shanaye Howe, Nick Hume,
Nikhil Shukla, Lucia Sinigagliesi,
Nataliia Solovei

Event Production: Fiona
Gruchy-Craven

Commercial Marketing: Amina
Addow, William Baxter-Hughes

Records Management: Andrew
Fanning, Apekshita Kadam,
Christopher Lynch, Francesca Raggi

Americas Consultancy
Carlos Martinez

Commercial Account Services:
Mackenzie Berry, Brittany Carpenter,
Carolina Guanabara, Ralph Hannah,
Kim Partrick, Michelle Santucci,
Joana Weiss

Commercial Marketing: Alexia
Argeros, Nicole Pando, Ana Rahlves

Records Management: Raquel Assis,
Maddison Kulish, Alba (Niky) Pauli,
Callie Smith, Carlos Tapia Rojas

Tokyo Consultancy
Kaoru Ishikawa

Brand Communications: Kazami
Kamioka, Masakazu Senda

Commercial Account Services:
Minami Ito, Wei Liang, Takuro
Maruyama, Yumiko Nakagawa,
Nana Nguyen, Yuki Sakamoto,
Masamichi Yazaki

Commercial Marketing: Hiroyuki
Tanaka, Eri Yuhira

Event Production: Yuki Uebo

Records Management: Fumika
Fujibuchi, Aki Ichikawa, Mai McMillan,
Momoko Omori, Naomi-Emily Sakai,
Kio Shijiki, Lala Teranishi, Aynee
Toorabally, Kayo Ueda

Picture credits

1 Atlantis Dubai; **2** Shutterstock; **4 (UK)** Richard Poynter; **6 (UK)** BBC, GWR; **7 (UK)** Graeme Robertson; **4 (US/CAN)** Zachary Fu & Dustin Ong, Kristen Stephenson/GWR; **6 (US/CAN)** Brittany Hirst/GWR, Lee Gumbs/SILLAR Management, Jon Enoch/GWR; **7 (US/CAN)** Aaron Snaiderman, Kevin Scott Ramos/GWR; **5 (AUS/NZ)** Lisa Burd/Stuff, Shutterstock; **6 (AUS/NZ)** Romina Amato/Red Bull Content Pool; **7 (AUS/NZ)** Adam Kenna/GWR; **4 (MENA)** Ammar Abd Rabbo/ABACAPRESS.COM; **9** Glenn Gratton/GWR; **10** Shutterstock, Kat Ku/GWR, Paul Michael Hughes/GWR; **11** GWR; **12** Jess Burges Kerikeri; **13** Rachael Woosley, Abby Taylor, Alamy; **14** Thomas Pesquet/ ESA/NASA, Getty Images; **15** Shutterstock; **16** Shutterstock; **17** The Maltings Partnership/www.maltingspartnership.com; **18** Shutterstock, Getty Images; **19** Tom St George, Shutterstock; **20** Alamy, Shutterstock; **21** Shutterstock, Caroline Power; **22** Getty Images, Shutterstock, Wilson Bentley, Alamy, Konrad Steffen/University of Colorado Boulder, Dr Juerg Alean/Science Photo Library; **23** Alamy, BBC; **24** Getty Images, Science Photo Library, Alamy, Shutterstock; **25** Getty Images, Shutterstock; **26** Thea Magerand, D. V. Palcu, Arbindra Khadka/National Geographic, NOAA, Shutterstock; **27** Kenneth Libbrecht, Getty Images; **28** Kip Evans Photography, Kip Evans Photography, OAR/National Undersea Research Program (NURP); **29** Alamy, OAR/National Undersea Research Program (NURP); **30** naturepl.com, Matt Testoni, Birch Aquarium at Scripps Institution of Oceanography; **31** Alamy; **32** Alex Pang, Alamy, naturepl.com; **33** Getty Images; **34** Shutterstock, naturepl.com, Ganesh Chowdhury/Sanctuary Asia; **35** Suthep Kritsanavarin, Imago Images, Sinsamout Ounboundisane; **36** Getty Images, Alamy; **37** Getty Images, Shutterstock; **38** Alamy, naturepl.com, Shutterstock; **39** naturepl.com, Shutterstock; **40** Alamy; **41** Andrei Savitsky, Getty Images, Michael Wolf, MBARI, Jérôme Mallefet, Alamy; **42** Dr Alan Jamieson, naturepl.com, NOAA, Alamy; **43** Alamy, Dr Alan Jamieson; **44** Shutterstock, Schmidt Ocean Institute, Turbosquid; **45** Shutterstock, Turbosquid; **46** Shedd Aquarium/Brenna Hernandez, Getty Images, Shutterstock, Gomes-Pereira *et al*; **47** Alamy, Shutterstock; **48** Cats Protection, Shutterstock, Brittany Hirst/GWR, Abigail Mook/GWR; **49** Brien Adams/GWR; **50** Ian Witlen/Red Bull Content Pool; **51** Getty Images, Shutterstock; **52** Paul Michael Hughes/GWR; **53** Sue Ryder/SWNS; **54** Illustration by Joanna Butler BA(Hons) (www.medical-artist.com), Shutterstock; **55** Science Photo Library, Science Photo Library; **56** Yoni Brook, Shutterstock, Lingkopings Parachute Club/Joppe de Kort, Alamy; **57** Scott Lloyd/GWR, Getty Images; **58** Alamy, GWR, Paul Michael Hughes/GWR, Erik Isakson/GWR, Teresa Slosar; **59** Wade Payne/GWR, Ken Blaze/GWR; **60** Ranald Mackechnie/GWR, Alamy; **61** Zach Machen/GWR, Paul Michael Hughes/GWR, Alamy, Getty Images; **62** Christy Jordan, Mustapha Azab/GWR, Riccardo Cellere/GWR, Erol Gurian/GWR, Trevor Johns, Jean-François Rioux/GWR, Paul Michael Hughes/GWR, Getty Images; **63** Mustapha Azab/GWR; **64** Shutterstock, GWR; **65** Abdellah Azizi/GWR, Simon Ashton/dmg media licensing; **66** Allison V. Smith/Guardian/eyevine, Shutterstock; **67** Jose Garcia (Garciartist) and Griffith University, Tim Maloney; **68** Sammy Tillery/GWR, Alberto Bernasconi/GWR; **69** Banijay/Mediaset; **70** John Wright/GWR, Henny Boogert; **71** Hungry Bear Media, wimhofmethod.com; **72–73** Cameron Spooner/GWR; **74** Turbosquid/Shutterstock/Gian Marco Rizzo, Getty Images, Shutterstock; **75** Shutterstock; **76** Edwin Koo/GWR, Richard Bradbury/GWR, Paul Michael Hughes/GWR; **77** Ioannis Vlachiotis; **78** Edwin Koo/GWR, Reuters; **79** MUSAN/Jason deCaires Taylor, MUSAN/Costas Constantinou; **80** Disney, Alamy, Sony Pictures; **82** Alamy, Shutterstock, Getty Images, Dick Rutan and Jeanna Yeager; **83** Shutterstock; **84** Xpogo, GWR, Ranald Mackechnie/GWR, Xpogo; **85** Maryna Cotton & Sarel van Staden, Julie Kerbel, Ian Bowkett; **86** Tony Fisher Puzzles, Moses Latigo Odida; **87** Artur Frost/Technische Universität Braunschweig, Philipp Carl Riedl/Red Bull Content Pool, Joerg Mitter/Red Bull Content Pool, Tomislav Moze/Red Bull Content Pool; **88** Shutterstock, Alamy, James Weber; **89** Robert Engelbrecht, Robert Engelbrecht, Nancy Thornton, Shutterstock; **90** Yash Moradiya; **91** Manuel Orts Lloris/GWR; **92** Dong Jianwen, Rod Penn/GWR; **93** Alamy, Elizabeth Nida Photography; **94** Shutterstock, Maryna Cotton & Sarel van Staden; **95** Nick DiGiovanni, Cheryl Clegg; **96** Shutterstock, Paul Michael Hughes/GWR, Maryna Cotton & Sarel van Staden, Ranald Mackechnie/GWR; **98** Richard Bailey; **99** Shutterstock, Adam Kenna/GWR; **102** Shutterstock, Busy Beaver Button Museum, Brien Adams/GWR; **105** Alberto Bernasconi/GWR; **106** James Dadzitis/SWNS; **108** Paul Michael Hughes/GWR; **111** Heritage Auctions, Alexandre Montesinos/GWR; **113** Alamy, Shutterstock; **114** Steve Benjamin/The Lewis Pugh Foundation; **115** Kelvin Trautman/The Lewis Pugh Foundation; **116** Alex Pang, The Five Deeps Expedition; **117** The Five Deeps Expedition; **118** Amrit Ale, Iamthanes; **119** Shutterstock; **120** Lat35, Corrina Ridgeway; **121** Danya Schwertfeger, Shutterstock; **122** Juan Enis, Deja Vu/Maggie Jackson, Shawn Heinrichs, Gabriel Leiva; **123** Marketing Adventures, Olga Ryngert-Yüjnaya/SAMOENS, Alamy, Shutterstock, Getty Images; **124** Arik Thormahlen, Richard Bradbury/GWR, Pemba Sherpa/Red Bull Content Pool; **125** Enrique Alvarez, Blue Origin, Atte Miettinen; **126** Alamy, Dick Rutan and Jeanna Yeager, Shutterstock, Getty Images; **127** Shutterstock; **128** Emirates Team New Zealand/James Somerset; **129** Benjamin Jordan & Lyndsay Nicole/Fly Monarca; **130** @slacklinepaysbasque, Chantal Grondin, Smiley Photography; **131** Quirin Herterich, Nicolas Baudier; **132** Maryna Cotton & Sarel van Staden, Ilaria Cariello Photography; **133** Jesse Major; **134** Ben Gibson/2023 HST Global Limited/Rocket Entertainment, Shutterstock, Alamy; **135** Shutterstock, Helen Maybanks/Disney; **136** Bob Marshall, Shutterstock; **137** Shutterstock; **138** Shutterstock, Alex Pang, Alamy; **139** Shutterstock; **140** Jean-Claude Golvin/Éditions Errance, Olaf Tausch, The Metropolitan Museum of Art, Shutterstock; **141** Science Photo Library, *The New York Times*, Shutterstock, Alamy; **142** Shutterstock, Alamy; **143** Getty Images, Alamy; **144** Disney/Jerry Bruckheimer Films/Infinitum Nihil/Alamy, Shutterstock; **145** Gregory Manchess, Getty Images, Alamy, Disney/Jim Henson Productions/Shutterstock; **146** Shutterstock, Alamy; **147** Shutterstock, Alamy; **148** Shutterstock, BBC, Alamy; **149** Shutterstock, Alamy; **150** Shutterstock, Alamy; **151** Shutterstock, Alamy, Lincoln Financial Foundation Collection, Roger Tomlin; **152** GWR, Alamy; **153** Netflix/Alamy; **154–155** Philipp Schmidli; **156** Fabian Oefner, Daimler AG; **157** Mercedes-Benz Group AG; **158** Shutterstock, Daniel Keating, Alamy; **159** Dreamstime.com, Alamy; **160** Getty Images, PoliMOVE, Porsche, Shutterstock; **161** Jorrit Lousberg/Light at Work Photography, Shutterstock; **162** USS *Gerald R. Ford* (CVN 78), Delphine Ménard, Allseas, Klaus Jordan, Boskalis; **163** Royal Caribbean, Royal Caribbean; **164** Svenska Ostindiska Companiet, Sail Training International, Getty Images; **165** Richard Sibley, Andre Marton Pedersen; **166** NASA/JPL-Caltech, NASA/ESA/CSA/STScI, Axiom Space; **167** NASA/Johns Hopkins APL, ASI/NASA, NASA/Johns Hopkins APL/Ed Whitman; **168** Justin Garvanovic; **170** ZARM/University of Bremen, NSO/AURA/NSF, ESRF/Stef Candé; **171** Jacqueline Ramseyer Orrell/SLAC National Accelerator Laboratory, Rubin Observatory/NSF/AURA, SLAC/Rubin Observatory, SAFRAN; **172** Shutterstock, Courtesy Saildrone and NOAA; **173** Kegan Sims/Agility Robotics, Oregon State University, Shutterstock; **174** Alamy, Shutterstock, SpaceX; **175** Shutterstock, Anderson Industries; **176** Shutterstock, @JohnPhotography, Getty Images; **177** Getty Images, Shutterstock; **178** 20th Century Studios, Mark Fellman/20th Century Studios/Disney; **179** Mark Fellman/20th Century Studios/Disney; **180** Alex Pang, Amblin/Universal Pictures/Shutterstock, Universal Pictures, Stan Winston Studio; **181** Stan Winston Studio; **182** Netflix/Alamy, Netflix/Shutterstock, HBO; **183** MGM/Universal Pictures/Alamy, Zed Jameson/BACKGRID, Splash News, Warner Bros./Alamy, Universal Pictures/Alamy; **184** John Zabrucky, Rock Island Auction Company, Shutterstock, Mark Cartwright, Alamy; **185** The Earl Hays Press, Tokyo National Museum, Shutterstock, Alamy, Bonhams; **186** HBO, Shutterstock, Netflix; **187** Warner Bros. TV/Alamy, StarPlus, Hajime Isayama, Kodansha/AOTF, HBO, Amazon Prime, Netflix, VH1, Nickelodeon; **188** YouTube, Netflix/Alamy, Ruby Okoro (@Rubyokoro), Getty Images; **189** Beth Garrabrant, Beth Garrabrant, Shutterstock; **190** Shutterstock, Alamy; **191** Hello Content, Shutterstock, Alamy, Getty Images; **192** Studio Ghibli/Alamy, The Pokémon Company, Aniplex/Alamy; **193** Fuji Television Network/Toei Animation/Alamy, Alamy; **194** Getty Images, Reiner Pfisterer, Isa Cherry, Leif Norman; **196** Shutterstock, Universal Pictures/Alamy, Alamy; **197** Alamy, Todd Rosenberg Photography, Paul Michael Hughes/GWR, Shutterstock, Getty Images; **198** Ana Dias, Brendan Meadows/WarnerMedia, Shutterstock, Alamy; **199** Ian Bowkett; **200** Getty Images, Global Creatures, Shutterstock, Disney/Alamy, Alamy; **201** Shutterstock, Getty Images, Alamy; **202** Ubisoft, Obsidian Entertainment/Games Press, Sony, Square Enix/Games Press, Cloud Imperium Games/Games Press, Games Done Quick, The Pokémon Company/Games Press, Shutterstock; **203** Greenfield Minecraft; **204** Elias Gammelgård/Red Bull Content Pool, Dale Tidy/Red Bull Content Pool, Blizzard Entertainment, Capcom/Games Press, Getty Images; **205** Colin Young-Wolff/Riot Games, Colin Young-Wolff/Riot Games, Lance Skundrich/Riot Games, Riot Games/Games Press; **206** Phillip Burgess, Shutterstock, Alamy; **207** Ranald Mackechnie/GWR; **208** Nintendo/Games Press, FuturLab/Square Enix, Hello Games/Games Press, Marvel/Second Dinner Studios; **209** Bandai Namco; **210** Devolver Digital/Games Press, Shutterstock, Microsoft/Games Press; **211** HBO/WarnerMedia, Getty Images, Niantic Labs; **212** The Bryan Museum, Getty Images; **213** Shutterstock, AGBO/Ley Line Entertainment/IAC Films/A24 Films/Alamy, Disney/Marvel Studios/Alamy, Paramount Pictures/Alamy; **214** Ranald Mackechnie/Camera Press, Getty Images, Alamy; **215** Getty Images; **216** Getty Images, Simone Castrovillari; **217** Fabio Cetti/Castrovillariphoto; **218** Getty Images; **219** Getty Images; **220** Getty Images, Shutterstock; **221** Shutterstock, Getty Images; **222** Getty Images; **223** Getty Images, Shutterstock; **224** Alamy, Getty Images, Shutterstock; **225** Getty Images, Shutterstock; **226** Shutterstock; **227** Alamy, Shutterstock, Getty Images; **228** Alamy, Getty Images, Shutterstock; **229** Getty Images, Daan Verhoeven, Alamy, Dean Treml/Red Bull Content Pool, Romina Amato/Red Bull Content Pool; **230** Getty Images, Alamy, Shutterstock; **231** Shutterstock, Alamy, Getty Images; **232** Shutterstock; **233** Shutterstock, Getty Images; **234** Alamy, Getty Images, Shutterstock; **235** Marcelo Maragni/Red Bull Content Pool, Getty Images, Shutterstock, Jamie Schwaberow/X Games; **236** Shutterstock, Alamy; **237** Shutterstock, Getty Images; **238** Marc Gewertz/NHRA, United Autosports, Getty Images, Shutterstock; **239** ONE Championship, Getty Images; **240** SWpix.com, Shutterstock; **241** Shutterstock, Getty Images, Howie Stern; **242** Alamy, Getty Images, Shutterstock; **243** Shutterstock; **244** Getty Images, Shutterstock; **245** Shutterstock; **256** Rod Hunt

Every effort has been made to trace copyright holders and gain permission for use of the images in this publication. We welcome notifications from copyright holders who may have been omitted.

Official adjudicators

Osman Alwaleed, Camila Borenstain, Emma Brain, Joanne Brent, Jack Brockbank, Sarah Casson, Swapnil Dangarikar, Brittany Dunn, Kanzy El Defrawy, Michael Empric, Pete Fairbairn, Victor Fenes, Christine Fernandez, Michael Furnari, John Garland, Şeyda Subaşı Gemici, Andrew Glass, Iris Hou, Monica Hu, Louis Jelinek, Kazuyoshi Kirimura, Lena Kuhlmann, Maggie Luo, Mike Marcotte, Rishi Nath, Mbali Nikos, Hannah Ortman, Kellie Parise, Pravin Patel, Justin Patterson, Glenn Pollard, Susana Reyes, Alfredo Arista Rueda, Paulina Sapinska, Tomomi Sekioka, Brian Sobel, Hanane Spiers, Richard Stenning, Claire Stephens, Sheila Mella Suárez, Natalia Ramirez Talero, Raafat Tawfik, Anouk De Timary, Sonia Ushirogochi, Lorenzo Veltri, Xiong Wen, Peter Yang, Jacob Yip

Acknowledgements

55Design (Hayley Wylie-Deacon, Tobias Wylie-Deacon, Rueben Wylie-Deacon, Linda Wylie, Vidette Burniston, Lewis Burniston, Paul Geldeart, Sue Geldeart), Abu Dhabi Tourism (Bahaa Alameddine), All Saints' C of E Primary School Blackheath, Arizona Science Center (Guy Labine), ATN Event Staffing, Banijay Italia (Silvia Martini, Max Giammarrusti, Gabriela Ventura, Riccardo Favatto, Alessandra Gerra, Paola Spreafico, Benedetta Ferraro), Susan Bender, Brand Vista, CBBC, Cepac, Codex Solutions, Electric Robin (Ross Brandon, Bob Fletcher, Jacqui Saunders), Ezoic (Claire Johnson), Patrick Feldman, Luca Fiore, FJT Logistics (Ray Harper), GWR Hollywood (Nick Norman, Kirin Sundher, Raubi Sundher, Tej Sundher), GWR San Antonio (Sonny Marston, Davis Phillips), Imagination Station Toledo (Jim Repolsek, Andi Roman), Integrated Colour Editions Europe (Roger Hawkins, Susie Hawkins), Marcus Jacobs, Michelle Jacobs, Juliet's brownies, Left Brain Games (Andy Keplinger), James Lloyd, Alex Lopreino, Torquil Macneal, Matt Hillman Graphic Design, MediaSet Italia, Meta (Dan Biddle), Mirage Entertainment (Eric Bohnert Bones, David Draves, Debra Draves), Mohn Media (Astrid Renders, Kevin Sarney, Karolina Kelc, Maximilian Schonlau, Jeanette Sio), MSC (Steve Leatham, Andrea Correale, Matteo Mancini, Mihaela Carlan, Thiago Lucio Santos Vieira, Carlos Ponzetto), Rob Partis, Ping Leisure Communication (Claire Owen), Prestige Design (Jackie Ginger), The Production Suite (Beverley Williams), Propworks (Emma Banwell), Redhouse, Ripley Entertainment (William Anthony, Tacita Barrera, John Corcoran, Jim Pattison Jr.), Devonte Roper, The Schultz Creative (Carl Schultz, Darlene Retief), Schwa, Science North (Marc Gareau, Kris Gurnsey, Katherine Huneault, Ashley Larose), SELA (Thana'a Almashat, Ibrahim Mohtaseb, Ali Almutawakil), Snap (Lucy Luke), Steinbeis Papier GmbH, Tim Stuart, TikTok (Ella Neale), Julian Townsend, Sally Treibel, Twitter (Heather Bowen), Uplause (Veli-Pekka Marin, Jussi Marin), Zoe Vaux-Thompson, Lorna Williamson, YouTube (Camilla Krum)

Abbreviations

ABW	Aruba
AFG	Afghanistan
AGO	Angola
AIA	Anguilla
ALB	Albania
AND	Andorra
ANT	Netherlands Antilles
ARG	Argentina
ARM	Armenia
ASM	American Samoa
ATG	Antigua and Barbuda
AUS	Australia
AUT	Austria
AZE	Azerbaijan
BDI	Burundi
BEL	Belgium
BEN	Benin
BFA	Burkina Faso
BGD	Bangladesh
BGR	Bulgaria
BHR	Bahrain
BHS	The Bahamas
BIH	Bosnia and Herzegovina
BLR	Belarus
BLZ	Belize
BMU	Bermuda
BOL	Bolivia
BRA	Brazil
BRB	Barbados
BRN	Brunei Darussalam
BTN	Bhutan
BWA	Botswana
CAF	Central African Republic
CAN	Canada
CHE	Switzerland
CHL	Chile
CHN	China
CIV	Côte d'Ivoire
CMR	Cameroon
COD	Congo, DR of the
COG	Congo
COK	Cook Islands
COL	Colombia
COM	Comoros
CPV	Cape Verde
CRI	Costa Rica
CUB	Cuba
CYM	Cayman Islands
CYP	Cyprus
CZE	Czechia
DEU	Germany
DJI	Djibouti
DMA	Dominica
DNK	Denmark
DOM	Dominican Republic
DZA	Algeria
ECU	Ecuador
EGY	Egypt
ERI	Eritrea
ESP	Spain
EST	Estonia
ETH	Ethiopia
FIN	Finland
FJI	Fiji
FRA	France
FSM	Micronesia, Federated States of
GAB	Gabon
GEO	Georgia
GHA	Ghana
GIB	Gibraltar
GIN	Guinea
GMB	Gambia
GNB	Guinea-Bissau
GNQ	Equatorial Guinea
GRC	Greece
GRD	Grenada
GRL	Greenland
GTM	Guatemala
GUM	Guam
GUY	Guyana
HND	Honduras
HRV	Croatia (Hrvatska)
HTI	Haiti
HUN	Hungary
IDN	Indonesia
IND	India
IRL	Ireland
IRN	Iran
IRQ	Iraq
ISL	Iceland
ISR	Israel
ITA	Italy
JAM	Jamaica
JOR	Jordan
JPN	Japan
KAZ	Kazakhstan
KEN	Kenya
KGZ	Kyrgyzstan
KHM	Cambodia
KIR	Kiribati
KNA	Saint Kitts and Nevis
KOR	Korea, Republic of
KWT	Kuwait
LAO	Laos
LBN	Lebanon
LBR	Liberia
LBY	Libya
LCA	Saint Lucia
LIE	Liechtenstein
LKA	Sri Lanka
LSO	Lesotho
LTU	Lithuania
LUX	Luxembourg
LVA	Latvia
MAR	Morocco
MCO	Monaco
MDA	Moldova
MDG	Madagascar
MDV	Maldives
MEX	Mexico
MHL	Marshall Islands
MKD	North Macedonia
MLI	Mali
MLT	Malta
MMR	Myanmar
MNE	Montenegro
MNG	Mongolia
MNP	Northern Mariana Islands
MOZ	Mozambique
MRT	Mauritania
MSR	Montserrat
MUS	Mauritius
MWI	Malawi
MYS	Malaysia
NAM	Namibia
NER	Niger
NGA	Nigeria
NIC	Nicaragua
NIU	Niue
NLD	Netherlands
NOR	Norway
NPL	Nepal
NRU	Nauru
NZ	New Zealand
OMN	Oman
PAK	Pakistan
PAN	Panama
PER	Peru
PHL	Philippines
PLW	Palau
PNG	Papua New Guinea
POL	Poland
PRI	Puerto Rico
PRK	Korea, DPRO
PRT	Portugal
PRY	Paraguay
QAT	Qatar
ROM	Romania
RUS	Russian Federation
RWA	Rwanda
SAU	Saudi Arabia
SDN	Sudan
SEN	Senegal
SGP	Singapore
SHN	Saint Helena
SLB	Solomon Islands
SLE	Sierra Leone
SLV	El Salvador
SMR	San Marino
SOM	Somalia
SRB	Serbia
SSD	South Sudan
STP	São Tomé and Príncipe
SUR	Suriname
SVK	Slovakia
SVN	Slovenia
SWE	Sweden
SWZ	Eswatini
SYC	Seychelles
SYR	Syrian Arab Republic
TCA	Turks and Caicos Islands
TCD	Chad
TGO	Togo
THA	Thailand
TJK	Tajikistan
TKM	Turkmenistan
TMP	East Timor
TON	Tonga
TTO	Trinidad and Tobago
TUN	Tunisia
TUR	Türkiye
TUV	Tuvalu
TZA	Tanzania
UAE	United Arab Emirates
UGA	Uganda
UK	United Kingdom
UKR	Ukraine
UMI	US Minor Islands
URY	Uruguay
USA	United States of America
UZB	Uzbekistan
VAT	Vatican City
VCT	Saint Vincent and the Grenadines
VEN	Venezuela
VGB	Virgin Islands (British)
VIR	Virgin Islands (US)
VNM	Vietnam
VUT	Vanuatu
WSM	Samoa
YEM	Yemen
ZAF	South Africa
ZMB	Zambia
ZWE	Zimbabwe

WHERE'S WADLOW?

This year's book features the fourth and final artwork from the award-winning illustrator Rod Hunt. To complete the theme of "Discover Your World", Rod takes us down into the depths of the ocean. Can you find Robert Wadlow swimming alongside the maritime pioneers and the menagerie of exotic sea life?

From his illustrator's cabin overlooking the busy waters around GWR Island, Rod has been hard at work depicting hundreds of record-breaking people, animals and objects for this year's cover. Almost every detail of his aquatic artwork has a record associated with it. Fittingly, for the final part of his quadrilogy, Rod has made it even harder to find the

tallest person ever – as Robert Wadlow (USA) has squeezed his 272-cm (8-ft 11.1-in) frame into a scuba suit, to protect himself from the elements.

To add to the fun, Rod has also selected 20 more record holders below that appear somewhere on the front and back covers – from colossal crustaceans to medieval siege engines. How quickly can you find them all? *Check the endpapers for the full artwork.*

2023

2021

2022

To see the "Discover Your World" poster in full, join this year's cover with those for 2021, 2022 and 2023!

GUINNESS WORLD RECORDS 2024

Largest seadragon
Weedy seadragon: 45 cm (1 ft 5 in). *See pp.30–31*

Oldest depiction of a witch on a broomstick
Flying heretic in *Le Champion des Dames*: 1451. *See p.150*

Farthest distance walked barefoot on LEGO® bricks
Sonny Molina (USA): 8.89 km (5.5 mi). *See p.100*

Fastest 20-m contortion roll
Sofia Tepla (UKR): 10.49 sec. *See p.105*

First person to walk a marathon distance underwater
Lloyd Scott (UK): 9 Oct 2013. *See p.78*

Most swords swallowed underwater
The Space Cowboy (AUS): four. *See p.78*

Largest wooden trebuchet
War Wolf: 90 m (295 ft) tall. *See pp.136–37*

Most drumbeats in one minute
Pritish A R (AUS): 2,370 beats. *See p.104*

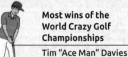

Most juggling catches in one minute (five balls)
Simeon Graham (UK): 423 catches. *See p.108*

Largest marine crustacean (width)
Taka-ashi-gani, aka Japanese spider crab: leg span of 3.69 m (12 ft). *See p.40*

Most wins of the World Crazy Golf Championships
Tim "Ace Man" Davies (UK): five titles. *See p.88*

Fastest woman to climb the higher 8,000ers
Kristin Harila (NOR): 69 days. *See p.119*

Largest underwater mermaid show
Atlantic Sanya (CHN): 110 mermaids. *See p.81*

Largest waterlily leaf
Victoria boliviana: 3.2 m (10 ft 6 in) across. *See p.47*

Largest collection of *One Piece* memorabilia
Lam Siu Fung (CHN): 20,125 items. *See p.193*

Most profitable sea pirate
Samuel Bellamy (UK): £120 m ($147 m) in two years. *See p.145*

Largest octopus
Giant Pacific octopus: at least 71 kg (156 lb). *See pp.32–33*

Most expensive movie prop sold at auction
Robby the Robot: $5,375,000 (£4.06 m). *See p.184*

First magician to saw a person in half
P T Selbit (UK): 17 Jan 1921. *See p.198*

About the illustrator
Not surprisingly, Rod Hunt was passionate about comics as a child. They inspired him to start drawing, and by the time he was a teenager he had begun to consider a career as an illustrator. Over the years, Rod has honed his artistic technique. Firstly, he mulls over the project and doodles simple pencil sketches; then he creates a more complete drawing. Next, he scans this into his computer and builds it up, layer by layer, using digital-illustration software. Find out more about Rod at **rodhunt.com**.

Most expensive car
Uhlenhaut Coupé: €135 m ($142.3 m; £113.6). *See pp.156–57*

DISCOVER YOUR WORLD